Robert Hughes

Cae Mor
Ffordd yr Orsaf
Llwyngwril LL37 2JS

THE RURAL POOR
IN EIGHTEENTH-CENTURY WALES

The Rural Poor
in Eighteenth-CenturyWales

DAVID W. HOWELL

CARDIFF
UNIVERSITY OF WALES PRESS
2000

© David W. Howell, 2000

British Library Cataloguing-in-Publication Data
A catalogue record for this book is available from the British Library.

ISBN 0-7083-1613-1

Typeset at the University of Wales Press
Printed in Great Britain by Dinefwr Press, Llandybïe, Dyfed

CONTENTS

LIST OF MAPS, FIGURES AND TABLES

For

Angela

and

Emma Angharad

ACKNOWLEDGEMENTS

Over the lengthy period this book has been in the making I have benefited from the guidance and support of many, some whose friendship, dare I say, I have risked in the process. Staffs of the various Welsh county record offices and of a number of libraries have been generous in their advice and assistance, none more so than that of the National Library of Wales, among whom Glyn Parry has been extraordinarily helpful in answering queries relating to the Great Sessions gaol files. For his help in choosing the jacket illustration for the book I am grateful to my friend, Dr Huw Owen, Keeper of Maps and Prints at the same National Library. I owe a special debt of gratitude, too, to Bryn Ellis of Holywell for so selflessly allowing me to use the valuable transcript he has made of the eighteenth-century Denbighshire Quarter Sessions Rolls. Sarah Lowrie, also, helpfully placed her legal expertise at my disposal in my work in chapter 10 on indictable offences. As with these criminal records so, too, with demographic data I have relied heavily on others, in particular on the expertise of my colleagues Brinley Jones and Nicholas Woodward.

Other scholars who have given readily of their specialist knowledge include Matthew Cragoe, David Eastwood and Prys Morgan. I owe a special debt to the scholarship as so much else of the late David Jones, whose passing has left an unfillable gap. All my work on Welsh rural society over the years has benefited from the advice and encouragement of Gordon Mingay and Michael Thompson. My research students over the years, too, have plied me with references and opened new vistas; to them all – Wilma Thomas, Leslie Baker-Jones, Melvin Humphreys, Mark Matthews, Eric Morgan and Robert Smith – I record my gratitude. Of course, all errors of fact and of interpretation are my responsibility alone.

Thanks are also due to my supportive head of department, David Eastwood, and my college for granting me sabbatical leave in 1997–8, which greatly facilitated the completion of this study. What was then the Social Science Research Council was generous in funding a year's leave of absence in 1981–2, enabling me to spend much time at the National Library of Wales. Theirs was truly a long-term investment. Our departmental secretaries, especially Mrs June Morgan and Mrs Jane Buse, have been patient and skilful in word-processing the untidy handwritten manuscript of a scholar time-warped in the bow-and-arrow stage of technology. Equal thoroughness and professionalism have been shown by the staff of the University of Wales Press, above all by Ceinwen Jones and Liz Powell.

On a personal level I have had wonderful encouragement throughout from my friends Gareth Elwyn Jones, Ieuan Gwynedd Jones and James Thomas. As the dedication acknowledges, my greatest personal debt is to my wife Angela and our daughter Emma, without whose encouragement and tolerance this work could not have reached fruition.

ABBREVIATIONS

AHE&W, IV	*Agrarian History of England and Wales*, vol.IV, ed. Joan Thirsk
AHE&W, V	*Agrarian History of England and Wales*, vol.V, ed. Joan Thirsk
AHE&W, VI	*Agrarian History of England and Wales*, vol.VI, ed. G. E. Mingay
Ag. Hist. Rev.	*Agricultural History Review*
Arch. Camb.	*Archaeologia Cambrensis*
BBCS	*Bulletin of the Board of Celtic Studies*
Econ. Hist. Rev.	*Economic History Review*
GS4	Great Sessions gaol files at the National Library of Wales
Jnl. Mer. Hist. and Rec. Soc.	*Journal of the Merioneth Historical and Record Society*
Mont. Colls.	*The Montgomeryshire Collections*
NLW	National Library of Wales
NLW Jnl.	*National Library of Wales Journal*
PVB	Parish Vestry Book
Trans. Angl. Antiq. Soc.	*Transactions of the Anglesey Antiquarian Society*
Trans. Cymm.	*Transactions of the Honourable Society of Cymmrodorion*
Trans. RHS	*Transactions of the Royal Historical Society*
WHR	*The Welsh History Review*
WWHR	*West Wales Historical Records*

Introduction

That the lower orders of eighteenth-century Wales, as in all other areas of Britain and the European mainland, endured a harsh and insecure existence is well known. Yet Welsh rural dwellers remain largely hidden from posterity, a secret people who seldom recorded their own feelings. Such a want of self-expression even among those of the lower orders who were literate – and very few were – sprang from the absence of a sense of individuality in Welsh society, the first autobiography of a poor peasant, that of John Thomas of Rhayader, appearing only in 1810.[1] Perhaps the nearest we come to the authentic voice is the deposition before a magistrate in a criminal case to be tried at the Quarter or Great Sessions. Faced with this want of accessibility, it is well-nigh impossible to get inside the minds of these poor people in order to gauge their attitude towards their hard fate, to discern if they harboured any strong feelings of resentment, to identify any particular grievances they had and to judge their attitudes to those many in control of their lives. The problem is even worse when we attempt to understand the often appalling lot of women; indeed the historian is confronted with nearly complete silence. Whatever the gender, we are left so often to surmise. Notwithstanding these difficulties, this study will attempt to provide a fuller understanding of the various hardships faced by the poor – small farmers, craftsmen and the landless making up the lower orders – and to examine the nature of the response to their predicament.

A volume concerned wholly with the lower orders of society does not require a chapter on the landed gentry and aristocracy; yet as the owners of much of the land, and as the political and social rulers of their communities their influence was all-pervasive and they will accordingly receive consideration throughout the pages of this book. The contemporary term 'the lower orders' is used advisedly to get away from any confusion that may arise through use of the generic category 'peasant', often employed to describe people who had connections in one way or another with the land.

The term was variously used by contemporary commentators on the Welsh scene; by some to describe the farm labourer as distinct from the farmer, by others to include both the small farmers and the labouring poor and by still others to embrace the country-dweller in general. Similarly, historians have found it difficult to reach agreement about the validity of the term; John Beckett argues that 'when historians use "peasant" as a descriptive term for rural society in general, they are using it in an unhistorical way'.[2] While avoiding the designation, it is at the same time necessary to be on guard against viewing more precise categories like farm labourers, tenant farmers, craftsmen and small freeholders – we shall leave the 'yeoman' for the moment! – as exclusive occupational categories; tenant farmers might do some day-labouring, craftsmen were often small farmers, and small freeholders often rented neighbouring farms.

The introductory chapter examines the landscape, land use, landownership and occupancy, population change and social hierarchy which constituted the economic and social framework within which country-dwellers lived and worked. The scene once set, there follow two distinct parts to the volume. The first seeks to discover the particular experiences and standard of living of each subgroup making up the lower orders in rural communities. Throughout sticking to the old adage that 'saving is getting', Welsh country-dwellers above all survived by practising thrift, and we shall look at the ways in which they purposely sought not to spend, and, complementing this, the manner in which they made the most of the natural resources of their environment.[3] In the harsh conditions of the eighteenth century some could not survive through their own efforts, and an examination will be made of the bleak existence of the paupers' twilight world and of the way in which growing numbers of them from the 1770s pushed whole neighbourhoods into crisis. Bringing this first part to a close is an assessment of the relationships between the various groups owning and working the land which is intended to evaluate the degree of harmony in working situations and to identify any particular grievances nursed by the different occupational groups.

Part II examines the various individual and social experiences of the lower orders by looking in turn at their popular culture, their religion and superstitious beliefs, the nature of their political involvement, their popular protest, the level of theft and the degree to which they lived together peacefully. As the title of part II, 'Rough and Rebellious Communities', suggests, there will be a strong focus on the rowdy and boisterous nature of the popular culture; the proneness to riotous behaviour while resisting encroachment on their customary rights by manorial lords above all, and the easy resort to violence in their dealings with neighbours who were perceived to have injured them. Questions will arise from this emphasis I lay on boisterous, defiant behaviour about the extent to which this protest and resistance were class-inspired, the role of women in such upheavals, the level of deference in the community and the degree of instability of eighteenth-century Welsh rural neighbourhoods. Of course, the distinctiveness of the Welsh experience in all areas of community life can only be properly assessed by drawing comparisons with other cultures in Britain and beyond, and this I have attempted, even at the risk of oversimplifying.

It will be apparent that the whole body of the work is supported by the scaffolding of other scholars' writings. In particular I am indebted to the three works that deal extensively with the lower orders of Welsh rural society, those of Melvin Humphreys, Glyn Parry and Richard Suggett.[4] Much of the primary source data is drawn from landowners' estate papers – the letters, estate surveys and rentals – an indispensable source for a rounded investigation of the lower orders, parish vestry books, contemporary 'tours' and diaries, and legal records. As a large part of the study is concerned with relationships both between individuals and between different status groups within the close-knit, face-to-face neighbourhoods, my reliance upon court records, above all on the gaol files of the courts of Great Sessions, is necessarily heavy indeed. It is upon the uncovering and interpretation of this rich material – in particular the depositions of witnesses – that any claim to newness for this book must largely rest.

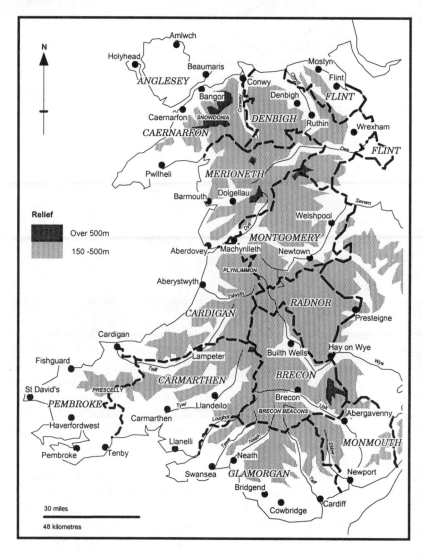

Map of Wales in the eighteenth century, showing relief and settlement

~ 1 ~

Prologue
Setting the Scene: The Land and the People

1. The Pattern of Farming

To a significant extent the configuration of the land and the climate in all areas of the world together determine the type of farming pursued and the pattern of settlement.[1] Its eastern border apart, Wales is surrounded by sea, and its relief comprises essentially a central highland block fringed by lowland, some of the latter stretching along river valleys far into the highland reaches. Diversity, of course, obtains within this overall pattern, which in turn dictates distinctive regional farming systems. The central highland changes character as it stretches southwards, the sharp mountainous terrain of the north smoothing out into the rolling uplands of the south. The lowland zone, too, between mountain and sea varies in extent. Apart from Anglesey and the Llŷn peninsula, the coastal plain in the north and west is narrow, contrasting with the more extensive lowlands along the south coast. Inland, the eastern border region comprises three main lowland areas which stretch as river valleys into the central uplands, along the Usk and the Wye in the south, the Severn in mid-Wales and the Dee in the north. The coastal lowlands, in places, too, penetrate far into the highland core along the river valleys. Whilst in the west the lower reaches of the valleys are narrow, those running north and south broaden out as they approach the coast.

That the lowlands comprise only a small proportion of Wales and Monmouthshire is a crucial determinant of the overall pattern of Welsh farming. Given that nearly 60 per cent of total land lies above 500 feet,[2] the most important factors limiting farming practice are rainfall and the amount of sunshine hours and temperature, the last two controlling the length of the growing season.[3] Its moist conditions dictate that Wales is naturally suited to growing grass, and this largely explains the predominantly pastoral character of Welsh farming over the centuries. Wide differences in quality, however, obtain between the natural grasses of the lowlands and those of the hills and moorlands of Wales. The dominant grass of the lowlands of under 700 feet is *Agrostis* which is not of good quality, and so on the lowlands as on the hills and uplands, the raising of store livestock for fattening on the lusher grasses of the English Midlands and south-eastern counties has always been the dominant pattern of pastoral farming, even after the coming of railways in the mid-nineteenth century. Above this lowland zone is found a belt of heathland, ranging from 700 to 1,000 feet, and higher still are moorland and mountain, their astringent pastures diminishing in nutritional value the higher the altitude.[4]

Such were the physical factors influencing the basic features of Welsh farming. Moreover, even in those few choice areas suited to fattening livestock, farmers had no option but to raise store animals for export. In the eighteenth century as in earlier times, the absence of a larger local consumer market for butchers' meat meant that fat cattle, in the absence of rail communication, had of necessity to be driven on foot to the centres of demand eastwards, which would have led to inevitable loss of condition on the journey. Walter Davies thus noted of the area about Laugharne (Carms.) in 1802: 'no better soil anywhere, full of white clover naturally excellent for dairy farms and for fattening, but this will not do here so distant from good markets.'[5] If the concentration on store livestock within mixed farming was limited in its profitability because of the slow turnover and the minimum amount of labour expended on the product,[6] Welsh farmers were obliged to persist with it until they were presented with new opportunities during the inter-war years of the twentieth century.

Such concentration on grass and livestock rearing does not mean, however, that corn-growing was everywhere neglected. On the contrary, in the favourable lowland areas significant amounts of corn were grown, and even in areas unsuited to its growth the peasant mentality of small farmers intent upon producing for themselves all the family requirements, together with the difficulties and consequent expense of importing it in the pre-railway era, ensured that most farmers grew some corn, principally oats and barley.[7] Moreover, a considerable extension in arable acreages occurred in Wales during the French and Napoleonic War years, when the high prices of corn led farmers to bring more and more land under the plough, as in the Vale of Glamorgan where farmers switched to tillage from dairying, in Cardiganshire where more barley was grown, and in Caernarfonshire and Radnorshire.[8]

Within this overall Welsh pattern of grass and livestock farming, distinctive farming regions have been identified by Emery for the period 1640–1750.[9] A clear arable type of farming was located only in the red soils of central Monmouthshire, which were suitable for both crops and grass. Here the average yeoman's wheat, oats and barley were worth a quarter of his goods. Distinctive, too, in the south-east was the coastal lowland stretching from Chepstow to Newport and pushing westwards to Cardiff, where, if less so than in central Monmouthshire, corn, especially wheat, was important, as, too, in this area of rich grazing and meadows, were dairy herds. Whereas the aforementioned 'Severn lowlands' concentrated on corn and cattle with an emphasis on the dairying branch, other areas like the Vale of Usk, the Vale of Glamorgan, Gower, south and west Pembrokeshire and Anglesey practised 'intermediate' types of farming systems which, based on corn and cattle, saw emphasis placed on either the dairying or the rearing side. Whilst the Vale of Glamorgan saw most of its arable given over to grain, half of it wheat crops, and within the livestock branch emphasis being given to the dairying herds which produced large amounts of butter and cheese for sale,[10] in the mixed farming of Gower and south and west Pembrokeshire the heavy corn cropping concentrated on barley, and dairying was less important than rearing of steers and bullocks.

Within the pastoral farming prevailing elsewhere in Wales, big differences obtained between the lowland areas – covering a wide swathe of Carmarthenshire, the coastal plain of Cardigan bay, the Llŷn peninsula, the Vale of Clwyd and the border lowlands – on the one hand and the upland core of the moorlands and mountains on the other. To take first the lowlands: corn was grown essentially for subsistence purposes, the farmers' main wealth deriving from cattle-rearing and, in more favourable districts, dairying and/or grazing. For instance, dairying was followed in the Vale of Tywi above Carmarthen. By contrast, on the upland tracts oats were the sole corn crop, and horses, cattle and sheep were reared. Caernarfonshire farmers, particularly those in the mountainous areas, were keeping increasing numbers of sheep over the middle decades of the century, especially when compared to the 1660s,

1670s and 1680s. In part as a response to the growing demand for
wool, especially from 1750, sheep came to displace cattle in the
mountainous areas, too, because they were cheaper and easier to
handle, and demanded much less attention than cattle, especially
dairy.[11] Likewise in mountainous Merioneth, at the close of the
eighteenth century sheep were the staple, though black cattle, too,
were reared in big numbers.[12] Besides the export on foot along
drovers' routes of store livestock, the production of cloth made in
the farmhouses and cottages of the poor constituted an integral
part of the upland farming economy of mid- and north Wales.

The eighteenth century is rightly associated with progress in
agriculture so far as the south-eastern and southern counties of
England were concerned, but no general marked improvement
took place in Welsh districts. That certain innovations, principally
clover and turnip culture, did manifest themselves from the last
decades of the seventeenth century and quickened over the course
of the eighteenth has been emphasized by Emery among others, but
such progress was mainly to be found on the home farms of the
aristocracy and gentry, on the small freeholds of enterprising
farmers and clergymen and on the holdings of a limited number of
substantial tenant farmers.[13] Some progress had come about, too,
in sheep farming with the introduction in the late eighteenth
century of improved English breeds onto both lowland and hill and
moorland areas, although farmers in the isolated mountainous
tracts of west Wales clung to the local sheep on the grounds of their
hardiness.[14] Mainly because of want of capital in Welsh farming,
only limited improvement was achieved in breed development of
cattle. What progress was made came about through the introduction of improved English breeds for crossing with local stock, a
development in the late eighteenth century most in evidence in the
river valleys of the Welsh border counties.[15]

As this last-cited reference to the borderland river valleys
demonstrates, the main areas undergoing improvement in the later
decades of the century were located in the fertile lowlands.
Remarkable in the north was the Vale of Clwyd, on which the
Revd Richard Warner at the close of the century conferred the
accolade of 'garden of the northern counties' and opined that
'clean fields, liberal manure, small close hedges and well-drained
meadows, evince a better agriculture than is generally found
throughout Wales'. Writing in 1794, John Fox similarly lauded the

Vale of Glamorgan: 'This part . . . is in general so fruitful, pleasant and populous, that it is called (and that too, I think, very deservedly) the 'garden of south Wales', as the Vale of Cluid [*sic*] is reckoned to be that of North Wales.'[16] While (awkwardly for the historian) dissenting from such plaudits, indeed viewing in 1803 the state of husbandry in the Vale of Glamorgan to be 'at a low ebb', the Revd John Evans lavished praise upon the area about Laugharne in Carmarthenshire with its 'very abundant crops of corn, pulse and grass: we were pleased also to observe a more rational husbandry than is generally seen in this part of the kingdom.'[17] If this last instance of improved farming questions the entire validity of Joseph Cradock's claim in 1770 that proximity to English farming was a crucial determinant of progress, there was doubtless point to his observation that:

> Several counties of Wales have made but a slow progress in agriculture. In many places bordering upon England, they have in a great degree adopted the English manner of tillage. In some parts of the counties of Montgomery, Denbigh and Flint, the lands are well improved. I have made this observation, that the remoter they are from the English counties, the less is there of the spirit of industry and improvement among the inhabitants.[18]

Although remoteness from markets and the unfavourable terrain in the western counties were the vital constraining factors on improved husbandry, the absence of English influences further westwards was certainly a drawback.

The tardy progress in farming practices which persisted in most areas of Wales before the beginning of the Napoleonic Wars is well documented, and David Thomas was led to conclude, 'there were few improvers and little improvement.'[19] That between Christmas 1749 and Christmas 1750 Wales, as one of twelve farming regions identified for England and Wales as a whole, contributed a mere 1.6 per cent of total cereal exports, and within that meagre contribution oats comprised over two-thirds of the cereals, is striking testimony to the poverty of Welsh agriculture.[20] Throughout the century the all-important proper rotation of crops was neglected, farmers simply taking corn crops, mainly barley and oats, one after another until the soil was exhausted and the crop yield negligible; turnips, vetches and other ameliorating crops were only scantily grown. Just one glorious exception out of a total 1,088 Caernarfonshire inventories for the years 1735–70 examined by Glyn Parry itemized turnips.[21] Little progress in this respect could be reported of the different Welsh counties to the Board of Agriculture in 1794. All too frequently, the native cattle, lacking the benefit of the new fodder crops and often grazing promiscuously on unenclosed commons and wastes, remained stunted in growth, and, in many western areas, unimproved in breed quality, an inferior condition encouraged by Welsh drovers allegedly because improved stock would have attracted more English dealers willing to pay with cash and so to be preferred to themselves, who perforce had to operate a credit system.[22] In addition, small uneconomic farm units and the frequent intermixture with adjacent ones, poor drainage, want of good roads, inferior implements, especially the ploughs and carts, costly carting of lime as a fertilizer, and inadequate farm buildings all acted as constraints on good husbandry. The degree to which landlords and tenant farmers were themselves contributors to this dismal state of affairs will be considered in chapter 2.[23]

2. Changes to the Landscape

'Whoever visits Wales, sees her nakedness', commented Hutton in the last years of the eighteenth century.[24] Woodlands had been gradually denuded over previous centuries, Leland noting in the 1530s the causes of deforestation yet at the same time recording that large areas of the Welsh countryside were well wooded. Considerable despoiling of trees had occurred in north Wales by the time Thomas Pennant was writing in the 1770s, a deforestation that quickened in the remaining decades of the century.[25] By that time the southern counties had likewise lost much of their timber cover, a laying bare most noticeable in Carmarthenshire and Pembrokeshire.[26] It was above all the great demands for timber for shipbuilding, for tanning – involving shipment of bark to Ireland – and for industrial undertakings that led landowners to fell trees at a gluttonous rate from the middle decades of the eighteenth century, for such sales crucially enabled them to meet pressing financial exigencies. But the lower orders, too, were in part to blame, tenant farmers especially despoiling the woodland on their holdings and cottagers 'stealing' it as their perceived immemorial right and sometimes out of sheer necessity.

The landscape was being transformed, too, by the ongoing process of encroachment and enclosure. Although enclosure of the arable common fields of the lowland Englishries stretching across the coastal plain of south Wales had been virtually completed by 1640, the piecemeal consolidation of strips in open arable fields in both Englishry and Welshry areas took place in a few districts in the ensuing years down to the end of the eighteenth century. Even so, at the commencement of the 1790s open arable fields were still to be found in areas like west Pembrokeshire, coastal Cardiganshire and the eastern vales and plateaux of Montgomeryshire, and there were also big stretches of unenclosed coastal bog and dune together with a certain amount of valley marshland given over to common grazing.[27]

Of course, by far the greatest amount of unenclosed land at the opening of the eighteenth century was to be found in the hill and moorland expanses, and over the course of the century there occurred a noticeable acceleration in the process of encroachment on, and enclosure of, these outlying tracts, which had begun in earnest in the late Tudor years. (Nevertheless, as late as 1800 roughly a quarter of the land surface was still common and waste.) Landowners themselves, as freehold or customary tenants of the various manors, made encroachments and enclosures of the commons and wastes. Often they individually encroached without consent from any party, either claiming – as on the Beaufort seigniory of Gower in the early eighteenth century – the property as theirs without any acknowledgement, or else they paid a fine in the manor court. Marauding activity on such a blatant scale by latter-day robber barons led Ellis Wynne in 1703 to denounce 'the great man who steals from the mountain half a parish' and 'robs the poor man of a living for his beast, and thereby a living for himself and his household'.[28] The avarice was certainly facilitated by the laxity and neglect prevalent in manorial administration in the late seventeenth and early eighteenth centuries. Slack administration in private manors allowed tenants, sometimes with the connivance of stewards, to encroach on common rights. Again, Welsh landowners acting as stewards of Crown lordships were nicely placed to make encroachments on the rights of the Crown, but many tenants of the Crown lordships, too, did likewise. Significantly, trials instituted by the Crown's lessee of the lordship of Cantremelenith (Rads.) in the 1770s against small encroachers like labourers, tenant farmers and lesser freeholders were held at Hereford, for it was doubted 'whether a Presteign jury may relish a prosecution for enclosing four acres when members have enclosed ten times as much'.[29]

As the last citation bears out, many small encroachments were being made in this century by cottagers, the squatters who built their *tai-unnos* (one-night houses) and subsequently enclosed a small acreage about them which they regarded as their freehold. We shall see that such encroachments were to reach a serious level in the last decades, reflecting the pressure of a rising population in the Welsh countryside with its non-elastic agriculture and paucity of alternative employment. Typically, at the opening of the 1790s Llanferres parish (Denbs.) contained in addition to forty-six houses, 'about 30 very small cottages, most of them erected of late years upon the common'.[30] Their hostility to squatters notwithstanding, tenant farmers, too, it will be shown later, were to add to their farms by making small encroachments on the waste, a creeping colonization doubtless enjoying the tacit acquiescence of their landlords.

A part of this encroachment was centred about the *hafod*, a small, rude summer dwelling with a few enclosed fields about it high up on the mountain slopes, from which base lowland farmers and their families supervised the grazing for their cattle and sheep on the *ffriddoedd* (rough pastures), returning with their livestock to the valley farmstead (the *hendre*) upon the onset of winter. For as pressure on land grew, it was natural that moorland and mountain wastes around the margins of the *hafod* should be encroached upon and enclosed, the *hafod* indeed over time becoming a separate farm. In turn the new farm often established its own *hafod* on the margin of the waste. The same development attached to the *lluest* – a simple shepherd's hut occupied in summer – which, rather than the *hafod*, was characteristic of the central uplands of mid-Wales. The metamorphosis from chrysalis *lluestydd* to independent sheep farms occurred in the late eighteenth or early nineteenth century. Elwyn Davies observes: 'they grew into farms by enclosure of fields from the waste in much the same way as *hafodydd* had evolved earlier.'[31]

For all the deterrence stemming from high costs, a certain amount of enclosure by private Act of Parliament had come about before the spur offered by the outbreak of war with France in 1793. Significantly once again, as border shires in touch with agricultual progress eastwards, Flintshire and Montgomeryshire were the two north Walian counties that experienced enclosure by private Act before 1790: Saltney Marsh in the former underwent enclosure following an Act of 1778, and the Severn and lower Vyrnwy valleys in Montgomeryshire experienced three extensive enclosures between 1780 and 1790. An important venture had also been undertaken in Anglesey at the close of the 1780s with the passing of two Acts in 1788 and 1790 for the drainage of Malltraeth Marsh, but completion was hindered by landed proprietors backing away from mounting costs.[32] Similar tardiness in parliamentary enclosure was to be met in the southern counties before 1793. In the three southwest ones, just two enclosures by Act of Parliament came about, both in Pembrokeshire and pertaining respectively to Narberth Mountain (1786) and Castlemartin Marsh (1788). One enclosure Act apiece for Glamorgan and Monmouthshire covering a total 1,530 acres constituted the entire parliamentary enclosure activity in the south-eastern counties before 1793.[33]

Whereas eighteen enclosure Acts for Wales and Monmouthshire before 1793 gave the go-ahead for enclosure of nearly 35,000 acres, some eighty-five between 1793 and 1815 legislated for enclosure of at least 213,000 acres. This period, indeed, saw the most feverish activity, for the later Acts between 1815 and 1885 dealt with the smaller amount of 166,000 acres.[34] Much of the post-1793 enclosure related to the vast tracts of upland moors, where newly enclosed large fields, bounded by either earth balks or dry-stone walls, were for the most part added to existing farms, or sometimes detached from the core of such holdings. These rectilinear enclosures contrasted with the irregular small old fields and their thick hedges found further down the slope; or at least this was what was intended, for as Colin Thomas cautions: 'examples abound in which the surveyors' neat lines never entered the real world.'[35] While enclosure facilitated improved farming in the lowland areas, little was done in the way of improving the upland pastures now often characterized by their geometric fields.[36] No doubt the principal motivation of these upland enclosures was the clarification and assertion of ownership, putting a stop to vexatious piecemeal small encroachments.[37]

3. The Distribution of Land

Much of the land was owned by large proprietors, comprising aristocrats, squires and gentlemen. At the time of the *New Domesday Survey* of 1873 estates of over 1,000 acres occupied 60 per cent of the total area of Wales. There was a significant swallowing up of small freehold properties of anything up to a hundred acres or so after 1814 by neighbouring landed families, so that by 1882 'The class of small Welsh owners who were numerous enough 100 years ago is comparatively limited now', but if this suggests that the concentration of land in the eighteenth century was rather less than later, nevertheless sizeable landed estates in the hands of the aristocracy and gentry were a key element in the rural economy and society.[38] In his rich study, Melvin Humphreys has calculated for Montgomeryshire that 'the 132 gentry families owned all except some 25 to 30 per cent of the privately owned land of Montgomeryshire in the 1690s'.[39]

Estates, apart from the wealthy Glamorgan ones, varied in size at the opening of the eighteenth century to cover the very large ones owned by great landlords whose incomes stretched from £2,000 to £3,500 a year, while the estates of the wealthy gentry yielded yearly incomes of £1,000 to £2,000, those of the squires had annual incomes rising from £400 to £1,000, and the smallest, those of the lesser gentry, were confined to annual incomes between £100 or less and £400. Such incomes were smaller than those enjoyed by the corresponding groups of landed families both in Glamorgan and in the more commercialized areas of England.[40]

That the majority of Welsh estates were concentrated in the lower income levels is reflected in the Denbighshire spread of estate incomes in 1706 represented in table 1. Valuable as these data are in revealing the spread of incomes of estates in Denbighshire (a sizeable number yielding under £100 a year, a pattern equally discernible for neighbouring Merioneth), we should note that large owners here, as in other Welsh counties, would have derived incomes from estates in neighbouring and even distant shires.[41] Even with the swallowing up of a significant number of small properties in all areas of Wales by the 'Leviathans' from the late seventeenth century through to the close of the eighteenth, both through profitable marriages with heiresses of Welsh estates (a process facilitated by the remarkable if mysterious failure among

Table 1: Denbighshire estate incomes in 1706

Income of estate in £s	No. of owners	Income of estate in £s	No. of owners
Under £100	38	1000–1100	1
100–200	46	1100–1200	0
200–300	25	1200–1300	0
300–400	10	1300–1400	0
400–500	7	1400–1500	1
500–600	2	1500–1600	1
600–700	6	1600–1700	1
700–800	1	1700–1800	0
800–900	3	1800–1900	0
900–1000	1	1900–2000	0
		2000 + (= 3250)	1

Source: NLW, Wynnstay box 106, no. 23: the account given of some gentlemen's estate upon oath to be taxed for the militia.

landed families to produce male heirs at this time) and by the purchase of (frequently debt-ridden) estates,[42] the same profile of a land dominated by small estates is still discernible at the close of our period. In the 1790s the few great proprietors with estates yielding over £5,000 a year, and the somewhat larger group of wealthy gentry owning estates producing from £2,000 to £5,000, were heavily outnumbered by the large class of gentlemen with estates worth from £300 to £2,000 a year, and by the numerous group at the base of the property pyramid comprising the yeomanry, who, unlike the *rentier* gentry, were owner-occupiers possessing properties worth less than £300 a year or extending from around twenty to 300 or 400 acres.[43] In Montgomeryshire, small freeholders owned between 20 and 40 per cent of the county's cultivated land throughout this period.[44]

The consolidation of Welsh estates into the ownership of fewer families had far-reaching repercussions for the size and nature of the Welsh gentry, and indeed for the wider communities they had traditionally ruled. Contemporaries wistfully observed that the Welsh countryside in the late eighteenth century was bestrewn with 'withering' mansions, these old *plasau* deserted and falling into decay or inhabited by tenants. For Edmund Hyde Hall, writing of

Caernarfonshire at the beginning of the nineteenth century, the process amounted to no less than 'a revolution among country houses'.[45] If, as in Montgomeryshire, the abandonment of small mansions, often because the heiress of an ancient family moved to her husband's seat upon marriage, had no profoundly harmful effects upon county communities for much of the early eighteenth century because the new owners through marriage were frequently from the same county, from mid-century the increasing tendency over Wales as a whole was for Welsh heiresses to be snapped up by English landed fortune-hunters, and this brought about a significant and harmful growth in non-resident, absentee estate-ownership. *Pari passu*, the traditional residential native squires were a declining group in the landed society of Wales.[46] Once again, Edmund Hyde Hall was to comment on this phenomenon: 'English names indeed are creeping everywhere in the Principality . . . it is in truth astonishing to see how many old names run away in females with their properties in this country.'[47] This structural non-residence, far more so than a fancy on the part of the substantial landed families to spend time away from their estates in London and elsewhere, was to constitute the essence of absenteeism among the landed élite in late eighteenth-century Wales.[48] With the displacement of the native residential squirearchy, an important traditional support to Welsh rural communities was removed, not least in the hospitality afforded and the financing and encouragement of improvements to the local economy.

If we have no body of official statistics revealing the proportions of the cultivated land in Wales that were owner-occupied and tenanted (in 1887 it was 11.1 per cent to 88.9 per cent) we *can* calculate the proportion of 'tenements' that were owner-occupied and tenanted respectively from the late-century land-tax returns. Out of a total 2,596 'tenements' assessed for land tax in some ninety-nine Pembrokeshire parishes in 1786, for instance, only 468, i.e. 18 per cent, were owner-occupied. Preponderant among these owner-occupiers were small freeholders or yeomen, lesser gentlemen, and clergy. But the figures demonstrate that most of the land – over 80 per cent – was farmed by tenants.[49]

4. Settlement and Population

The people who lived in rural Wales were for the most part country-dwellers, the market towns which served their farming hinterlands striking contemporary travellers as generally small and unremarkable. Two basic types of settlement pattern in the Welsh countryside had become well established by this time. In the upland districts, to levels sometimes reaching as high as 300 metres above sea-level, the pattern was primarily one of scattered farmsteads and cottages linked by a network of footpaths, uneven cart tracks and indifferent roads, whereas in lowland areas like Anglesey, the coastal lowlands to the north and south and the wide river valleys stretching westwards from the English borderland, a combination of manorial occupation, greater tillage and the growth of com- merce had produced nucleated villages.[50] Nowhere was the latter settlement pattern more highly developed than in the Vale of Glamorgan, in whose nucleated manorial villages were to be found clusters of substantial stone-walled yeomen houses dating back to the early seventeenth century. If Iolo Morganwg is to be believed, they were to represent more than just material well-being: 'Farmers living in villages are generally much more affable and sociable, much less sullen and arrogant, and more intelligent than those who live more solitary lives in the middle of their farms.'[51]

Population densities varied, very low ones naturally obtaining in the bleak moorland and upland slopes given over to livestock rearing with scant tillage, where, for example, at mid-century on Mynydd Hiraethog (Denbs.) as few as 0.84 to 1.33 families per hundred acres were to be found. At the same time, in low-lying areas of the north-east, purely agricultural parishes of the coalfield had densities ranging from 2.5 to 3.7 families, the heavier densities doubtless reflecting a greater element of tillage and consequent increased labour requirements. Further west at mid-century, there was a sparsity of population in the mountainous parishes of Merioneth, contrasting with the greater density in the Vale of Edeirnion. Similarly in Glamorgan, in 1670 the tillage areas lying under the 400-feet contour had a slightly denser population than the area falling between the 400- and 800-feet contour which went in more for stock-rearing and a decidedly higher population density than was to be encountered in the *blaenau* or hill districts to the north of the county. As the eighteenth century advanced, greater density differences would emerge, of course, between industrializing and purely agricultural parishes in various areas of Wales; already by mid-century lead-mining parishes in Flintshire, for instance, boasting between four and six families per hundred acres, had higher densities than their purely rural counterparts.[52]

Whereas population histories of England, Scotland and Ireland are available in specialized monographs, comparatively little is known about the population history of Wales. Indeed in his study of 'British population change during the eighteenth century', Roger Schofield states that 'lack of comparable data for Wales means that it cannot be included in the discussion'.[53] Perhaps because of the special problems bound up with the survival and quality of the evidence, historians have only just begun to investigate Wales' population history scientifically in the pre-1801 period. At present there are just a few regional studies of parish register data[54] and nothing to compare with the advances made by the Cambridge Group for the History of Population and Social Structure, or even with Flinn's study of Scotland and Connell's work on Ireland.[55]

From the basis of Parish Register Abstracts Rickman estimated that the population of Wales in 1700 was 406,000. The figure had increased by 20.9 per cent to 490,000 by 1750, leaving the population to expand by 19.6 per cent to 587,128 between 1750 and 1801. On this evidence, the increase in the population of Wales was nowhere near as rapid during the second half of the eighteenth century as it was in England, Rickman's figures for England showing a population rising by 17.9 per cent during the period 1700–50, and by 38.8 per cent between 1750 and 1800. Wrigley and Schofield broadly support this picture, estimating that in England population rose by 14.1 per cent between 1701 and 1751 and by 50.1 per cent between 1751 and 1801.

Historians of Wales have always recognized that Rickman's figures need to be considered with a lot of caution; indeed Rickman himself stressed that his material for Wales was incomplete. It would thus appear that as many as a fifth of Welsh parishes may have been absent from the Parish Register Abstracts of 1801. The aforementioned regional studies available have begun to identify the extent to which Rickman's figures may be giving a distorted picture of eighteenth-century population growth in Wales. Brinley Jones in his ongoing work on Carmarthenshire – soon to be published – will argue that Rickman's figures convey a wholly erroneous impression of eighteenth-century population patterns: while Rickman's figures indicate a population growth of 5,317 between 1750 and 1800 (62,000 to 67,317), he has found (on the basis of aggregating baptism and burial figures from as many as 90 per cent of surviving Anglican registers) that there was a surplus of almost 15,000 baptisms over burials for the period. Using a sample of parish registers, Glyn Parry has likewise disputed Rickman's figures for Caernarfonshire. Whereas the latter represent a 45.8 per cent increase in the period 1700–50 and a mere 14.6 per cent increase during the second half of the century, Parry contends that population growth between 1750 and 1800 'was as fast as, if not faster' than, between 1700 and 1750.[56] Similarly, in his analysis of population patterns in Montgomeryshire, Melvin Humphreys has shown that Rickman's figures quite significantly exaggerate the degree of population growth during the first half of the century and underestimate the rate of increase during the second half. On the basis of these few regional studies, it seems likely, therefore, that there was a faster growth in population in Welsh areas from mid-century than Rickman's figures suggest. Indeed, there was, in certain areas at least, a greater growth than even the parish registers suggest, for the significant growth of Dissent in Wales threatens the validity of Anglican registers as records of births and deaths in parishes, especially for the post-1750 years. Humphreys inflates his figures by the same amount as do Wrigley and Schofield, who contend that by the 1790s 1.17 per cent of all burials and 3.68 per cent of all baptisms are to be found, if at all, in non-Anglican registers. But Jones insists that these figures, particularly those for baptisms, are too low as far as west Wales was concerned, emphasizing that there can be little doubt that during the later decades of the century the growth of Nonconformity had placed a 'sizeable' part of the population outside the baptism register of the Church of England. In certain east Carmarthenshire parishes, indeed, by the 1790s there were more baptism entries in Nonconformist registers than in the corresponding Anglican ones. Similarly, in Merioneth, the information for the bishop from the parish of Llanycil for 1782 stated that far more baptisms took place in the Dissenting chapels than in the parish church.[57]

From these same regional studies, and figures 1 and 2 based on them, it emerges that the crucial turning-point in eighteenth-century population history in Wales was the early to mid-1740s.

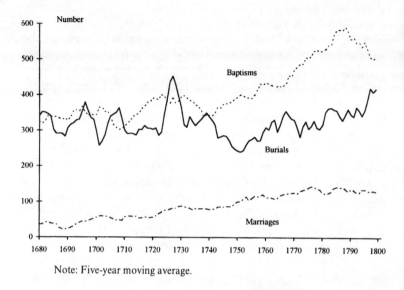

Note: Five-year moving average.

Figure 1: Baptisms, burials and marriages in Montgomeryshire, 1680–1805
Source: M. Humphreys, *Crisis of Community*, p. 72.

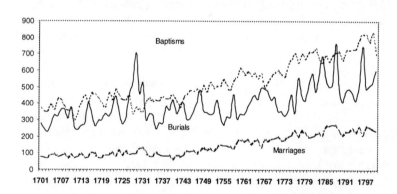

Figure 2: Baptisms, burials and marriages in west Glamorgan, 1701–1800
Source: Brinley Jones, *Glamorgan Historian, 12.*

Humphreys discerns a 'clear break around 1742' in Montgomery-shire. As in west Glamorgan, the population in Montgomeryshire in the years from 1701 to 1720 according to David Jenkins rose 'slowly but steadily', as shown in an overall surplus of baptisms over burials, but this was severely interrupted by the mortality crisis of 1728–30.[58] This serious setback was, however, reversed after 1742, for although there were intermittent high-mortality years thereafter down to the close of the century, they were not of sufficient impact seriously to set back the ongoing growth of population numbers shown in the secular trend of numbers of baptisms exceeding the number of burials.[59] Jones reaches the same conclusion for Carmarthenshire and west Glamorgan in regarding the mid-1740s as a crucial period. As mentioned in passing, he argues that the first two decades of the century witnessed a modest growth of population in west Glamorgan. Once again this small increase 'was not only brought to an end, but reversed by as much as a third' consequent upon the great surge in burials between 1728 and 1730.[60]

Parish registers reveal the grisly high mortality in Wales in 1698–1700, 1708–9, 1717, 1721, 1727, the astronomical number of deaths between 1728 and 1730, and the mortality crises in 1737–8 and 1742–3. During the black years of 1728–30 many parishes of west Glamorgan witnessed more than one burial on the same day, and frequently more than one death per family. In Caernarfonshire parishes, again, similar ravages were occurring: in eight sample parishes average burials between 1727 and 1729 inclusive were 111.3, compared with average burials over the three years 1724–6 of 60. The 1728–30 crisis was widespread in Wales as throughout Britain, and in a few Welsh parishes burial rates were as much as three times (in Penmorfa, Caernarfonshire, almost five times) as high as the average.[61]

It is rather more difficult to explain precisely these high death rates occurring in different years down to the early 1740s. In an important regional study David Jenkins has identified the cumulative effect of the run of poor seasons and bad harvests from the mid-1690s, bringing 'starvation and malnutrition' in their wake, as the cause of the high burial rate in Montgomeryshire parishes in 1699–1700, the most concentrated mortality occurring significantly in the late winter and early spring of 1699–1700. Not surprisingly, the most vulnerable were those at the frayed hem of society, the

dependent poor. A similar explanation has been advanced for
Flintshire's mortality crisis in these years. Here in west Britain, as in
Scotland, we are witnessing a Celtic-fringe phenomenon, no such
mortality crisis smiting English counties at this particular time.[62]

While starvation on its own does not appear to have been
generally the cause of high mortality peaks, the hinterland of
prevalent undernourishment in rural Wales made easier the grim
work of epidemic diseases like smallpox, typhus, dysentery, influ-
enza and, from the early 1740s, diphtheria, which, in a perverse
exacerbation, at times occurred simultaneously in a region, as for
instance in north Wales in 1739–42.[63] Smallpox, perhaps above all,
took a heavy toll, its one 'virtue' deriving from its preying on the
rich as well as the poor. 'All the children of these neighbouring
parishes [about Llanfechell, Angl.] are, or have been under small
pox and great many of them dye', was the forlorn jotting in
William Bulkeley's diary for 9 March 1738.[64] That same crisis year
saw the Lampeter vestry register (Cards.) replete with burial entries
of people who had become its victims. Again, in the high-mortality
year of 1742 Margaret Owen of Penrhos wrote to her husband on 9
September that 'the small pox is very rife in Anglesey'; likewise it
was raging between Aberystwyth and Machynlleth at Whit 1743.[65]

Faced with imprecise descriptions of them by contemporaries,
we are frequently left to guess the nature of the other diseases. 'It's
very sickly hereabouts and abundance dye', wrote estate agent
Griffith Parry from Clenennau (Caerns.) to his absentee master in
spring of the deep crisis year 1729, while it was recorded of
Carmarthen in August that many old people were dying of 'fever
and ague'.[66] Occurring in spring and early summer, it is feasible to
contemplate that this was an epidemic of dysentery or typhus.
Similarly, William Bulkeley noted on 9 February 1737 that 'Fevers
and Pleurises' were very prevalent in Anglesey, particularly in
certain parishes 'where they bury them almost every day' – an
illness that has been identified as an acute respiratory infection. To
the same diarist we owe the observation for 26 February 1740:

It is become very sickly in this neighbourhood [Llanfechell] and
generally all the country over, and the neighbouring country also . . . In
the neighbouring counties we hear that it is mortal and that they dye
very fast so that at Llanrwst Churchyard [Denbs.] there were at the
same time 11 graves open and 9 another time.

Given the time of the year, the disease could well have been typhus, which may have been brought over from Ireland, and in this instance it is clear that the starvation of the people weakened their resistance to it.[67]

While sometimes these 'great mortalities' occurred over widely scattered districts, at others they could be very localized, as for instance the epidemic of the 'bloody flux' – probably dysentery – which struck the parish of Llandygái (Caerns.) at the beginning of 1744. Obviously local factors were uppermost in triggering these outbreaks, with marshland areas, particularly those in Cardiganshire, succumbing to malaria, which was not experienced further afield.[68]

The epidemic diseases took their toll, too, in the second half of the century, sometimes raging, as earlier, at times of acute malnutrition, as did the fever in August 1758 in Anglesey and the 'malignant fever' in Llanidloes in 1800.[69] Grimmest of all was the continuing ravage of smallpox on the young. By the closing decades, when innoculation was increasingly available, many deaths were seemingly needless. Testimony to the reluctance of the poorer classes to recognize its efficacy is provided in a letter from Cardiganshire written in August 1796: 'To persuade them to innoculate their children is as difficult as to remove mountains. Upwards of six score little ones were buried of the small pox at Llanbadarn since it came to the neighbourhood – besides the great numbers buried elsewhere.'[70] Such epidemics would doubtless have accounted for the intermittent abnormally high-mortality years later in the century, including 1758, 1763–6, 1769–70, 1777, 1780–1, 1783–5, 1788, 1791–2, 1795–6 and 1799–1800. Llanelli parish in 1769 thus had fifteen deaths from smallpox, mostly infants; 'it has been a very sickly season and many have died lately in this town and neighbourhood', wrote George Morgan from Brecon on 23 February 1777, and the mid-1780s experienced many epidemic agues in Wales.[71]

It will be apparent that these later mortality crises were not sufficient, however, seriously to interrupt and halt the overall excess of baptisms over burials. Marriage aggregates, like those of baptisms, also saw a steady rise.[72] Population increase from mid-century was clearly a function of a rising birth rate and at times, as between the mid-1740s and 1760, a falling mortality rate. At best we can speculate about higher fertility. English evidence suggests that it was primarily due to declining age of marriage, and there is some tenuous evidence to point to the possibility of this having occurred in Welsh communities. For instance, writing from south-west Wales, schoolteacher Lewis Evans informed his brother in February 1791: 'The Sunday I was at home there were about twelve banns published at Llanbadarn. They marry younger and faster than ever anybody remembers. William Thomas the Clerk told me there are about 30 christenings for one or two burials which cannot be true.'[73] But it is also possible that it was due to rising marital fertility induced by improving living standards or changing nutritional patterns. Certainly in Wales *per capita* potato consumption was increasing. And here, perhaps the Welsh situation replicated Ireland's, where it has been suggested that the rise in fertility was a consequence of the increase in potato cultivation, which, being the responsibility of the woman, led to early discontinuation of breast feeding.[74]

5. *The Social Hierarchy*

That the Welsh rural community, as in all areas of Europe, was divided into finely graded status groups descending from the aristocracy and gentry at the apex of the social pyramid downwards through the ever-broadening ranks of professionals like attorneys, estate agents and higher clergy, freeholders, tenant farmers, craftsmen and artisans, labourers, and farm servants to the dependent poor at the base, is well established. Nor is any reminder needed that great sensitivity pervaded the members of the propertied élites, from the great titans to the mere yeomen and tradesmen, as to their 'rank and quality', and that every effort was made to parade and exalt the dignity of the family in the eyes of the covetous and status-conscious propertied community.[75] If not on such an ostentatious basis, a sense of rank and status was felt, too, within the massed ranks of those who were not landowners. Among the tenant farmers, those who held leases for lives basked in the glory of the status of freeholder at election times, entitled to vote at the hustings. Farmers of consequence, moreover, held seats in church; the observation on the Moreton chapel in the diocese of St Asaph in 1791 is significant: 'there are about 23 seats belonging to several different farms, and a large gallery, which is the place where menservants and cottagers sit in.' For all tenant farmers, their holding a farm bestowed a nice sense of independence. Contemporary observers were easily aware of the gradations of status within the lower orders. Thus the observation on the parish of Y Gyffylliog (Denbs.) for 1801 that there were '104 houses, and 460 inhabitants, almost all of whom are of the lower class, excepting some few respectable farmers and small freeholders' demonstrates both the preoccupation with 'respectability' and the contemporary view that only the minority of *substantial* tenant farmers along with the yeomen were of suitable consequence to merit separation from the 'lower class'. With any fluctuations in wealth, principally in the form of possession of land, came a corresponding change in people's status. Only in the nineteenth century do we witness this preoccupation with wealth as the bestower of status increasingly supplanted among the lower orders in Welsh rural communities by respect for a person's religious standing.[76]

Less is known about the size of the various hierarchical groups. Indeed, with the exception of two Montgomeryshire parishes for the 1790s, a want of reliable figures renders our knowledge of the precise social structure of individual rural neighbourhoods patchy and generalized. If we consider, first, the size of the propertied groups, it is calculated that the five baronets, fifty-nine squires and ninety-one gentlemen comprising the élite of Carmarthenshire society in 1710 constituted roughly 1.6 per cent of the county's total population. Similarly, the 219 Glamorgan gentry in 1690 represented a mere two or three households out of every 100 such units within the county. These figures accord with Peter Laslett's claim that 'the gentry were, at most, a twentieth of the population'.[77] Numbers of freeholders below the rank of gentleman were far more numerous; some indication of this is afforded by a list of Cardiganshire freeholders in four of the five Hundreds of the county compiled for election purposes in 1760. After taking out the lessees who were voters in the list along with those who were non-resident living outside the county, the eighty-eight squires and gentry were heavily outnumbered by the 642 non-gentry freeholders; among the resident Cardiganshire propertied groups, for every one gentleman or esquire there were seven yeomen.[78]

Very often parishes would contain no families 'of note', a term employed in the bishops' visitations to identify gentry and nobility. In these many cases, it follows that the standing of freeholders would have been enhanced. Llanbrynmair parish (Mont.) in 1791 thus had 'no families of note, excepting about 12 freeholders'. The situation was similar in Llanuwchllyn parish (Mer.) in 1795, the incumbent of the parish reporting thus: 'about 360 families of which number 130 paying taxes, no gentleman but one living in the parish, five freeholders'.[79] To differentiate themselves from the 'lower orders' certain of the more substantial yeomen freeholders were careful to appropriate to themselves the title 'Mr' or, again, to make provisions in their wills, as for the erection of superior tombstones on their graves, to reflect and enhance their social rank.[80]

That most of the dwellers on the land were below freehold status is typically reflected in the observation of Kinnerly parish in St Asaph diocese in 1791: 'none of more note than substantial freeholders, of which denomination there are a few. The others farmers, tradesmen and labourers.'[81] No clear pattern emerges as to the ratio of farmers' or landholders' families to those of labourers in the thirty-one Welsh parishes for which evidence is forthcoming from mid-century onwards. Whereas labourers' families outnumbered those of farmers or landholders in some twenty parishes, the reverse was the case in as many as eleven others, this last situation reflecting the high ratio of family to hired labour, and of indoor servants to outdoor married labourers on Welsh holdings.[82]

The meticulous counting of heads by Walter Davies in the two parishes of Llanfechain and Meifod in his native county of Montgomery in 1797 and 1798 respectively provides us with a unique picture of the social structure of rural Wales at this time.[83] The population of Llanfechain parish, which contained 107 families inhabiting a hundred houses, totalled 525 persons. Occupational groups were broken down by Davies as follows:[84]

Farmers, married, 26, with their wives	52
Ditto, widowers	4
Ditto, bachelors	1
Ditto, widows	1
Labourers in husbandry, married, 32, with their wives	64
Ditto, widowers	3
Housemates, married, 3, with their wives	6
Ditto, bachelors	2
Paupers, widows	18

Ditto, spinsters	1
Artificers, married, 19 with their wives	38
Ditto, unmarried	5
Inn-keepers, 2, with their wives	4
Professor of Music, 1, and his wife	2
Millers, 2, and their wives	4
Clergymen	1
Sexton and wife	2
Sons with their parents	106
Daughters with their parents	116
Men-servants (of which, men-servants employed on farms, 40)	50
Maid-servants (of which, maid-servants employed on farms, 38)	43
Insane persons, one of each sex	2
Total	525

Similarly, the population of Meifod parish was 'accurately taken' in 1798, its 293 houses containing 1,649 inhabitants. Although it is not possible to work the figures to the degree of precision as for Llanfechain, the breakdown of occupational groups nevertheless once again sheds valuable light on the social pattern of the Welsh countryside.[85]

Esquires	1
Clergy	2
Sexton	1
Schoolmaster	1
Farmers (including four freeholders)	98
Labourers in husbandry	82
Artificers, craftsmen	94
Millers	2
Inn-keepers	3
Butchers	2
Grocers	2
Drummers	1
Fiddlers	1
Gardeners	1
Male-servants (of which, men-servants employed on farms, 106)	140
Maid-servants (of which, maid-servants employed on farms, 84)	115
Widows	37
Widowers	1
Infirm	6

Reviewing the Meifod data, Walter Davies observed: 'The number of farmers, labourers, artificers, etc., may be nearly in the same proportion as in no. 23 [in Llanfechain]; and in all country parishes where agriculture is the main pursuit.' Table 2 reveals that his claim was near the mark so far as the two parishes were concerned. That craftsmen were only marginally less numerous than farmers underlines the self-sufficiency of these communities, a theme we shall explore in chapter 3. Male outdoor labourers and male farm servants outnumbered farmers by about 2:1 and (as revealed in table 2) by about 3:1 if maidservants are included. Within the farm-labouring workforce itself, there were marginally fewer male cottagers than male indoor farm servants living on the farm premises, and menservants and maidservants together outnumbered outdoor farm labourers by something like 2:1.

Table 2: Ratio of agricultural occupation groups in Llanfechain and Meifod parishes

	Llanfechain			Meifod		
Occupations	Numbers	Ratio to total	Occupations	Numbers	Ratio to total
Farmers	32	18.9	Farmers	98	21.1
Labourers in husbandry (i.e. outdoor labourers and indoor servants, males/females)	113	66.9	Labourers in husbandry (i.e. outdoor labourers and indoor servants, males/females)	272	58.6
Artificers	24	14.2	Artificers	94	20.3
Total	169	100.0	Total	464	100.0

Walter Davies provided details of a hundred houses in Llanfechain and of 293 in Meifod. As in pre-industrial English communities, the size of households was swollen by numbers of servants, and this would have applied more particularly to the better-off members. Indeed the cottagers' households would have been depleted by the early departure of their children to serve in

Table 3: Status and size of households

Status of household	Number of each group	Mean size of household	Range of sizes	Number of persons	Number of heads of household	Number of children		Number of servants		Relatives resident	Housemates
						m	f	m	f		
Gentry	1	16.0	–	16	2	0	0	8	6	–	–
Freeholders	3	6.3	8–5	19	6	6	5	2	0	–	–
Farmers	113	7.1	16–1	801	205	179	160	131	105	6	15
Artificers and tradesmen	91	4.5	9–2	410	177	98	91	21	12	3	8
Labourers	91	4.0	9–2	366	175	77	92	0	2	2	18
The poor	26	3.1	7–1	81	29	16	22	3	3	0	8

farmhouses and gentry residences. Table 3 breaks down Davies's
data into the principal occupational status groups for some 325 out
of the total 393 households whose occupations and status are
clearly signified. It is apparent that the mean size of households
was affected by the presence or lack of servants and that,
accordingly, gentry, freeholders' and farmers' households were
larger than those of the artificers, labourers and the poor beneath
them. It meant that while 208 (64 per cent) households out of the
total 525 were made up of tradesmen, labourers and the poor, yet
they comprised only 51 per cent of the total population. Peter
Laslett's insistence that our early-modern ancestors did not in the
main live in extended families is certainly supported by the
situation in the parish of Llanfechain as enumerated by Walter
Davies. Nevertheless, as Laslett concedes, elderly widows or
widowers would be housed in their last years of dependency, and,
in support of this, four of the hundred houses in Llanfechain parish
had a mother living in the household.[86]

Overall, there were on average 5.25 persons to each household in
Llanfechain and upwards of 5.5 persons to a house in Meifod,
statistics which perhaps explain Walter Davies's viewing the
multiplier of five used by the *Cambrian Register* in the 1790s to
translate the number of houses in a parish into the total population
'as much too small'. Mean household sizes were predictably smaller
in the late seventeenth and early eighteenth century, a time of more
static population. Schofield's contention that 4.25 was the likely
mean household size in certain English areas in the years
1650–1749 holds true for the Welsh situation, Bishop Lloyd's
Notitiae (1681–7) revealing a mean household size of 4.4 persons
for some 109 parishes in the diocese of St Asaph in the north-east.[87]

6. Welsh Towns and Town-Dwellers

Any study of agricultural communities must needs pay attention to
the towns which served them. Welsh towns were significantly
smaller than their English counterparts, so much so that Corfield's
minimum threshold figure of 2,500 for English and Welsh towns
during the eighteenth century is in the following discussion reduced
to 1,000 realistically to represent Welsh conditions.[88] That Welsh
towns were relatively retarded in growth is a reflection of low

population densities restricting demand, and of poor accessibility occasioned by indifferent roads.[89]

Even by 1801 there were many small towns like Lampeter, Hay, Llandeilo Fawr, Newtown, Knighton, Tenby and Conwy whose populations fell short of 1,000. Those of over 1,000 inhabitants in 1801 with a total population of 82,844 comprised a mere 14.1 per cent of the entire Welsh population of 585,128, a figure well below the 30 per cent of people in England and Wales living in towns with even a higher threshold of 2,500. Whereas the rank order in 1750 was in all likelihood pretty much the same as in 1670 when, according to Leonard Owen's figures, the hierarchy was Wrexham, Brecon, Carmarthen, Haverfordwest, Cardiff and Caernarfon, by 1801 that ordering had been crucially changed by the development of industry. If the earlier towns still occupied prominent positions in the rank order, with Carmarthen fourth, Wrexham fifth, Haverfordwest sixth, and Caernarfon seventh, by 1801 the first three positions went to Merthyr, Swansea and Holywell.[90]

Travellers were not impressed with the general run of Welsh towns they visited. Hutton, indeed, recorded of his visit to north Wales that upon entering Dolgellau, 'I found it was, like many of the Welsh towns, only to be viewed at a distance'. Though complimenting Caernarfon on its regular, well-paved streets, he caustically remarked: 'Most of the Welsh towns have the two faults of narrow streets and bad pavement.'[91] Similarly in the south, towns like Llandovery, Llandeilo, Tregaron, Lampeter, Llandysul and Narberth appeared to different travellers as poor, mean little places.[92] The often-cited sour comment of the traveller, the Revd Richard Warner, in 1797, on Brecon, 'Like most other towns in Wales, this place is interesting rather from what it has been, than on account of what it is now', indeed invites us to contemplate urban decline. There are problems in accepting this notion in its entirety, however. It is hence apparent that in this very instance of Brecon itself, the population of 1,914 in 1670 grew to 2,576 in 1801, a modest rise of 33 per cent. Just as certain towns remained stagnant, others forged ahead, a pattern that has been discerned for English country towns after the Restoration.[93] In north-east Wales Caerwys (Flints.) fell away in the shadow of Holywell's dramatic rise as an industrial centre over the course of the century, and such displacement by more robust competitors endowed with comparative advantages was a familiar occurrence in England and

Wales as a whole at the time.[94] Undoubtedly country towns in
England and Wales which thrived after the Restoration were those
which acquired a specialist role. Thus Holywell's rise as an
industrial town was matched by others like Swansea, Llanelli,
Neath, Merthyr Tydfil, Amlwch and Wrexham. Swansea was
likewise growing as an important seaside resort as, too, were
Tenby, Aberystwyth, Barmouth and, as a spa, Llanwrtyd Wells.
Other towns came to specialize as sea or riverine ports, places like
Haverfordwest, Carmarthen (the 'London of Wales' undergoing
much rebuilding), Cardiff and Caernarfon, or as centres with craft
specializations, as Denbigh in the manufacture of shoes and gloves,
or Dolgellau in the production of flannels, some twelve 'web
manufacturers' operating in the latter during the 1790s.

For all their small size compared with even middle-ranking
English towns like Devizes, Gloucester, Hereford, Hertford, Brid-
port, Tewkesbury and Newbury, Welsh towns were nevertheless
important in Welsh society as the economic, social and – so far as
the county towns in particular were concerned – political cogwheels
of their communities, and the abodes of the emerging middling
groups in society. Analysis of the 'principal inhabitants' of Welsh
towns listed in *The Universal British Directory of Trade, Commerce
and Manufactures, compiled for the years 1793–8* reveals a social
hierarchy paralleled elsewhere in English and European towns. At
the apex was a small circle of gentlemen and clergy, beneath them a
similarly small but significant and expanding group of medical men
and lawyers – whose supposed incompetence and rapacity
respectively came under the vitriolic lash of social commentators –
and in the lower reaches were the many 'traders'. Of the total 2,902
'principal inhabitants' of some thirty-five Welsh towns, some 245
(8.4 per cent) were gentry, 124 (4.3 per cent) clergy, ninety-one (3.1
per cent) medical men, a hundred (3.4 per cent) lawyers, and 2,342
(80.7 per cent) traders. Lawyers and medical practitioners were a
burgeoning group in English and Welsh towns alike; indeed, their
number in the 'poor, irregular' town of Llandovery struck one
commentator as 'incredible'.[95] The 'traders' included a range of
craftsmen and tradespeople like blacksmiths, coopers, saddlers,
carpenters, wheelwrights, shoemakers, spinners, weavers, hatters,
skinners, tanners, tailors, watchmakers, shopkeepers and merchants, and signifying their lowly ascribed status, schoolmasters.[96]
With the growth of foreign and domestic commerce over these

years there occurred a thickening in the ranks of the merchants, especially in the ports. Nineteen vessels belonged to the port of Carmarthen in the 1790s, trading with either London or Bristol; and reflecting the considerable commerce of the port the town boasted eight mercers, a timber merchant, a tallow chandler, a wine merchant and five general merchants. Some 252 individuals held accounts with one of them, Morgan Lewis, in the ten-year period 1797–1807.[97] Similarly, the port of Caernarfon housed seven general merchants, two mercers and a ship chandler. That farmers besides craftsmen were sometimes listed among the 'traders' of Welsh towns, if in small numbers, further underlines the close links between town and countryside in this pre-industrial era.

Family structures in towns are revealed in a census of Caernarfon in 1794 taken by Richard Griffith.[98] As in the countryside, servants and lodgers helped to swell the size of households. Of the total 2,613 inhabitants (excluding Town Liberty), these groups comprised some 15 per cent, a figure comparable with the 20 per cent in the rural parishes. So far as the incidence of nucleated families was concerned, once again such families were predominant: some 513, i.e. 82 per cent, of the total 629 houses in the town (excluding Town Liberty) were occupied by nucleated families. Besides the solitaries and no-family households (absence of a conjugal family unit), there were a small number of stem or extended families in the case of eleven married couples, who had either a father or mother living with them, and five married couples who had either brothers or sisters living with them.

Part I

Wresting a Mere Subsistence

~ 2 ~

Tenant Farmers and Small Freeholders

1. Tenant Farmers

In Wales as elsewhere in Great Britain most of the land was worked by tenant farmers. Although the typical Welsh tenant was in a very small way of business, even a farm providing no more than a meagre income was valued by him as bestowing a greater degree of independence than was enjoyed by the labourer beneath him. Moreover, possession of land, no matter what its extent, bestowed a certain status, thereby distinguishing the occupants from the remainder of the lower orders who obtained a livelihood through selling their labour. Important here in feeding the *amour propre* of possessors of land was the right to vote that went with it, a right granted not only to forty-shilling freeholders in the countryside but also to tenant farmers holding leases for three lives.

At the same time, it is easy to exaggerate the difference between those with and without land. For if farmers derived a quiet satisfaction from a sense of rank and status, and to lose their land brought a diminution in both community respect and self-esteem, there was no marked class division, no distinct gap between farmer and cottager. The observant Revd John Evans remarked in 1803 of the countryside about Troed-yr-aur in south Cardiganshire: 'The country is divided, for the greater part, into small farms, so that the farmer and his hind are nearly upon an equality, and precedency at table may easily be dispensed with.'[1] Arguably, a significant degree of assertive status consciousness on the part of small farmers had to await the decades leading up to the middle of the nineteenth century. Certainly Richard Williams, 'Poet of Vanity', echoed this growing sense of superior rank in his 'A new song illustrating the way of the world at the present time and the difference which existed in days of yore', published in 1850. Verse 11 ran, 'I remember that in former times the manservant and the maid sat at the same table for lunch as the husband and wife; now the husband and wife are in the parlour, beer being served to the husband and whey to the worker', and verses 13 and 14 continued in like vein:

> Formerly the master and manservant went on foot to the fair and the market, they were followed without vanity by the mistress, the maid, the son and the daughter. Now the husband and wife go on horseback, similarly the son with the daughter at his side, all of whom wear boots and spurs – no one goes on foot but the manservant and the maid.[2]

Symbolizing this widening gulf between farmer and labourer was the substitution in areas of north Wales around the mid-nineteenth century of the formal address 'Master' and 'Mistress' for the more intimate old terms 'uncle' and 'aunt'.[3]

Farms, most of them tenanted, were generally small, ranging for the most part from thirty to a hundred acres or so, perhaps around fifty acres representing the mean size.[4] Besides the important influences of the poor quality of land and distance from good markets, the small units were also in part a consequence of the earlier system of gavelkind, in operation in the Welsh hill and upland districts until the sixteenth century, whereby landholdings were equally divided among the sons upon the father's death. Such a system doubtless resulted in morcellation of holdings no less than of estates. Furthermore, as far as north Wales was concerned, the custom prevailing down to the close of the eighteenth century, the leasehold system of partitioning holdings amongst the lessee's family, certainly among sons but sometimes grandsons as well, resulted in the division of holdings into 'shares' after the original lessee's death.[5] Large farms, too, were simply out of reach of most prospective Welsh tenants, and perhaps English tenants with capital were deterred from taking Welsh farms by the barrier presented by the largely monoglot Welsh-speaking agricultural neighbourhoods. Significantly, the division into two holdings of Henllys farm in Pembrokeshire, part of the Bronwydd estate, was recommended in 1783 on the grounds that 'there are few tenants in this country of sufficient capital to undertake the management of such a tract of land as 398 acres 1 rood and 15 poles'.[6] Fertile tracts in the lowlands nevertheless boasted larger farms extending from 300 to 500 acres and sometimes above. Such unrepresentative farms even within the low-lying areas could be found notably in the Vale of Glamorgan, the Vale of Towy and south Carmarthenshire, south Pembrokeshire, the vales of Montgomeryshire and the Vale of Clwyd.[7] Thus in the Vale of Glamorgan, as Walter Davies recorded, there were a few farms ranging from 600 to 800 acres, and those between 300 and 500 acres were 'numerous'; even so, the general run of farms in the Vale in the late century would have fallen well short of 300 acres.[8]

Rights of grazing livestock on open commons and wastes effectively extended the scale of operations of many a tenant farmer with only a small farm, or for that matter, many a small freeholder. This being so, it is somewhat unrealistic to think in terms of size when considering upland farms, for these together with their sheepwalk, were assessed by the farming community not so much in terms of acreage but rather by the number of livestock they were able to support.[9] Tenant farmers possessed grazing and other rights on the commons by virtue of their landlords being lords or tenants, i.e. commoners, of the manor. Practices followed by tenant farmers in relation to grazing the commons and cutting turf differed from manor to manor, indeed from one common to another within a single manor, resting on customary arrangements entered into by the commoners within the particular manor concerned. In some instances, farmers could use any part of the common, usually (though not always) without stint, which gave rise to overstocking. In others, agreements were entered into by different landowners whereby individual tenants possessed the exclusive right of depasturing a specified area of the common, normally that lying contiguous to their boundaries, and the occupant could drive away livestock straying onto his or her 'liberty'.[10] Differing rights attached to farm holdings are reflected in a survey of the Wynnstay estate in Montgomeryshire in 1763. Some farms had grazing rights for a specified number of livestock – stint of common thus operating: for example, the sixty-eighty-acre Tyn y Nant farm in Noddfa township in Darowen parish had right of common for about eighty sheep and two or three horses; Melyn Dolgae – twenty-three acres in size – in Uwch y Garreg township in Machynlleth parish possessed right of common for sixty sheep on Park Hill, and the sixty-nine-acre Tŷ Mawr holding in Tafolwern township had a sheepwalk on Newydd Fynyddog for about sixty sheep. The total acreages given in the survey for other holdings included a specified acreage of sheepwalk, the entire extent of the latter belonging jointly to a number of neighbouring farms, often twelve in all. For instance, Pwlch Melyn in Rhiwsaeson township contained eighty-six acres, of which thirty-three were sheepwalk 'in proportion' with eleven other farms; of the 160-acre Y Wern in Rhiwsaeson township, some sixty-four acres were sheepwalk, again in proportion with eleven other holdings, and Tafolwern farm in Tafolwern township, covering sixty-six acres, included twelve acres of sheepwalk on Coryn Ffrydd proportioned between this and eight other farms.[11]

That these sheepwalks were a vital appendage to farms in this period and the century to follow was testified in 1892 by Tom Ellis, MP for Merioneth, when giving evidence before a parliamentary committee on small agricultural holdings: 'It came out distinctly in the evidence before the Committee that in Wales the small farmers in the hilly and mountainous districts were able to live a comparatively thriving life because they had, attached to their holdings, common pasturage on the hill and mountain sides.'[12] Even so, the uncertainty of the profits yielded by these sheepwalks represented a real drawback, depending as they did upon the mildness of the winter.[13]

Such was the smallness of some holdings that on certain occasions adjacent farms belonging to different owners were let together because it was hardly worth a tenant's while taking one without the other.[14] Some enlargement of farms took place over the course of the century by dint of landowners merging holdings. The process was often achieved by marrying small units, upon the expiration of their leases, with contiguous large ones. A crucial consideration emerges in John Harding's (agent to Powis Castle) advice to his master in 1702: 'there is two little tenements joyning to it which he will take the next year and if your Honour pleases convert it into one tenement to save Repairs.'[15] On the Wynnstay estate in the parish of Llanfrothen (Mer.), the farmstead of Tŷ Mawr and part of Llydiart y Wrach were joined between 1711 and 1713 with the remaining part of Llydiart y Wrach, and the two moieties of Maes Gwyr Llyn were joined in the same years.[16] Although marriage of farms was visible from the 1760s in the Vale of Glamorgan,[17] the process does not appear to have been rapid elsewhere in Wales. No doubt it was held back to some extent by the custom, widely practised by landowners, of allowing members of the same family to succeed a deceased tenant, no matter how small the farm.

When it did occur, consolidation was predictably not popular with peasant tenants, who harboured strong emotional attachments to what were often effectively 'family' holdings. What was stated by the Glynllifon estate steward to his employer, Lord Newborough, in 1827 about the proposed consolidation of his Denbighshire property applied equally to eighteenth-century Welsh peasant tenants:

> But if such thing was to be done there the dispossession of any of the old families would create such lamentations and woe as would be very little more than what your lordship's feelings and philanthropy could stand. Such doing is looked upon with a degree of horror by the country people in general.[18]

Thus Richard Vaughan of Derwydd (Carms.) wrote from London to his agent in April 1713:

> I very much approve your Endeavours to consolidate and unite distinct and several small tenements and you must not mind what Francis David Hugh or any other says or desire, but do that which you think is prudent and just as if it were your own case.[19]

Holdings were also being enlarged and new ones brought into being by enclosure and encroachments on the commons and wastes. Nor was this being done only by landowners, for tenants, too, played a part. Such was the case on Morva Hafod y Llyn in Beddgelert parish (Caerns.) between 1723 and 1745.[20] Indeed, the majority of encroachments made on the hills and mountainside within the lordship of Ruthin between 1749 and 1779 were made by tenant farmers, who enlarged their farms by taking in wastes.[21] Doubtless tenants were often encouraged in this by their landlords. Sometimes a tenant landed himself in trouble, as did Llewelin Williams, tenant of a farm belonging to a Mr Llewelin, whose enlargement of his holding from an encroachment around mid-century onto Cefn Erthan common in the Vaughan lordship of Perfedd (Carms.) and subsequent refusal to pay rent for it to the watchful John Vaughan, led to his being ejected by the sheriff.[22]

Welsh farm units were not only small; despite attempts on the part of landowners to bring some degree of tidiness and order to farm units, so rescuing them from the sorry mess of the late seventeenth century, down to the end of the eighteenth century they frequently remained fragmented and intermixed with other holdings. Such fragmentation stemmed from the intermixture of ownership of land in Wales, largely a consequence of the earlier operation of gavelkind. Farms which were composed of detached pieces lying interspersed among fields rented by other tenants were naturally difficult to run efficiently, and ill-feeling erupted from tenants trespassing on one another.[23] Intermixture of ownership sometimes entailed, also, certain holdings being jointly owned in shares by two or perhaps more parties, the tenant of such a joint-owned farm renting part from one owner and part from another.[24]

Sharing a tenanted holding among a number of the same family, which arose in north Wales, as we have seen, from dividing a farm upon a tenant's death and in accordance with his or her will, allegedly harmed its cultivation and general management. Of Yscubor Hên and Muriau Hên on the Vaynol estate (Caerns.) it was observed in a survey around 1800: 'the land being held by two or three parties (but same family) jointly – the rent paid jointly, and the hay and cows divided on the field – is the reason of the land being rather neglected.' Under the system it was simply the case that there were too many mouths to feed. Thus of Tyddyn y Priccia on the same estate it was noted in the survey: 'N.B. This farm would do well for one tenant, but the numerous family fed upon it now consume the whole crop if not more, and the houses all the straw.'[25]

It will be apparent that Welsh tenants were generally poor, lacking capital and barely distinguishable from their labourers in their standard of living. The very small size of farm units allowed men of such meagre capital to apply for them in the first place, and there was a strong urge among many in the community to take a holding, no matter how inadequate their capital. Thus Walter Davies remarked on the many farmers in north Wales who had secured leases of holdings worth £100 to £150 per year with just enough capital to work farms of £50 a year. Unfavourable comparisons were made with English farmers of substance. Writing to his estate steward in 1733, Paul Foley, owner of an estate at Almely, Herefordshire, took a dim view of them indeed: 'I am sorry to find nothing but Welsh tenants offer for Upcot – they are the worst of tenants, generally poor and without stock . . . you never yet procured me a Good Tenant since you was Steward . . .

Shropshire is a likely place to find a Tenant.'[26] Estate correspondence and surveys alike testify to the want of means of the Welsh tenantry. 'Most of the tenants upon the whole estate are already exceeding poor', was the reminder given the Margam estate owner, John Ivory Talbot, by his steward, David Rees, in June 1746.[27] A like dismal view of Welsh tenants' means was held by the steward of St Donat's Castle, Glamorgan, at mid-century: 'gentlemen here have been obliged to wait three or four years [for their tenants' rents] for there is no changing tenants in this country as in England, the country is so universally poor and changing is generally for the worse.'[28]

From his study of the wills of all farmers in the Welsh dioceses for the year 1800, numbering in all 240, Richard Colyer found that 84 per cent of the farmers concerned possessed personal wealth falling below £300; more specifically, approximately 12 per cent of the wills were from £1 to £50, 40 per cent from £51 to £100, 10 per cent from £101 to £200, and 22 per cent from £201 to £300. The remaining 16 per cent of farmers had personal estates worth between £300 and £2,000.[29] Such a distribution of wills points unmistakably to the scant means of farmers as a group. Again, in referring to the combined assets of three farmers in the township of Tre-wern (Mont.) totalling £1,200 upon their demise in 1717, Melvin Humphreys contrasts their comfortable lives with the 'slender' livelihoods endured by most tenants in the county.[30]

Small tenants' impoverishment, as distinct from the more opulent classes above them, was mirrored in their standard of living. In Glamorgan over the period 1660–1760 inventories reveal the household furniture of 'the ordinary farmer and farm labourer' to have been 'extremely modest and entirely utilitarian'. Writing in his diary for 21 April 1737, William Bulkeley noted how a small farmer holding a £15-a-year farm on his Brynddu estate and possessing goods worth not £30 had 'a mighty ordinary mean furniture'. Likewise, their diet. Commenting on south Wales, Walter Davies was careful to distinguish between the diet of the 'superior classes, and the more opulent farmers' on the one hand, whose tables were supplied with veal, mutton and beef, and the 'lower class of farmers, and the peasantry', on the other, who were 'seldom treated with "fresh meat"'. Moreover, bacon, salted and dried beef and occasionally mutton in the same condition, were mainly confined to their Sunday dinners.[31] The 'lower kind of farmers' in north Wales were similarly denied, having 'their tables as scantily supplied with the luxuries of salted bacon, butter, and cheese, as even those of the paupers they are forced to relieve'. The 'gloomy picture' continued: 'They find themselves, necessitated to sell almost the whole, as the means of payment of rents and taxes.'[32]

The term or length of tenures varied from one district to another and altered over time. While three-lives leases became increasingly common on certain estates in south-west Wales by mid-eighteenth century, elsewhere the tendency was for shorter terms; thus if in Glamorgan the three-life system was the most common tenure before 1750, tenancies at will were on the increase there from the 1680s, while northwards, in Montgomeryshire shorter leases at rack were the most common form of tenure by the early eighteenth century and on the Brynddu estate in Anglesey at mid-century farms were let for two, four, seven, eleven or twenty-one years.[33] By the later decades of the century yearly tenure had become the norm on north Wales estates, whereas in the south leases of varying terms were encountered; while they were commonly for three lives in the south-western counties, eastwards in Glamorgan they were granted for lives and also for seven, fourteen and twenty-one years.[34]

What were the tenants' responses to the leases they were offered? Commenting on the whole of north Wales in 1794, George Kay was in no doubt about the dissatisfaction farmers felt towards yearly tenures:

> This circumstance . . . accounts in a great measure for the very backward state of husbandry in those districts . . . I was repeatedly told, that the tenants were afraid of making the smallest advancement in this respect [i.e. improvement], lest they should next year be subjected to a rise of rent, or be turned out of their possessions.

The same criticism of yearly tenure at rack rent had been voiced earlier, in 1770, by Joseph Cradock in his *Letters from Snowdon*. One such instance of raising of rent of an industrious tenant indeed occurred during Kay's visit to Flintshire, when an enterprising farmer near Holywell found his improved farm attracted a much higher rent from a covetous neighbour, which offer tempted the landlord who informed the vexed trusting tenant that unless he paid almost the proffered rent he must quit the farm. There is some indication that north Wales farmers in the late century were willing to improve under twenty-one-year leases: Lord Penrhyn's tenants in Caernarfonshire prospered holding under such terms as did those on the Mawddwy estate of Mr Mytton.[35] On the other hand, there is evidence that tenants had mixed feelings about leases for lives. It was certainly the case that substantial tenants sought long leases as security for adventuring capital.[36] Again, John Vaughan, owner of the Golden Grove estate (Carms.) averred in 1757 that the granting of leases for lives was the method 'all the people chose and are well pleased with'. Contrariwise earlier, in 1726, certain of the Chirk Castle tenants met the agent, significantly 'in a body', to announce that the only way they would take leases was if they were granted for the term of twenty-one years instead of the term of the natural life 'as the leases are drawn'.[37]

Leases were being drafted in increasingly elaborate form in the eighteenth century, and the tightening control by the landlord over his property was reflected in the growing number of penalties for default.[38] In addition to the payment of a money rent either upon fine or at rack, tenants had to render certain duties primarily in the form of food payments and labour services, a part-survival of the manorial economy emphasizing the still relatively servile nature of the Welsh tenantry. Hens and eggs at Shrovetide were the usual food renders, while common labour services were a few days' reaping, a few days' service with a team for ploughing, harrowing or mucking, and carriage of coal to the landlord's mansion.[39] While commutation of food rents into money payments became general on Welsh estates over the course of the nineteenth century,[40] labour duties were to remain popular down to the 1890s, a reflection of the importance attached to them as a means of guaranteeing a sufficient workforce on the estate demesnes, particularly those of the smaller owners which were generally farmed for the market.[41] Tenants' obligation to work at harvest provided John Warren of Trewern (Pembs.) with some twenty-one 'customers' to work in his harvest alongside the thirty-five hired labourers in 1736.[42] Indeed, on the Brynddu estate in Anglesey the landlord covenanted his tenants at mid-century 'to work by the day when called upon'[43] – for which they were paid – over and beyond the normal reaping days. In similar vein, the Powis Castle lead mines were dependent in the late 1720s upon tenants of that and neighbouring estates turning ore carriers.[44]

Tenants also covenanted to pay a heriot of the best beast. Once again, by the close of the seventeenth century it had become usual for it to be rendered in kind or in money, at the choice of the landlord. Those who held of more than one landlord were hard pressed, for each owner expected payment.[45] Another covenant bound tenants to grind at a particular mill, making payment of the accustomed tolls. Sometimes they were enjoined to keep a hound. We shall see later that certain tenants found a number of these covenants irksome.

Such a significant amount of payment in kind in eighteenth-century Welsh agriculture was a consequence of the want of a sufficient supply of coins in the region.[46] Thus ironmaster John Morgan of Carmarthen was driven to minting his own coins at the beginning of the nineteenth century simply because there was insufficient small change in the local economy to be able to pay his own workmen.[47] Indeed, such was the want of ready money in the remote mountainous western districts of Snowdonia and Cader Idris that tenants down to the close of the century paid their rents to their landlords in cattle. Well into the nineteenth century indeed, the want of gold and silver in circulation meant that the north Pembrokeshire farming community made payment at stores for the provision of household goods not in cash but in such items as barley, wheat, cheese, butter, wool, pigs and geese.[48]

All too many holdings throughout the Welsh countryside were in a poor state of upkeep at this time. Responsibility for such repairs depended on the type of lease. Where tenants, as in north Wales, farmed their holdings at will, landlords were responsible for the upkeep of repairs and so much did they fall down on this that they were urged by George Kay in 1794 to pay attention to their tenants' 'bad' accommodation. In a letter to Arthur Young in 1792, Dr J. Simmons claimed that Squire Blayney of Gregynog (Mont.) was so generous towards his tenants in the way of providing buildings out of principle, 'being hurt by the behaviour of many of the Welsh squires, who grudge to floor the house of a farmer, that rents not more than £30 or £40 a year'.[49] In the south-western counties, on the other hand, the prevalence of three-lives leases meant that tenants themselves undertook to maintain the farms in good repair and so were, to some extent, responsible for the dilapidated farmsteads, albeit they had often taken them in a wretched state of repair. In contrast, landlords in Glamorgan and

Radnorshire agreed, either in their leases or under the general usage of their counties, to keep the buildings in repair. Yet again, in Brecknock and in 'several parts of other counties' in south Wales some compromise was being reached by the close of the century whereby expenses were divided between the parties, the landlords finding materials, the tenants doing the carriage and workmanship.[50]

Not only were repairs in a dilapidated state for much of the century; the general level of farming was low, even taking into account the constraints imposed by physical factors. 'Many of the errors so visible in the agriculture of this country, certainly arise from the ignorance, prejudice, indolence, and poverty of the tenants; but there are others, which attach to the proprietors of the estates.' That was the judicious summing up of the Revd John Evans in 1803 in his observations of the agriculture of south Wales.[51] Peasant-tenant farmers were certainly poor; lacking risk capital they farmed merely to get by and spurned the new progressive husbandry, claiming that they, too, could farm like their landlord if they had his purse. Reluctance to adopt new practices also sprang from 'ignorance' and the 'prejudice' which was rooted in their stubborn attachment to the ways of their forefathers. They hung back from trying out new English techniques, too, lest they should invite their neighbours' ridicule and be seen by the community as getting above themselves. Such attitudes cast some doubt upon the practicality of suggestions forwarded at the time towards promoting good husbandry: like that of the valuer of the Wynnstay estate in Montgomeryshire in 1763 of settling on the estate a few 'improving' English tenants as 'the most likely expedient to bring the Welsh farmers out of that dull, slovenly method they have been for ages pursuing', or Hassall's contention in 1794 that the successful practice of the green crop system by a few industrious tenants properly encouraged by the landlord would be the best means of recommending the utility of the new husbandry to the wider tenant community of Carmarthenshire.[52]

In too many instances landlords, for their part, fell down on their duties to promote good husbandry among their tenants. Joseph Cradock lashed those of north Wales in 1770 thus: 'Undisturbed with the spirit of enterprise and ambition, they follow the dull track of their ancestors, without thought and without remorse, and live and die unknown.' Writing in 1806, William Williams, a land surveyor, was similarly uncomplimentary to the general run of indolent landowners in Caernarfonshire.[53] It is likely that the growing number of non-resident absentee landowners were most culpable in this respect. Contemporaries drew attention to the problem. In his observations on the district of Dolbenmaen (Caerns.) at the opening of the nineteenth century, Edmund Hyde Hall prognosticated that the area 'now deprived of its resident gentry will probably for some time neither find nor make the necessity of this turnpike trust or any other improvement'.[54] To a lesser degree, the resident gentry for their part all too often neglected their estates and tenants. They were preoccupied with enlarging their estates rather than with improving them. Indebtedness of both small and great owners alike, frequently the product of extravagance and 'dissipation' and ending up in sales, was hardly conducive to investment in improvements;[55] and practices on the part of landlords – admittedly to be found in different parts of the Principality and at different times – like letting farms from year to year, letting by auction to the highest bidder, persisting in the south-west with the system of life leases at ridiculously low rents, together with their neglect to provide proper outhouses and failing to introduce progressive husbandry clauses into their leases, were all disincentives to improvements on the part of tenants.[56]

Although their role in promoting progressive farming has been downplayed by recent insistence that the real improvers were the lesser gentry, occupying owners and substantial tenants (to which group I would want to add certain clergymen), aristocratic and substantial gentry families also experimented with new husbandry techniques on their home farms.[57] As Richard Colyer has shown, this was especially so from mid-century, landowners calculating that by making improvements on their demesnes they would set an example to their tenants and, importantly, be perceived by their fellow landowners as benevolent and 'patriotic' landlords.[58] We can mention prominent and oft-cited examples like Thomas Johnes of Hafod, Thomas Lloyd of Cilgwyn and Colonel Lloyd of Bronwydd, all in Cardiganshire, John Vaughan of Golden Grove and the Rice family of Newton, Llandeilo, both in Carmarthenshire, John Mirehouse of Brownslade in Pembrokeshire, John Franklen of Llanmihangel in Glamorgan, Edward Corbet of Ynysmaengwyn and William Oakeley of Tanybwlch in Merioneth,

Paul Panton of Plasgwyn, Anglesey, Mr Myddelton of Chirk Castle in Denbighshire and Arthur Blayney of Gregynog in Montgomeryshire. If their improvements with drainage and reclamation, planting, growing new crops like turnips and clover and cross-breeding were decidedly more than Melvin Humphreys's begrudging depiction 'fashionable gestures', yet they were thin on the ground, not least because many large estates were in the hands of absentees. Moreover, for the kind of reasons we have rehearsed, the impact upon the wider tenant community of their home farms and the county agricultural societies which they sponsored from mid-century fell short of expectations. At the same time, the economies of local areas undoubtedly gained from the gentry-sponsored late-century turnpike trusts, canals (from the 1790s) and, even if very few in number, enclosure Acts.[59]

As was to be claimed of nineteenth-century Welsh farmers, no doubt their eighteenth-century forebears, likewise, when considering renting a holding asked themselves not whether they could make a living from the farm but rather whether they could pay the rent.[60] The first half of the century saw a modest rise in rents on Welsh holdings. In part, this was a response to improved methods of husbandry. Thus Thomas Lewis Esq. of Harpton Court (Rads.) informed his son around 1717 that 'the estates in these parts are much improved [in rents] of late years and are still rising by lime and water and also good husbandry'.[61] A more general cause of increased rents, however, was the practice of many landlords letting their farms to the highest bidders. Thomas Cradock wrote from London to Thomas Griffith at Margam (Glam.) in March 1725:

> Since it requires as much hast to let out this farm for the year and I am at this distance from you I must refer it to you to let it for this year as you think best for my Lord's interest only takeing sure you accept of the best offer soe it be made by a responsible person.[62]

Certain owners, too, reflecting a more businesslike approach to their properties, had their farms surveyed and valued. Indebtedness was a further spur prompting landlords to make the most of their properties. For instance, the London accountant for the owner of Powis Castle instructed the Welsh agent in 1724 to 'use all your endeavour to make the best of everything for unless you do that the estate will never clear off the great incumbrances that are upon it'.[63] For whatever reason, lands in Carmarthenshire by 1715 were 'much improved'.[64]

If, down to the 1760s, there was no general increase in rents to intolerably high levels as was to occur thereafter, the chronic shortage of capital meant that tenants were always slow in meeting their rents. William Vaughan, agent of the Ashburnham Brecknock estate, wrote in a tone of resignation to Lord Ashburnham in 1708: 'as for the old arrears in Mr Dalton's time I doubt they will never be received; for they are of a long standing and the defaulters make such plausible excuses that I despair to receive any of them.'[65] Lord Powis's London accountant wrote tersely to the Welsh agent, Humphrey Parry, in 1725 how his Lordship

> had as good be without tenants as have such as pay no rent; in fine I am
> resolved to bring those estates to the same custom as in Northampton
> and Middlesex to clear one half year before another is due; and not have
> whole volumes of arrears returned as has always been the custom of Mr
> Hughes and your father.[66]

That a similar frustration over slack payment of rents on his Montgomeryshire properties in the mid-1740s was felt by Charles Parry of Bradley Green, Worcestershire, was betrayed in his outburst to his agent: 'I want to know what is the matter my tenants pay me no rent for at this rate I had as good sell or else give away my estates as to keep them.'[67]

Given that recourse to changing backward tenants in a capital-starved society was merely wishful thinking,[68] landlords had simply no option but to indulge the 'system of arrears' and to permit their tenants to pay their rents in driblets. Yet such an accommodation led to some tenants finishing up totally ruined: 'When a tenant goes backward it is a kindness to him as well as a justice to the landlord to remove him before he be quite ruined and undone', Richard Vaughan of Golden Grove (Carms.) counselled his agent in summer 1715.[69]

In poor seasons or, worse, runs of poor ones down to the mid-eighteenth century, the situation for many tenant farmers verged on collapse and some were ruined. At the end of the seventeenth century much gloom was experienced in their ranks through the bad seasons in 1678–83, 1690–1 and 1694–9,[70] and farmers again suffered acute privation in the early eighteenth century during 1700–3, 1708–9, 1722–3, 1726, 1728, 1731–8, 1740–2, 1747–8, 1750–1 and 1755–6.[71] Various factors gave rise to these 'distempered times', but in a primarily pastoral farming region low livestock prices were often the reason for crisis. Thus cattle prices ruled low in Welsh fairs for much of the 1730s. Conditions in Denbighshire, for instance, were dismal in the mid-1730s, David Roberts reporting in October 1736: 'There is so much ground and lands unlet about here. Some years we may let and some may not and the fairs are very bad for selling beast in our country.'[72]

Given that Wales was an exporting region sending out store livestock to be fattened on lusher English pastures, a crucial factor affecting sales in Welsh fairs was the condition of the English grazing areas. June 1683, for instance, saw the fairs of north Wales doing poor business owing to the very wet weather which made graziers shy of purchasing until 'their ground by dryed up'.[73] Lack of 'a drover or strange butcher' at Caerwys on 5 March 1747 meant a very poor fair there, to the discouragement of the poor farmers of the district.[74] Equally vital, of course, was the availability of grass in Wales itself. The crisis in Monmouthshire in 1723 arose out of want of sales of cattle because of drought, shortness of grass and the poor prospect of fodder, and a lack of grass dampened sales of cattle about Cardiff in June 1731.[75] Dry seasons and poor crops meant low sales of cattle in 1740–1, barns even being unroofed in Anglesey to obtain old thatch for cattle.[76] In hilly areas where no corn could be sold to help with rents, slack livestock sales could be even more severely felt. Griffith Parry thus wrote from Clenennau (Caerns.) on 4 January 1742 to his master, William Owen at Porkington: 'the neighbours here are not allowed to sell their butter and cheese to go into south Wales as usual which is very hard with the mountainous tenants where there is no corn growing which makes rent more backward in payment.'[77] Hardship could also ensue for Welsh livestock farmers at times of very high corn prices for, at such times of scarcity, farmers – as those in Carmarthenshire in summer 1756 – were forced to buy their bread corn in the market, so robbing them of their ready cash.[78] For lowland farmers depending to a significant degree upon corn sales for meeting their rents, bad harvests were likewise damaging. Absentee Mrs Rice of Newton (Dynevor, Carms.) heard the gloomy news in late October 1735: 'I was in Carmarthenshire and met with but bad pay, their corn is in general grown and spoilt by the bad harvest and little or no price for cattle.'[79]

Although the normal convention was for owners to provide the land and the fixed capital and tenants the working capital, that distinction was often blurred in such times of crisis as occurred in late seventeenth- and early eighteenth-century Welsh farming. Landlords had no option but to come to their tenants' rescue by shouldering part of their losses. In the first place, arrears were permitted to mount to high levels, as on part of the Chirk Castle estate in Michaelmas 1744 where there were accumulated arrears of £1,265 on a rental of £926, arrears which rose to £2,027 a year later.[80] Moreover, payment in manageable amounts at different times of the year was permitted by landlords to enable tenants to take the best advantage of the periodic local fairs. For all the low esteem in which they were held, one suspects that it was the agents on the spot who often saw the necessity for a sympathetic approach towards tenants in arrears. The Revd William Vaughan thus wrote from Breconshire to Lord Ashburnham in London on 16 April 1708: 'and as I am oblig'd to be dutifull and faithfull to your Honour, so I think there is an obligation upon me the other side to be tender to your Lordships tenants: that times are bad and they do grone.'[81] Likewise, David Williams wrote on 26 February 1732 to the Hon. John Myddelton at Cefn y Wern, near Wrexham:

> It's hard times for money in these parts (Denbs.), I can get but little from tenants and indeed cannot expect much from your tenants till May for I am sure you are not inclined to put any of them to hardship and if severity was used everything is so very low it would be their ruin. All them that are in arrears at this time can pay but very little till they can get their cattle in order.[82]

For all that, tenants displayed a touching faith in their landlord's kindness in wishing to appeal to them over the head of their agents in matters like rent disputes.[83]

On some estates, furthermore, tenants were allowed to pay their rents partly or wholly in kind. In 1698, the poorest and weakest tenants on the Powis Castle estate were permitted to pay with corn; or bacon, cheese and butter; or an ox or a cow, and with work like ploughing and harvesting. Likewise, between 1699 and 1702 tenants on the Chirk Castle estate paid with cattle. As at Powis

Castle, so too elsewhere, tenants were sometimes allowed to clear their rents by doing work for the landlord. Thus Edward Daniel, tenant of the Bodewryd estate (Angl.), carried as much sand for the agent in July 1732 as was calculated would clear the previous year's rent. In like vein, the Margam (Glam.) agent, Thomas Cory, pressed his employer in 1712 to undertake repairs to a certain farmstead through his own workmen rather than grant money allowances to the tenant concerned, 'especially since your Lordship has several tenants so far in arrears that they will hardly ever be able to pay unless your Lordship will be pleased to employ them on such an occasion as this'.[84]

In the difficult years 1700–1 impoverished tenants on the Wynnstay estate had their holdings stocked by the landlord. For instance, in 1700 Ellis ap Richard and William David held separate moieties of Gweburnant farm in Penmachno parish (Caerns.) at rents of £10. 15*s.*, and 'in that those tenants grew poor and would have parted' the agent undertook to stock the holding with thirty young cattle, for the keeping of which over summer and winter they were allowed nearly 8*s.* a year for each animal. The agent commented: 'I found in *anno* 1700 that my master lost nothing by it but had some advantage.' Similarly in 1701 Hugh David, tenant of Croesor farm in Llanfrothen parish, Merioneth – 'being poor and lest it should stand vacant being all mountains' – was not only allowed to keep the hundred sheep which the agent had already put there in May 1700 without charge but was also sent another fifty-two, he receiving 6*d.* a piece for keeping them. Furthermore, his rent was reduced from £16 to £12, an earlier abatement of 40*s.* having been made in 1698.[85] Such abatements and reductions and, worst of all in the landlords' eyes, the prospect of vacant holdings, were avoided if at all possible not only by the aforementioned strategies but by making allowances to tenants for building or repairing outhouses, ditching and fencing – deployed on the Wynnstay estate in the last quarter of the seventeenth century – and, as on the Chirk Castle estate in the 1740s, by allowing taxes.[86] Even so, as we saw in the case of Hugh David's holding, abatements were sometimes forced on landlords during years of crisis.

For all the succour they received some tenants collapsed. 'Several gentlemen in Monmouthshire as well as other counties have trouble, vexation and loss with farms in hand that the tenants could not hold by reason of the times', observed Edward Riggs in

May 1723.[87] Agents were prompted into making distraints to prevent other creditors from getting in before the landlord.[88] Correspondence between agents and landlords sometimes portrayed a grim picture of the tenants' plight, none more so than the letter David Roberts wrote from Plas Eyton (Denbs.) to Chancellor Wynn at Bodewryd (Angl.) on 6 October 1732: 'about one and twenty tennants breake up in this parish [in Denbs.] besides great many others about here are Rueined no money sturs in the Country; four of Glanhesbin tennants I was forst to Shutt up theire barns and cease there Cattle yesterday.'[89] Gloomy news likewise, was sent to William Owen at Porkington by Griffith Parry from Clenennau on 4 January 1742:

> I seized upon your tenant at Ceven Coch and am busy in selling the stock . . . and shall next week seize upon the Tenants at Ceven Gwyn for both arrears unless I have money or security, I forebore with both of them too long which was owing to scarcity of money and hay last year.[90]

Writing from Margam on 2 November 1740, Watkin Jenkins told Lord Mansell that he had distrained on several tenants but could not sell their cattle.[91] It sometimes happened, too, that after the sale of tenants' distrained goods certain arrears were found to be 'desperate', i.e. irrecoverable. This was found to be so in 1707 in the case of Mathew Price of Llangorse and John Jenkin of Bronllys on the Breconshire Ashburnham estate, and the agent counselled Lord Ashburnham that it would be simply a waste of money attempting to sue them.[92] Generally, landlords either wrote the debts off or, as on the Wynnstay estate in 1695, recovered them in work like guttering and repairing.[93] Certain Wynnstay tenants with irrecoverable arrears in the 1690s resorted to begging, while still others on the Wynnstay and Chirk Castle estates 'fled the country'.[94] A few Wynnstay tenants who failed in the harsh years at the close of the seventeenth century were sometimes allowed to take a smaller farm on the estate, an indulgence that was again in operation there in the difficult years of the 1820s. For example, in 1692 Edward ap Richard, having grown poor and unable to work a £10 holding in Maenan, was removed to a smaller holding 'which another broken tenant had quitted', paying a rent of £5. 5s. 6d.[95] Doubtless most who failed at Wynnstay and elsewhere ceased to be farmers, some no doubt slipping down the status ladder to become farm labourers. Firm evidence survives of the unfortunate Thomas ap Robert of Isaf Commot in Caernarfonshire: his tenement, part of Tyddun y Tŷ Croes on the Wynnstay estate, 'was vacant *anno* 1691 the man broak his cattle dyed and all he had seized to answer part of the rent and arrears who now is a hired servant at Eglwysuan'.[96]

After the crisis of the mid-1750s farming conditions improved, though farmers faced further depressed prices in 1762 (in Montgomeryshire and Carmarthenshire),[97] in 1763 (in Brecknock and Glamorgan where, noted William Thomas in May, 'Daily distress are somewhere or other on renters')[98] and, more widespread, in 1780–5, which once again saw arrears in payment of rents.[99] Suffering among tenants on the far-flung sprawling lands of the Wynnstay estate in Denbighshire, Montgomeryshire and Merioneth was thus acute in the early 1780s, adverse seasons affecting both grass and corn crops. Tenants found it difficult to dispose of their cattle in spring and early summer of 1780 and 1781, and spring 1782 was horribly backward, Francis Chambre, the weighed-down agent, bemoaning 'a time of scarcity that memory can scarcely equal'. Such was the severity of the weather in late April 1782 in upland west Montgomeryshire that great losses were incurred among sheep and lambs. Most tenants there, both great and small, had to purchase their bread in May 1783, while their counterparts in the upper Vale of Clwyd had not only to purchase grain for spring seedcorn but also what was required to make bread for their families. Spring 1785, too, was backward, want of grass obliging tenants to lay out the money kept back for their rents in purchasing fodder for their cattle.[100]

Even so, in the second half of the century it was rather the marked increase in their rents which came at different times on different estates from the 1760s, prompted by increased prices, competition for holdings and letting of farms to the highest bidder, husbandry improvements and enclosure and rationalization of farm holdings through gradually getting rid of intermixed lands, which sparked resentment. For now the old leniency – partly born of laxity – on the part of landlords was replaced by more commercial attitudes with the aim of maximizing incomes. Not only, with the help of estate surveys and maps, were rents raised to unprecedented levels – so that in Montgomeryshire, for instance, increases between 1770 and 1800 generally ranged between 20 and 50 per cent – but, in Cardiganshire at least, certain owners from the start of the 1790s and possibly earlier abandoned the old indulgence with regard to arrears.[101] That the rent increases were to cause tenants to feel under pressure and to blame their landlords for what they, to an extent naively, believed to be harsh treatment was to be amply attested by contemporary commentators and will be discussed in chapter 6. A cautionary note needs sounding in the case of southern counties, however, for here, particularly in the south-west, tenants possessing leases for lives enjoyed 'absurdly' low rents.

In addition to their rents, farmers had to pay the tithe, of which two kinds were exacted: the great or rectorial tithes, of corn and hay, and the little or vicarial tithes, of calves, pigs, geese, lambs, wool, eggs, milk, cheese, honey, beans, peas and the like. Down to the close of the eighteenth century they were mostly paid in kind, though sometimes they were commuted to cash.[102] The mode of collection of the tithe of corn in the parish of St David's (Pembs.) was described in a bill in the Court of the Exchequer in 1721:

> That according to the Custom of the parish and all adjacent parishes, all farmers and occupiers of land are obliged to lay out the tenth sheaf of corn for tithes, and the tenth part being so laid out and severed, they are obliged to lay up the said tenths in stacks for the benefit of the farmer [i.e. the lessee of the tithes] and to preserve and secure the same for the space of 24 hours, or for some reasonable time till the farmer [i.e. the lessee of the tithes] might have an opportunity of carrying it away.

As in this instance and in the later suit in 1770 in the ecclesiastical court against a farmer in the parish of Penbryn (Cards.) for not making up the tithe sheaths in small heaps according to the custom of the parish, friction could arise over the methods of tithe payment, a more detailed consideration of which will follow later in this study.[103]

Beyond the hardship tenants endured from adverse seasons, high rents and irksome tithes, they were occasionally struck by natural calamities like cattle distemper and floods. Montgomeryshire farmers, in particular, but also those in Flintshire, Denbighshire and Radnorshire had to face up to contagious distemper among their horned cattle in 1749 and 1750 which killed their livestock. Furthermore, toll collectors fell into arrears, for as at Wrexham no cattle were sent to the markets.[104] Floods, too, from time to time

damaged certain tenants, as, for instance, two in the Towy Valley
(Carms.) in 1737, the Chirk Castle tenant, William Evans of
Gartherur, in the 1760s from 'the two rivers' flooding, and certain
tenants belonging to the Wynnstay and other estates in Merioneth
in summer 1781.[105] High tides, also, hit Golden Grove tenants
along the coast of Carmarthenshire early in the century, and
certain farmers on the Margam estate (Glam.) in the second
quarter of the century quit their holdings because of damage done
by spring tides.[106]

It was not uncommon for tenants to rely in part upon supplementary forms of income for payment of their rent and other
taxes. With most Welsh farmers requiring at least forty acres to
make a living for themselves and their families, it will be apparent
that those many tenants holding smaller units perforce relied upon
some extra means of support. Even allowing for superior land
quality in some situations, there is no doubting that thirty acres or
below would have constituted unviable units, and the ratio of these
to the total number of farms on a spread of Welsh estates was
noticeable: sixty-five out of the total 151 holdings on the Bodorgan
estate (Angl.) in 1725; as many as thirty-one out of the total thirty-
six farms in Glamorgan belonging to the Hon. Christopher
Mansell in 1731; forty-five of the seventy-nine holdings owned by
Sir Thomas Stradling in Glamorgan in 1732; six of the twenty-five
tenements on the Noyadd Trefawr estate in Cardiganshire in
1744–5; thirty-five of the forty-six holdings on the Caerhun estate
in Anglesey and Caernarfonshire in 1774; and twenty-three out of
the fifty-six tenements on the Slebech estate in Pembrokeshire in
1791.[107]

Flannel manufacture in the farmhouses scattered across the hills
and moorlands of mid- and north Wales was, indeed, an important
adjunct to farming, so much so that farm servants hired to work
the land were also expected to be proficient at weaving, work which
would be done on one or two looms located in an outhouse or lean-
to shed during the slack winter months in the farming cycle. Such
was the dependence upon woollen manufacturers by these farmers
that the Wynnstay agent gloomily forecast that poor sales of
flannels in the area about Machynlleth (Mont.) in spring 1783
would prevent payment of some farm rents there. Not all farmers
engaged in weaving were poor, however. Inventories point to some
of them in Merioneth and Montgomeryshire becoming quite

affluent, certain substantial farmers in Montgomeryshire, for instance, engaging spinners and weavers on a daily basis.[108]

Carriage of timber and other minerals was another source of extra income. With regard to timber, tenants of John Salusbury Esq. at Bodfari (Flints.) were in March 1746 to be given the refusal of becoming timber carriers at 'reasonable' wages. A half-century later, farmers in the parish of Llanferres (Denbs.) 'often' relied upon the carriage of lead ore to pay their rent. So much in the later decades did the tenants of smallholdings of ten to twenty acres involve themselves in carriage of lead ores, calamine and coal in the mineral parish of Whitford in Flintshire that local farming allegedly suffered, an injurious effect perhaps likewise suffered in the many other areas of the county where 'farmers were greatly employed' in carrying minerals. Of course, agriculture and extractive industry were carried on side by side on the landed estates and it is certainly the case that some of the work performed by tenant farmers – receiving the usual rates of payment – was at the behest of their landlords.[109]

Along the entire stretch of the Welsh coastline, many farmers, too, derived part of their income from involvement in sea-trading activities, their inventories often listing 'shares in a vessel'. Indeed, so far as the coastline of Glamorgan was concerned, many men who combined seafaring with farming chose to designate themselves 'mariners' and were nicely prosperous.[110] Some farmers, too, about the coast were involved in shadier dealings, linking up with smugglers in providing horses and carts on the beaches to convey the contraband goods inland. For example, a letter of May 1763 written by the collector of customs at Beaumaris (Angl.) to the Board of Commissioners reported that: 'in less than an hour's time [the smugglers] will land and carry the whole cargo into the country, as there are several farmers concern'd with them, which [*sic*] have their carts and horses ready for that purpose'.[111]

2. Small Freeholders

Given the tendency by contemporaries when designating occupational categories to interchange the terms yeoman, farmer and farm servant or labourer, it is unwise to draw a clear differentiation between tenant farmers and yeomen. Moreover, if we seek to uphold the division along the lines that yeomen were small freeholders occupying their own lands then we have to realize that many at the same time would have been tenanting some extra land from neighbouring owners. Although the economic status of a freeholder might often fall below that of a tenant-farming neighbour, in general terms the social division between mere tenant farmers and non-gentry freeholders in a neighbourhood was acknowledged. In particular, freeholders were intensely and conceitedly proud of being voters in elections (though tenants holding leases for lives enjoyed the same privilege) at a time when few around them were so fortunate. They, too, by virtue of their social status would be able to get good farms for their daughters by arranging successful marriages. As was the case later in the nineteenth century, 'the arranged marriage was a feature of the farming community; a spinster's marriage portion was often known, particularly if it had been provided for in a father's will.'[112] Their sons were quite frequently put into the professions.[113]

Freeholders below the level of the minor gentry would have obviously varied in their fortunes. Those at the top of their group stood out as is reflected, for instance, in a description of Gresford parish (Flints.) in 1791: 'upwards of 400 houses, 2400 souls or thereabouts. Besides 4 esquires, several substantial yeomanry.'[114] Glyn Parry has shown that the big non-gentry freeholders or yeomen of mid-eighteenth-century Caernarfonshire were sometimes as rich as neighbouring gentlemen. Take, for example, Thomas Parry of Plasnewydd, Llanfaelrhys, whose wealth at his death totalled a dazzling £775. 7s. 6d. (much of it in bills, bonds and ready cash) or, again, Richard Owen of Penmachno whose worldly possessions at his decease, once again largely in debts owed him, were valued at no less than £608. 13s. 6d. Significantly in a society where the size of a person's house accurately mirrored his or her wealth, these two prosperous farmers in each case resided in the demesne farm of a former gentleman's estate that had since been absorbed into the property of another estate-owner.

But such substantial freeholders were untypical. In Caernarfonshire the last-cited inventories were way above the average for the county of £84. 2s. Although this last sum was certainly respectable, it was less than half the average inventory of Caernarfonshire gentlemen.[115] Nonetheless the relative comfort of the small freeholders and more prosperous tenant farmers would have been ostentatiously demonstrated from the early decades of the eighteenth century in their possession of refinements like the looking-glass and clock.[116] And in an era when a wish to own land was a burning desire of most countrymen, they took pride in the family, were accorded due status by those around them, and propertyless neighbours derived pleasurable satisfaction in being able to claim a family connection.[117]

If the tendency from the seventeenth century in bequeathing small freeholds was increasingly away from partible inheritance towards primogeniture, nevertheless freehold farmers took care in their wills to provide for remaining members of their family. As far as Montgomeryshire was concerned, widows were left all the household goods, implements and stock, while younger children received money portions to be charged on the freehold property, which was left intact to the eldest son. Under these arrangements, widows often remained throughout their lifetimes on the family farm and acted matriarchally as the effective head of the household. Many of the younger children, unable to find a living from the limited resources of the family farm, were obliged to become labourers on the farms of relations or neighbours. Later, after marriage, their modest portions and perhaps frugal savings might just allow them to rent a small farm, but their feeling of consequence was nourished by the awareness of who they were.[118] In the closing decades of the century, however, it became increasingly difficult to get farms for children,[119] a foreshadowing of the land hunger of the century to follow, which doubtless meant that, as later, married sons and daughters had to wait for a farm, so that sometimes two or more families had to live in the family farmhouse. This passion for land no doubt also saw the same overcrowding in the farmhouses of tenant farmers, married children waiting for farms living alongside the unmarried youngest male who expected to succeed the parents in the occupation of the old home.[120]

It was the social status conferred and the administrative roles opened up to them by landownership which distinguished them, rather than any superior competence as farmers. Indeed, from a purely economic standpoint they lacked the support given by landlords to their tenants in difficult years. So concerned were they, moreover, with adding to their existing land that many neglected to make husbandry improvements. Remarking in 1794 upon the numerous occupying freeholders possessing from 20 to 300 and 400 acres in north Cardiganshire, the experienced farmer of that county, the Revd David Turnor of Wervilbrook, claimed that although one would expect under these circumstances to see the countryside under an improved state of husbandry, 'I am sorry to observe that these occupying proprietors are, in general, as backward in their improvements, as any of the tenantry. They are more solicitous to add acre to acre, than to improve what they already occupy.'[121]

Craftsmen and Artisans

Until the later decades of the nineteenth century local craftsmen and artisans were a vital element in the rural economy and the society it sustained. Lacking the capital and to an extent the enterprise to purchase new machinery and to embrace the latest husbandry techniques, most Welsh farmers well into the late nineteenth century performed their work tasks by using a wide variety of simple hand tools produced either by themselves or by country craftsmen. Skilled and taking pride in their craft, the latter designed their tools and implements, as, for example, the billhook, to serve best the particular circumstances and traditions of their neighbourhoods. Not only farm tools but furniture for the home, dairy and kitchen utensils, horse harnesses, clothes, boots and almost every other requirement were produced by each neigh- bourhood's craftsmen and artisans. Many of these like weavers, blacksmiths, wheelwrights, coopers, tailors, cabinetmakers, car- penters, hatters, glovers, tanners, bootmakers, cloggers, thatchers, basket-makers, saddlers, joiners, millers, bakers, brewers and stonemasons lived and worked in market towns while others practised their crafts in local villages and hamlets. Some, too, were itinerant, travelling to remote farms, sometimes putting up at a welcoming, gossip-hungry farmhouse for a short period to accomp- lish a large amount of work before moving on to another isolated holding. By far the most numerous of these trades in Cardiganshire in 1831 were carpenters, tailors, stonemasons and blacksmiths.[1]

But all were crucial in these self-sufficient localities. Angus McInnes has emphasized just how numerous they were in England between 1670 and 1820, and the same held true for Wales for those years and indeed, for some considerable time afterwards.[2] Stat- istical evidence for the 1790s demonstrates their relative import- ance *vis-à-vis* other occupational groups in town and countryside alike. In the small market town of Builth, of the total eighty-nine 'principal inhabitants' eight were gentry, one a clergyman, two attorneys, and the remaining seventy-eight 'traders etc.', of whom thirty-six were craftsmen comprising nine shoemakers, three saddlers, two smiths, two tailors, two carpenters, two malsters, two glaziers, and a breechmaker, watchmaker, hatter, weaver, joiner, currier, mantua-maker, cooper, glover, farrier, skinner, tanner, habit-maker, and soap boiler apiece. Denbigh, a bigger market centre, boasted 209 'principal inhabitants'; twenty-one were gentry, three clergy, three medical men, six attorneys and the remaining 176 were 'traders', of whom 102 were craftsmen, most numerous among whom were the eighteen shoemakers, seven tanners, seven milliners, six glovers, six flaxdressers, five tailors and five smiths.[3]

Turning to the countryside proper, we can revisit the rich statistical data available for the Montgomeryshire parishes of Llanfechain and Meifod. Of the total 633 workers involved with the land in one way or another during the late 1790s, 130 (20 per cent) were farmers, 118 (19 per cent) were craftsmen or artificers and 385 (61 per cent) were labourers in husbandry, this group including outdoor married labourers and indoor menservants and maidservants. The 118 artificers comprised ten shoemakers, three cobblers, three coopers, ten tailors, sixteen spinners, twenty-two carpenters, four thatchers, seventeen weavers, eight smiths, eight sawyers, three masons and slaters, one saddler, one wasper, one sieve maker, two towdressers, two tanners, one brickmaker, one engineer, two joiners, one skinner, one broomsman, and one flaxdresser.[4]

These skilled craftsmen have long been recognized as 'familiar and important figures in the countryside'.[5] Daniel E. Jones was to state (in translation) of the local craftsmen of the parishes of Llangeler and Penboyr (Cards.) in 1898: 'Nevertheless they were first of all agricultural workers. The farm was the big "spring" whence they and their families got their livelihoods.'[6] This applied equally to earlier times. Moreover, significant numbers of craftsmen plying their trades in rural hamlets and villages were integrated yet more closely in the agricultural community because farming smallholdings as a by-employment was a common feature of their livelihood. For instance, at mid-century on the Brynddu estate in Anglesey a carpenter, tailor and weaver each held a small farm, while on the Orielton estate in Pembrokeshire in 1773 John Phillips, cooper, leased a tenement in Minwear parish for three lives at £4. 10*s.* a year, and Richard Thomas, smith, leased the messuage called The Croft together with part of Kilne Parke in Martletwy parish, again for £4. 10*s.* per annum.[7]

In September 1758 tenant farmer Job Roberts was upset at
receiving notice from Richard Myddelton of Chirk Castle to quit
Glyn tenement, because without it he would be forced to part with
Mr Eyton's farm, 'for that itself will not keep a team'.[8] The small
tenements of the craftsmen-smallholders were certainly unable to
support a team of horses and so they were obliged to rely on local
farmers for the use of teams for ploughing and the carting of
manure and hay. Likewise they would have kept neither a bull nor
a boar, and so once again they had perforce to turn to a local farm
for these vital services. What was reported of the Builth Union
(Rads.) in 1893 was just as applicable to the previous century:
'There is constant interchange of services between regular farmers
and smallholders also, who supply each other's wants as occasion
offers without any payment of money.'[9] The 'debts' incurred by the
craftsmen-smallholders were repaid by working in the farmers'
fields at harvest.[10] In this way, they were intimately stitched into
the fabric of mutual interdependence between smallholdings and
larger neighbouring farms.

Certain craftsmen and artisans were hired by the year at the
mansions of the gentry and aristocrats to serve the requirements of
the house and home farm and to cater for the general upkeep of the
estate. Dr Simmonds recorded of his visit to Squire Blayney's home
at Gregynog (Mont.) in September 1792:

> He has always from 50 to 60 workmen employed taking in bricklayers,
> carpenters, joyners, smiths, as well as day labourers; in short, all trades
> seem to be carried on in one of his back courts. These persons are
> employed either in building or repairing farm-houses and cottages.[11]

Compared with the wages of husbandmen hired for work on the
home farms, the craftsmen and artisans did very well. At Mostyn,
for example, in 1743, Robert Edwards, husbandman, got £5 for
the year, whereas Hugh David, the smith was paid £8; at
Wynnstay, likewise, in 1736–7, Edward Jones the smith received
£10 for the year compared with the £5. 5s. paid to Robert Jones, a
wagoner.[12]

Still other craftsmen and artisans in the rural community were
hired by the day. Lewis Morris's information concerning daily
wages in the Cardiganshire parish of Llanbadarn Fawr in 1755
once again testifies to the superior position of the craftsman and

artisan: 'Labourers for ditching etc. 6d. a day on their own victuals, 3d. and victuals. Carpenters 6d. or 8d. and victuals, or 12d. their own victuals. Masons 12d. and victuals. Some 18d. Taylors 6d. and victuals.'[13] These skilled workers found increasing employment opportunities in the frequent building or rebuilding of the mansions of aristocrats and gentlemen alike in these years, in the rationalization and improvement of farms, including the erecting of farmhouses on them, and in the expanding industrial sector as in work on building canals. The Kymer canal at Kidwelly saw eight carpenters, two smiths, and four masons employed in its construction in January 1768: the majority of the carpenters got 1s. 2d. a day, one smith received 1s. 3d. a day and the other 1s. 8d., and the four masons were paid 1s. 2d. a day.[14] By the very nature of their work, however, most craftsmen and artisans were paid for piece work, receiving a lump sum for making an article or completing a job.[15] This would certainly have been so in the case of tanners, saddlers, tailors, shoemakers, cloggers, weavers and fullers. Such making 'to order' meant that there was a steady traffic between producer and consumer, business and gossip intermeshing, before the finished goods were ready.

Valuable insight into the personnel and economic position of these groups is afforded by probate inventories. The twenty-seven testators holding some land but preferring in their wills to designate themselves as tradesmen or craftsmen, who are contained in Humphreys's valuable sample of 560 Montgomeryshire inventories over the period 1690–1750, 'were in all respects the humble associates of the farming community'. Thomas James of Betws Cedewain, weaver, was representative of their poverty; at his death in 1706 his goods were valued at £11. 10s.; most prized were his loom and some wool and flannel, together worth £4. 8s., and in addition he possessed a quantity of corn and hay, four ewes and lambs and a cow. These twenty-seven testators pursuing a craft or trade and occupying some land compared poorly with the twenty-four yeomen-craftsmen, farmers (as we have noted earlier) who also had a craft or trade carried on at the farm premises like tanner or weaver: whereas the average total value of all goods belonging to the latter group was £98. 15s. 4d., that of craftsmen/tradesmen-smallholders was a mere £32. 16s. 7d.[16] The poverty of this last group is again highlighted by Emery in describing the possessions of William Prichard, a weaver of Llansteffan (Rads.), at his decease in 1690: all he possessed was a pair of looms together with a cow and calf, an old horse, a couple of pigs and hens, and corn worth £1.[17] More comfortably off as a weaver, though still relatively poor, was Evan Maddock, of Llangynwyd parish in Glamorgan; at his death in 1704 his possessions were valued at £23. 2s., which included looms worth £1. 5s. and 'two stones of wooll' valued at 10s., together with cattle, sheep, a horse and 'implements of husbandry' worth 6s. 8d.[18] Given that the average value of seventy-five Caernarfonshire tradesmen's and craftsmen's inventories between 1735 and 1770 stood at £36. 2s. 4d., this group (most of them based in the countryside and holding some land) was considerably poorer than the yeomen, whose average inventory was £84. 2s.[19] It will be apparent that they owned similar amounts of wealth as their Montgomeryshire counterparts.

Not only was this group of craftsmen/tradesmen-smallholders poor. There is some evidence that in north Wales certain types of craftsmen had grown poorer, and consequently declined in status, by the mid-eighteenth century. Seemingly it was overcrowding that had brought about this decline among weavers, shoemakers, corvisers and cordwainers in Caernarfonshire. The last three crafts all worked with leather, and, it appears, too many were jostling for a living in the leather trade by the mid-eighteenth century. Significantly, Denbighshire witnessed infighting in the 1730s between the various crafts involved in the leather trade.[20]

Such low incomes, too, were achieved only by long hours of work. Testifying about a theft of goods from his premises on the night of 26–7 January 1728, Luke Jones, a Denbigh dyer:

> says that about 6 a.m. of 27 January . . . having occasion to go into his workhouse or dyeing shop in Henllan street to look out some white cloth in order to be dyed this examinant missed one piece of white cloth containing 12 yards which he well remembered to have seen left in his shop or workhouse about 12 of the clock the night before at which time this examinant left off working for that night.[21]

Requiring considerable capital to practise their craft, tanners, unlike most of their fellow craftsmen, were in the way of making for themselves a modestly prosperous living. Standing at £134. 15s., the average value of Caernarfonshire tanners' inventories between 1735 and 1770 was well above those of the other tradesmen and craftsmen of the county and, indeed, exceeded the average yeoman inventory.[22] In the towns, tanners were, indeed, often relatively wealthy, and here they did not generally have some of their wealth tied up in farming. For example, Alderman Cradock Nowell of Cardiff (d. 1709), possessed £200-worth of stock in his tanyard, which comprised 20 per cent of his entire personal estate, valued at £910.[23] Walter Coffin senior became a rich man from his tanning business in Bridgend, ending up as a landed proprietor, as, too, did Joseph Fortune, tanner of Haverfordwest.[24]

Apart from the mainstream craftsmen and artisans found in all areas, another rural occupation closely tied up with the land in the south-west was that of lime-burner. With the extension of lime as the principal agricultural fertilizer in that region of Wales in the late eighteenth century, lime-burners, enveloped in a hellish world of evil-smelling fumes and dust, became important as processing craftsmen in the local economy. Kilns were erected at coastal villages and creeks of Pembrokeshire and Cardiganshire into which limestone was shipped from Milford Haven and elsewhere.[25] Pococke thus observed at mid-century that Fishguard was inhabited by fishermen and lime-burners.[26] Not only were limekilns important in providing a vital fertilizer; along with the smithies, their warmth rendered them meeting places for young men and in this way they can be viewed as essential to vernacular cultural development.[27]

Apprenticeships for the instruction of boys and young men into 'the art and mystery' of a particular craft, lasting from two years up to seven or more, were jealously insisted upon by craftsmen. Those who passed themselves off as skilled in a particular trade without having served the required apprenticeship were prosecuted.[28] Craftsmen's treatment of their apprentices was sometimes so harsh that they were taken to law. Denbighshire Quarter Sessions for Michaelmas 1711 were petitioned by Francis Appleton of Wrexham, joiner, to the effect that he had placed Thomas Appleton, 'a poor fatherless child', as apprentice to Thomas Cross of the same town, corviser, who often 'barbarously beat him' so that he was forced to quit. An order was issued by the Denbighshire Easter Quarter Sessions, 1718, to release Ellias Price from his apprenticeship to Edward Owens of Wrexham, weaver, 'he having been beaten and abused and not instructed in the trade'. Thomas Edisbury of Bersham, wheelwright, was requested by the

Denbighshire Easter Quarter Sessions for 1738 to appear to answer William Griffith, his apprentice, for not giving him sufficient meat and his 'immoderate' correction of him. One apprentice in 1757 was assaulted by his master, Hugh Hughes, a Wrexham hatter, with intent to commit sodomy.[29] 'Very bad to his apprentices when useing his Trade' was the unsparing comment of William Thomas about saddler John Richard of Llandough juxta Penarth when recording his burial on 17 November 1764. Clearly, by no means all craftsmen were the upright, rational leaders of eighteenth-century religious Dissent.

We have already encountered theft of goods from Luke Jones, the Denbigh dyer. The poverty of many craftsmen perhaps explains their tendency to steal raw materials from one another or from other non-craftsmen neighbours. Three Presteigne shoemakers were arraigned before the Radnorshire Great Sessions for having jointly stolen sole hides on 6 May 1735, while Alexander Bragger of Wrexham, tanner, was later prosecuted at the Denbighshire Great Sessions by another tanner of the town, one Edward Tomkies, for theft of leather and skins from his yard in September 1744. During a single night in spring 1748 John Edwards, a Llangollen weaver, helped by his two sons, stole yarn from a neighbouring yeoman and one other person of the same parish.[30] Moreover, the vulnerability of this group to economic fluctuations is reflected in their prominence in certain food riots of the period. We shall see later in this study that craftsmen and artisans – shoemakers, weavers, carpenters, blacksmiths and tailors – were out in force in the Denbighshire and Flintshire food riots of May 1740. They were a significant group, too, in the corn riots at the end of the century. In his study of food riots in Wales between 1793 and 1801 David Jones revealed that of the 103 rioters 'suspected, indicted and convicted of disturbances' before the courts of Great Sessions six were weavers, two were carpenters, and one was drawn from each of the crafts of slater, joiner, turner, blacksmith, currier, skinner, tailor and woollen-draper, making in all sixteen craftsman participants. Particularly harmed by the conditions of war interfering with the growth of woollen manufacture and so reducing their incomes, weavers were understandably prominent.[31]

On a wider basis, pinched by high prices and taxes, tradesmen and craftsmen were frequent participants in the many disturbances in the Welsh countryside in the war years from 1793 to 1813.

Shoemakers, tailors, weavers and carpenters in Montgomeryshire and Carmarthenshire, for example, played a leading role in riots during the war years. Of the 181 males appearing before the Great Sessions of the two counties between 1792 and 1813 suspected of rioting, assaults and destruction of property, some fifty-six were tradesmen and craftsmen. Given their occupations, they were ideally placed to spread news of forthcoming disturbances, and, furthermore, they appeared concerned to assist their hard-pressed country neighbours.[32]

Their suffering in the 1790s and also in 1800–1 was to drive some of their number, along with other groups like farmers and agricultural labourers and farm servants, to emigrate to the New World. In the cloth-making areas of Montgomeryshire and Merioneth, however, the wartime fall in the standard of living of weavers meant that in this region emigrants were drawn more heavily from among their ranks than from any other occupational group. Some of them thrown out of employment, and all gloomy about their prospects at home, these normally well-to-do artisans looked to America for a more prosperous future. Others among the artisans and 'mechanics' had also suffered unemployment through the wartime interruption of trade and were similarly lured to America; men like coopers, tailors, shoemakers, and also farmers who were facing high rents, heavy taxes and burdensome tithes. Disposing these middling groups all the more to leave was their attachment to religious Dissent which rendered them fearful of persecution at home, particularly in the highly charged, paranoid political atmosphere of spring and summer 1794.[33]

The Labouring Poor

Just as in rural England between 1700 and 1780 'the single most important source of wage-payment was farm labour', so, too, was this the case in the Welsh countryside.[1] In the two Montgomery-shire rural parishes of Llanfechain and Meifod in the 1790s labourers in husbandry outnumbered the other two main occupa-tional groups of farmers and artificers by 385 to 248. There were marginally fewer outdoor married male agricultural labourers living in cottages dispersed among the farmsteads and paid by the day than male indoor farm servants hired by the year or half-year (117 to 146). If we combine menservants and maidservants, both living in at the farmhouses, then the total of 268 farm servants far outnumbered the 117 male married outdoor labourers. Not that the two groups were entirely differentiated, for most of the latter would have received part of their wages in the form of board at the farmhouses.[2] A particular form of hiring obtained in the south-western counties of Cardiganshire, Carmarthenshire and Pem-brokeshire where labourers and their families were tied to working for their masters the whole year round, year in year out, at a fixed low rate per day, without food. Compensating the labourers for their low wages were a cottage, garden and the keep of a cow at a low rent, and the additional perquisites of setting a quantity of potatoes in a fallow and the receipt of bread corn at a fixed rate per bushel all the year round, though these last were far from general.[3] Such a mode of hiring bore resemblances to the hind system of Northumberland.[4]

1. Income levels

Unrecorded allowances in kind were paid to all types of Welsh farm workers, a reflection of the lack of a ready supply of circulating coinage. 'The farmer will always find it advantageous to

pay his labourers and tradesmen as much as possible in produce',
remarked Walter Davies in his observations on Pembrokeshire
farming in 1805.[5] Such perquisites paid to outdoor labourers, both
in board and in kind, varied from district to district and remained
numerous down to the mid-nineteenth century at a time when cash
wages were low. Common ones were a cottage and garden at a low
rent and fuel free of charge. Only with the increase in monetary
payments in the late nineteenth century did these perquisites
gradually disappear.[6] Even as late as 1918 we read:

> Turning now to the group of 19 budgets collected in Wales – in Wales
> family incomings frequently are more complicated than in England.
> Allowances in kind are often of more importance, while many Welsh
> farm workers obtain meals on the farms, – not important over the
> greater part of England.[7]

Such a significant level of unrecorded payments in kind con-
stitutes just one of the problems encountered in attempting to
assess income levels of the labouring poor in cash terms in this
period. For bedevilling such an exercise is also the significant
degree of dual occupations undertaken by people working on the
land, the seasonal pattern of farming activity encouraging on-the-
breadline workers to take other modes of employment in slack
periods. Furthermore, we are generally unable to come by the
contribution to the family income from wives and children,
whether through employment in farming work itself – apart from
harvest work, women assisted in weeding and stone-picking – or
such domestic activity as knitting performed by wives and
daughters.[8]

With these difficulties in mind, the amount and movement of
agricultural labour rates in eighteenth-century Wales will now be
discussed. Evidence of servants' and labourers' wages on the home
farms of landed estates is relatively plentiful. Table 4 records the
yearly rates paid to servants at Mostyn in Flintshire from the late
1730s to the early 1770s. While the rates of payment have to be
handled with a degree of caution because payment of an employee
varied with age and experience, it is clear that a hierarchy of
agricultural servants prevailed, all coming under a first husbandman or head ploughman. Of course, with rates dependent upon the
size of establishments at the various mansions, the degree of

Table 4: Servants' wages at Mostyn

	Wages (£ s. d.) for certain years												
	1737	1738	1739	1740	1741	1751	1752	1755	1756	1757	1767	1768	1774
First husbandman (head ploughman)	5.0.0								5.0.0	6.0.0	7.10.0		
Hedger	3.10.0	4.0.0					4.0.0						
Carter	3.10.0				4.0.0						7.0.0	7.0.0	
Second husbandman				3.10.0				3.10.0					
Cowman		2.10.0	3.10.0				3.10.0						6.0.0
Ploughboy	1.6.0		1.8.0			1.15.0	2.10.0				2.10.0		
Dairymaid		2.8.0					2.8.0						3.0.0
Poultry girl/woman	1.6.0							1.6.0				2.0.0	

Source: Bangor, University of Wales, Bangor Library, Mostyn MSS 6507, 6508, 6509.

geographical isolation, or proximity to industrial workings, and, as indicated, the age and skills of the servants concerned, those at Mostyn cannot be taken to represent estate servants' wages in general. It is apparent that movement in rates in the early years down to the mid-1750s was at best modest, but thereafter increases were more substantial.

From the 1790s this over-reliance on estate home-farm accounts is happily eased by the plentiful data on farm servants' wages provided in the Board of Agriculture surveys of the various Welsh counties. Want of a standard rate, arising from geographical location and the presence or otherwise of industrial ventures, is evident. Farm servants' wages in Glamorgan in the early 1790s thus ranged between £5 or £6 up to £8, £9 and £10 a year compared with the meagre £1. 5s. up to £6 or £7 paid to their counterparts in remote and non-industrializing southern Cardiganshire. Again, whereas a ploughman's annual wage on top of his receiving board and lodging from his master in Brecknock and Radnorshire was from £7 to £9, in remoter Carmarthenshire it ranged from £3 or £4 to £5. 10s. or £6. 6s., and in Pembrokeshire from £3 or £3. 10s. to £6 or £7. 7s. The higher rates of £6 to £10 a year with victuals paid to a husbandman in Montgomeryshire, depending on his skills, likewise contrasts with the lower ones obtainable in Caernarfonshire and Anglesey of £5. 5s. to £7. 7s.[9]

Day labourers' wages in the early 1700s were low and moved up only slowly before the third quarter of the century. At Bodidris in Caernarfonshire, belonging to Lady Lloyd, men during the years 1701–3 received from 3d. to 6d. a day for general work like carrying stones and harrowing for oats and for work in the hay and corn harvest. The daily rates for farm labourers with food provided by their masters as laid down by the Anglesey justices in 1718 hovered around 6d.: 'labourers in summer, 6d, in winter, 5d, mowers, 9d, and reapers, 6d.' Men working on the Abermarlais estate demesne in Carmarthenshire in the early 1730s were paid 1s. a day for mowing hay and 6d. a day in the hop yard and nursery. (As was generally the case, women received just half the male rate for work in the latter.) In the evidence communicated by Lewis Morris in 1755 about wage rates in Llanbadarn Fawr parish, it was stated that 'labourers for ditching etc.' received 6d. a day on their own find, or 3d. and victuals. Reviewing the Glamorgan evidence, A. H. John concluded that the daily rate for adult farm labourers during

the first half of the century ranged between 6*d.* and 8*d.*[10] That there
was no marked increase in day labour rates before mid-century is
suggested by wage evidence relating to St Dogmaels and
Whitchurch parishes in north Pembrokeshire: while in St Dogmaels
in 1737 4*d.* a day was being paid for harvest work and 2*d.* to 3*d.* a
day for other farm tasks, in Whitchurch in 1754 4*d.* a day was still
being paid for harvest labour and likewise 2*d.* a day for work after
the harvest.[11]

The third quarter of the century saw these lethargic daily rates –
as we shall see, well below English levels – pick up markedly.
Dissatisfaction among Anglesey labourers leading to wage
increases in the early 1750s moved one disapproving man to complain in 1753 that 'labourers in husbandry have become intolerable
in their wages which very much impairs the farmers' profits'.[12] We
hear again that agitation was afoot for higher wages among some
of Squire Philip Yorke's workmen at Erddig in Denbighshire from
early 1768, Thomas Birch in a telling observation informing the
absentee owner in February: 'All the Country has raised labourers'
wages, consequently yours begin to complain, Caesar says you
must give them a Penny a day more, and I fancy has talked with
them on that head.' In May 1769 two men working in the garden
there were requesting 12*d.* a day and on two consecutive Saturdays
refused their normal pay of 5*s.* a week, i.e. 10*d.* a day. In line with
the common practice among those who felt grievances under the
estate system, they were determined not to take up their wages until
they heard from the squire himself. Yorke was later informed that
if he decided to part with them he would have none under 12*d.* a
day.[13] But the demands fell on deaf ears, the squire of Erthig
spelling it out to his steward in 1770: 'I do think 10d. a day
sufficient, and nothing shall induce me to exceed it.'[14]

Daily rates for farm labourers had moved up appreciably by the
close of the 1760s. Visiting south-east Wales in 1768, Arthur
Young estimated that daily wage rates about Bridgend and
Cowbridge were 1*s.* and around Newport 10*d.*[15] Similarly, farm
workers on Glamorgan estates during 1775–7 earned 10*d.* to 12*d.* a
day, and women 6*d.* to 8*d.*, at hay and corn harvest.[16] By the time
Young visited west Wales in 1776–8 wages there too were stirring;
at the daily wage of 8*d.* in winter and 10*d.* in summer in Pembrokeshire, and 9*d.* all the year round in Carmarthenshire, rates had risen
considerably above their general level of 6*d.* in the 1750s.[17]

Such increases were confirmed in the various county surveys made for the Board of Agriculture in early 1794. Once again, the daily wage map of Wales showed rates highest in the areas of industrial development and along the eastern borders and lowest in the remote western counties. In Glamorgan, Denbighshire and in the district about Parys Mountain in Anglesey, areas of industrial growth, farm labour rates had risen appreciably: day labourers in Glamorgan got from 1*s.* to 1*s.* 6*d.* and sometimes 1*s.* 8*d.* a day, those in Denbighshire were paid 1*s.* 2*d.* to 1*s.* 4*d.* in winter and summer respectively and around the copper works of Parys Mountain they earned from 1*s.* 2*d.* to 1*s.* 4*d.* Significantly, elsewhere in Anglesey the general day rate was 10*d.* to 1*s.* without victuals. While day rates for the husbandman in an eastern county like Montgomeryshire were 1*s.* in winter and 1*s.* 2*d.* in other seasons, without victuals, except in harvest when he was allowed 1*s.* a day with food, or, again, in Radnorshire, 1*s.* 2*d.* a day, in western counties rates were decidedly lower: in Caernarfonshire the husbandman was paid 1*s.* in spring and summer and 10*d.* in winter, without victuals, and in Merioneth 1*s.* a day in summer and 8*d.* in winter on his own find. Lowest rates of all obtained in the south-western counties. Labourers in the upland northern and western parts of Carmarthenshire received 8*d.* a day in summer, on their own find, and as little as 6*d.* in the winter months. Reflecting Walter Davies's description of labourers and their families in this south-western region as 'heirlooms or appendages to the farms', certain farmers in this remote area of Carmarthenshire provided food for their labourers, and still others kept a cow for them or a few sheep, such perquisites lowering the money wage accordingly. In south Cardiganshire below the river Aeron labourers received 8*d.* in summer and 7*d.* in winter, whereas northwards they were paid 8*d.* in spring and summer and 6*d.* in winter – though 2*d.* a day more was given in certain northern parts as about Aberystwyth as an adjustment to the presence of lead mines. Similarly, while in south Pembrokeshire 10*d.* in summer and 8*d.* in winter, without food, was the payment received by farm labourers, their counterparts in the hilly north got 2*d.* a day less. Once again reflecting Davies's 'feudal' type of labourer, certain Pembrokeshire farmworkers were paid 8*d.* a day all the year round, with a cottage and garden to go with it, and in some instances the keep of a cow on easy terms was agreed between the parties.[18]

What happened to farm wages during the long period of war with France between 1793 and 1815? Alan Armstrong has concluded for England and Wales in general that 'the wages of farm workers rose significantly during the war years, though with considerable local and regional variation'. Indeed, wages of day labourers may well have nearly doubled in the war years, though he doubts if the cash element of the income of farm servants increased to anything like this amount. The principal explanation advanced is the relative shortage of male labour, especially in the busy farming seasons, owing to men being drawn into the armed forces in the war against France, either through service in the regular army or, more commonly, enforced service in the militia or local corps of volunteers. The *Farmers' Magazine* thus reported scarcity of hands in Essex, Staffordshire and Wales in 1803.[19] Writing on Cardiganshire in 1808, Samuel Rush Meyrick attributed the marked improvement in the labourers' position in the county since the beginning of the century to the reduction in 'the stock of labourers' consequent upon the need for men to serve in the armies.[20]

That alert recorder of the Welsh rural scene, Walter Davies, drew attention to the rise in labourers' wages from the mid-1790s. In his notes gathered for west Wales in 1805 he scribbled: 'Labour-wages very much advanced of late years.'[21] By 1814 male and female outdoor labourers in south-west Wales received 1*s.* and 8*d.* a day respectively in winter months and 18*d.* and 1*s.* respectively in spring and summer without victuals. In the better-farmed and more industrially developed south-eastern counties, daily rates were from 1*s.* 4*d.* to 1*s.* 8*d.* in winter and from 1*s.* 6*d.* to 2*s.* in summer, without victuals. In north Wales, the price of labour in areas of growing commercial and industrial activity advanced around 30 per cent between 1793 and 1799, particularly in busy seasons like harvest. Indoor servants' wages likewise increased over the course of the war years – in south Wales, indeed, far more dramatically than Armstrong suggests for England and Wales as a whole. 'Servants' wages', Davies observed of south Wales in 1814,

have undergone a more universal advance than the price of labour by the day, or by job-work. Old farmers, still living, remember their hiring servants . . . for from 5l. to 6l. a-year; and when a few came to demand 7l., the world was thought to be near its end. Now the average of the whole district, from 18 years old and upwards, may be twice that sum, or 14l., though most waggoners, undertakers of some care, etc., hire for from 15 to 17 guineas.[22]

The level of wages in Wales – patchy and incomplete though the data are – were low compared with English areas. In their respective studies of south Wales both D. J. Davies and A. H. John were careful to point to the considerably lower wages – at 6*d.* to 8*d.* a day – that obtained there than the average wage of 1*s.* to 1*s.* 6*d.* a day and occasionally higher that prevailed across areas of England down to mid-century.[23] That this poorer rate persisted into the later decades is corroborated by Arthur Young who, observing the wage to be 10*d.* a day throughout the year on the tract between Newport and Cowbridge, added: 'the cheapest I have anywhere yet met with', a truth verifiable in Bowley's reproduction of Young's wages for England and Wales as a whole for 1767–70. The 5*s.* to 6*s.* a week rate reckoned by Young for south-east Wales compared unfavourably with the 7*s.* 9*d.* mean wage for farm labourers that he calculated for the southern counties of England and Wales as a whole.[24]

These relatively low wages have, nevertheless, to be set against the cheap cost of living in Welsh communities. Robert Morgan, the Carmarthenshire ironmaster, writing to a correspondent at Bristol in 1761 concerning the hiring of a good clerk for the Carmarthenshire works, reflected: 'if he has a family they can live better here for £50 p.a. than with you [at Bristol] for £80 p.a.' Similarly, on his visit to north Wales in 1795 J. Hucks was to observe of Bala in Merioneth: 'every necessary article of life is here more than commonly reasonable; fifty pounds at Bala would go as far as an hundred in most parts of England.'[25] Whereas in 1757 even on the English border at Wrexham butter was selling at just 3½*d.* a pound and beef and mutton for as little as 1½*d.* a pound, at the same time Welshmen in London were shocked to find themselves having to pay for their butter 5½*d.* to 6*d.* (indeed, as much as 7*d.* to 10*d.* if fresh), for beef 4*d.* to 4½*d.* and for mutton 4½*d.* to 5*d.*[26] Although the prices quoted for Glamorgan by Arthur Young in 1768 were not markedly below the average for the southern counties of England, he recognized that if he had ventured deeper into the Welsh countryside where turnpike roads were absent, 'I have no doubt but I should have met with a great change in everything'.[27]

Such a want of good communications with the expanding centres of population eastwards exerted a severe constraint on the volume of sales, a depressing influence on the local market exacerbated by the self-subsistent nature of the Welsh farmer, craftsman, artisan and labourer alike.[28] Despite the cheapness of most goods and food in Wales, Arthur Young's 'average prices of corn' between 1771 and 1784 reveal that wheat and barley prices in Welsh districts were frequently as high, sometimes higher, than English ones, the necessity for rising imports after 1770 doubtless explaining such high levels. Prices of oats in Welsh markets, on the other hand, were always well below English levels.[29]

Where does this leave us in terms of real wages? In the second quarter of the eighteenth century, with low agricultural prices prevailing, English farmworkers, as other groups, lived through what has been described as a golden age, and there is no reason to believe that the Welsh agricultural labourer did not similarly enjoy this quiet prosperity.[30] The situation as far as English labourers were concerned changed for the worse, however, from mid-century. Given that farmworkers' wages, though rising, failed to keep pace with the sharp increase in prices after 1755, and that there was no adequate compensation from other forms of income to offset this adverse trend, the inescapable conclusion is that for most of them there was 'a perceptible trend towards a declining standard of living in the later eighteenth century'.[31]

There are insufficient data on wages and prices of a precise nature to enable us to assess the movement of real wages in rural Wales in the later decades of the century. Of course, the big element of living-in servants, of boarding outdoor married labourers and mixed payment in cash and perquisites shielded labourers from any big increases in prices that may have occurred. Again, the Welsh peasantry would not generally have purchased the most expensive corn bread, wheat, and would, indeed, have enjoyed relatively cheap oats prices. Moreover, their diet was so sparse that any increase in meat prices would have had less of an impact than a similar rise in the price of oatmeal or cheese. The garden-produced potato, too, was quickly becoming from mid-century a vital substitute for bread corn in times of high prices. These mollifying factors notwithstanding, the lives of the labouring poor were increasingly pockmarked with poverty *before* the crisis decade of the 1790s. Some were losing rights of grazing their livestock on and taking turf from commons and wastes. Others were suffering from the growing scarcity of jobs in the wake of a rising population. We thus discover Elizabeth Middellton in summer 1777 imploring Richard Myddleton of Chirk Castle to put her husband 'in a way of getin bread', he

> bein out of work all winter and three of us to be metained. I cant recover the Det that I went in the winter as my Husband was so long out of work as he cant done all sort of work but Labour for Slatters . . . he is very willin to doe enything that he cane.[32]

Want of employment, however, would doubtless have been more acute but for the sprouting of many industrial concerns in the way of coal, copper, slate and lead mines throughout Wales in these later decades. From the evidence of four labourers' budgets for the year 1788 presented by the Revd David Davies for Denbighshire and Merioneth parishes we see that, even on a distinctive Welsh regime of cheap foods – barley or oatmeal rather than wheat as bread corn, and no meat – and in communities where the emphasis was on self-sufficiency, families failed to make ends meet and fell into debt. Apart from the main item of expense – food and other household provisions covering barley or oatmeal, butter, milk, potatoes, sugar, salt, soap and tallow – they incurred further outlays on rent of cottages, fuel and clothing. The indebtedness in each of the four families was as follows:

	Family one (of 8 persons) £ s. d.	Family two (of 6 persons) £ s. d.	Family three (of 6 persons) £ s. d.	Family four (of 8 persons) £ s. d.
Total annual expenses	27 14 4	21 0 8	24 2 2	25 13 10
Total annual receipts from men's, women's and children's earnings	20 3 0	16 18 0	19 10 0	20 16 0
Annual deficit	7 11 4	4 2 8	4 12 2	4 17 10

Source: David Davies, *Labourers in Husbandry*, 188–91.

The decades of the French Wars in Wales witnessed not only an acceleration in wages. Prices in these abnormal times escalated so that there was a marked catching up with other higher-price areas. Walter Davies observed for north Wales in 1810: 'Provisions, in general, are a little under the London prices; corn somewhat dearer, but seldom [to the extent of] more than 5d. to 6d. per bushel.'[33] For verification of rising prices we can cite Eden's evidence for Llanferres (Denbs.) and Wrexham at the close of 1795 and early 1796: beef, mutton, 3*d.* to 5*d.* a pound, salt butter, 8*d.*, fresh butter 9*d.* a pound, wheat from 13*s.* to 14*s.* a bushel, barley 6*s.* 6*d.*, oats from 3*s.* 6*d.* to 4*s.*, and bacon had risen in price from 5*d.* (in 1781) to 1*s.* in 1797.[34] 'The dearness of provisions in Wrexham parish', Eden remarked, 'is attributed to monopolizing farmers.' By 1813 prices of provisions in north Wales were nearly twice their pre-war levels, and certain commodities cost four times as much as in 1760.[35] Worse inflation was allegedly experienced in the south, a Cowbridge correspondent averring in 1811 that all items apart from house rents and firing were even more expensive than in London.[36] Although wages were increasing substantially, it appears that price increases outstripped them, and so it was probably not the case in Wales, as has been contended for English areas, 'that wage-paid labour in agriculture just about succeeded in holding its own during the French Wars'.[37] Perhaps indicative of falling living standards in Wales was the 'humble petition' in 1813 by the labourers and workmen of the Golden Grove estate demesne (Carms.) to their employer, Lord Cawdor. Pointing out that most of them had wives and children to support and had perforce to live on 7*s.* a week, they went on to request a higher weekly wage 'because of the present high price of corn and every other article necessary to the nourishment of the generality of the suffering poor – Barley is 9s. 6d. a Winchester Bushel, cheese and every other article proportionately higher and in all probability may become still higher.'[38]

There is no mistaking the suffering of the labouring poor in Wales in the 1790s, a consequence of the fast-rising population, wartime inflation and a run of poor harvests whose consequences were rendered the more critical by hoarding farmers and middlemen in the corn trade. Reports to the Board of Agriculture in early 1794 contained concerned comments about the labourers' increasingly fragile position. Of south Cardiganshire it was observed: 'Their pay bears no proportion to the price of provisions, or the labour they perform', and similarly bleak was the comment on Glamorgan:

> The lowness of husbandmen's wages at the present period, appeals persuasively to humanity for redress: where they have wives and young families, the price paid for their labour is insufficient to procure them the common necessaries of life. It may be said, that if this be the case, their respective parishes must, and in many cases do, give them relief proportionate to their wants.[39]

Poignant in the extreme was the depiction by Eden in November 1795 of a Presteigne (Rads.) agricultural labourer's family:

> He is 40 years of age; has a wife, and 5 children of the following ages; 9 – 7 – 5½ – 3 – and 1½ years old. The wages and employment of the father are extremely various at different times of the year: in summer, he receives from 1s. to 1s. 6d. a day; in winter, from 10d. to 1s. a day. He is allowed his board, in harvest; but not at other times, except while he works for a gentleman, which occurs about once a week. He is, sometimes, prevented by wet weather from working; and, often, cannot procure employment: so that, upon the whole, he thinks the average of his earnings does not exceed 6s. a week. His wife, occasionally, assists a neighbouring family in baking, and earns about 9d. a week. The oldest children nurse the youngest. This family never received relief from the parish till last winter, when they were allowed, in the severest part of the season, about 3 pecks of wheat, and 5s. in money.[40]

Yet it was not the farm labourers but the colliers and other industrial workers who formed the core element of the food riots of the 1790s and earlier decades. It has been emphasized earlier that a significant number of farm labourers in Wales as elsewhere were in receipt of perquisites which helped to shield them from the worst consequences of high prices. 'During the dearth of late years', commented Walter Davies in 1814, 'many of these feudal labourers had their barley for 3s. 6d. a provincial measure, which would have cost them 12s. in the market; and in the year 1800, fifteen shillings'.[41] Accordingly, of all the members of the labouring poor, it was the farm labourers who suffered the least privation from the consequences of poor harvests.

Industrial workers like lead miners and colliers nevertheless retained close links with the land, especially during the early and middle decades of the century. Modest numbers were engaged in working the lead mines located in Cardiganshire, Carmarthenshire and Montgomeryshire. Wages were low. Perhaps reflecting the want of alternative employment in Cardiganshire, earnings there were lower for most of the eighteenth century than in the north-eastern counties of Flint, Denbigh and Montgomery. Wages at Llangynog (Mont.) in the 1730s ranged from 17*s.* a week earned by a few miners on piecework, to 1*s.* a day for other miners, down to 6*d.* and 8*d.* for labourers. Thus even the latter were receiving rates comparable to those of farm labourers while miners were earning considerably more. Miners in Cardiganshire were for just a short period at mid-century paid better wages than their counterparts in the north-east, those at Esgair-mwyn in the 1750s getting 1*s.* to 14*d.* a day and labourers 8*d.* to 11*d.* compared with the 10*d.* to 1*s.* a day paid to lead miners at Nant-y-ffrith, near Wrexham. In the parish of Llanbadarn Fawr (Cards.) in 1755, meanwhile, 'labourers for ditching etc.' were on a relatively paltry 6*d.* a day on their own victuals or 3*d.* and victuals. However, wages in mid-Wales soon fell behind those of the north-east again, lead miners in 1788 now earning only 10*d.* a day. If this compared unfavourably with the 6*s.* a week paid to road menders at that time, the rate was still higher than that paid to farm labourers in mid-Cardiganshire at a distance from the mines, who received a mere 6*d.* to 8*d.* a day. In all lead-mining concerns, living standards for workers fell during the Napoleonic War years.[42]

Not only were lead miners' wages low; they were paid irregularly, miners going without their money for lengthy periods. Moreover, as was experienced among English workers like weavers and cutlers, the truck system operated in the Welsh lead-mining industry in Cardiganshire and also at Rhandir-mwyn in Carmarthenshire to the detriment of the workforce. Just how cynical the manipulation of the system had become by the end of the century is conveyed in a communication of J. Johnes from Aberystwyth in November 1781:

> Have here two or three Pretended miners . . . [who] are inclined to get all the mines into their own hands if they can, but as it is now they supply the works with all articles the miners want, and the poor People suffer as they are charged exorbitant price in every article they sell.[43]

Such unsatisfactory rates paid to the lead workers necessitated supplementary incomes – a feature shared by other occupational groups in the lower orders. Family labour in the mines was for this reason not uncommon, women and children performing the 'lighter' tasks of carrying the ore out of the mines and washing and preparing it for market. Women employed in washing ore at Llangynog (Mont.) in 1732 got 9*d.* a day compared with male miners who earned 1*s.* a day – though labourers at the mine had to make do with 8*d.* and 6*d.*[44] In addition, facilitated by the miners' short working day, an important by-employment was work in farming like potato planting, corn and potato harvesting, harvest work which seriously interrupted the smooth operation of lead mining.[·] Doubtless many who performed farm work in this way were in fact small-scale farmers. Indeed, in the lead mines of Lord Cawdor in Rhandir-mwyn small adjacent tenants were expected to provide labour: the agent wrote to the heavily indebted Cawdor in 1799 counselling against the sale of neighbouring small farms 'as the small tenantry could certain afford to work them [the mines] much cheaper than strangers, and I have often seen the times that we could not have carried them on without the command of the tenantry to carry timber, ore and etc.'[45]

Closely tied up with the land in the first half of the eighteenth century were the colliers; indeed on the Pembrokeshire coalfield this relationship was to persist throughout the century. The Glamorgan collieries producing for the sea-borne coal trade in the early century were small and numbers of colliers working in them correspondingly few. A. H. John pointed to a 'nucleus of the basic industries producing for a market outside the county' growing up along Swansea Bay from Baglan to Swansea in the early decades of the century, significantly adding, 'But even this was an industrialism set very much in an agricultural background.'[46] As with lead mining, so, too, with coal mining and the other basic industries, at sowing and harvest labourers drifted back to agricultural work, emphasizing the overriding importance of farming in the local economy and the close links between agriculture and other local occupations. Part of this stemmed from the very fact that industry furnished a ready means of part-time employment for local farmers, whose very seasonal activity lent itself to multiple occupations, thereby providing a living throughout the year.[47]

Even closer ties obtained between colliers and the land westwards in Pembrokeshire and Carmarthenshire.[48] Collieries in

Pembrokeshire were throughout the century only small concerns: the relatively substantial mining activity at Hook was worked by just sixty-five to ninety labourers in 1785–6, while a decade earlier sixty-four worked at Begelly colliery, thirty-eight at Moreton and seven at Ridgeway. Certain of the colliers and carters would have been small tenant farmers; the Picton Castle estate leases, for example, bound various tenants to work in their landlord's coalmines at the accustomed wages and, less often, to keep carts to carry coal and culm. Carting of coal was likewise enjoined on Lord Ashburnham's tenants about Pembrey (Carms.) late in the century.[49]

Rates of pay were higher in coal mining and other forms of industrial employment than in farming, although employment in the latter was arguably more regular. Day rates for unskilled labour in industrial concerns in early-century Glamorgan ranged from 8*d.* to 10*d.* a day. Sales on credit meant that colliers, making up the largest contingent of the relatively small group of industrial workers in south Wales at this time, were normally paid subsistence at each weekend and received the balance due to them at the end of a month, or six weeks or an even longer period. If they were relatively well-off, their resources did not stretch to keeping themselves in times of slack trade. That they could then undergo the sharp pinch of hunger is revealed in a telling communication sent to Lord Mansel, owner of the Briton Ferry estate, by his steward in March 1709:

> Whole troops of them [colliers] followed in ye streets of Swansea last Saturday and humbly acknowledged your goodness in saving their lives by corne before hand, they added there had been no trade for six weeks last past some of them declaring that they had no bread in nine days, but live on cockles. I'm sure some of them look more like skeletons than men . . . the poor children being almost famished their case being so miserable.[50]

Of the small numbers of the labouring poor in industrial enterprises but having some links with the land, uncomfortable lives in the extreme were lived by those at the very margin. It is not difficult, for instance, to envisage the bleak experience of cottagers on the Black Mountains of Carmarthenshire who had encroached on the commons and dug coal and whose activities were encouraged by that ruthless exploiter of his estate's resources, John Vaughan of Golden Grove, in the late 1750s. Writing from London in January 1758 he craftily directed his local agent:

> As to the Cottagers that have Dug on the Waste Coal I think you have acted very Prudently and leave to you to pay the People for what coal they have landed, tho you and I will know they where trespasters yet I desire the may be paid in such a maner that they shall not know from whom or for what which I hope will be a means to make them Aid and Assist in Discovering where the Veins of coals ly by which means many of them may be Imployd In Carrying this work on and I hope will make many of them whose Cots are vacant Come and Inhabit And likewise Come and repair those that are in a great Ruinous Condition.[51]

2. Props against Indigence

To a certain extent the lid was kept on the discontent of the labouring poor by virtue of their being in receipt of poor relief. From the 1780s in particular, we shall discover in the next chapter, there was a big increase in casual, temporary relief as distinct from the traditional long-term allowances paid to the infirm and the aged. Important, too, were the subscriptions of large landowners, if for a variety of motives not all altruistic, to ward off crisis. It is well known that in the food crises of the mid-1790s and 1800–1 they responded by subscribing as a group in a county or district so that large supplies could be bought up and sold at reduced prices to the hungry. A like response on the part of the gentry and aristocracy occurred in north-east Wales in the starvation year of 1783 – the result of the poor harvest of the previous year – on the receipt by the owner of Wynnstay, Sir Watkin Williams Wynn, and other gentlemen of requests for help from areas of Denbighshire and Montgomeryshire where they held property.[52] Besides efforts to provide increasing supplies of cheap grain for the poor in times of acute want, other charitable initiatives were forthcoming in an effort to ameliorate the situation. At its meeting of 26 February 1801, the Haverfordwest Common Council resolved that '£20 be paid towards purchasing provisions for making soups for the use of the Poor'.[53] That same miserable year saw Lord Cawdor allow the 'labouring poor' to set twenty-three acres of potatoes in his plantations in St Petrox parish, 'to their great relief'. A similar provision was made by the Tredegar Park agent in spring 1800, whereby potatoes grown on the home farm were cut small and given to the estate labourers to plant in their gardens.[54]

Another prop against indigence was the friendly society, an innovative form of self-help in English and Welsh counties in the last third of the eighteenth century. Meeting in public houses, these friendly societies or box clubs imaginatively combined the opportunity for conviviality with the need for mutual insurance against poverty and indigence arising from sickness or death in an age when the only alternative was parish poor relief.[55] Just as parish officials connived at poor people erecting small cots on the commons, thereby shielding themselves from added claimants to poor relief, as early trustees of these societies it is likely that the local gentry and aristocracy encouraged them as a means of imposing some check on the fast-rising burden of parish poor rates. Respectability was stamped all over such institutions; only law-abiding, sober men were to be members, they were to attend club meetings regularly, and were not to swear at such meetings nor engage in discussion of politics. Members, all aged between eighteen and around forty, were to pay a sum varying between 6d. and 1s. into the Society Box 'towards raising a fund for the good of the fraternity' and an extra 2d. was to be spent that evening on ale.[56]

Table 5: Friendly societies in Welsh counties in 1802

Counties	Number of friendly societies	Number in such societies
Anglesey	2	161
Brecon	22	1555
Cardigan	11	800
Carmarthen	77	5676
Caernarfon	7	715
Denbigh	18	2221
Flint	18	3307
Glamorgan	123	11178
Merioneth	4	145
Montgomery	13	1139
Pembroke	21	1628
Radnor	9	605
Totals	325	30130

Source: PP, 1803–4, xiii, 1714–15.

The Poor Returns, 1802–3, represented in table 5 show the numbers of friendly societies and their membership in the twelve Welsh counties.[57] Writing in 1814 of south Wales, Walter Davies remarked that these beneficial clubs or friendly societies 'were not uncommon 50 or 60 years back' but that in the decades immediately following down to the 1790s a number had fallen through: some admitted too elderly persons from the beginning while others granted assistance before they had accumulated sufficient capital, either or both of these tendencies giving rise to frequent insolvency. Still others had their funds embezzled by dishonest borrowers. Sir Frederick Eden, in observing in early 1796 that friendly societies in Denbighshire were not as numerous as they had been twenty years earlier, pointed to some three or four having been dissolved in the district of Llanferres owing to dishonesty of certain people in defrauding them of their funds.[58] Others in that county, though surviving, had, according to Eden, fallen into disrepute by over-much political discussion – which is hardly surprising given the serious and respectable type of membership.[59] Government intervention in 1793 with the 'Act for the Encouragement and Relief of Friendly Societies' placed such societies on a firmer footing and from then on they grew in number.[60]

For all the early difficulties and failures, there is no mistaking the achievements of a number of them by the close of the century. Eden thus remarked of the one at Narberth (Pembs.) founded in 1772: 'It is in a very flourishing state; maintains it's [*sic*] own Poor; and has a surgeon and apothecary by the year, to attend the sick and hurt.'[61] Unfortunately lists of members' occupations do not survive, but in the more rural-based counties outside Glamorgan and Flintshire there can be no doubt that members would have been drawn from a variety of trades and callings.[62]

One palliative for labouring families of the poor was to move up the hillsides onto the marginal wastes and common lands and, with the pressure brought to bear by a rising population on non-elastic agricultural resources and in a rural economy lacking alternative employment, encroachments occurred from mid-century at a much faster rate than hitherto. It is well known that this encroachment was encouraged by the Welsh custom whereby if a *tŷ-unnos* (a one-night-shack) was built on the common in a single night and smoke seen to rise from the chimney at dawn, freehold rights to the cottage and a small plot of land about it were established.[63] The

quickening was felt in Radnorshire, where by 1758 small encroachments of wastes and commons had been made over the past twenty
years or so without permission in the Crown lordship of Cantremelenith by the neighbouring inhabitants who, according to
Richard Austin Esq. of the City of London in his report to the
Lords Commissioners of His Majesty's Treasury, 'in process of
time will encroach the whole wasts unless prevented by your Lordships authority'.[64] Alun Eirug Davies has examined the process of
encroachment in Cardiganshire, a hillward migration that was
irritating both the Crown as owner of extensive wastes in the
county and private landowners from mid-century onwards. Such
was the acceleration in the 1780s that Lord Lisburne, absentee
owner of the Trawsgoed estate, sought legal advice in 1797 on how
best to prevent additional encroachments and to procure the
destruction of cottages already erected.[65]

As mentioned earlier, the labouring poor were sometimes encouraged by parish vestries to erect cottages on the waste so that
they would not become a burden on the poor rates. In September
1789, Joseph William of Whitechurch parish (Pembs.), 'being of a
very poor and narrow circumstances and obliged to quit his house
on last Michaelmas, having no place to go', built with the assistance of his neighbours during night-time a small cottage on the
common in Whitechurch parish. He bore a letter on 12 March 1790
to Thomas Lloyd Esq. of Bronwydd, lord of the manor, requesting
his favour that he should retain it rent-free; significantly the letter
was written on his behalf by the curate and a churchwarden of the
parish, who certified that Joseph William was poor, belonged to
the parish and 'bears a good character for Honesty, Sobriety and
Industry'. Again, the poor-law guardians of certain Caernarfonshire parishes in the first decade or so of the nineteenth century
were encouraging the labouring poor to build houses for
themselves on the common in order not to become chargeable on
the rates.[66]

Another prop to the domestic economy of the poor here, as
throughout the rest of the British Isles and many areas of Europe,
was seasonal migration for work to supplement family incomes.
Upland and remote areas of Wales would see men walk to harvest
corn in the English Midland counties or to the Vale of Glamorgan,
returning to work in the slightly later harvests of their home
districts. Cardiganshire inhabitants, for instance, went as reapers to

the harvest fields of Herefordshire. Again, William Marshall reported around 1790 that among the itinerants working in the hop fields of Kent were people from Wales. Growing opportunities for itinerant harvesters came in the years 1793–1815 with the shortage of hands in farming districts as a consequence of the calls on men for military service. Thus Welsh people, along with Scots and especially Irish, were to be found in the Lincolnshire harvest fields in 1800.[67] Surveying Europe as a whole, Olwen Hufton concluded that by far the most mobile section of the population in search of work were women, particularly unmarried ones, and she cites the celebrated case of young unmarried girls and married women from mid-Cardiganshire, picking up extra migrants from north Brecknock along their route, walking during April to London for work in the expanding market gardens of the late eighteenth-century metropolis and returning in September. Known to their local contemporaries as 'merched y gerddi' (the garden girls), most were the daughters of small farmers, while others were domestic servants, day labourers' wives and even the wives of farmers.[68] Measured by the level of earnings available in their home areas, their wages were high, and doubtless afforded a vital supplement to family incomes and, in the case of farmers' daughters and wives, often, no doubt, helped render viable otherwise uneconomic farm units.[69]

Women were also crucially involved in a vital by-employment in Welsh farming communities, namely, woollen manufacture in one form or another. J. Geraint Jenkins has emphasized the importance of the woollen industry in the counties of Montgomery, Merioneth and Denbigh in the eighteenth century and its dependence upon domestic production in the cottages and farmhouses of the region. Whereas cottagers, mainly the housewives, did the carding and spinning, weaving was left to neighbouring farmers who, unlike cottagers, were able to afford the relatively expensive looms. Indeed, in this stretch of countryside covering mid- and north Wales farm servants, as we have noted, were hired as much for their weaving skills as for their suitability for farming tasks.[70] Elsewhere in Wales in this period of local self-sufficiency, domestic manufacture of woollen cloth was necessary, not only to meet the immediate needs of the family but also to satisfy local requirements. As in Montgomeryshire, Merioneth and Denbighshire, these domestic tasks of carding, spinning and weaving were carried out as part-time occupations, cottage-women doing the carding and spinning and supplying weavers and knitters with yarn.[71]

Knitting of stockings was a common pursuit in the homes of the poor, a cottage industry that was to remain important for many families down to the close of the nineteenth century and beyond. Merioneth, in particular, was famed for its women stocking knitters. The traveller Hutton in the late eighteenth century observed of its recognized centre, Bala: 'The women are everlasting knitters of stockings; sitting, standing, or walking, the pins are in motion. We may fairly conclude there is not an idle female in the place; nay, I have seen them employed while *riding*.'[72] The actual sphere of zealous knitting activity based in Merioneth was well defined, embracing a mountainous expanse of terrain some eighteen miles long and twelve miles wide where men and children as well as women were so occupied. Indeed, the Revd John Evans in 1804, when describing the knitting activity about Bala, made a significant claim with regard to its importance to the cottage economy: 'Knitting being the common employment of the neighbourhood, for both sexes of all ages, even the men, frequently take up the needles and assist the female in the labour, *where the chief support of the family is derived*' (my italics). This Merioneth district extended across the county boundary into Betws-y-Coed in Caernarfonshire and into parts of Denbighshire, particularly the district around Llanrwst and Ysbyty Ifan.[73]

Towards the south, Cardiganshire was likewise an important region for knitting. The sharp eye of the Revd John Evans once again observed of the district about Llanddewi Brefi:

> In this country there is no particular manufacture, each family making their own apparel, except that of *knitting*, in which they are so expert, that it has been observed they can knit a stocking while a goose is roasting, or a pot boiling; however they will knit more than a pair in a day. The custom we observed in north Wales of meeting in each other's houses, from a view of sociality and economy, is observed here . . . Large quantities are got up, and sent to the *English markets*.

His journeying in the same county brought him in touch with a cottager's wife near Strata Florida who, with the help of her two eldest girls, one five and the other seven, could earn 5*d.* a day from knitting, as much as, if not marginally more than, she would have gained from field work. Meanwhile, her husband dug peat, an occupation which, depending on the weather, brought in 6*s.* or sometimes 3*s.* or 4*s.* a week.[74] Domestic stocking manufacture was widely practised, too, in Brecknock and Radnorshire for much of this period, though it went into decline in the last quarter of the century. Stockings were sold in the local markets for 8*d.* a pair, and a woman, busying herself to the task, could card, spin and knit four pairs in a week. However, with the raw materials of each pair costing 5*d.*, she received just 3*d.* for knitting a pair or 1*s.* a week.[75]

3. Material Conditions

The poverty of the Welsh labouring poor was reflected in their diet, housing and firing. The food they ate was at best meagre, and at times of poor harvest and near-starvation they were driven to riot. From the weekly budgets of the five poor families in Merioneth and Denbighshire in the 1780s and 1790s provided by Davies and Eden, we learn that between 60 and 70 per cent of expenditure went on barley or oat meal.[76] The latter two cereals comprised the main bread corn in Wales as a whole and were indicative of the poverty of the country and its people. E. J. T. Collins's table showing the 'equivalent' percentage of the population in Great Britain consuming different cereals in 1801 demonstrates the overwhelming majority of households in Wales as living on barley (60 per cent) and oats (20 per cent), just 15 per cent living on wheat, whereas for England and Wales as a whole 65–70 per cent of households lived on wheat. The Welsh situation was closely akin to Scotland's, where 82 per cent of households lived on barley or oats, though here the proportions were reversed strongly in favour of oats (72 per cent) over barley (10 per cent).[77] Just as barley was prominent in most areas at the end of the century so, too, had it been equally popular in earlier decades: thus Lewis Morris remarked in 1763: 'Barley bread is, to this Day, the common household bread of Anglesey, Pembrokeshire and some other Corn Counties of Wales.'[78] Oats, too, and rye, were popular in certain areas throughout the century. According to Pococke, in the mountainous parts of the north generally, oaten cake and rye bread were popular at mid-century, while a mixture of rye and barley was noted by the same traveller as being popular in Caernarfonshire.[79] A like

mixture of rye and barley or simply rye on its own was preferred in
Cardiganshire in the 1780s and 1790s.[80] Although wheat as bread
corn was far behind barley and oats in Wales as a whole, it was
nevertheless the principal bread corn in the Vale of Glamorgan and
other vales of the south-eastern counties in the opening years of the
next century. In the same period, it enjoyed some consumption,
too, in the lowland areas of the Marcher counties and the Vale of
Clwyd, but elsewhere in the north it was eaten only sparsely.[81]

William Bulkeley noted in his diary as early as May 1735: 'At
Llanvichell market [Anglesey] a great asking for potatoes and sold
for 9d. and 10d. a cibbin.'[82] They became increasingly popular as a
staple item in the diet of the lower orders in Wales from mid-
century. Pococke noted their common use in Caernarfonshire in
the 1750s, and Pennant observed of a parish in Flintshire in 1773
how every cottager had his potato garden 'which is a great support'
and 'a conveniency unknown fifty years ago'.[83] According to the
traveller Dr J. Simmonds, writing to his friend Arthur Young on 16
August 1792, Mr Holland of Conwy in 1754 supplied the farmers
of his district with potatoes on condition they would horse-hoe
them, but meeting with a lukewarm response he sent a man to do
the work for them, 'since which time they have followed this
practice, and vessels have long come from Barmouth, Liverpool to
carry them to London. Indeed they are universally well-cultivated
in Wales, even by the meanest cottager.'[84]

Potatoes were likewise commonly grown in mid-Wales and the
south. By the 1790s in north Cardiganshire they were, along with
barley bread, 'the chief sustenance of the poor' and in Pembrokeshire, too, they were a regular part of the labourer's diet.[85] So
common had they become in the south by the turn of the
nineteenth century that Walter Davies was to remark in 1814 that
in seasons of scarcity of bread corn 'they are its best and cheapest
substitute.'[86] While they were a cheap crop to produce, offering a
more secure subsistence for the peasantry, in the long run they
allegedly harmed the physical well-being of the Welsh people, Dr
Hunter commenting in the 1860s: 'The decline of the physical
condition of the population seems to date from about 80 years ago,
when the introduction of the potato caused the neglect of the most
nutritious crop these poor lands could produce – the oat.'[87]

Bread and, from mid-century, potatoes were supplemented by a
few other basic foods. At mid-century the diet of a north Wales

cottager comprised principally milk, cheese and butter and, in coastal areas, fish.[88] The north Wales labourers' budgets for the 1780s and 1790s reveal that apart from expenditure on bread corn and potatoes, money was also laid out in purchasing butter and milk. A frugal fare similarly obtained in southern areas, Eden noting in 1797 that the usual diet of labouring people in Narberth parish (Pembs.) was bread, cheese, potatoes and porridge and a thick flummery made of coarse oatmeal, while that of an agricultural labourer's family he encountered in Presteigne parish in Radnorshire in November 1795 comprised for breakfast onion-pottage, for dinner bread or potatoes, and the same for supper.[89] A few years later, the Revd John Evans, observing south Wales as a whole, gave as the peasantry's chief fare barley cakes, potatoes mixed with skimmed milk, and either buttermilk or the liquid called 'dodri-gryafel' – a fermented liquor from the juice of the wild service tree.[90] Fish, we have noted, were a 'great plenty' in Caernarfonshire at mid-century, and doubtless they were important in other coastal areas, Malkin observing in 1803, for example, that in the area about Fishguard herrings and potatoes constituted the food of the lower classes.[91] But fresh meat was seldom eaten by the smaller farmers and the labouring population. Increased harvest earnings, however, saw the two labourers' families in Llanferres parish (Denbs.) investigated by Eden able to afford butcher's meat, beyond their reach in January and doubtless at other times outside the harvest period. In such 'normal' times, the families of the lower class of farmers and the peasantry were restricted to eating bacon, salted and dried beef and sometimes mutton in the same state, on Sundays, and occasionally on weekdays.[92] For the Welsh lower orders in rural areas there was to be little improvement in their diet before the mid-nineteenth century, a consequent undernourishment which led Clare Sewell Read in 1849 to compare the standard of work of the west Wales peasant adversely with that of his English counterpart.[93]

Accommodation was wretched for all categories of the lower orders. Single-storeyed cottages inhabited by outdoor married farm labourers and other wage-earners and craftsmen were damp, dark, cramped and uncomfortable. Contemporary observations brimmed with strictures. Arguably, the worst dwellings of all were those many cots erected on the waste and commons increasingly over the course of the eighteenth century, and the huts dotting the hillsides inhabited by shepherds and peaters. One such peat

worker's hut near Strata Florida in the Plynlimon range in
Cardiganshire was described by the Revd John Evans in 1803:

> It was partly formed by an excavation in the slate rock, and partly by
> walls of mud mixed with chopped rushes, covered with segs, and having
> a wattled or basket-work chimney. The entrance was at the gable end,
> facing the south east, which was defended during the night, or in very
> cold weather, by a wattle hurdle, clothed with rushes. A wall of turf for
> fuel served as a partition for the bedroom, furnished with a bed of heath
> and dried rushes in one corner. The furniture was such as necessity
> dictated: some loose stones formed the grate; two large ones, with a
> plank across, supplied the place of chairs; a kettle, with a back stone for
> baking oaten cakes, answered every culinary purpose; and two coarse
> earthen pitchers stood by for the preserving or carrying water and
> dodgriafel, the usual beverage of the family.[94]

Some improvement in the structure of Welsh cottages was achieved
by the late 1840s for now the walls were being made of stone and
mortar and the roofs of slate, but they were still darkly lit, poorly
ventilated and too confined for health and comfort.[95]

Covenant servants hired by a farmer for a year lived in at the
farm, women and girls sleeping in the farmhouse itself, men and
boys in the lofts of outhouses. These farmhouses were of mixed
quality, those in west Wales running westwards of a line stretching
roughly from Conwy to Neath of a poor standard of construction,
farmhouses in Cardiganshire and north Carmarthenshire, indeed,
having walls made of earth. In sharp contrast, east of the line were
to be found the good-quality timber farmhouses of the north-east
and the stone ones of the south-east.[96] The accommodation of
farm servants obviously depended a great deal on the quality of
structure of the farmhouse and its premises in which they were
domiciled, but in general terms this standard of comfort was low
and frugal. Conditions experienced by male servants were de-
plorable in late nineteenth-century Wales, and would have often
been worse in this earlier period. After all, many farmhouses in
Cardiganshire were entirely rebuilt from the 1830s, replacing what
one commentator chose to call 'miserable mud hovels'.[97]

The labouring poor frequently burned turf for fuel and so were
heavily dependent upon cutting turf from the commons and
wastes. The cost of turf or peat comprised an important item in
the expenditure of the poor, those in the Lower District of

Cardiganshire in 1793 paying 1*s*. 10*d*. or 2*s*. a load, and each family requiring six loads a year. Reflecting the necessity for a substantial element of payment in kind in these societies where circulating money was in short supply, the expensive carriage of each load in farmers' carts over distances of five to six miles was generally paid for by four days' labour at harvest. In these reckonings, moreover, the time given to digging the turf and carting it was not taken into account.[98] Carting turf was out of the question on steep slopes, and procuring it could be hazardous; according to Pennant, men from the vale of Mawddwy carried a light sledge on their backs up the mountain side to the remote turbaries and, filling it with a big load, dragged it, by means of a rope placed over their breast, to the brink of the slope, where, transferring themselves to the front of the sledge they proceeded to draw it downwards, the load sometimes overturning and dragging the hapless individual along with it.[99]

Because of the poor state of road communications, coal was burned in the cottages of the poor only in those areas where access to it was relatively easy and cheap.[100] Walter Davies was to indicate in early 1814 that owing to its 'very unequal' distribution its price of necessity varied considerably from area to area; in parts of Radnorshire the price was fifteen times and in parts of Cardiganshire twenty times dearer than at the pits.[101]

When increasingly from mid-century enclosure of commons and wastes or the reassertion of their perceived rights by the lords of manors interfered with the access of the poor to turbaries or the taking of wood or coal,[102] suffering ensued in England and Wales alike and the lower orders petitioned their 'betters' against such hurtful activity.[103] It was interference of this nature by John Morgan of Tredegar House, Monmouthshire, with the freedom of the poor inhabitants to cut timber on Coedmoeth common in the parish of Bedwellty (Mons.) that led them in November 1791 to petition him to withdraw from his declared intention of cutting into cordwood all the wood remaining on the common.[104] Again, a dispute arose between tenants of the manor of Gower Suprabocus and the lord of the manor, the 4th duke of Beaufort, in the 1740s over the latter's determination to charge the tenants for coal they dug on the commons. Hitherto, they had been allowed to dig turf and coal in the nature of estovers in those commons adjoining their tenements without payment, and the duke's vigilant steward, Gabriel Powell, contended in the late 1740s, 'had they not talk't of

Setting up a Right I believe they would have been indulged in the same manner to this Day.'[105] In both these cases, it was a clash over differing views held by tenants and lords of manors over their respective 'rights' which caused problems for the poor over continuing access to fuel. Competing rights, too, between neighbouring parishes to taking turfs from commons further intensified inter-parochial bitterness. For instance, unauthorized encroachment on Cilcennin parish (Cards.) for the purpose of cutting turf for firing prompted the parish vestry of 11 June 1755 to appoint John Llewelin, a fellow parishioner, to be overseer to look after the moor, and the vestry members agreed to share the expense of prosecuting offenders.[106]

~ 5 ~

The Dependent Poor

In a century when there were few safeguards against falling into penury beyond the help received from family and neighbours, the number of paupers – those who were indigent and destitute, unable to maintain themselves and their families – swelled alarmingly in times of scarcity and epidemic. At such times of crisis, increasing numbers in a neighbourhood had perforce to fall upon the parish for succour, as, for example, in the awful years of suffering between 1729 and 1731, in 1767 and again during the starvation years of the mid-1790s. At the beginning of March 1729 John Meller Esq. and John Lloyd, local magistrates, after informing the churchwardens and overseers of the poor of Wrexham parish that 'the poor who are settled inhabitants of the parish of Wrexham are of late greatly increased partly by ye Extraordinary price of bread corn and partly by the Sickness which hath long continued in these parts', charged them to levy an additional rate of twopence per pound in order to support this increase in the needy. Forlorn likewise was the jotting William Thomas scribbled in his diary for January 1767 about the crisis in the Vale of Glamorgan: 'People fall daily on parishes from the Dearness of provisions and continual Lingring after the last Autumn fever.'[1] A similar rise in the numbers in receipt of poor relief and the amount spent thereon occurred in the difficult years of the mid-1790s and 1800–1, when there were food riots. The parish of Dolgellau (Mer.) experienced a dramatic increase of 'new' recipients in 1795–6 and, more particularly, in the awful years of 1800–1. Summer 1795 was to see a like resort to relief by the able-bodied in Presteigne parish (Rads.), and there Eden recorded in November 1795:

One of the parish-officers says, that, last summer, during the very high price of corn, the earnings of labourers were so small here, that the Poor were literally starving; and that 2 people, who came to crave relief from him, were in such a state of unfeigned distress, that they actually fell down in his house, through hunger.[2]

Poignant reminders of the vulnerability of the poor in hard times and the consequent need for parish relief are provided in letters sent to local magistrates requesting assistance. In the harsh period of the early 1780s Benjamin Morgan was moved to importune John George Phillips Esq. of Cwmgwili on behalf of a poor neighbour thus:

> The Bearer Rees Williams is a poor man and his settlement in the Parish of Abergwilly [Carms.] has himself a Wife and four Children to maintain. The weather has been so unfavourable that he got very very little these three last months, and all the articles of life are very dear for he can't buy a dish of Barley under 1s. 4d. and can't maintain his Family with Bread only order 3 dishes per week which will cost 4s, and he cannot get by his labour when he works what he always does when the Weather permits more than 2s. a week so he must want which I will know. Therefore beg you will take his case into your serious consideration and give your orders to Mr Davies of Pentre . . . one of the overseers of the poor to pay him so much a week during these hard times.[3]

Thomas Lewis wrote imploringly in July 1793 to the Revd H. W. Eyton of Leeswood (Flints.), vicar of Mold and a prominent magistrate:

> I pray with you all day and night because I had nobody Els in the paris but you will take none of my part . . . indeed sur Evry thing is Verry dear my wife is the doctors hand Sens two year go and down Lay in Sickness Sins twelvmonth and indeed sur am allmost naced i had nothing to put on only you see I had only one Shurt . . . I borrow Coat and I must pay six pence. I am use to go to churge evry Sunday i am so poor Evry body take me in a Sport. I see myself go Very ould and near to the grave. I am born Sins the year of our Lord 1714. I hope to god that any of you will Sorry. I beg your faver all of you to bit of Cloths. I got only one Coat Sins one and twenty year if you will help at this time.[4]

As throughout eighteenth-century Britain and mainland Europe, a basic level of pauperism was present in Welsh communities outside the years of crisis, although, given the absence of reliable runs of statistics, there is a frustrating want of knowledge of the precise degree of pauperism in the whole society. Only with the Poor Returns, 1802–3, do we acquire some crude sense of the percentage of the population of England and Wales in receipt of poor relief. Yet, an impression of the depth of poverty towards the close of the seventeenth century is conveyed in the hearth-tax returns of 1670. After a list of the householders liable to pay the tax there followed a list of those considered too poor to be chargeable, albeit they were listed in various ways, which renders the data somewhat unsafe.[5] In some forty-two local Caernarfonshire administrative units, mostly parishes, the extent of pauper householders to total householders ranged between nil and 62 per cent, the percentage of poor householders to total ones of all forty-two units being 43 per cent. In Montgomeryshire, similarly, as many as 57 per cent of households were deemed to have insufficient means to pay the tax in the years 1671–4. Likewise, in south Wales, 47 per cent of households in Pembrokeshire fell into the category of 'paupers certified', as distinct from 'persons lyable', the proportion of pauper householders to total householders over the entire 102 local units (mostly parishes) ranging between nil (in five units) and 78 per cent (in Rosemarket parish). Cardiganshire hearth-tax returns for 1670 give a combined total of 2,083 of 'discharged' and 'receivers of alms' as against 2,442 taxpayers, so that once again it is likely that the substantial figure of 46 per cent households were perceived to be poor. Of the hearth-tax entries/households of the *rural* regions of Glamorgan, 24 per cent were 'not chargeable' and as such likely to have been considered poor.[6]

That levels of poverty were remarkably high is the inescapable conclusion thrust upon us by the hearth-tax figures, yet parish vestry books reveal that down to the mid-eighteenth century few indeed in their parishes were in receipt of poor relief. In 1729 the sole deanery in the entire diocese of St Asaph which levied compulsory poor rates was, significantly, the populous mining area of Wrexham. Furthermore, as late as 1776, some thirty-eight out of a total of sixty-nine parishes or townships in Anglesey had 'no poor' or 'no assessment' and twenty-one such units out of a total of seventy-one in Caernarfonshire had 'no assessments'. Certainly down to mid-century the relatively limited overall population compared with the later decades renders it feasible that the myriad local communities coped with their poor through traditional ways like kindred and neighbour help, gentry charity and church 'gatherings' or collections.[7]

The parish was prodded into making extended provision in the face of the accelerated population growth from mid-century in a

Table 6: Amount of monies expended on the poor . . . in several selected years of those for which returns were required by Parliament

Counties	Average of three years to Easter 1748, 1749, 1750 £	Year ending Easter 1776 £	Average of three years to Easter 1783, 1784, 1785 £	Year ending Easter 1803 £
Anglesey	–	169	930	6,532
Brecknockshire	1052	2408	4238	10456
Cardiganshire	302	1085	2248	7631
Carmarthenshire	1279	2948	5671	13452
Caernarfonshire	–	472	1579	7158
Denbighshire	1139	5365	9762	19954
Flintshire	873	4044	7076	13442
Glamorgan	2224	5301	8818	23136
Merioneth	311	1037	2256	7944
Montgomeryshire	1383	5509	8971	20858
Pembrokeshire	1009	3049	5151	15019
Radnorshire	957	2254	3889	9220
Totals of Wales	10529	33641	60589	154802

Source: British Parliamentary Papers, HC, xliv (1839), 8–9.

primarily agricultural economy offering little alternative employment, albeit enclosure of certain favourable lowland fields did
create more individual farmsteads offering greater employment
opportunities, and industrial ventures, too, soaked up a certain
amount of the surplus population.[8] If we measure the extent of
pauperism – those who were dependent upon charity for their
survival – by the ratio of those in receipt of relief from the poor rate
to total population, the figure of 9 per cent for Wales as a whole (11
per cent for England and Wales) is provided in the Poor Returns,
1802–3.[9] The rising absolute amounts expended on the poor in each
Welsh county in the second half of the eighteenth century are given
in table 6.[10] Percentage increases in various later years over the
mid-century amounts expended reveal progressive acceleration, the
fastest rise occurring from the 1780s. Not only did poor
expenditure rise absolutely in England and Wales, but also in *per
capita* terms from the 1750s onwards.[11]

Parish vestry books reflect the growing urgency of the situation
from the mid-1750s and especially the early 1760s onwards,[12]
followed by the dramatic surge in pauperism from the late 1770s.[13]
The year 1761 was critical for Henllan parish in Denbighshire, its
February vestry agreeing that 3*d*. in the £ be further assessed
towards relief of the poor 'as they are becoming very numerous'.[14]
But it was the surge in demand from the late 1770s which brought
the greatest pressures on parish rates. Constant reassessments
upwards that vestries had to bring themselves to make were
typified in the deliberations and decisions of successive meetings of
the vestry of Aber-nant (Carms.):

Year	per pound	Year	per pound
1768	3*s*. 6*d*.	1790	8*s*.
1769	4*s*.	1794	8*s*.
1777	5*s*.	May 1796	8*s*. 6*d*.
1779	6*s*.	Dec. 1796	9*s*. 6*d*.
1784	8*s*.	1797	10*s*.
1788	7*s*.	1798	12*s*.

A like rise in rates took place in Meifod parish in Montgomeryshire:[15]

Year	per pound	Year	per pound
1763	0s. 7d.	1788	1s. 6d.
1768	1s.	1789	1s.10d.
1777	1s. 2d.	1792	2s.
1780	1s. 3d.	1796	3s. 6d.
1782	1s. 4d.	1800	6s. 6d.

The pressing demands for poor relief in numerous Welsh parishes can be instanced in the Lampeter vestry stipulating in November 1786 that 6d. in the £ be added to the poor rate as an addition to the 3s. already rated on the parish towards supporting the poor, 'as they do increase'.[16] Such a big increase in numbers of paupers which parishes were experiencing from the late 1770s can be seen in the case of Newchurch parish, Carmarthenshire:[17]

1776	9	1781	27	1790	30	1796	42
1777	16	1784	34	1792	34	1798	44
1778	21	1786	39	1794	45	1799	43

Melvin Humphreys has revealed for Montgomeryshire that: 'After the 1770s . . . the numbers of dependent paupers increased at an ominous rate, outstripping the related population growth of the century.'[18]

The growing demand for relief felt in Welsh counties developed, in turn, a defensive, sometimes hostile, mentality in the vestries. It was demonstrated in the stringent measures taken to safeguard against potential paupers gaining settlement, such as the cynical arrangement of marriages so that a female pauper was moved to her husband's parish;[19] or the removal of women suspected of being pregnant to their parishes of settlement;[20] or, as in the case of Cenarth parish (Carms.) which had found it necessary to raise its poor rate from 1754, prominent parishioners engaging themselves in May 1760 in going to law to defend themselves

> against all paupers that shall pretend to be intruders in this parish and that whatever expense we shall be at to defend ourselves in such cases shall be paid without exception, and that no person this day absent shall screen himself from the payment of his dividend of the said expence,

and as in the case, likewise, of the overseers of Henllan parish (Denbs.) complaining in 1759 to the magistrates and applying for orders to remove 'several Poor people that are come to inhabit in the parish of Henllan without gaining any legal settlement there'.[21] Vestries, too, like those of Lampeter in February 1780 and Llanfihangel Ystrad (Cards.) in May 1798, resolved that those men who resorted to employing a substitute to serve for them in the militia should not choose someone with a wife and children for fear they would become chargeable to the parish.[22] Greater insistence on the poor wearing (shaming) badges denoting their status as paupers was yet another manifestation of vestry rigour in holding down expenditure. Such unpitying sentiments towards those luckless mortals likely to prove an added burden to the parish resulted in an undignified trafficking of the unwanted, be they pregnant women or vagrants, across parish boundaries to their place of settlement. Moreover, if the behaviour of the constables of Abergele (Denbs.) was in any way typical, then the very process of conveying vagrants could be cruel in itself, many complaints having been made against them in the 1730s, including 'broken pates and empty stomachs'.[23]

Forms of poor relief in Welsh counties were diverse, but certain common elements can be discerned. In the later decades of the century a basic division became increasingly apparent between those who were elderly, widowed, infirm or insane – the chronic paupers – who were in receipt of weekly rates over long periods, and those who were merely temporarily thrown on the parish through loss of work, sickness or accident and who were recipients of *ad hoc* casual relief.[24] Testifying to their vulnerable position in society, the first category of chronic paupers always contained a significant number of widows and (often) their dependent children. Of the seventy-two on the weekly rate in Abergwili parish (Carms.) in 1790 as many as twenty-six were described as 'widow'.[25] Similarly, those twenty-two people relieved by a weekly allowance in Henllan parish (Denbs.) in 1760 included nine widows – six of whom had two or three children to maintain. Others in that group of twenty-two comprised four – one of them a poor orphan – who were blind or dim-sighted, one who was 'sickly and subject to fits' and another, a widower, who was referred to as 'sickly and two small children'.[26]

Those 'pensioners' of Henllan in 1760 were all paid yearly sums of money, frequently at the rate of 1*s.* per week, and sometimes, in addition, the rent of their house: thus Lowry Jones, a widow with two children, was granted 1*s*. a week and 7*s*. 6*d*. to pay her rent while Griffith Jones, eighty-one and blind, received 1*s*. 6*d*. a week together with 8*s*. for his house rent. A similar pattern of allowances is discernible elsewhere: the Erbistock parish vestry (Denbs.) for 26 September 1762 ordered 1*s*. 6*d*. a week be allowed Eleanor Lloyd, widow, for maintenance of herself and children, and in 1766 Mary Randles was granted by the same vestry 6*d*. per week, and 8*s*. for house rent and a load of coals;[27] in Caernarfonshire, the Llannor parish vestry agreed on 24 August 1780 that 2*s*. per week be paid to Jane Thomas, a pauper, till All Saints Day, towards her support and that of 'five young helpless children'.[28] In some instances, the parish would find a house for the pauper and pay the rent, such renting of cottages in a neighbourhood for the reception of the poor constituting the preferred choice of a parish over the alternative one of building a workhouse or poorhouse.[29] One of the agreements reached by the Lampeter parish vestry on 11 October 1786 reads: 'Allowed to find a house for Mary Lloyd at a moderate rent and 1s. per week towards her maintenance and also 2 cwt loads of turf for the whole year', while another of the Llanfair-ar-y-bryn vestry (Cards.) of 8 October 1793 was entered in the vestry book: 'requested the churchwardens to provide a house for Elizabeth, wife of Rees David Daniel and her three children. Also an old rug and an iron pot, her weekly allowance of 2s. per week be continued till further orders.'[30]

Sometimes the money allowance granted to a pauper would be paid to one of the parishioners for taking care of that person. For example, the Aber-nant vestry (Carms.) granted Martha Thomas, singlewoman, £3. 10*s*. for the year 1774, proceeding on 30 May to make an agreement with William Thomas for maintaining her for that amount.[31] Family relatives would sometimes be in receipt of relief for looking after their kin, children taking care of their parents or one brother maintaining another for example. In the aforementioned parish of Llanfair-ar-y-bryn in 1798, James Lewis was settled with his son, the latter receiving £3. 10*s*. from the parish for his maintenance, and David Thomas was cared for by his daughter who was paid £1 for looking after him. On 23 November 1769 Llanrhystud parish vestry (Cards.) recorded an agreement made with Rees Evan of the parish of Llangwyryfon in that county earlier in the year for looking after his brother David for 18 months at the rate of £3 a year, the said Rees Evan having received 20*s*. to clothe him. Reflecting on a society whose members wore dress to conform with their station in the finely graded social hierarchy, Rees agreed that at the time of his leaving, David 'shall at that time be decently clothed and clad at my expense as it shall be thought requisite and reasonable for a pauper to be'.[32] Such payments to family relatives were necessary at this time of widespread poverty among the labouring poor and emphasizes how families could survive only by dint of all members – apart from young children – contributing to the income of the household; indeed the elderly were in the nineteenth century forced to end their days in the workhouse because making savings for old age was not possible and because their children could not afford to support them, release from this sad circumstance coming only with the Old Age Pension in 1908 which, handed over to their children, enabled them to take their parents into their homes.[33]

Every community had a few 'idiots' who, helpless, frequently depended on the parish for survival. Llanfair-ar-y-bryn parish vestry, for instance, ordered on 3 May 1796 that 2*s*. 3*d*. a week be continued to Hester Morris 'who is insane'. To its credit, the Lampeter vestry took good care of 'Evan the Idiot' from the late 1770s through to the 1790s: in 1787 a vestry of 17 April allowed him a pair of wooden shoes and an old blanket; the vestry of 27 November agreed with Jane Thomas a payment of £4 for the keeping and nursing of Evan for the ensuing year, and, besides proceeding to allow him a flannel shirt, resolved that the churchwardens 'for the time being are to see and examine that the said idiot is to be us'd properly'; 10 December saw the vestry allow him a pair of wooden shoes, a hat and a pair of breeches.[34] In Cardiganshire it was general practice for such pauper idiots to be boarded with parishioners, though some were left with family or friends.[35] One parish vestry there, Llanfair-ar-y-bryn, indeed showed a decidedly enlightened attitude towards idiots. Its meeting of 30 June 1795, after directing that Margaret Rhydderch, an idiot, should be and remain with her mother and stepfather at the weekly allowance of 2*s*. 6*d*. for the year, added: 'and we are of opinion that Idiots in general unless sent to a Madhouse should be with their respective Relatives unless they refuse to take them upon reasonable terms'.[36]

Over and beyond the allowances granted a pauper parent – often a widow – for maintaining themselves and their children, a significant amount of the poor relief granted to chronic paupers went on payment to different parishioners towards providing care for pauper children, either because they were orphans or, for one reason or another, their parents could not look after them, or else because those children were – in the parlance of the time – bastards. Treatment of such children put out to nurse was often so appalling that, according to diarist William Thomas, many died in infancy.[37] Once old enough, such pauper children, many orphaned or deserted, were apprenticed to masters like farmers, tradesmen, craftsmen or artisans.[38] Parish vestries were keen on arranging such apprenticeships, for thereby they avoided the expense of maintaining their destitute children.[39] Masters were chosen by the vestries, and in order to protect themselves against the not unlikely eventuality of an apprentice running away before the expiration of the agreed term – from two to as many as eleven years – they usually paid the masters the premium at regular intervals rather than in one lump sum. The apprentice was provided with meat, drink and washing by the master, while the parish for its part gave money towards clothing.[40] It has been shown that cruel treatment was sometimes meted out to apprentices.

While granting regular sums of money as allowances was for the most part restricted to the aged and infirm, widows with or without children, orphans and the like, the size of the relief given to individuals and their families in the late decades of the century ranging from 6*d.* to 2*s.* 6*d.* a week depending on circumstances, casual *ad hoc* relief dispensed to the temporarily indisposed or out of work took the form of money or payment in kind. The expanding scope and variety of the casual relief allowed in the later decades of the century – first brought to our attention in the Welsh context by T. I. Jeffreys Jones – mirrors the growing demand for succour on the part of the poorer sort in the community, now not just, as hitherto, largely the old, infirm, widows, orphans and the like, but increasingly people who were able to work but who because of want of employment, accident or illness, were forced onto the parish. The surge in poor-relief expenditure from the late 1770s would certainly have been driven to an important degree by this new demand for casual relief from the short-term unfortunate.[41] The problem of coping with growing numbers of needy families was exacerbated by the influx of outsiders to areas of industrial growth like, for example, Mold in Flintshire, where the opening of collieries in the last three decades of the century saw a corresponding rise in the poor rate from £400 to over £1,400. According to A. H. Dodd, the chief difficulty posed to the parish authorities in Montgomeryshire in relation to industrial development was the displacement of traditional cottage labour – women suffering especially in the process – by spinning and carding machinery in the last years of the eighteenth century, poor rates mounting steeply in the affected areas like Llanidloes, Llanbrynmair and Welshpool after 1790. From the 1790s, too, the call-up of men for war service meant that their families were likely to need poor relief. J. Hucks observed in 1795 of Holywell: 'The town and its neighbourhood, as might be expected, abound with numbers of poor women and children, who are left starving, whilst their husbands, fathers and brothers, are gloriously signalising themselves in the service of their country.'[42]

It is likely that most of the casual relief was in the form of cash payments, but paupers were also provided with turfs (for fuel), loads of coal, shoes, clogs, clothes, blankets, barley, potatoes, pots, pans, buckets, and money to repair and thatch houses.[43] Relief in the form of medicines, medical appliances and attendance, and loads of fuel, would have gone to the recipients of regular and casual relief alike. Examples of casual relief highlight the fragile and insecure existence led by most of the lower orders in these years and the narrowness of the line between self-maintenance and dependence on poor relief and charity. Henllan vestry on 9 March 1760 ordered its overseers to pay David Davies 7s. 6d., he and his family 'having been sick of a fever'. On 2 January 1786 Lampeter vestry allowed John James a peck of peel corn and a peck of barley towards his support 'during this inclement weather'; later, on 3 May 1790 it granted Thomas Williams of Wern 2s. a week 'till such time as he can have work' and on 24 February 1800 it allowed him, now old, 'a little barley and a pound of butter now and then when occasion requires'. Llandyfaelog vestry (Carms.) on 18 December 1786 ordered '1s. per week to Thomas John during his present illness and the parish to apply to some gent. of the Faculty for a cure to him', while, on 6 April 1789, Llangyndeyrn vestry (Carms.) granted '2s. per week to Robert Owen and wife during their present illness'. On 12 June 1793 Llanfair-ar-y-bryn vestry agreed that £1. 11s. 6d. be given to Rees David, surgeon, for healing the leg of William Jones, smith, who was to be allowed 6s. per week for three weeks for the support of himself and his family while unable to work. Once again mirroring the importance of the income of both husband and wife to keep the family afloat, casual relief was given when a wife could not work. At its meeting on 29 November 1791 the Lampeter vestry allowed Thomas David William, weaver, 'owing that his wife is ill and unable to earn her bread', one peck of peel corn and 2s. in money towards her support while, on 20 June 1793, it granted Simon David 8s. for support of his wife, 'being very infirm and quite impotent to do anything towards her subsistence'. A large number of dependent children, too, as in all peasant societies at this time, could make all the difference between buoyancy and submersion: in late 1789 the same Lampeter vestry ordered 'one quarter of barley to John James, saddler, as he has so many children and being so very indigent'.[44]

Yet another mode of casual relief for the able-bodied was the prudent outlay of money by the vestry to provide the unfortunate with the means to come by work.[45] Llandyfaelog parish vestry (Carms.) in December 1782 ordered 'a mattock to William Rees' and on 1 December 1789 it agreed to allow David Davies the necessary tools and materials for him to set up his trade of clog maker, granting him also 1s. 8d. for the first week and 1s. for the second. Thomas Anthony was on 8 July 1795 granted by the same vestry £3. 2s. for a horse instead of a cash allowance, and a later meeting of 8 September 1797 allowed 'Edward the Tinker 30s in order to buy half a box of tin with which he promised to support himself and his wife for two years to come without being troublesome to the parish'. In like manner, Llanfair Dyffryn Clwyd vestry (Denbs.) in 1761 gave spinning wheels, and Llanyblodwel (Salop) in 1756 and 1784, stocks of wool, hemp or flax.[46]

Vestries also contrived at putting paupers to work by ordering certain of them to circulate each farmstead in the parish, spending one or as many as three days at each one. Down to the end of the century at least, unlike the operation of the roundsman system, wages were not paid to these paupers for the odd jobs they carried out on the farms they visited – they were simply allowed to go about the parish to do work for board and lodging, usually in return for clothing given by the vestry.[47] Ann Thomas, by order of the Llandysiliogogo vestry (Cards.) on 6 May 1778, was to be allowed 'to go about the parish, that every farmer is to keep her one day for every two pounds Survey [that they are charged to the

Land Tax], to begin at Erwan-fach'. Again, the Llanrhystud vestry (Cards.) of 28 February 1770 'ordered then John David Richard go from house to house in the Hamlet or Parcel of Mevenydd, and remain so many Days at such Houses as their respective Surveys will admit of at one night at every Pound'. Upon becoming a pauper of Aber-nant parish (Carms.) Margaret Samuel, as the vestry agreed on 11 October 1796, was to circulate to each tenement in the parish for the space of three days at each.[48]

Most poor relief was given on an outdoor basis in England and Wales throughout the eighteenth century notwithstanding the early-century efforts at encouraging the erection of workhouses to house the poor. As the 'Workhouse Act' of 1722 did not lead to those in need of relief entering workhouses, in Welsh as English counties before 1750 'the vast majority of relief was in monetary payments outdoors'.[49] Increasingly as the labour surplus in England and Wales manifested itself in the late eighteenth century, the authorities came to realize that outdoor relief had to be given to the unemployed or underemployed, and so, it is argued, Gilbert's Act in 1782, by sanctioning monetary outdoor relief to the able-bodied, merely recognized the new conditions prevailing and the practical responses already in operation to deal with the problem of labour surplus.[50] So far as Wales was concerned, in 1776 there were some nineteen workhouses 'capable of accommodating' 536 persons: eleven of the nineteen were to be found in Pembrokeshire, some six counties had no workhouse, and, with the exception of centres like Cardiff (200), Swansea (100), Wrexham (70) and Llansilin (40), the numbers which each could accommodate were small, thirteen having a capacity of ten or under. By way of contrast, the typical workhouse in English counties could boast a capacity of twenty to fifty paupers.[51] Some growth in workhouse provision had occurred in Wales by the end of the century, the 1803 Poor Returns revealing that some sixty parishes or places 'maintained all, or part of, their Poor in Workhouses'. In the year ending Easter 1803 some 722 were so maintained, a very small number when set alongside the 50,793 persons relieved out of workhouses besides the 3,945 who were not parishioners, most of whom would have been vagrants.[52]

Many of those listed as workhouses in the official parliamentary returns would not have been workhouses in the true sense of the term. Indeed J. S. Taylor avers: 'When the term is used in parliamentary returns, it means any residential relief respondents thought fit to mention.'[53] Some were doubtless workhouses, like the one in Wrexham built within fourteen years of the passing of the 1722 Act, although decline was to set in following Gilbert's Act of 1782, so that it soon became inhabited mainly by infants, the old and the infirm. Again, we may cite the ambitiously conceived Forden House of Industry (Mont.) built in 1792 under a Special Act of Parliament whereby eighty parishes in east Montgomery-shire and adjacent Shropshire were incorporated and their poor were to be sent to the one establishment. Completed in 1794, its directors set out to make it a going concern as a house of industry providing work for the inmates in carding, spinning, weaving, tailoring and shoemaking. Between 300 and 400 inmates were to be found there in the years before 1800. A promising venture was, however, by 1805 ruined by wartime conditions.[54]

But most of the 'workhouses' listed in the parliamentary returns would have been simply 'poorhouses', a term used often in the parish vestry books, and were essentially a late eighteenth-century innovation reflecting the growing worry on the part of parish vestries at the steep rise in poor-relief expenditure and their efforts to contain it.[55] Such poorhouses were mostly a row of cottages 'intended and used merely as a more economic means of paying the house-rents of paupers'.[56] Even so, at least some of these poor-houses aimed to exact work from their inmates, like those in Llan-narth (Cards.), Llawhaden (Pembs.) and Llandyfaelog (Carms.) in the last decade or so of the century.[57] What were conditions like for paupers in these houses? Uncomfortable, not to say grim, surroundings were the lot of most, it seems. The approach of the Llawhaden parish vestry to the running of its poorhouse offers an insight into the harshness that informed the attitudes of at least some parish authorities in that period. At a meeting of 2 January 1787 it was resolved that

> All the Paupers belonging to the said Parish do come into the Poor House built for their reception where they shall be properly provided for on the 1st day of March next ensuing and that they shall have no relief in money after that Day (unless another Vestry shall order those that are bed-ridden or other persons of incurable disorders to be relieved by money) and that they are to be put to work by the Overseers of the Poor every Day and in case of their refusal to work in each Manner as

directed by the Overseer and as they think them able to perform or being refractory in any respect by contradicting the Orders of the House or not obeying them, that they are to be confined in a dark room provided for that purpose until such person or persons shall promise to perform the work allotted for him, her or them.

N.B. It is apprehended that all the several paupers will be able to get their own living if blind or lame and not bed-ridden.

(At the same time, where to draw the line in terms of discipline was seemingly no easy matter, the very want of authority on the part of the governess of Knighton workhouse (Rads.) in the 1790s leading to the poor 'often' beating her.) Discontent on the part of the inmates at their lack of 'sufficient maintenance and proper treatment' in the house of William Morgan, butcher, provided for the poor of Llanfair-ar-y-bryn parish (Cards.) – where they had been lodged between May 1793 and May 1794 – led to the vestry of 30 June 1795 ordering Lewis Price and Esther Adam to give evidence as to their former treatment by the said Morgan before a local justice. If the inmates' complaints were indeed to be adjudged legitimate, then the poor were not to be allowed back to his house.[58] Similarly, the report by Henry Mathias Esq., a Pembrokeshire justice, on his visit to Johnston poorhouse, near Haverfordwest, on 22 July 1800, made at the request of a pauper inmate, Evan Harry, made dismal reading.[59] He found it

in a very ruinous state, the Roof being much out of Repair and the House filthy and unhealthy in a great degree then having a quantity of Ashes and dirt in it and in some parts open at the Roof, and tho' by no means fit and proper for the Reception of the Poor I found removal to and then placed there six persons viz. Martha Davies, widow, the said Evan Harry, Mary his wife, Ann Harry, George Harry and James Harry the children of the said Evan and Mary Harry and one Bed only in the said House which was the property of the said Martha Davies she alone occupying it and not even a bit of straw or anything else whereon the other Poor Persons could lay their Heads . . . the said House in its present state is not fit for Human Beings. (8 October 1800)

It is difficult to discern any merit in these poorhouses of the late eighteenth century.

Yet, Taylor argues, as receptacles for the 'impotent' poor children, the elderly and all sorts of handicapped people, they provided a social service: 'Misery was indeed resident in the pre-1834 workhouse . . . but the unreformed workhouse, for all its inadequacies, fulfilled a social need, and may have done so better than has hitherto been suspected.' For all that, it is just as well that most Welsh parishes with workhouses/poorhouses/almshouses did not make it a condition for distribution of relief that paupers should be sent to these institutions. On the contrary, relatively very few paupers were housed within their walls. The poorhouse seems to have been a place of last resort for those incapable of redemption in terms of ever making it to self-subsistence. Indicative in this respect was the thinking behind the Cardiganshire vestry of Llanfair-ar-y-bryn's decision of 14 May 1793 that outdoor relief be given to any in a distressed situation 'if by such relief they . . . find that they will prevent their coming to be a constant burden in the Poor House'.[60]

For the very poor and dependent, there were other ways of keeping alive apart from the safety net of parish relief. As in all areas of western Europe, beggars were a common sight on the roads and lanes of town and countryside alike in these years, a crucial component of 'the economy of makeshifts' in eighteenth-century France so fascinatingly portrayed by Olwen Hufton.[61] Such was the necessity for poor children to beg in the opening years of the eighteenth century in Anglesey that it was claimed there was no chance of getting them regularly to attend schools founded by the SPCK. Dean John Jones informed the society in 1716 that

> It is impossible in those parts to fix the poor Children constantly and regularly at School, because they must go for ever and anon to beg for victuals, – there *being no poor rates settled in these parts* [my italics], it is the constant method to relieve the poor at their doors and the houses of the several Parishes being scattered about at considerable distances from each other increases the difficulty the poor children labour under.[62]

Children begging remained sufficiently common into the late eighteenth century – despite the expanding provision of poor relief – to catch the eye of Henry Wigstead when touring through north Wales in 1797: of the Llangollen district in Denbighshire he observed: 'The natives have scarcely understood a word of the English language: the children have, however, been instructed to beg; and "give me a penny" is to be heard from twenty little surrounding tongues at the same time.'[63]

Adults, too, especially in the more difficult years, were sometimes forced to turn to begging. Harsh, indeed, were the mid- and late 1690s for Welsh farmers, when broken tenants in Llanfrothen and Llanfor on the Wynnstay estate in Merioneth were forced to become beggars.[64] During the hard times in and around 1740 Anglesey people had no option but to beg, William Bulkeley noting in his diary for 9 December 1741: 'The market at Llanerchmedd much risen, and abundance of the poor going about like last year.' At such a time beggars would have been a familiar sight elsewhere; thus Monday, 8 March 1741, saw 'some begging people' call at the house of Elin Tannatt of Trebryd (Denbs.) seeking alms.[65] Rising populations in the different counties from mid-century would have seen their numbers swell. Old people living in north Wales were to recall in 1812 how in rural areas 'fifty years ago it was common for upwards of twenty young people . . . to go begging for want of employment'.[66] Towns, in particular, were natural collecting places for beggars; Arthur Young mentioned streets of towns like Carmarthen being 'infested with beggars',[67] while the Revd John Evans, in his journeyings in 1803, wrote identically of Carmarthen: 'The streets of the town are infested with beggars', and added, 'indeed mendicity seems systematically pursued, both here and in many parts of south Wales.'[68]

Once parish vagrants were brought to their attention by the overseers, the local magistrates were responsible for deciding upon their place of legal settlement. Suspects were placed in the house of correction or the gaol (the two institutions were virtually indistinguishable in the early century) by a single or pair of justices and in due course they were examined. Those unfortunates who were adjudged by the justices at Quarter Sessions to be rogues and vagabonds were sent back to the house of correction or gaol to be detained and, on the next market day, stripped to the waist and publicly whipped 'until their bodies be bloody'. Thereupon they were conveyed by the parish officials back to their place of settlement, sometimes at a considerable distance. The houses of correction, those in Wales sheltering just a handful of inmates in the early 1770s, aimed to house the poor who were debtors and, in eighteenth-century parlance, rogues, vagabonds or sturdy beggars and other idle and disorderly persons, and they were sent there for 'correction and hard labour'.[69]

If the parish ratepayers sought to rid themselves of potential paupers by zealously returning vagrants to their legal places of settlement, the magistrates for their part saw them as a threat to property and public order. Pembrokeshire Michaelmas Quarter Sessions for 1743 resolved that a general warrant be issued to all high constables for taking into custody all vagrants, the county 'being much infested with strangers and dangerous rogues', some of whom here, as in Caernarfonshire and Denbighshire, would have been Irish. Similarly, the Cardiganshire Quarter Sessions in May 1773, noting that 'several very alarming robberies and burglaries' had recently been committed in Cardiganshire and in neighbouring counties, ordered the justices in their respective neighbourhoods to implement a more careful searching out of 'all vagrants, strollers or other suspicious persons wandering, begging or doing any other act of vagrancy within the county'.[70] So concerned were the Pembrokeshire justices in the 1780s at the presence of vagrants in the county that some of them, acting as individuals in their own districts, were making the considerable payment of 10*s*. to any person who brought before them a vagabond. Thus George Bowen of Llwyngwair, near Newport, ordered payment to John Lloyd, yeoman, of 10*s*. for bringing before him Elinor Evan, widow, a 'rogue and vagabond' found wandering and begging in the parishes of Newport and Nevern, while, in the south of the county, Charles Swann Esq. of Merrixton, ordered the same amount to be paid to Lewis Smith, yeoman, for taking up Edward Savage found begging in the parish of Ludchurch.[71]

The sheer destitution of this marginalized group – many, no doubt, very elderly – comes across from the bleak plight of Thomas Martin, at whose inquest on Christmas Eve 1766 in St David's parish (Pembs.) it was stated that 'he was going about seeking relief and on the road from St. David's homewards the deceased failed being about 80 years of age – and either through hunger, cold or inclemency of the weather Thomas Martin expired'. Just a few days earlier indeed, the body of James Leadbeater had been found in a roadside ditch in Ruabon parish (Denbs.) around 8 p.m. by a nineteen-year-old youth, the inquisition *post mortem* supposing him to have perished 'through extreme poverty and the inclemency of the weather he having been seen begging that day and some days before in the neighbourhood'.[72]

Certain of the old folk customs, too, which did so much to bond
communities and to bring a touch of conviviality, however fleeting,
to lives of toil and privation, served as a veritable legitimizing of
begging. From early morning till noon on New Year's Day
children thus went from house to house collecting 'calennig' or a
New Year's gift. Sometimes the gift comprised food and the
children of north Pembrokeshire and Cardiganshire brought a bag
to carry it. Customs associated with Twelfth Night also levied
contributions. Thus females from among the Pembrokeshire poor
would practise what was termed 'souling' or 'sowling', which
consisted of their calling on their wealthier neighbours and
demanding 'sowl', that is, cheese in particular, fish or meat. Other
customs which similarly served as a communally sanctioned means
of raising funds to help the needy were those of *cwrw bach* and the
pastai.[73]

Landowners' charity, sometimes in response to begging, played
some part in alleviating the misery and degradation of the poor.
Arthur Price, agent of the Golden Grove estate in Carmarthenshire, distributed to the poor of Llanfihangel parish in each of the
years ending Michaelmas 1718 and Michaelmas 1719 the sum of
£20, and he distributed to the poor in the vicinity of Golden Grove
£20 and £21. 10s. respectively in the years ending Michaelmas 1723
and Michaelmas 1724. Likewise in June 1774 Richard Vaughan of
Golden Grove gave out beef from his mansion to the poor, and he
sent money to those who had failed to present themselves on that
occasion. Again, twelve bushels of barley off the Golden Grove
home farm were given to the poor in 1780. Lists of poor persons
who were to receive money at Christmas 1767 in the borough of
Brecon from the Morgan family of Tredegar House in Monmouthshire numbered some eighty-four, each to have 6d. or 1s., the sum
total reaching £3. 6s. 6d. Later, Sir Charles Morgan, Bart. of
Tredegar distributed twenty-nine suits to poor men and twenty-
eight gowns and petticoats to poor women of neighbouring
parishes at Christmas 1794, while, in early December 1798, clothes
were ordered to be made for seven men and seven women in six
different parishes. In the north, the Chirk Castle accounts noted on
17 June 1773: 'List of the poor at Llangollen and Trevor Traians to
receive bread at Chirk Castle.' The Williams Wynn family of
Wynnstay likewise gave to the poor of the neighbourhood: on 26
May 1737 a local tailor was paid 10s. for making twenty coats for

'old poor people' at Llanfihangel; the difficult farming years
1737–43 saw the family distribute charity money to 'poor decayed
tenants', and at a later harsh time for the poor, January 1776, Sir
Watkin Williams Wynn issued instructions from Wynnstay that
both the poor of Oswestry and their counterparts in Wrexham
should be given ten guineas out of consideration of 'this very
inclement season'.[74] Of course, such charity, we shall see later, was
partly motivated from considerations of a family's political interest
and was paltry when compared with sums spent in pursuit of con-
spicuous consumption and in striving to cut a figure in the world.

In addition, charitable bequests were made by gentlemen and
ladies and sometimes by small freeholders to the poor of their
respective parishes. Returns for 1786 show the total annual
produce issuing from charitable donations in the form of money
and land for the benefit of poor persons in all twelve Welsh
counties was £6,236, ranging from a mere £63 in Cardiganshire to
£1,369 in Denbighshire. Legacies were laid out by parish officials
upon bond to certain local private borrowers at interest of 4 or 5
per cent or laid out at interest on land or turnpike security.[75]

There is some indication that the old tradition of dispensing
hospitality at mansions was in decline in the late eighteenth
century, however, at a time when the needs of the poor were
growing ever more clamorous. First Lord Newborough was on 22
January 1793 complimented by Thomas Evans for 'no doubt'
keeping up 'with the true spirit of antient times' the festivities of the
season at his mansion:

> It is a laudable custom to retain them. They harmonise a neighbour-
> hood; they add comforts to the lower classes of Society, who ought to be
> comforted; and (what is most of all) produce many many a 'gardawd ar
> [*sic*] mwyn Duw' [alms for the sake of God] – a phrase now familiar to
> your ears.

Later, on 31 December 1793, Thomas Holford wrote to him from
London:

> The Country people must be happy to observe their young Lord and
> Master's wish to keep up the hospitality and give bread to many of their
> families as in old times, and no doubt will toil to repay it, in improving
> their farms to the utmost of their endeavours.[76]

The inference is that too often such hospitality was dying out. Partly, as land surveyor William Williams bemoaned in reporting on Caernarfonshire in 1806, this was a consequence of the noticeable incidence of 'withered' mansions in that and, we have seen, other Welsh counties, their weighed-down annual tenants no longer able to keep up the hospitality and charity once dispensed by the native gentry owners. The new Caernarfonshire landlords, strangers to their neighbourhoods, were, if sufficiently opulent, absentees, enjoying themselves 'in the town, spending their time on all kinds of dissipation, neglecting and forgetting their duty as men and Christians'.[77] B. H. Malkin, writing on north Cardiganshire in 1803, similarly pointed to the adverse impact that absenteeism had on hospitality and local employment.[78] That there was a real measure of truth in this charge of absenteeism we have already emphasized, but its adverse impact was to some extent at least softened by the fact that landowners' agents took care to keep up the family's donations for good political reasons. In addition to these harmful influences on the level of charity, the tradition of Welsh gentry hospitality itself may have succumbed to the growing Anglicization of the Welsh squires and the virtual abolition of the ancient customs. According to a traveller in 1808, this had indeed been the case in Montgomeryshire.[79]

If the parish poor rates did provide a level of relief which enabled people at least to stay alive and if, indeed, a quite humane treatment was accorded the totally impotent like the blind, the usual allowance of just 1s. to 2s. 6d. a week across the later decades of the century, with perhaps the cottage rent thrown in as well, was wholly inadequate to ensuring even the barest modicum of comfort and dignity.[80] It certainly fell below the lowest level that a day labourer working on a farm on his own find would have earned in the early 1790s, namely £3s. 6d. to 4s. a week. Part of the problem stemmed from the disinclination on the part of parishioners to pay higher rates. Several persons in Cenarth parish (Carms.) refused or neglected to pay the poor rate in 1749 as, too, did certain inhabitants of Henllan parish (Denbs.) in 1761–2, perhaps because of the 3d. in the £ rise agreed in the parish vestry in February 1761. We have noted, too, the steep climb in rates in Aber-nant parish (Carms.) from the mid-1790s; parishioners' grumbles concerning allowances given to people for caring for paupers were sufficiently loud to push the vestry into justifying itself. One such declaration read:

that John William, Cilwen, is to have £3 for the maintenance, clothing
etc. of Evan Rees from 11 October 1796 to 11 October 1797 and in case
any of the parishioners not present at the aforementioned vestry (11
October 1796) should think the above sum extravagant, then John
William do promise to deliver up the said Evan Rees to any person who
will undertake to keep aforesaid Evan Rees for a less sum, on Ascension
Thursday 1797.[81]

Such niggardliness was exacerbated by the sour and begrudging
attitude displayed to their paupers on the part of the parish
authorities, who did all they could to drive questionable claimants
to relief out of the parish, and to shame and make feel unwanted
those many who remained. In an age when people accepted their
station and lot in life with a degree of resignation, for the poor to
complain of conditions in the poorhouses surely signifies atrocious
neglect on the part of those in charge! Such was their privation that
it is small wonder that some paupers turned to theft as the only
means of staying alive. When Ann Lloyd, spinster, of Corwen,
Merioneth, confessed before the court of Great Sessions for
Denbighshire in autumn 1796 to stealing 4½ guineas, a cloak
and butter from a farmer in the parish of Llanrhaeadr-yng-
Nghinmeirch (Denbs.), she put forward as her defence the fact that
her mother lived at Corwen, in poverty, and there being no food in
the house, she, Anne, went begging, and not meeting with relief,
she stole.[82]

Matters were made worse on account of the lax and inefficient
administration of parish poor relief in Welsh counties. 'And here
permit me to observe', wrote John Paynter from Hafod (Cards.) in
1770,

that *our* poor laws, defective enough in themselves, are, in a manner,
totally neglected, useless and misapplied. The assessments for the Poor
are partial, unproportionate and irregular – never approved of by the
magistrates, nor the overseers were call'd to an Account! Monthly
meetings, as in England, would contribute to cure this evil.[83]

(In this last respect it is significant that parishes like Llangyndeyrn
(Carms.) and Llangedwyn (Denbs.) were convening monthly
vestries from the 1790s.) That laxity had prevailed in Llanfair-ar-y-
bryn parish is on record: its vestry meeting for mid-June 1795,

noting that the balances due from the several churchwardens were not properly stated, agreed that two justices be asked to attend to investigate the accounts at the end of the month. Magistrates were certainly not as vigilant as they ought to have been. When referring to the poor rates in Carreg township in Machynlleth during his tour of north Wales in 1797, Walter Davies volunteered: 'The idleness of the poor and the negligence of the magistrates go hand in hand.'[84] Yet they, too, were in a difficult situation when faced with reluctant parish authorities, indeed having on many occasions to chivvy them into fulfilling their obligations in allowing relief and to serve as overseers. John Price, a Denbigh alderman, deftly conveyed the feelings of frustration on the part of authorities and the poor alike as early as 1770 when writing on 2 November of that year:

> This day I gave up my office as alderman, troublesome it has been enough, as the care of the Poor lies upon us, the overseers not caring to proceed without particular orders from the aldermen, besides making up innumerable disputes and quarrels among the inferior sort.[85]

Such ill-feeling aroused among the poor extended to the distribution of charity in general. A widow of Llywel parish in Breconshire indeed found herself arraigned before the Great Sessions in 1730 for the murder of Mary Powell by striking her with a chamber pot, although the blow had been intended for Elizabeth Roberts, whose recent allocation of charity money among the poor of the parish had failed to make any provision for the indignant widow.[86]

~ 6 ~

Relations in Working the Land

1. Relations between Landlords and Tenant Farmers

No great fissure opened up in this century between landlords and
their tenants over religious and political persuasions. We shall see
later that tenants were expected to support their own landlord's
political interest and that, while there were occasional clashes, most
tenants complied. Only on the linguistic front was there a real
parting of the ways, large landowners spending increasing amounts
of their time 'in town' (London) and distancing themselves from
their language and the traditional patronage of native culture and
the bardic craft. Geraint H. Jenkins thus succinctly concludes:
'Many of them avidly pursued the manifold pleasures and temptations of sophisticated life in London, and as the century unrolled
they became indifferent or even hostile towards Welsh culture.'[1]
Criticized by leaders of Welsh culture for such betrayal they most
certainly were,[2] but it is unlikely that this resentment was as yet
deeply felt in the lower orders.

In the eighteenth century it was the more immediate economic
conditions and circumstances which sometimes gave rise to
strained relations and hostile perceptions. Predictably, trouble
could arise when a tenant was given notice to quit a holding in
favour of someone else who may have offered a higher bid for the
farm. Job Roberts of Yale thus wrote in pained tones to the agency
at Chirk Castle in September 1758 over his receiving notice to part
with the Glyn tenement. Reminding Richard Myddelton that he
could not recollect ever offending his honoured landlord or
himself, he complained: 'I think it very unjust for anyone to covet
to reap my Improvement . . . it lies in your power to give the person
who covetts it an Immediate answer.'[3] Insistence on clearing rent
arrears, too, could spark resentment. The no-nonsense, businesslike approach of John Vaughan of Golden Grove (Carms.) in
insisting on the speedy wiping out of arrears on the estate in the
difficult farming years of the mid-1750s led tenants, in his agent's

words, to 'murmur greatly' and to create 'a great noise in the country' in 1755.[4] While sometimes, as shown earlier, agents took a sympathetic approach towards hard-up tenants, on other occasions they were unduly harsh. Writing to the owner of Chirk Castle in July 1724, clergyman Thomas Wynne of Llanrwst interceded on behalf of one tenant thus:

> The bearer is a parishioner of mine, a tenant and old servant of the Castle, Mr David Williams [the agent] and he disagree in their accounts, and truely Mr Williams used him hard, in so much that he seized his cattle . . . If you can prevail with Mr Williams to let him continue in his Tenement I dare say he will in a short time be able to clear his arrears.[5]

That agents were prone to feathering their own nests at the expense of tenants when making distresses was alleged in 1756 by one of their own number, Lewis Lewis, agent for John Vaughan, absentee owner of Golden Grove.[6]

The process of distraint itself often met with much resistance, both verbal and physical.

> Hugh Jones [of Penygelly farm on the Mostyn estate] has been very free with me in his hearty curses, both in the presence of the bayliff and my own servant, lays all the fault at my doors, that I was the occasion of his goods being seiz'd upon,

reported Roger Mostyn from Cilcain to Sir Roger Mostyn, Bart. at Mostyn sometime before 1739.[7] Physical encounters, we shall see in chapter 10, sometimes led to cases being brought against resisting tenants in the assize courts.

The issue of repairs could give rise to resentment. In 1737 tenants of the Mackworth estate in the parish of St Mellon's, Cardiff, were ready to throw up their small farms because they were out of repair, particularly with regard to ditching.[8] By the early 1740s many farms on the Margam estate in Glamorgan had fallen into disrepair through 'neglect of not doing what ought to have been done many years ago', and to avoid the dismal prospect of much land falling into hand the owner had no choice but to lay out large sums of money.[9] Several tenants of the Chirk Castle estate were complaining in 1754 that their buildings were badly out of repair.[10] Once again, failure to act promptly in earlier years over carrying

out repairs meant a crisis for the Wynnstay estate management in
the late 1770s and 1780s. A memorandum drawn up in 1777 for Sir
Watkin Williams Wynn was terse:

> The Reason of the advanced rents not coming to immediate profit is
> owing to the shameful neglect in letting the buildings run to ruin during
> Sir Watkin's infancy when they might have been stopped for a trifle are
> now in general to be built new or the tenants cannot possibly live in
> them.[11]

By this time a hardening attitude on the part of tenants towards
run-down holdings was discernible. Their becoming noticeably
more clamorous for repairs was a response to the high rents that
were being charged them from the 1770s. On the Wynnstay estate
they had come to *expect* repairs from summer 1776.[12] Likewise,
Chirk Castle tenants requested repairs following the rent increases
of the late 1780s, a number of them complaining about the lack of
adequate farm buildings or about dilapidated premises. A letter of
May 1790 from the agent predicted with a degree of trepidation: 'It
will be some time before tenants reconcile themselves to their
advanced rents and I shall find it a difficult matter to satisfy their
wishes as to repairs etc.'[13]

Sometimes giving rise to bitterness was the tenants' complaint
that their landlord had not given allowance for repairs which they
had carried out. Disgruntlement had certainly come to colour
Simon Humphrey's attitude by 1728 when contemplating under-
taking repairs to Cefn Caire, a tenement he rented off Sir Griffith
Williams: 'I have so often been burnt in the hand', he complained
to the Revd Hugh Wynne of Doleychowgrid [*sic*], 'by making
repairs upon other men's lands and have had no allowance for it
that I am now quite disheartened.'[14] Monmouthshire assizes at the
close of the century saw an action brought by a Mr Howkins
against his tenant, John Phillips of the Gare, for a whole year's rent
for the holding, Phillips, however, pleading an allowance for
mason work which he had been promised by Howkins. The dispute
lay over the amount of work involved.[15]

Similarly, tenants who had carried out husbandry improvements
felt the need to petition their landlords for permission to continue
in their holdings. That there was an element of uncertainty there
can be no doubt. For example, Jane Williams of Ruthin, widow,

importuned Robert Price in summer 1727 to beg her landlord, John Myddelton, living at Cefn y Wern, that she might continue as tenant for the year in the two parcels of land she occupied, considerable expense having been incurred by her in mucking and providing seed wheat. Likewise, William Watkins, a considerable farmer and, like his father and grandfather before him, tenant to the duke of Beaufort of a farm called The Demesnes in Grosmont parish (Mons.) at £68. 10*s.* a year, petitioned his Grace in the 1740s against being turned off for refusing to pay £21. 10*s.* more for it at the behest of the agent. Claiming that his grandfather, at the rent of £68. 10*s.*, built a dwelling house, barn, stable and wainhouse at his own expense, he complained: 'I found too late to my cost that the Building and improvement and good husbandry that was done on the said Farm, was the occasion of enhancing the rent of it.'[16]

Rent increases, for whatever reason, certainly produced much friction in the later decades of the century. There is evidence from a variety of sources of tenants' resentment. The independent-minded Evan Evans in his Introduction to his *Casgliad o Bregethau* (Collection of Sermons), 1776, denounced in Old Testament fervour: 'Have not most of our gentry thrown away all regard for religion and morality, and are become as slaves to their vile lusts; and in order to pamper them, rack their poor tenants?' and thundered, 'Great Self is the object of all their aims and wishes; and thousands load them with curses for raising exorbitant rents.'[17] Travelling through north Wales at precisely the same time, Joseph Cradock remarked that the 'exorbitant demands' of landlords were leading to 'great complaints'.[18] Geraint H. Jenkins observes that popular ballads from the 1770s 'complained of soaring rents, high taxes and a general fund of resentful bitterness'.[19] The verse of Hugh Jones, Maesglasau, bemoaned rents being doubled, rates increasing and mounting debts to shopkeepers.[20] If less prone to criticize the élite in society, the agent of Chirk Castle, we have noted, frankly recognized in 1790 that tenants would take some time to come to terms with the increases in their rents. In the wake of the rent increases of the 1770s, the low-price years of the early 1780s were especially painful ones; the agent of the Wynnstay estate acknowledged in 1786: 'taking advantage of the value which land bore to the occupier at the time, have perhaps advanced [in 1777] his [Sir Watkin's] rents to a degree that many of the farms will not bear at present.'[21] Tenants of the estate in the Lordship of

Cyfeiliog in Montgomeryshire actually entered a 'most iniquitous conspiracy' in 1783 against paying advanced rents, which the agent boasted of having 'fortunately crushed' before Christmas, significantly in the process finding it necessary to make 'some examples'. To such an extent had rent increases sparked resentment among tenants on the Caernarfonshire estate of Lord Newborough, that at an unknown date between 1776 and 1807 some eighty of them jointly petitioned Edward Lord Thurlow, the High Chancellor of Great Britain, complaining against the 'oppression' of the receiver of rents on the estate, Samuel Price Esq., in raising rents considerably above their earlier level.[22]

Indeed, trouble had been brewing among the Wynnstay tenants from the moment of the general increases made in 1777. William Morris held out in defiance of his landlord, insisting on paying only his old rent of £36 and refusing to quit the farm, albeit the holding had been let on Lady Day 1777 to a new tenant at £50 per annum. To prevent the 'wrong' message going to other tenants, Francis Chambre, the agent, directed a bailiff to arrest him, and he clumsily did so in open market at Wrexham.[23] Randle Jones, tenant of Park Eyton, chose to quit the holding in 1778 rather than pay the advanced rent and subsequently refused to pay a year's rent of £80 due at Lady Day 1777, on the grounds that the succeeding tenant entered before he had any right. According to Chambre, he had given consent to the new tenant to enter and so he made the 'pretence for the purpose only of being a Rogue', adding darkly, 'I will immediately arrest him and learn him to be honest.' In early 1779 a certain Langford of Eglwysfach tenement on the estate held out against paying £60 for the farm – at which rent it had been let to a new tenant – offering only £50 and, in justification, claiming it was his improvements that had brought the farm to its present value. Chambre counselled his master, Wynn, to refuse the offer, lest others should apply to have their rents lowered on the same pretext.[24]

The extraordinary conditions of the war years of the 1790s saw burdens on tenants mount as never before and a small number emigrated to the United States. Apart from the political pressure faced by Dissenters, an Independent minister of Caernarfon maintained, people were emigrating in autumn 1793 because of high rents, burdensome taxes and heavy tithes. Certain of the twenty-one-year leaseholders on the Vaenol estate in Caernarfonshire had emigrated before their leases were due to expire in 1799. Impoverished farmers in south-west Wales, too, particularly those of south Cardiganshire, left for the new world in the 1790s and in 1800–1.[25] There was clearly a great dissatisfaction among many tenants with the high rents their landlords were charging them.

Of course, insofar as the whole agrarian system was (and is) based upon sharing of good and bad times, it was perfectly natural that rents should have risen in a time of prosperity like the late eighteenth century. To some extent the complaints by tenants and, for all their social compassion, poets and radicals against the rise in rents from the 1760s were manifestly naive.

There is some evidence that tenants found certain other covenants in their leases intrusive. September 1756 thus saw the Golden Grove (Carms.) agent inform his absentee master, John Vaughan, of his having had disputes with many tenants over duties. The background to the trouble lay in Vaughan's determination in the 1750s to end the earlier slackness by which duties had lapsed into a nominal 1*s.* and some others were not collected. His instructions to his agent in 1755 were twofold: that the duties and heriots 'ought to be in proportion to the rent, as is the general rule' and that, as had been the custom, duties were to be had in kind or in money, at the landlord's choosing. Neglect of payment on one occasion in the 1730s led to an assault on the tenant: William James, tenant of Charles Richards Esq., Penglais, near Aberystwyth, had sent his landlord but one horse instead of two to work in his harvest, whereupon the violent squire had beaten him with a stick.[26] We sense some resentment, too, over heriots in the letter written by John Morgan to Thomas Bryan, agent of the Tredegar Palleg estate (Brecknock), in October 1764:

William David one of the Tenants died last summer and I seized a cow of his for a heriot, he had but two in all of his own; his son is come to give you satisfaction, and desires to keep the cow, and that you will deal with him favourably; I suppose if he did pay every man his due, that he should have but very little to pay nobody.[27]

Once again, with regard to the covenant enjoining tenants to keep a hound, there was some friction: Sir Watkin Williams Wynn of Wynnstay was informed by his agent in August 1776 that his tenants in the Vale of Clwyd 'rather growl at keeping such large

Hounds as the Major sends'. The duty to grind at the lord's mill, too, may have been felt irksome. Certainly David Jones of Llanbrynmair parish (Mont.) was sufficiently angry to arraign a miller of the same parish before the Great Sessions for the county in 1785 for 'extorting oats' from him 'by the colour of an ancient custom' whereby all the occupiers of land in the township of Tirymynach were bound to bring all their grain to be ground at the accused's mill. We learn from the indictment that the miller was allowed to take out one peck and a half out of fifty pecks of oats 'upon the first shelling'. Although a verdict of not guilty was returned by the court, this prosecution may well have mirrored the feelings of the wider farming community.[28] While evidence for the eighteenth century of widespread truculence towards these various duties on the part of the tenantry is patchy, by 1825 , according to one observer, they had become vexatious as symbolizing a certain degree of servility.[29]

Preservation of game by landlords, sustained by the Game Laws which forbade freeholders of under £100 a year and leaseholders worth less than £150 a year to take game, was doubtless irksome for tenants, although actual evidence is scant. Given the assumptions we hold of courts of law upholding the landowners in their sole right to game if challenged, it is reassuring to discover that on hearing a case brought before the Glamorgan Great Sessions in August 1793 by a farmer of Penlline against the gamekeeper of the local estate-owner, Miss Gwinnet, for spoiling a barley field the previous September through beating about for game, the judges after a five-hour hearing found in favour of the plaintiff.[30]

Finally, with the growing value of timber over the course of the eighteenth century, landlords sought to protect their woodlands. Such a policy engendered much ill-feeling between landlords and those tenants who cut down trees despite provisions forbidding it in their leases. Concealment was obviously aimed at, tenants on the Cwmgwili estate (Carms.) in the years before 1785 covering over the roots of felled trees with grass to avoid discovery. Indeed, for Melvin Humphreys, tenants' misconduct in this respect constituted one of the most serious rifts in landlord/tenant relations in these years.[31]

There is no mistaking the expectation on the owners' part that tenants would behave dutifully and respectfully. As we shall see, this involved using their votes properly and rallying to the military defence of their counties in the 1790s. More generally, any display of independence and want of deference was deemed to be 'impudent' and could have unfortunate consequences. Henry Parry, tenant at Coedmarchan on the Chirk Castle estate, was allegedly 'very pressing and impertinent' on leaving his farm in 1725 concerning allowances he would receive for compost on the holding. He was accordingly cautioned by the agent that provided he carried himself 'civil and thankful' he could remove what muck he had on the premises to wherever he chose.[32] A notable instance occurred on the Mostyn estate when Robert Price, tenant of Pengwern Hall near Llangollen, which the family had farmed for over fifty years, was turned out of his holding in 1768 by Sir Roger Mostyn. According to the Revd Evan Lloyd, he had by virtue of a good education 'derived a spirit too great to stoop and cringe to agents', and, seizing his chance, a covetous, 'undermining neighbour by perpetual applications to Sir Roger's agent, and all the dirty underhand work usual in such negotiations' at last succeeded in gaining the farm.[33]

As this last-cited instance demonstrates, part of the problem of mistreatment of tenants lay with estate stewards and agents. Twm o'r Nant was in no doubt that tenants were ground down by twin oppressors:

> Between the laws of stewards and the vanity of great men
> A tenant is caught between the devil and his tail,

while Lewis Morris lashed unsparingly: 'Thou shalt worship the estate agent for he is the graven image of thy master and a demigod. Obey him through fire and water, watch lest thou offend him, and woe be to thee if he frown upon thee.'[34] There was much truth in these strictures. We have alluded earlier to their feathering their own nests when making distresses upon tenants. The dishonesty of some in abusing their office for gain was found out – men like George Higgins, gent., steward of the Llwydiarth estate (Mer.) who was dismissed in 1699 for having dishonestly returned tenants in arrears and for having fraudulently used his master's money to buy cattle and purchase a small estate; Stephen Howard, agent at Margam, who was sacked in 1711 for failing to return proper arrears; John Parry, agent at Glyn (Mer.) to the owner, Owen of Porkington, who came unstuck over taking ridiculously large earnest from tenants and who, after a legal hearing, was in 1753 paying back money to tenants whom he had wronged; and John Hosier, agent at Chirk Castle in the 1740s and 1750s, who defrauded his employer by failing to return all the rents.[35] Nor is it difficult to point to thoroughly unpleasant bullies like, for instance, John Lewes, estate agent of Lewis Pryse of Gogerddan (Cards.), who made certain tenants' lives a misery in the 1770s and 1780s for having dared to vote against the Gogerddan interest.[36]

Yet to condemn them out of hand as a class would be to ignore decency among certain of their number. Reference has been made earlier to some of them counselling a soft approach towards tenants in arrears. The same leniency was sometimes manifest on those few occasions when tenants whose effects had been distrained fled with part of their stock. John Owens thus wrote on 19 November 1735 to his absentee employer, Madam Rice of Newton (Dynevor, Carms.), how a tenant of his master in Llandeilo parish, who had fallen £8 in arrears and whose goods were distrained upon, conveyed all his stock, household stuff, corn and hay at night-time 'out of the way'. Constables and 'spies' were deployed in tracking down the missing goods. The tenant was taken in the first week of December following, and, upon his uncovering all the missing goods, the agent turned him loose. That same crisis period of the mid-1730s likewise saw Cadwallader David of Plas Ucha, about to have his goods seized by the agent, drive away certain of his stock in early February 1736. Although he lost the holding through debt, sympathy was once again evinced by the agent, who wrote: 'I must beg you would pardon him and let my mistress or yourself give me orders to give his wife a cow or two.'[37]

After what can be viewed as an indulgent 'landlordism' in Wales in the early decades, when, as in Ireland, a veritable 'moral economy' prevailed of lax estate management which included long leases, ridiculously low rents and tolerance of arrears, there is no mistaking the anxiety on the part of landowners to make the most of their properties from the middle decades onwards.[38] At the same time some were careful to stop short of hurting their tenants, and to exercise lenience towards those who were particularly vulnerable. Foes Lochart farm on the Bronwydd estate in north Pembrokeshire was out of lease in 1775 but was not to be raised because 'the tenant is old and poor'.[39] Emphasis has been laid earlier upon the upset and grievance felt among Wynnstay tenants at the general rent increases of 1777. Yet Sir Watkin instructed his agent concerning one complainant: 'if it is only the common complaint against the advanced Rent you know how to proceed, but if it is a case of *distress* I would have you be merciful to them.' George Morgan, agent to Charles Morgan of Tredegar Park, was in early 1777 despairing of his master's generosity and, frustrated at the latter's willingness to let Abergawdy farm in St David's parish go cheaply, exclaimed: 'At this rate it will be out of my power to make any improvement in your Honour's rent roll.'[40] In expressing their gratitude in 1879 to the owner of the Gwydir estate for her timely help to them in the difficult farming times of late, the tenants also adverted to

the benevolent deeds of your illustrious ancestors, notably during the long continued and disastrous depression consequent upon the American War of Independence, when, after repeated remissions of rent, the Gwydir tenantry were finally disembarrassed and relieved by the cancelling of all arrears, an act of clemency the fondly cherished household traditions of which has been handed down to us from our forefathers.[41]

Tenants' love of the 'family' holding and their keen wish to continue as occupants was a feature of this as of the following century. Applications for renewal of leases sometimes directly alluded to the family's stake in the farm. 'I am desir'd by the bearer Mr Powell to give your Lordship the trouble of a letter in his behalf', wrote Charles Penry from Brecon to Lord Mansell of Margam in 1722; ' . . . he is desirous of continuing your Lordship's tennant in the House where his father liv'd forty years.' John Roberts, tenant of a holding on the Chirk Castle estate in the parish of Y Gyffylliog, wrote to his landlord in 1726 requesting a reduction in the proposed new rent, urging, 'I have no mind to part from the place that I and my ancestors lived some hundred of years ago.'[42] That many landlords indulged this sentimental attachment is a token of their community spirit. Significantly, Sir Watkin Williams Wynn intimated to his agent in March 1781: 'I always wish to continue the successors of my Tenants if possible instead of letting them to strangers.'[43] The snag was that by this time there were so many desperate to secure tenancies that landlords all too often allowed self-interest to prevail over sentiment.

That tenant farmers resented paying tithe is mirrored in the frequent obstruction they offered to its collection, a resistance which brought them into conflict with both the clergy of the Church of England in Wales and landowners as tithe impropriators. Tithe disputes occurred in the parish of Llangadog and chapelry of Llanddeusant (Carms.) in 1736, at Llanfechan (Mont.) in 1736–9, and obstruction to collection of tithe again took place in the parish of Monmouth around mid-century.[44] Illustrating the willingness on the part of farmers to resort to petty obstruction, an action was brought in 1757 by the rector of Mathry against a farmer who withheld permission for the rector's cart to cross the fields to secure the tithes unless the oxen were muzzled to prevent them from eating his grass, and a suit was heard in 1770 in the ecclesiastical court against a farmer in the parish of Penbryn (Cards.) – a fiercely anti-tithe parish, later, as in the 1890s – for not making up the tithe sheaths in little heaps according to the ancient custom in the parish.[45] As examples of the way that disputes could cast a shadow over the harmony of a parish, John Longford, vicar of Hanmer (Flints.) informed two of the county's JPs in 1760 that 'a long list of persons' (seventy-five were named) were refusing to pay or compound for small tithes, while later, in 1800, a legal case was fought between the vicar, Thomas Watkins, and the inhabitants of the parishes of Llandyfalle, Crucadarn and part of the parish of Bronllys, the latter backed up by John Macnamara of Llangoed Castle, over the exaction of tithe hay and the validity of a composition for tithe corn which was claimed to have been imposed by the vicar on unwilling parishioners. As yet, opposition to payment was based on financial considerations and methods of payment, not religious grounds. Frank indeed was the outburst of Richard Howell in a letter of 1780 to William Bassett Esq. regarding tithe payment in the parish of Llantrisant (Glam.):

> If the tithe gathirers is not put a stop they will rewin the Poor Farmers if they go on at this rate but by and by it will fall on the landlords and they are the only people who ought to take care that no imposition of the kind should take place.[46]

The frustration felt, of course, was not all on one side. Parish incumbents, frequently short-changed by lay impropriators, nurtured a sense of grievance at tenants' unwillingness to pay the full amount of the tithe. For instance, vicar Humphreys complained to Lady Owen at Glyn in January 1721 of how her tenants at Craigie-forchog had over the past eight years given only what they pleased in tithe wool, not even the twentieth part, let alone the tenth due.[47]

Although untypical of their group as a whole, there were wealthy, prospering tenant farmers in all neighbourhoods, and their numbers were on the increase in the later decades of the century. For these hard-working and productive men the lowly status they enjoyed *vis-à-vis* what they perceived as the unproductive, lazy, parasitic landlords, rankled. One late eighteenth-century ballad voiced their resentment thus (in translation):

> You the gentry who cough and grow fat
> We, dazed, fare poorly.
>
> I can assure you that were it not for the tenant
> You would not prosper so well.
>
> You the gentry oppress to your utmost ability
> And trample fathers of families in their homes.

According to Glyn Parry, the conflict and tension among substantial tenant farmers found an outlet in Nonconformity and, in Caernarfonshire certainly, in Methodism.[48]

2. Relations between Gentlemen and Estate Servants

Relations between both home-farm and house servants and their gentry and aristocratic employers at the mansions were close, such servants taking pride in 'their' family's consequence. Yet, here too, tensions could arise. The extravagant, largely absentee Sir Watkin Williams Wynn of Wynnstay (Denbs.), fearing the harm it was doing to his local standing, particularly at election time, was much exercised in the late 1770s and early 1780s over his chief agent's failure to keep up the payment of servants' and workmen's wages at Wynnstay. Tongues were wagging, leading Sir Watkin to complain to the besieged Francis Chambre on 12 May 1781:

Without you can do something for the People in the Neighbourhood of Wynnstay it will be absolutely impossible for me to come down there this year. You promised me that all the Rents in the Neighbourhood should be appropriated to that use. I am afraid the non compliance with that request of mine has made the poor People *impatient* and apparently *saucy*.

Earlier, in June 1779, Sir Watkin had feared literally a 'hue and cry' upon his coming to Wynnstay.[49]

If rare, the show of 'independence' on the part of home-farm labourers at Tredegar Park in February 1800 is further testimony to the resentment that sometimes arose at the mansions. At this time of acute scarcity of corn supplies, trouble was sparked by the proposed reduction in the distribution of wheat to the workmen. Significant in revealing the harsh retaliation visited by the landed families on perceived troublemakers and ingrates, those two or three home-farm labourers who were allegedly instrumental in persuading the entire workforce to assemble in the upper court 'in a body' on 15 February to protest at the proposed reduction were 'immediately discharged' by the bailiff, Henry Brown, the rest going 'very quietly and satisfied to their several occupations'. Brown reassured his master that many of them repented 'having been so foolish as to be prevailed upon to join in such a scheme but fear operated on the minds of many of them they having been threatened to be beat unless they would come forward'. (Given the level of intimidation that was at work in many popular disturbances at this time, perhaps their explanation was genuine rather than merely a convenient excuse.) Similar intolerance of any resistance on the part of estate employees was revealed by Lord Mansel of Margam in 1711. In reply to his agent's report that Ann Wiles objected to his Lordship's instructions about the pigs and angrily demanded to be discharged and paid her wages, Lord Mansel wrote: 'Pay her off immediately and anyone else that desire to go or are impertinent.'[50]

Ill-feeling would have arisen, too, when a number of servants at the various mansions stole money or goods from their employers, a tendency which is observable from an inspection of the Great Sessions gaol files and which will be noted in chapter 10.

3. Relations between Farmers

The popular image we adhere to of Welsh farming before the advent of harvest machinery in the last decades of the nineteenth century is of farmers co-operating among themselves and with their labour forces in farm tasks at busy seasons of the farming year like haymaking, corn harvest and sheep-shearing. Custom was a powerful lubricant that oiled the wheels of neighbourhood cohesion, and in this instance of co-operation in farm tasks the custom of love-reaping entitled a farmer to call upon his neighbours to assist him for one day.[51] Moreover, co-operation could extend beyond mutual help at busy seasons: tenants on the neighbouring Chirk Castle and Wynnstay estates even reciprocally assisted each other in the payment of rents whenever there was a deficiency.[52]

Yet given the jealousy with which farmers of all descriptions protected their property rights, there were inevitable irritations and disputes between neighbouring farmers over a range of issues which must lead us to query the degree of harmony which obtained.[53] Griffith Parry wrote from Clenennau (Caerns.) on 21 May 1729 of 'little trifeling quarrels' occurring among William Owen's (of Porkington) tenants about turf 'which is frequent at this time of year'.[54] Disputes between tenants arose too, as mentioned earlier, as a consequence of the intermixture of ownership of land, whereby tenants held farms whose fields were intermixed with land rented by a different tenant. Predictably, tenants trespassed on one another. To some extent at least, landowners attempted to ease the problem either by exchange of lands or by letting such intermixed farms together to a single tenant.[55] Another potential source of friction was the conflicting claims to unenclosed common land. Upset at not being allowed to rent Caernolwr (Caerns.) off William Owen of Porkington, which would allegedly have given him some pretext for encroaching on Owen's rights of common, Edward Roberts of Glan y Dŵr in summer 1742 resorted to such bullying conduct towards his neighbours in building a large sheep fold higher on the common in Owen's sheepwalk, and rebuilding it after it was thrown down, that Owen's tenants gave up their farms.[56]

Want of hedging or walls between contiguous tenements, too, gave rise to disputes. A sense of the nuisance, indeed menace, of predatory neighbours in this respect is conveyed in the following communication of estate agent John Parry from Brynsanon to William Owen at Porkington in summer 1748:

> This night came here your tenant Ellis Powell of Plas yn Pennant in a great concern for that Mr Knight his next neighbour of Gilfach turned into his hey grounds five heads of cattell in order to claim the same as belonging to him and assaulted and very much abused his wife your tenant who endeavoured to turn them out and are continually troublesome and abusive to your said tenant in worrying and killing their sheep upon the Waste and never join in lineing or fencing the boundaryes between them though continually in a civil manner requested so to do.[57]

Trouble sometimes erupted also over disputed rights of way, a problem that was no doubt exacerbated by the frequent inter-mixture of landownership. In 1754 Jane Davies, widow, of Bailie farm in Cellan parish (Cards.) prosecuted Thomas John of Llanlas Issa in that parish for breaking down the gate of a close on her farm and treading down the grass in the close. In his defence, John stated he was justified in his action, for until Jane's recent locking off the close with a gate he had enjoyed the right of passing along a road leading through the said close linking his farm with the village of Cellan. Of course, tenant farmers would often be drawn into disputes of this nature because of objections on the part of their landlords to right of way over their land. Such was the case when in February 1762 the landowning parson of Llanystumdwy (Caerns.) encouraged one of his tenants renting a holding near Tir-hir to stop an old road that tenants of William Vaughan Esq. used for access to church and market.[58]

Neighbouring farmers' quarrels over land sometimes led to serious litigation. Brecknock Great Sessions for spring 1742 tried a case of dispute between neighbours Howell Powell and Ann Watkins, spinster, of Llangorse, over Powell's renting a farm, no doubt desired by Watkins herself. The latter was alleged to have stated on 3 March 1741 that she would make Powell 'curse the hour he ever rented a tenement and lands at Llangorse called Eligro'; the following night sure enough saw the barn and two wainhouses, and all the corn, grain and goods stored therein, set on fire.[59] Later, at the 1767 spring Great Sessions for Caernarfonshire, it was testified that Gaynor Jones of Penrhose, widow, before inciting her daughter Jonnet to set alight a neighbour's corn and hay, which she had duly put to torch on 6 December 1766, had been heard to curse all the Walter family because they had taken her land from her. Mary Roberts, widow, having likewise urged on Jonnet, told a witness for the prosecution: 'Neither man nor devil burnt the corn and hay, but it was God who had so ordered it, to revenge on them for taking away their neighbour's land.' 'What, don't you know', she said, 'that God revenges on such occasions, and this is but a small revenge in comparison to what will happen to the family; they are a very bad people.' John Edwards of Rhydonen, gent. in the parish of Llanynis (Denbs.), having been evicted from the farm called Plas yn Llanynis and replaced by one Richard Davies, took every opportunity in the years that followed to quarrel with Davies and abuse him, so much so that the latter prayed for sureties of the peace against him at the Great Sessions in spring 1757.[60]

To the fore among those quarrels between neighbouring farmers were disputes over straying livestock and their impounding. The Great Sessions court records bear witness to the prevalence of such quarrels which not infrequently led to forceful rescue from custody of the livestock impounded. Illustrating the 'reciprocity of enmity' among farmers, quick to take offence and intent on asserting their self-interest and self-respect, the pounding of livestock in Glamorgan and doubtless elsewhere in Wales led to counter-pounding, and conciliation in impounding disputes was difficult and only short-term, so that Richard Suggett likens the protagonists to those caught up in an enduring blood feud.[61] So common was the practice in Glamorgan in the third quarter of the eighteenth century that the diarist William Thomas commented on the 'daily pounding' of one another's cattle among the small farmers of the village of Dinas Powys, a vengefulness which saw the 'ruination' of many there through going to law.[62] Moving away from the ample evidence for the Vale of Glamorgan, bitter indeed was the quarrel between Anne Roberts, spinster, of the parish of Penrhosllugwy (Angl.) and Richard Hughes, a yeoman of the same parish, which saw them on one occasion in 1753 physically assault one another, Hughes sustaining injury from a reaping hook. According to Anne and her combative widowed mother, the ongoing quarrel arose from Hughes's cattle straying onto Anne's land 'and that when she impounded any of his cattle for the trespass done her, he used to

break the pound and taking away the cattle therein impounded
without paying any damages for their trespass'. On the other hand,
she averred, when her cattle were impounded by the said Richard he
made her pay heavy damages, especially the 5s. for the trespass
done by a mare and gelding for about half-an-hour in late
November 1754. Attempts by attorney David Williams of Llan-
edwen (Angl.) to get Richard Hughes to settle the dispute amicably
failed, whereupon the attorney brought an action against him in the
Anglesey Great Sessions, the upshot of which was that Anne
Roberts was convicted at Beaumaris in 1755.[63]

Finally, and in the late eighteenth century in particular when
prices for agricultural produce were rising to unprecedented levels,
farmers outbidding one another for holdings must have given rise
to resentment. One such auction at the Angel, Cardiff, for the
leasing of Sweldon farm in the Vale on 28 June 1766 led William
Thomas to record: 'Farmers undermining one under the other daily
by receiving such prices for all things.'

4. Relations between Tenant Farmers and Labourers

A further question to be considered in this survey of relations in
working the land is the degree of harmony or otherwise that
prevailed between tenants on the one hand and their servants and
labourers and the wider labouring community on the other. We
have shown earlier that there was no significant conscious assertion
of class separateness on the part of the farmers. Farm servants and
labourers often assisted their masters in breaking down fences on
commons. Again servants would assist their masters in discovering
thieves, and also in pilfering from others. For instance, on 13
February 1790 Rowland Evans, servant at the farm of Sherri
(Angl.), tenanted by Hugh Owen, assisted the latter on their
journey home by cart from Amlwch market to steal iron borers and
iron plates from the works on Paris Mountain.[64] Periods of service
with the same employer extending sometimes over a number of
years naturally forged close personal relationships. Servants were
regarded very much as part of the family, the master's responsibility extending to moral oversight as, for example, seeing to
it that they, like their own children, were prepared for public
catechizing at Lent.[65]

Tension and conflict were none the less present. Twm o'r Nant in *Bannau y Byd* claimed that farmers set about keeping the price of corn up when it was at a low level, and likewise, they kept wages low at harvest.[66] Farmers, too, were sometimes ordered to appear before Quarter Sessions for not paying the wages of their servants. For their part, covenant servants were sometimes guilty, for whatever reason, of refusing to remain in the service of a farmer or a gentleman employer for the duration of one whole year, a breach of contract which saw some arraigned before the courts. Owen Williams was presented before the Anglesey Great Sessions of 1734 for failing to serve out his term of one whole year as servant in husbandry with Margaret Wynne of Trejorwerth (Angl.), widow, at the rate of £4. 10s. wages.[67] Servants sometimes stole from their employers or erstwhile masters. When a farmhouse was robbed, servants were the first to be suspected and examined by the farmer. One Richard Holbrook, servant to Richard Jackson, of Gresford parish (Denbs.), gave himself away by changing colour when the servants were examined following a theft on 29 January 1740. David Hopkin, farm servant, attacked and robbed his master David Price of Cray in Devynock parish (Brec.) while fetching him home from drinking at Tavarn y Garreg in that parish on Saturday afternoon, 21 January 1769. As far as theft by 'knowledgeable' erstwhile farm servants was concerned, we can cite by way of example the stealing of a mare on the night of 3 March 1753 from the farm of Lewis Herbert of Crickhowell (Brec.), yeoman, by Morgan Lewis, some time previously his servant. Casual labourers working by the day or just over the harvest period were also known to steal from their employers. For instance, William Jones of Llanfillo parish (Brec.), hired by Job Prosser of Talgarth (Brec.), tailor and small farmer, one day in late April 1786 to prepare ground to plant potatoes, found the opportunity to steal money from the house while the family were scattering muck on the meadow land.[68]

Inevitably, personal relations between servants and labourers and their employers, for whatever reason, would sometimes become embittered. Some extreme instances of this can be cited. Farm servants at the remote holding of Nantstalwyn, near Abergwesyn (Brec.), thus poisoned their master in 1770.[69] Similarly, a few years earlier, in February 1766, Rowland Jones, farm servant at Cil Euruch (Mer.), had attempted to poison his master, Robert

Jones, yeoman, and others of the household by putting arsenic or some other poisonous drug in the flummery which they ate for supper. Found guilty, he was sentenced to five years' imprisonment.[70] For their part, farmers were sometimes guilty of excessive conduct towards their labourers; 29 July 1785 thus saw a Monmouthshire farmer murder his workman while in bed, so angered had he become over the victim having wrongly informed him a few days earlier that the horses were not in the field.[71] Just as apprentices were often poorly treated, it is not unlikely that farmers were sometimes cruel to their young servants. Such was his ill-treatment of his eight- or nine-year-old servant in depriving him of sufficient food, clothing and shelter, which led to his death no less, that John Webborn, a Rhosili farmer, was indicted for murder at the Glamorgan Great Sessions, found guilty, and executed at Cardiff on 26 March 1799.[72] Perhaps the circumstance which occasioned most tension between farmers and cottagers, and which led to open hostilities over the continuance of fences, was the farmers' (freeholders and tenants like) dislike of encroachment on the commons by cottagers and squatters, a subject to which we shall return in chapter 9.

Part II

Rough and Rebellious Communities

~ 7 ~

Popular Culture, Religion and Alternative Belief

1. Popular Culture

The increasing permanent migration of young men to London in search of work (drawn particularly I suspect from the ranks of the craftsmen families who faced a growing scarcity of jobs in their home villages from the mid-eighteenth century), the short-distance movement of industrial workers from one Welsh county to another chasing higher wages, the settling in Bristol and its hinterland of Glamorgan people through growing commercial links, and the seasonal migration of men and women to English corn harvests and the London market gardens, all betokened a growing mobility in Welsh society during the eighteenth century.[1] But lacking the option of easy migration later afforded by railways, the large majority of country-dwellers spent their entire lives within their own intensely local and inward-looking neighbourhoods. Enhancing their character as close communities was their continuing use of the native Welsh language throughout the century, to the extent that perhaps as many as 90 per cent of the people of Wales spoke it as late as 1801. Furthermore, 'possibly as many as 70 per cent of the inhabitants were still monolingual by 1800.' Apart from the historic Englishries of south Pembrokeshire and peninsular Gower, the English language was making creeping advances only along the Welsh borderland. Naturally, monolingual inhabitants were to be found in the isolated western counties of Anglesey, Caernarfon, Merioneth, Cardigan and, somewhat less so, Carmarthen.[2]

It is difficult to strike a balance in assessing the levels of literacy in eighteenth-century Welsh communities. On the one hand, a true break with the 'rudimentary' education afforded to the poorer classes in earlier centuries came with the remarkable achievement of Griffith Jones's circulating schools in the decades of the mid-eighteenth century where, it has been estimated, perhaps as many as 250,000 people, both children and adults, learned to read the Scriptures and other religious texts.[3] While the lives of vast numbers in the agricultural districts, farmers, cottagers, servants and labourers alike, were in this way vastly improved, and in the very process we witness the laying of the foundations of that later important sociocultural dichotomy in Welsh rural society, *buchedd* A and *buchedd* B, at the same time the ability to write on the part of Welsh men and women remained low by English standards. Whereas, according to Schofield, 40 per cent of men and 60 per cent of women in certain English parishes signed their marriage certificates with crosses in the 1750s,[4] the figures in south-west Wales were significantly higher at 54 and 77 per cent respectively. With respect to males, some improvement had come about in the latter district by the 1830s, the figure having fallen to 42 per cent, but at 73 per cent the position with regard to women remained virtually the same.[5]

While the growth in reading literacy in Wales facilitated the spread of Methodism, quickened Anglican church life from the 1750s and nurtured a taste among literate members of the lower orders for Welsh bibles and other works of piety,[6] the popular culture participated in by most was far less respectable. That the eighteenth century in Britain as a whole was a fun-loving, sensuous, rowdy, boisterous, cruel and unsqueamish society, its amusements often fortified with alcohol, is well documented. The many whose drab lot it was to spend lives largely given to hard labour sought instant and intense relief and escape, no matter how fleeting, in spontaneous merriment and gaiety – amounting in contemporary Methodist eyes to licentious abandon – through high-spirited activities like alehouse-centred dancing, singing and playing dice, and watching and acting bawdy interludes in which hated characters such as the miser or the land agent came in for satirical attack. Important, too, in helping people come to terms with, and make sense of, the uncertainties and insecurities of life – an existence so vulnerable to killer disease and all the exigencies of the weather – was the Christian religion and, arguably more important, an alternative belief which was, to use Bushaway's definition, 'an holistic structure in which the labouring poor sought to reinforce their view of the external world and which provided a means of dealing with the chance incidence of personal loss, illness, economic hardship and the uncertainties of life'.[7]

It is useful to categorize the diversions of the ordinary people in eighteenth-century Wales into two distinct groups along the lines employed for pre-industrial England by Robert Malcolmson. In the first place, there were the everyday recreations.[8] The vast number of alehouses, licensed and unlicensed,[9] afforded a common mode of relaxation and merriment – until as late, indeed, as 3 or 4 a.m. – through drinking, gossiping, playing dice, playing at cards, singing and dancing, although they had their darker side in the frequent brawls that occurred and in a small number of people literally drinking themselves to death.[10] That public houses, too, caused secondary poverty through drinking and gambling can be inferred from William Bulkeley's entry in his diary for 15 February 1737: 'As scarce money is, people find it to get drink and play dice, for there was no less than 100 people last night and today at Llanfachell [Anglesey] at that sport.' Although the alehouses were mainly visited by the male population, women were occasionally to be found among the company.[11] Other daily diversions during winter were the evening gatherings of neighbouring women at one of their houses sitting round the fire – saving fuel thereby – and while knitting indulging in gossip or listening to an old tale or an ancient song or to the harp being played. In illiterate groups in pre-industrial European societies, traditional songs and stories, which passed from one generation to the next, comprised a vital and enjoyable part of popular culture. While the women were involved in these *cymmorth gwau* (the knitting assembly), no doubt the husbands were to be found in the alehouse, a situation matched in French villages where women gathered for *veillées* while their menfolk were in the tavern.[12] Gossip, too, took place in normal day-to-day routine commercial activities, as at markets and fairs when business transactions were mixed in with exchange of news with dealers and craftsmen or when itinerant craftsmen visited outlying farms, and storytelling was part of the very work process among harvesters and other groups like servants.[13] Singing and dancing, too, at the workplace was common just as it was in the alehouse and private dwellings. Describing his journey through Merioneth, Pennant remarked that 'numbers of persons, of both sexes, assemble, and sit round the harp, singing alternately pennills, or stanzas of ancient or modern poetry. The young people usually begin the night with dancing, and when they are tired, sit down, and assume this species of relaxation.'[14]

In the second place, as both Malcolmson and Bushaway demonstrate, there were the major seasonal festive events of the traditional 'holiday calendar' or 'local customary calendar', the nature of which was essentially determined by the twin influences of the seasonal rhythms of the farming cycle and the celebrations of the Christian Church. Accordingly, these public festive occasions were those of Christmas – extending from Christmas itself to Twelfth Day – Shrovetide, Easter, May Day, Whitsuntide and harvest. Thus in the calendar of work, determined by the farming cycle, harvest was particularly important, the various 'harvests' occurring across summer and autumn giving rise to feasts, starting with those of hay harvest and sheep-shearing feasts and ending up with corn-harvest supper. In addition, festivities and entertainments were associated with the annual feast days celebrated in many towns and villages and also the many local fairs. Finally, there were the many sports and pastimes indulged in by the common people, some – like football on Shrove Tuesday – associated with a particular holiday.[15]

The many folk recreations growing from within the bosom of each tight-knit, face-to-face community mirrored, as did the prevalence of mutual aid, the strong community spirit of this pre-industrial era. Clearly expressing the community sense of solidarity in English and Welsh communities alike, for example, were the many sporting competitions between neighbouring parishes, none more so than the football matches.[16]

Popular diversions and entertainments on festive occasions were boisterous. Football, in particular, was a violent and dangerous game which left players with broken limbs and, indeed, if Rhys Cox's recall of his early days in Anglesey in the second quarter of the eighteenth century is to be believed, some mortally injured.[17] Besides Shrove Tuesdays, the village Saint's Day with its annual wake (the *gwylmabsant*) was the occasion for football matches between neighbouring parishes and, more important in Glamorgan, bandy play, an early form of hockey, as, too, for competitions in leaping, running, wrestling, hurling, bull-baiting and cockfighting. Open house prevailed at wakes, those who had left their homes for service elsewhere returning to visit their families and renew old friendships. Such was the ritualized drunken brawling and fighting between the youths of adjacent parishes on these occasions, however, that certain clergy attempted to suppress the festivals or at least to prevent them from taking place on the Sabbath.[18]

Richard Suggett has arrestingly argued that the *gwylmabsant* was no mere rowdy, secular 'survival' from the earlier religious festival, which was finally to succumb to Nonconformist strictures in the early nineteenth century. Its eighteenth-century form as an annual parish festival was, rather, a 'new phenomenon' that grew up from the later decades of the seventeenth century, its customs that emphasized the particularism of the parish symbolizing the competitive, hostile relations between neighbouring parishes that emerged in the wake of the parish becoming a secular, autonomous unit of local administration. Nowhere was this inter-parochial strife more intense than over the vexed problem of the relief and removal of paupers following the Parish Settlement Act of 1662. The *gwylmabsantau* at this time, as 'symbolic representations' of the competing relationships between parishes, are best understood as occasions when solidarity and parochial 'patriotism' were aggressively displayed in response to the hostility from neighbouring parishes. Significantly in this respect, they came in following the Settlement Act of 1662 only to fall away with the end of the old poor law. The same social significance, he argues, can be attached to the Maypole or the 'summer birch', whose essential feature was the defence of the birch from theft by a neighbouring parish, William Thomas recording the violence on 29 June 1768 between neighouring parishioners of St Fagans and St Nicholas in the Vale of Glamorgan when St Nicholas people attempted to steal the 'painted wooden God' from St Fagans and were stoutly and successfully resisted with guns and clubs by the folk of St Fagans and Llandaff.[19]

It is an oft-made observation that many of Georgian Britain's diversions and pleasures were streaked with blood. Animal sports like bull-baiting and cockfighting were cruel but much-enjoyed recreations. While bull-baiting had become far less popular in south Wales by the end of the eighteenth century, cocking lost none of its earlier appeal and, as in English counties, a contest would be watched by all ranks of men.[20] Often the gentry provided the cocks and they and clergymen were prominent gamblers at the contests. Frequent theft of gamecocks from the gentry by members of the lower orders testifies to the popularity of the sport.[21] From the frequent cockfights which took place within individual families they ascended in importance to the village ones held about once a month, to the one fought alongside other games on the parish feast day, to the week-long county fight which occurred around Eastertide. Contemporary

commentators denigrated Welsh cockings for their greater barbarity
even than those elsewhere, where individual pairings were the norm.
The Revd S. Pegge thus wrote feelingly in 1775:

> It consists, we will suppose, of sixteen pairs of cocks: of these the sixteen
> conquerors are pitted a second time; the eight conquerors of these are
> pitted a third time; the four conquerors a fourth time, so that (incredible
> barbarity) thirty-one cocks are sure to be most inhumanly murdered for
> the sport and pleasure, the noise and nonsense, nay, I may say, the
> profane cursing and swearing of those who have the effrontery to call
> themselves, with all these bloody doings and with all this impiety about
> them, Christians.[22]

Gambling and drinking were powerful stimulants to excitement.
Contests were held at inns, often in conjunction with horse-racing
events, and frequently in churchyards, for the soil of the latter was
deemed to be especially efficacious in warding off spells rival
owners might seek to cast upon the birds of an opponent. Cock-
fights, indeed, sometimes took place after church service.

Churchyards were the venue for many other pastimes, and as
such were bustling and beckoning centres for local inhabitants.
That secular enjoyment preceding and following Sunday religious
observance was in no way regarded as profane and ungodly is
reflected in the recall of Matthew Owen of Llanrhwydrys (Angl.)
who was born in 1769. He remembered 'going to the churchyard,
before the service, to tell tales, to compete in kicking the football,
wrestling, throwing the stone, and so on; then, in we went to the
service. In the afternoon, we would go to play tennis against the
church roof.' Dancing to the accompaniment of the harp or violins
was also carried on in the churchyards of many districts.[23]

Fairs were sometimes festive occasions, albeit information about
their social dimension, as for English ones, is limited. Certainly hiring fairs and harvest ones were occasions for pleasure and gaiety.[24]
The particular participation of young people at such fairs, as in so
many other festive occasions and notably May Day ones, was
indicative of the important milieu they provided for courtship. At
the same time, fairs were not simply occasions for happy courtship
and relaxed conviviality for, in a period wanting the civilizing
agencies of mass Nonconformity, popular education and temper-
ance, excessive drinking and fighting were equally marked attributes.

Amusement and diversion, again sometimes boisterous, even cruel like the barbaric 'holly-beating' on Boxing Day and 'thrashing the hen' and 'throwing at cocks' on Shrove Tuesday, were certainly afforded by these customs and rituals, but they had an importance beyond mere festivity. Crucially, as we shall discuss later, they helped ordinary people to cope with the crises and insecurities that capriciously beset them. Again, in so far as they often gave poor families relief in the form of gifts of drink, food or cash, such customs as collection of *calennig* on New Year's Day, carrying of wassail bowls on Twelfth Night, collecting pancakes on Shrove Tuesday, collecting eggs in north Wales by means of wooden clappers on the Monday before Easter, and May Day dancing before farmhouses in Denbighshire and Flintshire, were a form of legitimized begging. Moreover, such bounty tied up with these old rituals, as Bushaway demonstrates, strengthened social cohesion: these acts of largesse, coupled with commensality on the part of farmers, as at harvest and, again, their giving a feast to small farmers and cottagers on Christmas Day in north Pembrokeshire and on New Year's Day in Carmarthenshire, emphasized and promoted the ideal of community solidarity.[25] Similarly, the harvest custom of 'carrying the neck' or the ritual of the last sheaf, common in Welsh and English areas alike, mattered to labourers, it has been argued, 'because it reflected the co-operation between master and men and reinforced, at least for another year, the sense of community prevailing in the village'.[26] So far as *gwylmabsantau* and Maypole customs were concerned, however, it is not so much their role in promoting harmonious relationships within individual parishes that needs stressing; they were rather demonstrations of parish solidarity and patriotism *vis-à-vis* competing neighbouring parishes.[27]

This popular culture in Wales and England, rightly emphasized as exhibiting 'both continuity with past centuries and parallels with other European societies', came under attack from Evangelical clergy in the established Church and the Methodists alike.[28] Although certain Anglican clergymen in Wales, like the pious Parson Ellis in Anglesea at mid-century, had opposed the excesses of the wakes associated with Saints' Days and succeeded to an extent in curbing the worst abuses,[29] seemingly most clergy were happy enough to join in the festival. Their ease with the situation was shared by the gentry. After all, if Elizabeth Baker's contemporary observations on Merioneth are to be believed, Welsh gentry and lower orders freely mixed in a variety of social situations, and so they attended parish revels and other festivities as a matter of course. Thereby, too, through the patronage they dispensed, local deference would be nicely buttressed.[30] It has been contended that it was the influence of the Methodists that was by the end of the century to effect a marked decline in Sunday sports like playing hand- or football and other enjoyable pastimes like parish games, dancing, playing cards, Maypoles and May songs.[31] Yet, having referred to the 'sour spirit' of Methodism harassing games and amusements, Edmund Hyde Hall proceeded to observe around 1810 that another motive undermining pleasurable recreation was the growing spirit of commercialism and profit-seeking which rather sought to channel people's energies into the accumulation of wealth. Such an insistence on the duty of men to work was encountered throughout Britain and reinforced the attacks on the morals and customs of the people by the Evangelicals.[32]

Apart from the aforesaid influences in causing a decline in the traditional festivities and the interludes, the growth of 'respectability' in the late eighteenth century similarly worked against them. Perhaps in the towns in particular, middling groups and gentry alike were keen to stamp them out. After Joseph Lord Esq., mayor of Pembroke in 1788, had given public notice forbidding the playing of football through the streets of the town on Shrove Tuesday of that year, but to no avail, eleven of the offenders were prosecuted before the spring Great Sessions of 1789. Later, six men of the same town were arraigned before the spring Great Sessions of 1792 for playing football in the streets for three hours 'to the great disturbance and common nuisance of subjects of the king'.[33] According to Richard Suggett it was the growing disorder associated with the festivals which influenced the gentry into deliberately distancing themselves from them at the close of the eighteenth century, a withdrawal of patronage that might well explain Peter Roberts's observation that by 1815 wakes in Denbighshire were 'mostly confined to the lower orders'.[34] Yet it is Suggett's interesting contention that, for all the preaching against revels by the Methodist and Nonconformist preachers and the 'movement of social distancing' on the part of the gentry from around 1800, the revel did not come to an end because of suppression by Nonconformists or gentry but because it was abandoned by the revellers themselves. With the decline in the inter-parochial rivalries following the abandonment of the old poor law came the inevitable falling away of wakes as 'the symbolic markers' of parochial differentiation.[35]

The want of domestic comforts so far as the lower orders were concerned rendered such public leisure pursuits as the alehouse, fairs, parish wakes, games and sports the more compelling. Yet if information about the private domain of people's lives is scant, this does not mean that it was unimportant in the life of the individual. Even if children left home quite early in their teens, some even younger, for domestic service, farm labour or apprenticeship, family life for many may well have been satisfying and compassionate. If Joseph Cradock is to be believed, married women in north Wales were, after a time of pre-marital sexual freedom, faithful to their husbands.[36] Certainly life in the cottages and farmhouses was busy, women, on top of their normal domestic duties, having to help the menfolk in outdoor work. Any spare time saw them knitting or spinning. Domestic abodes, too, were regularly visited by a stream of 'callers' ready to gossip or tell tales through the medium of the native Welsh tongue. For the slightly better-off, singing and dancing in their own homes into the morning hours were convivially shared with neighbours.[37]

At the same time, husbands exercised a firm control over wives and children, physical punishment being accepted as part of the normal pattern of things. In a few instances husbands so abused and terrified their wives that recourse was had to the courts to restrain these brutes. If, on the other hand, wives were found to have abused their husbands, then forms of popular, rough justice came into play within the community. Breakdown in relationships occurred when the normal mutual 'expectations' were in some way disappointed: men thus looked to their wives to prepare meals and to see to it that the home was well run, while the wives in turn expected their husbands to keep in regular employment and provide a wage. Something of the strain felt in households with dependent children is reflected in the occasional desertion of wives and children by husbands, some nine married men, for instance, being recorded in the Denbighshire Quarter Sessions rolls between 1719 and 1791 as having abandoned their wives and families. A typical order was made by the Michaelmas court of 1750 'to seize sufficient of the estate of Robert Burton, saddler of Llangollen, to indemnify the parish he having gone away and left his wife and children to the charge of the parish'. Wife-sales, moreover, were resorted to in eighteenth-century Welsh communities, the transaction taking place at fairs or markets during which the wife wore a halter round her neck and endured the listing of her virtues and faults by her husband in his search for bids. Nevertheless, they were far fewer than in certain English areas, the lack of large urban centres rendering them less likely and, furthermore, the tradition of broomstick marriages in Wales, we shall see, furnished a ready means of informal divorce.[38]

Courtship and marriage, as death, were important rites of passage, surrounded by various rituals and customs.[39] Partners were usually drawn either from the same parish or neighbouring ones. Marriage ceremonies themselves, as in other parts of Britain, were frequently informal, clandestine or irregular, not conforming with the full requirements of Church and common law, a state of affairs which persisted to some extent even after Hardwicke's Marriage Act of 1753.[40] Indeed, according to Gillis, 'a sizeable part of the English and Welsh labouring classes' legitimated their marriages after 1753 not in church following the due reading of banns, but under alternative secular forms of 'common law' unions.[41] Several explanations can be advanced for the popularity of clandestine marriages. Welsh clergy, notoriously impoverished, had no choice but to follow the wishes of their parishioners because of their dependence upon their offerings. The cheapness of clandestine marriages (private betrothals or 'little weddings' as distinct from 'big weddings' preceded by banns and surrounded with much festivity and ritual) only partly explains the resort to them by the poorer sort. As much appeal lay in their facilitating quick and convenient marriages and also the avoidance of the much-hated callings of banns.[42] Part of the attraction, too, was their affording secrecy and the opportunity presented to the young of outflanking family opposition.[43] Although the influence of religion had allegedly dampened down this kind of informal marriage in south Wales by the time that the Revd John Evans was writing in 1803, his observations on both the north and south firmly establish the 'little wedding' as part of the popular culture of the Welsh countryside.[44] Moreover, in writing on the 'little wedding' in north Wales, his reference to the 'trial' – albeit making for ambiguity in claiming that it *preceded* this form of wedding – suggests yet another reason for the popularity of clandestine marriages, and both Gillis and Parker emphasize that the notion of trial is vital to our understanding of the 'little wedding'. Children were important in certain rural communities as they could be put to work at an early age and, moreover, parents saw them as eventual providers for them in their declining years.[45]

The custom of bundling (courting in bed), common in the seventeenth and eighteenth centuries not only in Wales and Scotland but in England and a range of other European areas besides,[46] was tied up with this 'little wedding' betrothal and was clearly a form of trial.[47] As in all aspects of courtship, rules regulated conduct, but there is evidence that the earlier restraint was giving way to greater sexual freedom in bundling by the end of our period.[48] Nevertheless, in the case of pregnancy, marriage followed, such an arrangement constituting a community-imposed sanction to safeguard itself against unprovided-for children becoming a burden on the rates.[49] That with this understanding the neighbourhood accepted the practice is attested to by an early nineteenth-century doctor who described Cardiganshire people's courting 'on the beds . . . in the sight and with the approbation of their mutual friends and relations'.[50]

A popular form of clandestine marriage in certain parts of Wales was the besom marriage or broomstick wedding, a public, secular form whereby both self-marriage and self-divorce were available to couples from the lower orders.[51] Folklorist Gwennith Gwynn argues persuasively from evidence in the christening register of the parish of Llansantffraid Glyn Ceiriog and adjacent parishes in Denbighshire between 1768 and 1799 that besom weddings comprised 61 per cent of all unions in those thirty-two years. This conjugal arrangement was to be found, too, in certain other areas of north and south Wales, in parts of England and among gypsy couples across the European mainland.[52] Although Gillis discusses them as an alternative form of marriage growing up in response to the 1753 legislation, there is no reason to suppose that they did not occur in earlier years.[53]

Besom weddings, like other forms of alternative marriage, contained the proviso of 'trial', but the marriage seemingly had to be made void within the first twelve months. The knot was untied by the disappointed party jumping backwards over the besom from the house into the open in the presence of witnesses. The annulment so achieved, both parties were at liberty to remarry, and the sometime wife meanwhile enjoyed the status of a virgin or a widow. Another attraction of the besom marriage was that it protected the standing of the female, for the notion of *cydfydio* (cohabitation) implied partnership, not ownership; the wife therefore did not, as in official church marriages, become wholly subordinate to the husband, but rather retained her property and her maiden name.[54]

Marriage in the peasant and artisan world of early modern Britain and Europe was a public institution, the establishment of a household bringing with it social obligations. Accordingly, orderly conduct in marriage was regulated by the manorial and Church courts, the latter in eighteenth-century Welsh dioceses enforcing, for instance, conjugal rights among married couples.[55] Paralleling them were the unofficial customary sanctions of the community. Shaming rituals emerged involving mockery and ridicule; the most elaborate form of British rough music coming to the fore in the seventeenth century was called variously Skimmington and Riding the Stang, whose Welsh version later became known as *ceffyl pren*.[56] The skimmington or skymmetry court was the vehicle for popular, rough justice in Glamorgan and the other border counties in the eighteenth century. Thus the eccentric Glamorgan diarist, William Thomas, recorded for 15 March 1765:

> Was acted with much Noise and Riots in Wrenston and Wenvoe, Skymmetry, on the Occasion that Morgan Daniel his wife abused him after a merry night of dancing at their house in Wrenston the 13th of February last past. Here John Bevan acted John y Nel, and Jenkin the Butcher of Eley Mawd Marriwn, John y Sais one of the Judges, Thomas David of Burden's Hill, Blacksmith, Shiriff, etc.[57]

This form of popular justice was to persist in Glamorgan down to the mid-nineteenth century.[58] Similarly, rough justice in eighteenth-century Ruthin (Denbighshire) was administered through a court styled Court Beans after the name of its founder, Richard Beans. Held during the town's wake, and presided over by two annually appointed judges dressed in the livery of their different trades and wearing white wigs and tattered gowns, the trials were preceded by the court, in imitation of the courts of Great Sessions, processing as far as the church gates before returning to the court located on an elevated rock. Typically, one of its laws enacted that 'when it is proved that a man has become beaten by his wife, he should be carried about the town in a chair fixed to two poles, on the shoulders of four men [the *ceffyl pren*]; and exposed to the ridicule of both sexes', a reflection of the fact that in this early-modern period the henpecked husband throughout Britain was ritually mocked and humiliated for his failure to control his wife.[59]

2. Religion

The secular diversions enjoyed on the Sabbath, some in the churchyards themselves, and the disinclination on the part of many to marry in church, signifies a society wanting in religious fervency. Yet there was a quiet affection for the established Church among a minority of parishioners, partly rooted in tradition, familiarity and, in the Welsh-speaking areas, in the Welsh-language services. Failure on the part of the Church to take sufficient care over the provision of Welsh services[60] in Welsh-speaking areas led to trouble between the parishioners of Bettws (Carms.) and their bishop in the mid-1770s.[61] The people clung to their old Church, too, because of the comfort it brought in the midst of a harsh and insecure world.

Arguably, also, their very affection can be explained to some extent in terms of the easygoing, non-challenging nature of the Church's witness. Apart from the mechanistic homilies delivered on proper moral standards, no great calls for self-discipline and self-sacrifice were made on the flock. They were free to combine with easy conscience full-blooded enjoyments and simple piety. Poverty-stricken, especially those in southern dioceses, many curates failed to set an example in pious living. Indeed, barely distinguishable from their parishioners in their standard of dress and general decorum, too many were to be found drinking in the alehouse alongside their flock. In his sensitive portrayal, Geraint H. Jenkins informs us: '"Disorderly living and drinking" was a common charge brought against impoverished curates in church courts, whilst rhymesters dubbed them "sow-gelders and alehouse-keepers".'[62] Certain outrageous excesses would have scandalized neighbourhood susceptibilities, yet most curates would not have been guilty of the grossest kinds of misbehaviour to merit their being hauled before the Church courts. It is doubtful if the main body of churchgoers were upset at the familiar neglect and worldliness of their curates; arguably they would have felt more at ease, and no matter how simple, habitual and formalistic their piety, they would nevertheless have derived comfort and reassurance from the sermons and *halsingod* (religious carols).[63]

It is likely that in any clash between loyalty to their religion and the calls of the secular world the latter prevailed. Thus on one occasion a Sunday football match between Llanbedr and Llanllechid in Anglesey saw the latter team's smaller numbers swollen by the dispatch of a supporter to the Llanllechid church service, whose alarming news of impending defeat saw male members of the congregation leave hurriedly to join their fellow players, thereby turning the game round to victory.[64]

Most parishioners, however, did not attend church.[65] Divine services on the occasion of Church festivals, which generally fell on weekdays, had ceased being held in Caernarfonshire by the 1770s at the latest for the want of congregations assembling.[66] More importantly, apart from Easter communion and other sacraments celebrated most commonly in association with the other two great festivals of the Church and after the gathering of the harvest, Sunday services were but scantily attended. Figures that exist for Caernarfonshire for 1778 suggest that 'well under half of the population were regular [Anglican] Churchgoers'.[67] Very poor levels of attendance were also the prevailing pattern in 1755 in the archdeaconry of Carmarthen. Basing church attendance on the number of communicants – which gives an optimistic picture – percentage bands of Anglican churchgoers to total populations in some fifty-five parishes were *roughly* as follows:[68]

Percentage bands of church attenders	Number of parishes
1–5	5
6–10	11
11–15	15
16–20	8
21–5	8
26–30	2
31–5	3
36–40	2
41–5	0
46+	1

If most were simply apathetic, some were downright hostile to religion; Henry Williams of Llanfwrog (Angl.), yeoman, was thus alleged to have blasphemed in his native village in early 1732 by stating in Welsh that God meant no more to him than a blade of grass, while John Catheral of Hawarden parish (Flints.), tailor, walked naked through the streets of Hawarden on several Sundays at the close of 1759, which led to his being described as 'an impious and irreligious person' at the 1760 Great Sessions.[69]

A small minority of thoughtful Welsh rural dwellers belonging in the main, but not exclusively so, to the 'middling sort' of people, comprising successful farmers and freeholders, and thriving tradesmen, craftsmen and artisans, were to join the ranks of the Methodists.[70] Acquiring reading skills and literacy mainly through the celebrated circulating schools of Griffith Jones, their desire for family religious devotions had been largely met by the Anglican Church through the publications of many religious books in Welsh, a quickening in piety facilitated by the development of Welsh provincial presses.[71] But their wish for a more personal religion which would impart to them warm personal counsel and encouragement was not, and simply could not be, met within the Anglican Church, whose mission was centred on the body of parishioners as a collective group rather than the individual.[72] Such people would doubtless have found the Anglican services very dull and non-uplifting, and for them the neglectful, worldly conduct of too many of the clergy would have been distasteful and offensive. Richard Morris reported that the Methodists' progress in Anglesey was 'greatly attributed to the indolence and it is to be feared, ignorance of too many parochial ministers', while the diarist Elizabeth Baker noted in 1781 of the society about Dolgellau: 'What to me is offensive is the excessive drinking that their [the native Welsh] Clergy are in general addicted to – which is one reason the Methodists yearly increase.'[73] For those thoughtful, pious individuals seeking a more individualistic religion, Methodism, with its emphasis on salvation through personal repentance, holiness and continuous zealous striving against the power of Satan, was a natural home. Spellbinding sermons delivered by charismatic young men, fervent hymn singing and warm fellowship together wondrously satisfied the spiritual yearnings of the middling, respectable groups in rural society.[74] Arguably, too, hitherto minor gentry and substantial freeholders who, by dint of their properties having been swallowed up by the great Leviathans, had been forced downwards into the ranks of mere substantial farmers, professional men or craftsmen, found new respectability, status and fulfilment in Methodism.[75] This, however, should not blind us to the fact that a small number of gentry families themselves were to be found in Methodist circles.

While essentially a religion of the middling sorts, whose ranks furnished the dynamic spiritual and organizational leadership in each neighbourhood, rural labourers, too, in the last decades of the century and perhaps earlier, were set on fire by the new, dramatic movement. 'Of the servants of this county [Caernarfonshire]', wrote the unsympathetic George Kay in 1794, 'a great number are Methodists; and it is very common practice when they engage with their masters, to contract for smaller wages, that they may have the liberty of attending at all times the Methodist meetings, which are very frequent' – albeit no such custom obtained elsewhere in north Wales.[76] Lead miners in the district around Rhydfendigaid in mid-Cardiganshire, too, were mostly Methodists at the close of the century.[77]

One further notable trait of its membership was the appeal Methodism made to young people, and young women were especially prominent. Serious-minded, pious young females were afforded an outlet for individual participation denied them in both Anglicanism and other walks of life, while the handsome, magnetic young preachers would certainly have aroused more than just spiritual feelings. The intimacy of fellowship of like-minded people provided opportunities for cultivating close friendships and forging marriage partnerships, and offered, too, a means of coping with feelings of sexual guilt by confessing spiritual and pre-marital experiences within the privacy of a small group. Predictably, Methodism's critics were quick to latch onto the occasional sexual indiscretion that surfaced in these groups of young people.[78]

The movement's growth was nevertheless 'a slow, uneven and fitful process'.[79] Perhaps reflecting the harsher poverty of the southern dioceses and the consequent greater neglect of parishes, early Methodism made more headway in this part of Wales and, in particular, in those communities experiencing the powerful preaching of Griffith Jones, Daniel Rowland and Howel Harris, about Llanddowror, Llangeitho and Trefeca respectively. Welsh Methodism was, furthermore, a mainly rural phenomenon, making but little progress in the unwelcoming towns.[80]

Other serious-minded, pious individuals from the middling sort were Dissenters, whose lives were made somewhat easier under the provisions, however grudging, of the Toleration Act of 1689. Whereas the power of the Anglican Church in north Wales resisted the implantation of both Dissent and Methodism to any significant extent, in the southern counties, above all Glamorgan, Dissent took firm root, although it was never more than a small minority of the total population. Even at an optimistic count, in the second decade of the eighteenth century Welsh Dissenters comprised below 5 per cent of the country's population. Numbers grew appreciably from mid-century, however, in response to Dissenting preachers adopting the evangelical style of the Methodists. Throughout the century they were popular in town communities, appealing to merchants, tradesmen, artisans and craftsmen, while in rural areas the majority of Dissenters comprised freeholders, humble farmers, craftsmen, artisans and labourers.[81]

If in the eyes of the law second-class citizens, Dissenters after 1689 were able to practise their faith more or less free of the persecution they had suffered during the bad old days of the penal code. That vulnerable tenant farmers had nevertheless to watch their step is mirrored in the instance of William Prichard of Pwllheli, an Independent, whose defiant befriending of one of Griffith Jones's schoolmasters and criticism of a sermon by the popular, if dictatorial, Chancellor Owen of Bangor led to his being evicted from three farms in succession before finding shelter under the Anglesey landlord, William Bulkeley of Brynddu.[82] Methodists constantly faced this kind of harassment. Their preachers, indeed, especially in the towns of north Wales, 'were often met with a stream of obscenities, stripped of their clothes, shouted at, heckled, stoned, pelted with rotten fruit, and thrown into ponds and lakes'.[83] Landowners and clergymen, mistakenly if perhaps understandably believing that Methodist zealotry harboured erstwhile Levelling doctrines, called into being violent mobs of youths to intimidate evangelizing intruders.[84] Furthermore, landowner-magistrates were well placed to crack down on the holding of Methodist conventicles, as did the Denbighshire Quarter Sessions in 1747 with regard to those held at Rhosllanerchrugog and Lloft Wen.[85] Farmers, moreover, whose houses were used for Methodist meetings, were evicted, only to repeat the 'offence' upon gaining another farm. On one occasion, a group of neighbouring Methodistical Anglesey farmers were summoned before the landlord's agent and the local clergyman and presented with the choice of either giving up their Methodism or leaving their holdings. If certain of their number gave in to such bullying, this was not so with the valiant-spirited Richard Hughes who, savouring the opportunity of being persecuted for conscience's sake, clapped his hands and proclaimed, 'Blessed be God! Hosannah to the Son of David.' After repeatedly trumpeting this refrain he departed, mouthing defiantly: 'Farewell, dear brethren; whoever is willing to sell an everlasting kingdom and a glorious crown for a poor farm at a high rent, it is not I; no, by the help of the Brother for adversity, – *no, never!*' Their historian, the Revd William Williams of Swansea, added: 'And there were many and many in those days who, in similar circumstances, said again and again, "*No, never*".'[86]

3. Alternative Belief

More important for the majority of Welsh country-dwellers, even for many of those who attended a Christian place of worship, was their attachment to a coherent structure of folk beliefs, an alternative belief which coexisted with orthodox Christian belief; indeed in certain respects the Christian belief in Hell and the Devil could be said to have reinforced such folk beliefs. This interrelated body of unorthodox, locally specific knowledge and belief drew within its embrace folk tales, weather lore, belief in witchcraft or being 'overlooked', divination rituals, belief in ominous occurrences, faith in the efficacy of a range of protective devices against evil and in popular cures and charms, life-crises rites of passage, calendar and work customs, and formal magic.[87]

Underlying so many of the superstitions, rituals and popular cures was the belief in the existence of supernatural forces and agencies in the terrestrial world. Writing in 1779, the Revd Edmund Jones, 'the Old Prophet', believed fervently in 'apparitions and agencies of spirits' like fairies who were 'evil spirits belonging to the kingdom of darkness', citing individuals known to him in his earlier years who had experienced their presence.[88] Down to the close of the century this widespread belief in fairies, the reappearance of departed spirits, and the roaming of the devil after dark rendered many afraid to go out of doors at night.[89] Different customs marked the three spirit-nights (*y tair ysbrydnos*) of All Hallows Eve, May Eve and St John's Eve when spirits roamed abroad. It was the custom in many districts on St John's Eve, for instance, to place over the doors of houses sprigs of St John's wort, or second best, the common mugwort, thereby purifying the dwelling of evil spirits.[90]

Moreover, on these three nights associated with the roaming of supernatural spirits it was quite natural to seek their help in revealing the future, in particular the appearance of a maid's future husband.[91] Given the uncertain life spans of individuals, the insecurities of existence for both humans and animals and the fragile situation facing most, in which the death of a family member gave rise to economic problems, it is not difficult to see why the lower orders were preoccupied with anticipating the future – which tradition taught them it was possible to do so in certain ways – and once that was done, either to take avoiding action wherever possible or, more commonly, simply accept one's fate with a sense of resignation in keeping with the disadvantaged material lot they were expected to bear.[92]

Besides divination beliefs and practices (as well as supernatural methods, some, too, were based on the interpretation of natural phenomena or on random choice) there was an obsession with ominous signs, particularly those foretelling impending death. Thus a bird flying into a house was such an unnatural occurrence that it was taken to portend illness or even a death in the family. Belief in the corpse candle (*canwyll y corph*) as a precursor of death was widespread, while in south Wales many would claim to see a coffin and burial train making its way towards the churchyard at dead of night from the house of a person soon to die.[93]

Misfortune, it was believed, befell persons who were foolish enough to ignore observing correct rituals. Thus they might offend the fairies coming into their houses by omitting to provide clean water for them or by leaving a knife near the fire, for want of which propitiation many were hurt by them. Or again, as in Montgomeryshire, a good crop of corn would be denied the farmer who failed to place the ashes of the yule log in the first hopper with the seed corn to act as a charm. When explanations of this kind failed to account for a particular misfortune, people could fall back on the scapegoat of the witch.[94]

Such was the hold of these beliefs on the common people that Hyde Hall observed of Caernarfonshire at the opening of the nineteenth century: 'The powers of Methodism have not yet been able to set quite at rest the influence of witchcraft.'[95] Old women supposed to be witches could, it was widely believed, bring misfortune on families, induce sickness, and put a curse on both men and animals.[96] People, believing themselves or their families to be bewitched, resorted to cunning men, conjurors or astrologers in the hope of finding remedies, for example by being given charms. Besides removing the spells cast by witches they could, it was believed, reveal the future and discover the identity of a thief. John Price of the parish of Llansanffraid (Rads.), for example, threatened to go to a conjuror to find out who stole money from him in summer of 1788. Peter Roberts accordingly wrote in 1815:

> A fortune-teller, or astrologer, is resorted to by the ignorant; when anxiety as to the future, is excited whether by hopes or fears, to learn what may be gained, or to recover what has been lost; and the power the imposters have over some minds, is sometimes prodigious.

On occasion, a dissatisfied client might sue such a cunning man, a fate which befell Robert Darcy of Wrexham, for instance, who was brought before the Denbighshire court of Great Sessions in spring 1741 to answer to his claim 'to practice a diabolical occult and crafty science to discover where great quantities of linen yarn stolen on 16 April 1740 might be found'.[97]

So inbred and tied up with everyday experience were these superstitions and rituals that it is not difficult to comprehend their taking pride of place over orthodox Christian belief. It is thus significant that William Bulkeley noted in his diary for 27 July 1740:

> Very few people in Llanfechell Church to-day, occasioned by the old superstition of the people of all sexes going to Llaneilian wakes to visit a dry skull, scraping an old stone and playing other gangling tricks in the Myfyr and ye Cwppwrdd.

Methodists themselves could not break free. Geraint H. Jenkins reminds us: 'As late as 1800, fraught Methodist chieftains were still having to urge their brethren to desist from dabbling in magic and witchcraft.'[98] While on the one hand certain of the rituals and superstitions struck fear, even terror, into many of the meaner sort, on the other they were a valuable 'coping mechanism', a means by which people could face up to and deal with life's crises and uncertainties.[99]

~ 8 ~

The People and Politics

1. The Politics of Reform

The quarrels waged between Whigs and Tories in their own counties, boroughs and local neighbourhoods down to the 1760s, boisterous, often violent, and perhaps wanting in genuine ideological content on both sides, were confined to the narrow gentry and aristocratic élites, who often unleashed their toadying servants and dependants to secure their goals by force.[1] Although the old Whig and Tory rhetoric would persist down to the close of the century, a significant change in Welsh politics came about from the 1760s fuelled by the growing anger felt by the independent country gentlemen and freeholders at the arbitrary power built up and vaunted by absentee Leviathans. Modern-day historians have recognized that while many of the old Tories became 'Church and King' loyalists in the 1760s, returning to their natural role of conservative upholders of the state as presently ordered, others of them in the masonic lodges, like Sir Watkin Lewes (Cards.), John Pugh Pryse of Gogerddan (Cards.) and Robert Morris of Clasemont (Glam.), were Wilkite radicals wedded to ideas of reform which would shield them from overbearing plutocrats. Whereas there were just six freemasons' lodges in Wales in 1760, ten years later there were sixteen.[2]

There were, indeed, new alignments forming in Welsh politics in the later decades of the century which brought in social categories hitherto excluded. For emerging in these decades was a new group of reformers, a loosely knit but remarkable alliance of gentry and industrialists (frequently erstwhile Tories or Jacobites) alongside liberal or radical Dissenters, the latter mostly men of independence like craftsmen and small freeholders. Quickening their radicalism was their response to the struggle for freedom of the American colonists, some of whom were of Welsh stock; believing that the tyranny exercised there by an overmighty Westminster executive would soon be imposed at home, they favoured a mild dose of

parliamentary reform. They drew inspiration from and gave support
to the Wilkite Society of the Supporters of the Bill of Rights and the
later Wyvill Petitioning or Association movement of 1779–82. Other
reforms, too, united this group, such as the cleansing of self-
perpetuating borough oligarchies, the call for more 'liberal' views in
Anglicanism, and the weakening of that Church's control over
religious life.[3] For instance, in 1787 some sixteen members of the
Carmarthen Corporation sent an address to their member of
Parliament, J. G. Philipps, requesting him to support the Protestant
Dissenters in their intended application to Parliament for the repeal
of the Test and Corporation Acts.[4]

If there was, for reasons we shall examine later, only a poor and
patchy response among Welsh people to the reform movements
associated with Wilkes and Wyvill (only Flintshire, Denbighshire
and Brecknock sent petitions to Parliament in the early 1780s)[5] there
was nevertheless significant resistance among small gentry and freeholders to the oligarchic control of politics by the magnates
(absentee and often non-native) in the later decades of the century.
Spearheading such resistance were sometimes the new reformers; by
doing this they brought a new flavour to campaigns, for though the
contestants they supported were still the traditional landowners the
discourse they deployed was progressive – 'populist, anti-
aristocratic, and pro-religious toleration'.[6] Their support was
discernible in a number of elections in the 1780s. Denunciation of the
growing influence of 'villainous', 'despotic', absentee magnates was
made during the Glamorgan election of 1780 by an 'Independent'
faction, prominent among whom were Robert Jones of Fonmon and
Robert Morris of Clasemont, both erstwhile supporters of Wilkes, in
response to the 5th duke of Beaufort's nomination of Charles Edwin
of Llanmihangel for the vacant county seat. Similar 'Independent'
campaigns took place in Pembrokeshire in 1780 and in Glamorgan
in 1789, the latter witnessing songs composed for the Wyndham
campaign for 'liberty' against the aristocratic duke of Beaufort. One
song encapsulated the anti-aristocratic spirit informing the populist
'new politics' thus:

> The man who lives happy, from cities remote
> In his stockings of yarn and his brown russet coat
> If he has but enough to live decent and neat
> Is a fool if he cringe to the rich and the great.

Elsewhere, in the Monmouthshire election campaign of 1771 and the 1774 Montgomeryshire election, similar protestations on the part of gentry and freeholders against the arbitrary power of alien lords were forcefully aired. However, while the Independent campaigns of the 1780s were clearly populist, seemingly inspired by the political debate surrounding the Association Movement of 1779–82, the struggles against absent magnates in Monmouthshire and Montgomeryshire manifested no clear traces of political radicalism in their rhetoric.[7]

The democratic stirring in Welsh politics in the 1760s, 1770s and 1780s embracing the ideals of the Wilkite and Wyvill reform movements were largely confined to a minority of articulate and rational middle-class Dissenters. Such notions did not inform the thinking and outlook of the overwhelming majority of the Welsh people. Scraping a living only by dint of much toil left little time or incentive for politics. Again, just as later *The Times* for 18 August 1843 concluded, 'It is difficult to stuff the head of a Welsh farmer, who speaks and reads only Welsh, with the political crotchets of Chartism', the language barrier must have placed eighteenth-century radical political ideas beyond the reach of most Welshmen. Moreover, the landed gentry and aristocracy, their clergymen and schoolmaster allies, and Methodist preachers and teachers were all intent on reminding the people of their proper place in the divinely ordained social order. Finally, whether through a ready-given habitual deference or through a sullen acceptance of their position of dependence together with their awareness of the dire consequences of insubordination, the Welsh people accepted their lack of political rights.[8]

To some extent a change was to come about under the extra-ordinary conditions of the 1790s. High rents and corn prices, enclosures, and growing poverty among the masses, reflected in mounting poor rates which themselves further squeezed rate-paying farmers, all made for instability. On top of this economic malaise came the traditional grievance of militia service, but now sharpened by the Acts of 1795 and 1796. If the many country riots of the 1790s were essentially fuelled by economic factors, at the same time there is no mistaking the democratic ideas which excited *some* members of the mob. Such a manifestation of Jacobinical sentiment among some of the lower orders, vividly exposed by David Jones and Gwyn A. Williams, has meant a shift from our earlier view that the Jacobins in Welsh political life in the 1790s were exclusively a small minority of middle-class Dissenters.[9]

One such 'pernicious and seditious' man among the meaner sort was John Ellis of the parish of Llanbrynmair (Mont.), yeoman, who on 17 December 1796 was alleged to have uttered in 'a loud voice' in his mother tongue:

> I mae yr Tylawd yn cail eu gwascu gan y Cywaithog ag i mae ne wedi resolvio y gael rheiolaeth arall ag ny dydiw ddim yn power Gwirboneddigion y wlad ei rhwystro ne ag ys gwna nhw fe geiff fod yn waed am waed.

> (The poor are oppressed by the rich and we are determined to have another government and it is not in the power of the gentlemen of the country to prevent it; if they do, it shall be blood for blood.)

Gwyn A. Williams contends that this was only part of a general flare-up of anti-government feeling in the winter of 1796–7 throughout Merioneth and Montgomeryshire catalysed by the new Militia Act of November 1796 but growing into a wider 'subversive' protest. In its stormcentre of Llanbrynmair and district in particular, there was a spate of anti-government outrages and public meetings, leading to the indictment of several small farmers of the parish for 'raising insurrection'.[10]

Another centre of 'republican principles' was Llannerch-y-medd in Anglesey; 'seditious' pamphlets were circulating there in the crisis of 1796, and in the starvation year of 1800 one John Phillips, a small farmer of Llangefni, publicly uttered the following declaration: 'I am a Jacobin and a Republican and know a Republican Government will be a much better one than the present . . . that the present king is a bad man and a sinner.' According to Gwyn A. Williams, 'republican principles' were widely propagated among the small farmers of north-west Wales as a whole during the crisis years 1800–1, with farmers much embittered by the Militia Act and high grain prices.[11]

Again, during the disturbances at Denbigh in late March 1795 associated with the previous Act of Parliament for manning the navy, a member of the 400–500-strong mob, one John Jones, a small farmer of Aerden, in response to the attempt by magistrate Lloyd of Wigfair to explain it to them in Welsh, replied that 'they did not want to have the Act explained to them, that Lord Camden had maintained in the House of Lords in the year 1775 or 1776 "that no Britton could be taxed without the Consent of the People" '.[12] The enclosure riot at Hope in north-east Wales in 1793 similarly revealed an underlying general dissatisfaction with the prevailing established order. Anti-ruling-class feelings were present, too, in the food riots in Pembrokeshire in the mid-1790s.[13]

Clearly the 1790s saw *some* of the Welsh lower orders, no doubt the moving spirits behind many of the disturbances and certainly a minority, embrace notions of a radical kind in response to unprecedented suffering and privation. While I am inclined towards caution, according to Gwyn A. Williams the true extent of such democratic Jacobin sentiment has been concealed from historians by the departure of many for a better future in America; but their letters from Wales were 'full of the prices, the rents, the poverty, the iniquities of landlords and the Church, full of irritation at the endless anti-American propaganda in the British pulpits and newspapers'.[14]

We have shown earlier that farmers and craftsmen left villages like Llanbrynmair and elsewhere. Suffering at home and the hope of a better life in the New World drove them to take this momentous step, though it is clear that they also espoused vague notions of democracy in response to their resentment of the established order. That Welsh landlords by the 1790s were widely unpopular is palpably clear, although in their defence some of the problems arising from wartime conditions were not of their making. To their credit, they did try to take the sting out of the suffering of the poor by raising subscriptions for the bulk purchase of grain to be distributed at less than market prices. Indeed, Cardiganshire landlords were commended by the Revd John Evans in 1803 for having done their best to preserve their tenantry from becoming paupers, and perhaps from being lured by American agents into emigrating during the French Wars by taking on every kind of tax.[15]

2. Securing the Votes of the Lesser Men

It is by turning to examine electoral politics at their grass-roots level within the individual constituencies that we can best discover the way in which politics impinged on the lives of ordinary people below the ranks of the gentry. On the face of it, there was a total control in all the Welsh constituencies by small groups of squires and aristocrats, who, like their English counterparts, kept contested elections to a minimum out of considerations of expense and the harm they did to the 'peace' of the county. Control on the part of the Welsh landed families over the county constituencies was rendered even more secure than that enjoyed by their English counterparts by virtue of the smaller electorates (ranging from 500 to 2,000), by the absence – compared with England – of contests between gentry and peerage families, a reflection of the lack of a wealthy aristocracy in Wales, and by the want of a sizeable commercial industrial class of wealthy men to pose a threat to the Welsh gentry families. Finally, as will be shown, the relatively high ratio of leasehold-tenant voters to freehold ones in Welsh constituencies made such electorates more controllable by the landed families. Threats of eviction, O'Gorman contends, were commoner in Wales, as was resort to the creation of temporary leases.[16] 'When you give me assurances to move in your behalf I will grant leases enough to secure a large majority', were the glad tidings sent by Edward Loveden Esq. of Gogerddan to Squire Powell of Nanteos on 17 January 1787 in connection with the forthcoming Cardiganshire election. Further irregularity can be seen in the entry in the Chirk Castle accounts for 16 April 1722: 'Pd. Mr Thomas Ffoulkes at Llangwm for engrossing 8 leases from freeholders to their sons in those parts in order to Qualifie them to vote at the Election.'[17]

Welsh gentry control over the borough constituencies was even more secure. They were assured of hegemony by the want of competition both from English patrons, who showed little interest in the less attractive Welsh borough constituencies, and from local commercial or industrial middle-class families, who docilely followed their superiors. The fairly large size of the Welsh freeman borough electorates, together with the clearer separation of municipal and parliamentary politics in Wales, accounts for the absence for the most part of the blatant excesses of bribery and corruption encountered in English borough elections. The Welsh gentry exercised control over the eleven freeman boroughs – only Beaumaris, the twelfth, was a corporation borough – by their domination of the borough corporations. As the right to vote was vested in burgesses for whom residence was not a requisite qualification, the patron in control of the corporation could create any number of burgesses from among his friends and dependants. Of course, the group constituencies (that is, where contributory boroughs were united electorally with the shire town) of Caernarfon, Cardiff, Cardigan, Denbigh, Flint, New Radnor, Pembroke and, down to 1728, Montgomery, were harder to control than the single ones of Brecon, Carmarthen and Haverfordwest, for during election periods rival patrons of the different boroughs in the group constituencies created numerous new burgesses. Such conduct was brazenly resorted to in the Cardigan borough election of 1768 when Pryse of Gogerddan's alleged creation of a thousand burgesses between Cardigan and Aberystwyth was matched by Sir Herbert Lloyd of Peterwell's appointment of a thousand burgesses for his borough of Lampeter.[18]

In England and Wales alike, the minority who had the vote, comprising tenant farmers who possessed leases for lives, small freeholders, lesser gentry and town burgesses, were gathered into the political interest of one or another dominant landowning family. Yet no matter how secure the control of the landed families over their constituencies, especially in Wales, they were not in a position to take votes for granted. Rather, they and their election agents (who were their estate stewards) had to exercise constant vigilance in the effort to earn and keep the goodwill of constituents. Only by bestowing their patronage and favours on 'friends' throughout every layer of the enfranchised community could the 'great folk' who comprised the tiny body of parliamentary candidates and MPs ensure that men would vote for them at the polls. In this way electors were bound by close vertical ties of a reciprocal kind into one interest. Frank O'Gorman has stressed that 'Every election contest took place in a highly specific social situation, its proceedings fuelled by ideas of reciprocal obligation.'[19] Particular care was taken to win the good opinion of the lesser gentry, who could deliver not only their own votes but also those of their tenants and other dependants.

Tenants with leases for lives were directed by their landlords for whom they were to vote; to all intents and purposes theirs were 'tied' votes. Their sheer numbers rendered their votes vital at the polls, and these numbers were maintained in south Wales down to the close of the century and beyond. Richard Jones Lloyd of

Pantglas (Carms.) informed J. G. Philipps of Cwmgwili (Carms.) in
1789: 'Mr Rice goes on successfully but the other party are very
sanguine of success by weight of base metal, the Freehold Leases.'
In the Pembrokeshire elections of 1765 and 1768 leaseholders for
lives comprised as many as two-thirds of the county electorate.[20]
Landowners were anxious to extract as many votes as they could
from their tenantry and busily looked for means whereby their
leases would allow them to vote. The Chirk Castle owner was
accordingly advised in 1739:

> If you do abate to some of your tenants some 20s. some 30s., some 40s.,
> a year to qualify them for a vote perhaps it will be above £200 a year out
> of your estate which will be easier spared than spend £2,000 or £3,000
> treating and not certain then, and don't doubt your timber and coals
> will make that small gap up.

Disappointment would have been felt in mid-June 1771 by John
Morgan Esq. of Tredegar Park at Thomas Phillipps's acquainting
him: 'I looked over both the leases you sent me and [am] of the
opinion that nothing can be done to them now to make either of
them operate as freeholds so as to entitle the lessees to vote.'[21] At
the time of the actual polls, tenants were carefully regimented
under the watchful eye of the estate agent. Activity such as that
recorded by the Wynnstay agent for 10 July 1747 was common:
'My expenses going and coming to Carnarvon election, and to
bring in the freeholders that was my master's tennants . . . 0. 7s.
0d.'[22]

On one level, we can think in terms of the political servitude of
the tenant farmers. On some estates electoral loyalty was a
precondition of tenants taking farms; indeed on the
Montgomeryshire Wynnstay lands they were made to swear an
oath upon entering their holdings that they would support their
landlord, Sir Watkin, at the polls.[23] Control was exercised just as
firmly on the Margam estate in Glamorgan. Watkin Jenkins
assured Lord Mansell (absent in Kent) on 5 October 1740 with
reference to the next election in which his uncle was standing
against Mr Edwin: 'all persons that holds any lands under your
lordship [on the Margam estate] is safe and will obey your
directions for they dare do no otherwise – therefore I never gave
myself any Trouble about them.'[24] The same held true for Margam

tenants in earlier years. In spring 1708 Moses Evans of Hendreowen, Llangnywyd, Llewellin William, Lewis Reece and David John were instructed by John Nash that upon being informed of the days that they chose 'knights of the Shire and Burgesses for Cardiff' they were to go to Cardiff and attend the Hon. Sir Thomas Mansel and vote as he or his agent directed them. The request carried a warning sting in the tail: 'PS. Take care and doe your duty well and you will oblidge, but if any of you get drunk and neglect your Duty that person loseth my friendship for ever.'[25] Later, on 8 May 1722, John Watkin of Cevenbrynych besought Lord Mansel not to remove him and his wife 'at this great age' from his farm, a tenement he had held for sixty years, one of Mansel's under-stewards having threatened to evict him because he had voted in the last election for Jones of Buckland,

> a thing I always refused to do until forced to it by the frequent and personal solicitations of my other landlord Mr Morgan of Tredegar who (besides his agents) was with me no less than four times to press me to give my vote, and still denied until he Assured that your Lordship would not be angry and at Last was carried up to the court betwixt him and his brother.

His unfolding apology carried some quiet criticism of Lord Mansel's want of personal involvement: 'I do assure your Lordship had both my Landlords appeared in person I should not have failed to choose your Lordship but being attacked so violently by Mr Morgan and your Lordship being at too great a distance to defend me I could not resist.'[26]

One north Walian owner, J. Trevor, was perhaps in a minority of those who refused to resort to eviction: while assuring John Myddelton of Chirk Castle in 1740 of his readiness to engage his tenants in the Chirk Castle interest and of his confidence that they would comply, he expressed his unwillingness 'to give authority for any violence towards them'.[27] That Chirk Castle nursed no such qualms can be seen in the complaint of R. Richardson to the estate agent, Joseph Lovet, on 15 June 1757 of how Hewet, the previous agent, had served him with ejectment which forced him into arrears of £60:

> Which arrears I have paid to you and all brought wrongfully upon me
> and my poor family and by Mr Hewet wrongfully shuing me . . . and is it
> reasonable for a whole family to be wrongfully ruined and stripped and
> turned out of all their substance . . . for as I can prove I never was short
> of wanting of goodwill and peforming it to the whole Family – for at the
> last election I voted for my landlord, Mr John Myddelton and
> prevented 5 tenants from voting against him . . . and all the reasons I
> ever could receive was Robert Edwards wife informed Mr Hewet a pack
> of malicious, scandalous and false lies that I should be at Holt and at
> Wrexham rejoicing for joy that Watkin had won the election.[28]

Such punishment by eviction was meted out to disobedient tenants
elsewhere in north Wales, Lord Newborough viewing it as a
'disagreeable necessity'.[29] Their temerity in voting for the Chirk
Castle interest in the 1742 election led to the eviction of John
Edwards and his father-in-law, tenants of the substantial holding
of Cerrig Llwydion, by their landlord Mr Lloyd of Mold, and they
were spitefully put 'to all cost and inconveniences' possible on that
score. Simply nothing was left undone on the part of Sir Watkin
Williams Wynn's watchful agents to enforce the obedience of
tenants and dependants in the bitterly fought Montgomeryshire
election of 1774. Even if a landowner stopped short of eviction,
spiteful retribution could be visited in other ways. For instance on
28 April 1724 Richard Vaughan of Golden Grove (Carms.)
instructed his agent to inform tenants who had voting rights that
they would not have any coal because they had voted against his
interest.[30]

In Wales where, in contrast to the English situation, both county
and borough constituencies were single-member seats, the seeming
political servitude of Welsh tenants was all the more marked. For
they had no opportunity to cast their vote for the second member
with perhaps greater freedom of choice, as indeed happened in
England.[31]

On another level, it is unlikely that tenants in general felt any
strong wish at this time to vote against their landlord's interest.
Only patchy evidence exists for tenants voting according to
ideological conviction. Significantly, a Monmouthshire Dissenter
defied his landlord, the 4th duke of Beaufort, at the poll in 1742 out
of principle. Again, October 1789 saw Thomas Jones of Cwmcoch
(Carms.) write to the liberal-minded J. G. Philipps of Cwmgwili: 'I

will give you my vote for the town of Carmarthen at the next election for all I am Tenant to Mr Hodgkin and Lady Stepney.'[32] Arguably, by far the great majority of tenants were content, as 'clansmen battling for their chieftain', to support their landlords at elections loyally, zealously and uncritically, receiving in return the food, drink and entertainment bountifully on offer at the polls. Moreover, in a status-conscious society, the fact that their leases for lives bestowed upon them at election times the prestige of being perceived as freeholders of the county doubtless rendered many of them well-disposed towards their landlord's interest.[33] The sheer desire, too, to secure a holding rendered more than one applicant for a farm, on the Chirk Castle estate at least, ready enough to pledge his political support and to press his past loyalty. P. Maurice thus wrote to the Hon. Robert Myddelton at Chirk Castle requesting that his wife be given the tenancy of his mills which had been taken from Madam Mostyn upon her public declaration in favour of Mr Watkin Williams: 'I know not what advantage it may be to her, but how great soever it proves, I am ready and willing to spend more than an equivalent in promoting and advancing your interest, wherever I have any influence.' Writing from Llanrwst on 6 September 1722 to John Myddelton Esq. at Chirk Castle in support of Evan Jones's (of Cerrig-y-drudion parish, Denbs.) desire to rent Plasyollin demesne, the Revd Thomas Wynne emphasized, 'he is a True Stickler for the Castle Interest and commands some votes besides his own.' The Hon. John Myddelton, steward to his brother's Chirk Castle estate, was reminded in January 1727 by Robert Wynne of St Asaph: 'the bearer . . . I do assure you has voted for your Brother the last Election and so has his father who lives in Llanfair parish . . . he is quite idle for want of a farm . . . he says you have promised him your assistance.'[34]

What of the small freeholders in the electoral interests of unreformed Wales? Substantial landowners in Montgomeryshire – and doubtless elsewhere – with an eye to electoral advantage looked to the land-tax meetings to get those freeholders, previously not considered to be worth 40s., assessed and so qualified to vote, that is, once such freeholders when canvassed declared themselves in support of their interest. Contrariwise, those small men unfavourable to their interest were to be blocked from being assessed through persuading their parishioners that by being rated they would gain a settlement.[35]

Viewed from one perspective, the smaller freeholders gave their support to a neighbouring big landowner's interest through a feeling that a show of community solidarity was desirable.[36] Just as potent an influence in their voting behaviour was their standing in awe of the dominant landowning families in their neighbourhood. 'This whole Country is governed by fear and those of large Estates do as much awe and tyrannise over the lesser Gentry as they do over the Poor', wrote the Erddig estate agent on 30 December 1720 to his master Philip Yorke concerning Flintshire politics. Everywhere, non-compliance brought the risk of heavy-handed retaliation. Stubborn small freeholders were thus threatened with being 'marked men' by being pursued through the courts at some unknown future date, or else they were put in fear of being forced into holding parish offices incurring expense and trouble. Those among the lesser gentry vaunting the coveted office of justice of the peace were warned that opposition would see them turned out of their commissions. The vain clash of titans in the 1774 Montgomeryshire election saw small freeholders who were disposed to support the Powis Castle interest threatened with the loss of immemorial rights to cut turf or graze sheep on commons and wastes in the Wynnstay manors.[37] Information about the behaviour of freeholders and, for that matter, tenant farmers with voting rights, was collected by a system of paid informers. With the approaching Montgomeryshire election in mind, Sir Watkin Williams Wynn instructed his agent to

> employ some people who can give you *certain Intelligence* what they [his opponents, Lord Powis and Mostyn Owen] are about. We must have some agents but not the profusion which we had last time, they should be good understanding people, you should employ one or two as steady spys immediately.

Earlier, in 1774, Sir Watkin had paid a Mr Cotton ten guineas as 'gossip money'.[38]

But this is only one aspect of the securing of freeholders' support. Equally important, and mirroring the reciprocal nature of the vertical ties which bound men into a political interest, parliamentary candidates and MPs were expected to reward gentry and freeholders with local offices and church livings, and to procure positions for their sons. Pressing requests for favours were showered upon them by the enfranchised, constituting what Frank

O'Gorman has termed 'the "moral economy" of electioneering'.[39] As part of this process, freeholders' sons seeking to make their way in London were expected to be given a helping hand by the MP: typically, James Lewes reminded Thomas Pryse of Gogerddan (Cards.) on 28 June 1744 of the necessity of looking after the son of Griffith Jones of Llwyndynis, a firm adherent to his interest: 'I know these things must be irksome to you, but you must also know that I dare not refuse writing, or they'll murmur the whole country over.'[40] In an age, we have noticed, when the office of JP was the coveted prize among the many hungry for consequence, making someone a magistrate was a specially effective guarantee of attachment to a particular interest.[41]

Again, so far as landholding itself was concerned, freeholders as voters could expect favours either in procuring tenancies or, if already tenants, in receiving some indulgence that might otherwise be refused. John Parry, estate agent to the Owen family of Porkington's lands in north Wales, wrote to his employer in 1743 of his support for William Owen as the would-be tenant of Glan y Môr in Merioneth, reminding him that 'being a voter, he will expect your favour'. Requesting assistance in 1764 to help him with charges incurred in erecting buildings on his holding, William Rees, tenant on the Tredegar Castle Palleg estate in Breconshire, was at pains to impress upon the chief agent that he was 'a voter with Mr Morgans in his election'.[42]

A favour of a more unusual kind was asked of Richard Myddelton of Chirk Castle in autumn 1756 by Thomas Mesham, who possessed a landed estate and tenants but was in Flint Gaol awaiting a court appearance to answer his wife's mother for debt. Myddelton's assistance was sought to help procure his release from custody, 'for I well know if your worthy father was living he would soon because I was acquainted with him and sollicited votes for him at the great Elections against Sir Watkin and struck off some voters against him'.[43]

Besides using their influence and extending their 'friendship' to promote the careers, boost the egos and satisfy the desire for tenancies of those in a position to vote for their interest, prominent families sought to win the support of the gentry and freeholders by giving periodic freeholders' dinners, subscribing to balls, assemblies, hunts and race meetings, attending Quarter Sessions regularly and by making charitable donations to the poor.[44] Failure to recognize this last obligation could harm the family's chances at the poll. John James wrote with quiet satisfaction from Harpton Court in Radnorshire on 5 August 1774 to his employer, John Lewis, in London:

> Mr Edward Lewis is gone to Wells. He gave the Radnor people *half a guinea* for ringing for him when he came to Downton, but has been several times since, and has not given anything to the Poor or anybody he scarce speaks to any of them, which they all take notice of and swear they'll never vote for him if he is opposed.[45]

Charitable donations included subscriptions raised in times of food scarcity. In the food crisis in north-east Wales in 1782–3 as in the later crises of the 1790s and 1800–1, landowners, prodded by their agents, were concerned to be seen as public-spirited in order to enhance their political and local standing and to guard against being outshone in the eyes of the community by opponents of their interest. Francis Chambre, the Wynnstay agent, informed his master, Sir Watkin Williams Wynn, on 13 April 1783 of his being told in Wrexham that 'the distress of many individuals made it necessary to open a subscription immediately, and that it was wish'd you should take the lead rather than suffer the Dean and his party to begin upon it, which was said they intended doing early this week'.[46]

Credit in the eyes of the poor was again to the fore in the thinking of Henry Brown, agent to the Morgan family of Tredegar, in deciding upon the type of grain to be distributed to the poor in April 1800. Given that barley was 'exceedingly bad' and just as scarce as wheat, he decided there was more advantage to the poor in their being served just wheat, which they could mix with such barley that they themselves could come by at the local farmers' houses. He added significantly: 'at the same time this measure [will] add more to your credit by being held in high estimation among the Poor People.' Predictably, Brown's pen dripped jealous bile when referring to the efforts of others. On 26 March 1800 he brooded darkly of Mr Kemeys: 'there is no doubt but great care will be taken to trumpet about his munificence', while later, on 21 April, he reflected sourly of the 5th duke of Beaufort: 'There are some Folks, who when they do a thing, like to have it trumpeted forth.' What had upset him was the duke's encouraging his tenants to release supplies of grain by publicly offering them a guinea for every load brought to either of the market towns of Monmouthshire and there to be publicly sold. Brown complained: 'the offer seems calculated to make a sound.'[47]

Edward Lewis's virtual ignoring of the electors of Radnor in 1774, and the ire it evoked, point to the obligation on the part of the great families to pay proper attention to the individual susceptibilities of freeholders and burgesses, men fortified by a keen sense of status, lest they be offended and through pique switch their loyalties. Frank O'Gorman, David Eastwood and Matthew Cragoe have all emphasized the importance of the canvass in satisfying and bolstering the pretensions to status and influence on the part of the voter. In anticipation of a forthcoming election for Carmarthen, Herbert Lloyd of that borough fittingly cautioned J. G. Philipps of Cwmgwili in 1784: 'There are many burgesses you have not seen, even those in our interest which you should not neglect otherwise they will be against.' Indeed, constant vigilance was advisable. Notwithstanding J. G. Philipps's eventual return unopposed for Carmarthen Borough in 1784, his wife Anne was writing from Cwmgwili to him in London on 12 February 1785: 'You forgot to write to Mr Scurlock [of Blaencorse] before you went away. I therefore wrote a note myself and sent it today. I thought it was better to write, as it would have seemed very neglectful had we taken no notice of them.'[48]

Far from being quiescent followers of the great landowners' lead, freeholders in the growing industrial economy of Glamorgan saw an opportunity to bargain for their votes. Walter Vaughan, gent., testified at Swansea in 1748 that Mr Price of Penlle'r-gaer 'hinted strongly' to him that because of the forthcoming election, 'now is your time to insist upon the coal under Wain Gron which is part of the copyhold lands in the fee of Trewyddfa, Gower, belonging to the Duke of Beaufort'. Vaughan actually refused. Corroborating testimony was provided by John Mathew of the parish of Llandeilo Talybont (Glam.), yeoman, who swore at Swansea on 7 December 1748:

that he was told just before the last General Election by several of the Freeholders of the parishes of Llandilotalybont and Langevelach that they had been sent to by Mr Price of Pennllegare not to promise their votes with the Duke's Interest unless they should have their coal for nothing, of which this Deponent then informed Mr Gabriell Powell. And this Deponent further saith that he heard severall of them say that it would be foolish to vote with his Grace's Interest unless they had it.[49]

Freeholders, too, were not to be ridden roughshod over by Leviathans in a matter close to all landowners' hearts, namely encroachments on manorial rights and enclosures of commons. The Morgan family of Tredegar's attempt to recover the lost right of collecting 'commortha' rents in the manor of Brecon in the second half of the century led to a confederacy of freeholders to dispute the right at law. With the issue waxing 'warm' on both sides in 1784, the Morgan camp was advised by Bowyer of Lincoln's Inn in December: 'It therefore behoves Mr Morgan to proceed with circumspection and to be on safe ground before he attacks so formidable a Confederacy, and particularly as he is member of the County and many of the Bondsmen [i.e. the Combination members] are freeholders.'[50]

Similarly, the freeholders of Devynock Hundred (Brec.) were involved in a struggle with Morgan, as Crown lessee, over his claim to the right of depasturing strangers' cattle from the neighbouring counties on the Great Forest of Brecon, the freeholders declaring that they believed that as 'both your tenants and *constituents* [my italics] they were entitled to indulgences of depasturing more than strangers had a right to expect'.[51] In like vein, John Lewis of Harpton Court was aware in the election year 1768 of the advantage that might accrue to his opponent, Edward Lewis, attendant upon his (John Lewis's) task, as steward of the Crown lands, of rooting out encroachers. Later, in 1774, he was urging:

We must preserve the general good opinion of the country by convincing them of the reality of our intentions, ever was, and is now to recover his Majesty's rights, and down with the least hardship to any man – though the contrary has been most unjustly and falsely represented. This cannot I think be too much propagated as many are concerned from above Rayader to Presteign.[52]

This same sensitivity to rights of common on the part of freeholders and burgesses, and its political repercussions, can be seen, too, in the politics of the Carmarthen Borough in 1768. Contemplating in early February 1768 the imminent declaration of Mr

Gregory for the borough seat, John Hensleigh of Panteaugue (Pembs.) sourly imagined his agent haranguing the populace: 'Mr Gregory is come to relieve you from slavery and oppression. If you elect him he will redeem your Commons, which are enclosed and arbitraryly kept from you, and will lay them open to you as your old right.' Again, in the Glamorganshire election in 1798 Mr Wyndham was opposed by Mr Windsor, who was backed by Lord Cardiff and the duke of Beaufort. An election address on behalf of Wyndham entitled 'Hundreds of Langefelach and Swansea, Rights of Commons and Courts Baron' sought to assure the freeholders and customary or copyholders that, despite the contrary claims of the Beaufort interest, they were entitled to rights of common in the district.[53]

3. Local Issues and Politics

Apart from the contentious issue of encroachments and enclosures, Welsh voters, like their English counterparts, were involved in the political process by virtue of their interest in securing local improvements by Act of Parliament in relation to harbours, roads, canals, gaols and houses of correction, paving and lighting of towns and the like. Such local Acts – involving the MPs for those respective districts sitting in committee – were passed in response to petitions from the propertied groups of the area concerned. Behind these petitions would have lain much local discussion, some doubtless at cross-purposes; the views of local electors would perforce have to be listened to by the great landowners, and the parliamentary performance of the latter would be scrutinized and held to account. Pressure from local freeholders thus secured exemptions from tolls on the carriage of coal and lime, an example of this occurring in autumn 1776 when twenty-eight freeholders sent a memorial to George Rice of Newton (Carms.), MP, voicing their objection to the payment of such tolls along the proposed turnpike road from Llandeilo to Trecastle. That the very building of turnpike roads was a vexatious matter which could split communities is conveyed in William Thomas's diary entry for 12 January 1764:

Was a meeting in Cowbridge about the Turnpikes, being the sixth here and there about that affair this three months past, and here they agreed for a General Turnpike, but Esqr. Jones of Fonmon and Mr Turberville of Wenny did stoutly oppose them for the good of the County.[54]

The issue of encroachments on Crown lands in Wales mobilized an all-Welsh political response among the large territorial magnates and small gentry alike in 1778–9. Collectively aware of their past illegal, hidden encroachments on the vast Crown wastes in the Principality, unease, indeed panic, set in among their ranks at the intention of Lord North's ministry in late 1778 to inquire into encroachments of private landowners onto Crown lands in Wales. In order to effect this survey the lords commissioners of his Majesty's Treasury under its warrant of 20 November 1778 appointed John Probert as an assistant to the revenue officers with powers to manage the waste lands as the Crown officers saw fit, and also to enclose as Crown property waste and uncultivated lands. No particular resentment would have been voiced over the aim of better managing the Crown revenues in the Principality of Wales, for hitherto such an administration had been notoriously slack, leading to widespread arrears of rents, but the enclosure provision, as Peter D. G. Thomas has observed, was a different matter altogether.[55] The likelihood of past depredations coming to light in the course of the inquiry and the consequent forfeiting of certain of their estates was not lost on the Welsh gentry and aristocracy, and a flurry of angry accusations against what Lord Bulkeley termed the 'tyrannic intentions' of the administration quickly followed. Such memorials from landowners from the different counties of Wales chimed in with the current mode of protest against the tendency of the Crown to act arbitrarily, and this was encapsulated in Dunning's famous resolution in the House of Commons in April 1780. Even so, the furious response to this Treasury warrant contrasted markedly with the mute response by Welsh landowners to the broader nationwide campaign for economical reform associated with the Petitioning Movement of 1779–82.

The aforementioned Lord Bulkeley, the young MP for Anglesey, was the moving spirit behind the campaign of protest in his circulating an address to his fellow Welsh MPs and all others having 'landed interest' in Wales on 19 December 1778. Prominent, too, in north Wales was Sir Watkin Williams Wynn of Wynnstay. Separate county meetings of landowners of Anglesey,

Caernarfonshire, Denbighshire, Merioneth and Flintshire met in January 1779 to protest against this Crown high-handedness, which was deemed to be 'illegal and unconstitutional'. Less urgency was manifested in the south, only Brecknock holding a meeting on 20 January.[56] Nevertheless, at the Cardiganshire Quarter Sessions of 12 January a representation was drawn up and submitted to the county and borough MPs. After claiming that Probert's powers would deprive the commoners of their undoubted rights, it continued:

> We cannot help considering this appointment as preparatory to a general inspection into the titles of our estates and an attempt to enlarge the powers of the Crown at the expense of the subject inconsistent with these principles of liberty this nation so proudly boasts of – the precedent is there and formidable and at a time when so universal a discontent prevails in this Kingdom may have a fatal tendency to alienate the affections of a brave and loyal people.[57]

There followed out of these county meetings two general meetings of Welsh MPs and other gentlemen in London on 23 January and 6 February 1779 to draw up a memorial 'of Freeholders of the Principality of Wales' to be sent to the Treasury Board.[58] Objecting that the implementation of Probert's powers might 'prove injurious to their property', it called for the warrant to be suspended.[59] The upshot was a compromise, testifying to the political clout of the Welsh squires; in return for their going along with the original aim of the warrant to collect arrears of Crown rents in Wales they achieved their principal objective of checking the inquiry into their erstwhile encroachments on Crown lands. (In practice, it was to be the men and women of smaller properties who were to feel the pinch through enforced payment of such arrears, some farmers about Newtown (Mont.), for example, having their cattle distrained in December 1779.) Likewise, Burke's Welsh Bill introduced on 5 July 1780 as part of his campaign for economical reform, although a watered-down version of his original intentions, was ultimately dropped essentially because it displeased the Welsh gentry.[60]

If the normal channels of political participation were denied to the non-propertied, it should not be concluded that they lacked any outlet for political bargaining. On the contrary, as the next chapter will show, rioting took place over vexatious issues perceived as posing threats to local welfare like balloting for service in the militia and high corn prices; in face-to-face riotous confrontation and bargaining with well-known and familiar local magistrates certain concessions were sought and sometimes won. For Bohstedt, writing of England and Wales in the years 1790–1810, 'riots were doubtless the most common form of popular political action in this period'.[61]

~ 9 ~

Riots and Popular Resistance

No easy conclusion can be reached about the degree of harmony in the eighteenth-century Welsh countryside. From one perspective we can posit peaceful neighbourhoods. To a considerable extent the dependent, vulnerable and land-hungry rural dwellers were reduced to servility through a mixture of paternalism and bullying on the part of local gentlemen and aristocrats. Pondering the 'submissive' disposition of the 'lower class of people' in north Wales in 1770, the visitor Joseph Cradock mused: 'I know not whether to attribute it to their manner of life, or to the great power the squires exercise over them.'[2] Again there is no mistaking the strength and succour of kinship within communities, the reciprocal ties between neighbouring farmers, the fellowship between farmers' families and their menservants and maidservants, the folk customs and religious beliefs, 'commortha' and the distribution of poor relief, all which served as props to community stability and harmony. Yet there was a darker, more angry side to relationships in the rural world. Court cases above all, but an array of evidence besides, point to a violent, unsqueamish, brutal society easily given to lawlessness and physical affray, a breakdown in public order which the magistrates and their helpers, for all their often brave intervention, were unable to do much about. Indeed, a significant amount of the lawbreaking and resort to violence involved rioting justices themselves.

The rural community had its own standards and sense of right and wrong which often conflicted with statutory law. Corn riots were sanctioned by the poor as a legitimate defence of a traditional right to purchase food at a 'fair' price, and likewise smuggling, wrecking, poaching and the exercise of a whole range of common rights were cherished by the lower orders as customary rights succouring them in their struggle for survival. Attempts to interfere with the enjoyment of these rights on the part of the authorities led to conflict. In particular, new forces afoot in the eighteenth century such as the engrossing and forestalling of the market by profiteering middlemen, and the reassertion of manorial franchises as their perceived legal right on the part of manorial lords, would inevitably spark riot and disorder on the part of the poorer sorts of people. The crop of militia laws, too, that came onto the statute book from the mid-eighteenth century were injurious to the meaner ranks of society and met with determined resistance. Another irritant to the countless traditional, highly localized neighbourhoods that made up Welsh rural society was the intrusion of strangers from outside into their midst, newcomers who were resented as a threat to community order and accordingly stoutly resisted. Public disorder, too, was the frequent product of the strong partisanship inflaming both parliamentary election contests and borough politics. Finally, disorder sometimes erupted over the attempts by officials to arrest certain wrongdoers, neighbours in the process rallying to the defence of one of their own.

1. Food Riots

Food riots were a frequent occurrence in different parts of Wales, as in England, throughout the eighteenth century. Recognizing this, David Jones commented: 'the riots from 1793 to 1801 were therefore remarkable only because they were so numerous.'[3] Corn riots had taken place in earlier decades in 1709, 1713, 1728, 1740, 1752, 1757–8, 1765–6, 1778, 1783 and 1789, all years of scarcity and high prices, such disturbances demonstrating the working population's heavy reliance, as we have shown, upon bread as a staple food. This impoverished working population scraped a living in normal times, but a bad harvest meant local famines, out-of-reach prices and awful deprivation. Typically, the winter of 1739–40 experienced 'the great frost' in north Wales which, lasting from 23 December 1739 to 10 February 1740, saw prices for corn rise and food riots erupt in May; again, the food disturbances in Anglesey in 1757 and 1758 occurred against the backdrop of the 'remarkable' season of 1756–7, which produced 'dearth and scarcity' in corn.[4]

As mentioned, this fragile situation arising from the vagaries of the harvest was rendered worse throughout Britain by the increasing tendency over the course of the century for corn factors, badgers, millers, large farmers and others seeking to engross and forestall the market. Testimony as to the harmful impact on ordinary people of this practice is ample. For instance, in August 1741 Mary Richard and Humphrey Griffith Owen, both of Dolgellau parish, Merioneth, were prosecuted at the Great Sessions for having in the previous June engrossed 200 bushels of barley at Llanelltid parish and sold it at a profit in Dolgellau market, 'which illegal practice . . . tended . . . to the enhancing of the price of corn at Dolgellau and several other places in Merioneth to the very great prejudice of several of the inhabitants of the said county'.[5] Cardiff Quarter Sessions in early October 1766 responded to the 'Dearness of Corn' by putting a stop to Jobbers 'about the Country that buys corn to sell it at Bristol under hand and not in Marketts'.[6]

It is not surprising that at periods of bad harvest labouring people should have turned their anger against those who were making the situation worse by buying up grain for export. As Edward Thompson so forcefully argued, at these moments of crisis the working population resented what they perceived to be illegitimate behaviour which did violence to the old moral economy of the lower orders with its notions of a fair or just price for bread as a traditional right. Corn riots, while certainly sparked off by hunger or fear of hunger, were informed by this popular consensus of traditional rights and the need to defend them.[7] Such attitudes extended to other vital provisions and at times of deprivation the people also stole butter, cheese and beans and prevented their export. The years 1757 in north-west Wales and 1795–6 in Pembrokeshire, in particular, saw high prices for butter which led to disturbances in those areas. In the light of Sir Thomas Mostyn's letter from Gloddaeth (Caerns.) in early December 1756 that 'Butter w^{ch} *our Country people live on* is very dear' (my italics), it is small wonder that riots in north-west Wales in 1757 and 1758 were as much concerned with its exportation as with corn.[8]

It was this anger over the export of grain and, on some occasions, other foodstuffs from local areas in times of scarcity which partly determined the location of disturbances. Food riots frequently occurred in the coastal and riverine ports of England and Wales and in the market towns that supplied London and the new manufacturing centres.[9] In the years before the corn riots of the 1790s and 1800–1 in Wales, disturbances which have been examined by David Jones, food riots erupted in and around Wrexham in spring 1709, at Loughor and Swansea in February 1713, at St Asaph and elsewhere in Flintshire and at Beaumaris in summer 1728, at Pembroke, Denbigh, Rhuddlan, Rhyl, St Asaph and Prestatyn in spring 1740, at Caernarfon in April 1752, at Holyhead, Laugharne and Carmarthen in early and mid-1757, at Redwharf, Llanbedr-goch and Beaumaris (all in Anglesey) in winter 1757–8, at Caernarfon, Conwy and Pwllheli in early 1758, at Llanishen, Ely and Fairwater in the Vale of Glamorgan in February 1765, at Flint in 1778, at Aberystwyth in 1783 and across the entire north Wales coalfield in 1789.[10] That the riots flared up more frequently in north Wales than in the south can be explained by the proximity to the manufacturing and commercial centres of Lancashire and Cheshire.

Perhaps as important in giving rise to food riots in Wales, as in England, was the presence in the disturbed areas of groups of industrial wage-earners like colliers, lead miners, slate quarrymen and the like, and of craftworkers like shoemakers, tailors and weavers.[11] These groups were all exposed to the sharp price fluctuations in the open markets of the towns and, as we have shown, were far more vulnerable than 'protected' agricultural labourers. Moreover, by 'the force of custom' the latter were more deferential to their masters than were the non-agricultural workers. Roger Wells's insistence that the majority of eighteenth-century food riots were not comprised of rural agricultural workers is well taken, albeit some of the industrial workers in Welsh riots were living in rural townships and parishes.[12] Colliers were a very important group in many Welsh corn riots, both in the north and south; again, lead miners rioted at Aberystwyth in 1783 in protest at the high corn prices, and slate quarrymen comprised the rioters at Caernarfon in spring 1752 and again in early 1758.[13] Craftsmen and artisans, also, were prominent in the food disturbances in Denbighshire and Flintshire in May 1740. Of the 130 people arraigned before the Flintshire Great Sessions in August 1740 for taking part in the riots at Rhuddlan and its vicinity in May, apart from the fifty-three colliers and miners there was a strong contingent of shoemakers, weavers, carpenters, blacksmiths, tailors and the like.[14]

In the determination to stop shipments of corn and other produce, sometimes vessels would be boarded and the cargo stolen, as at Beaumaris in late June 1728, at Pembroke on 23 May 1740 and at Lawrenny creek in Milford Haven on 16 February 1757.[15] The following winter, 1757–8, indeed witnessed the theft of 'several shiploads' of corn, butter and cheese about to leave Anglesey.[16] On other occasions specific houses were visited by perambulating groups intent upon stealing corn destined for export. Friday, 23 May 1740 saw men breaking into several private dwelling houses at Rhuddlan and destroying as well as dividing among themselves large amounts of corn intended for shipment. Similarly on Thursday, 29 May 1740 a group of people from around Denbigh made for the house of John Morris of Launt in Denbigh parish, a miller, and took away about three hobbets of wheat. Likewise, a mob broke into a house at Rhydbont, Anglesey, on Tuesday, 3 January 1758 intent upon stealing the butter and cheese of Edward Rimmer of Warrington, maltster, and proceeded to break up the cheese butts into pieces and share them among themselves (estimated to be about a hundred persons). That the sole motive of the rioters, as Edward Thompson has demonstrated, was not just to obtain desperately needed food but sometimes merely to express outrage at the violence being done to traditional moral assumptions by greedy middlemen, and to punish them, is reflected in two of these instances cited, for at Rhuddlan corn was destroyed and the corn stolen from Morris of Launt was left 'some in the high road and some in the fields' near his house.[17]

Yet many of the same mob that visited Launt had the previous day, Wednesday, 28 May, stolen five hobbets of wheat already sold for export from John Edwards of Henllan parish, a farmer, and the next morning one of their number proclaimed at the Denbigh cross that its price was to be 10*s.* a hobbet, at which level it was sold that morning. The proceeds were then divided among the group, each receiving 3*s.* In all this we glimpse the complexity of food riots: the corn stolen at Launt was simply left, but the same group earlier in the day had set the price, albeit the money they received was not returned to the original owner, John Edwards. Lowering the price was again in evidence in the Caernarfon riot of February 1758, William Morris informing his brother on 13 February that local quarrymen had the previous week made for the town, broken open the storehouses and sold the corn, butter and cheese at reduced prices. Likewise, in Anglesey, of the shiploads of corn, butter and cheese stolen in the winter of 1757–8, 'the greatest part of it [was]

never sold at all and what was sold was next to nothing – Barley at
1s. a Pegget, Butter 1d. a pound and some for 1/2d. a pound and
cheese at the same rate.'[18]

In a couple of instances certain townspeople, without resorting
to actual riot, resisted the high prices in difficult years by seeking to
control market prices, as was likewise to occur in the corn riots in
south-west England in 1800–1. Late May 1740 thus saw various
people who went to Bala market (Mer.) to buy oatmeal being
forcefully taken before Charles Vaughan of that town, styled by his
accomplices 'recorder', and being allowed to take their oatmeal
home only on swearing on oath that they had not purchased it for
export or to be sent out by sea. Having paid variously 2d. to 4d. for
their oaths, they were handed tickets signifying they had been
sworn which had to be produced at the outskirts of the town as a
condition of their being able to leave unmolested. Community
solidarity was shown in Pembroke town in early 1796 when the
townspeople entered an agreement among themselves not to buy
anything till the prices fell, resolving that they would not give more
than 4½d. per lb. for beef or mutton or 9½d. for fresh butter.[19]

Edward Thompson's claim that provision riots had specific aims
and that these were pursued in a disciplined manner sometimes
holds true in a Welsh context throughout the century. Many of the
riots were free from random, indiscriminate looting and wanton
destruction of property or physical assault.[20] Lowering the price on
some occasions and, again, as Glyn Parry indicates, the scrupulous
behaviour of the Denbigh rioters on 28 May 1740 in taking corn
from any one place only if the quantity there exceeded three
hobbets is testimony to the specific aims shared by the rioters in
Wales, as was the case elsewhere in Britain and western Europe.[21]
Yet, following Bohstedt, food riots in Wales were often 'disorderly'
in the sense that on many occasions food was taken from the
owners without payment. Even when a lowering of the price
occurred – and this was far from being general – there is some
evidence, as in the case of theft from John Edwards of Henllan,
that the proceeds of the sales were not returned to the owners.[22]

In addition, physical violence was by no means a rarity. To some
extent of course the propensity to violence was related to the size of
the assembly. Many riots were small affairs, ranging from just a
handful of people to twenty or so. Others were much larger: a
crowd variously estimated at between 700 and 1,300 rioted at

Rhuddlan on Friday, 23 May 1740, and some 400 the following day; the Denbigh mob who marched on Llanfydd parish on 30 May 1740 numbered no fewer than thirty and perhaps as many as 150; an estimated 150 people marched from Beaumaris and Llannerch-y-medd to Holyhead in January 1757, and on 17 June 1758 around a hundred colliers raided a Carmarthen storehouse. It was among these big crowds that discipline sometimes broke down. The Rhuddlan disturbances in May 1740 certainly got out of hand when on 23 May the 'infatuated' mob ransacked the houses of three merchants who were too frightened to enter the town. The mob, indeed, carried five pikes with them, boasting that four were to carry merchant George Colley's quarters and the other his head, and they also swore that they would pull magistrate David Ffoulkes 'limb from limb and his house about his ears'.[23] The march of the Denbigh 'gang' on Llanfydd led to a fracas in which one Llanfydd man was shot dead by a member of the gang, Thomas Evans a Denbigh shoemaker. After breaking open storehouses in Caernarfon in February 1758 and selling corn, butter and cheese for low prices the quarrymen got drunk 'and played misrule'.[24] In the ensuing scuffle with the authorities several rioters were shot, one mortally. Highway robbery and theft of money on the part of six men occurred during the course of the Denbigh food riot on 1 April 1795, and during the riot three magistrates were assaulted. These last instances should certainly caution us about too readily thinking in terms of orderly crowd behaviour even in Bohstedt's 'small agrarian villages' of up to 3,000.[25]

E. P. Thompson pointed to some particular provocation sustained as the likely explanation for the collapse of crowd discipline.[26] In the case of Rhuddlan in 1740, merchant Colley's action on the first day, 21 May, in apprehending five rioters, and the follow-up by David Ffoulkes Esq. in placing them under arrest, inflamed the situation. But political party rivalries, too, played some part in this riot. K. Lloyd Gruffydd has persuasively argued that with the approaching parliamentary elections of 1741 there was an element of political faction at work ready to take advantage of the economic crisis: the Tory Sir Thomas Mostyn's colliers were prominent participants at Rhuddlan, chanting on their arrival 'A Mostyn', and arms were provided for the rioters by John Wynne, the steward of Sir Thomas, at Mostyn Hall itself. Significantly, magistrate Ffoulkes observed on 25 May that the mob were 'encouraged and have money given them by gentlemen around Holywell'.[27] Similarly, in the politically turbulent borough of Carmarthen it is possible that the collier-rioters in June 1757 were stirred up by one of the factions.[28]

That troops were called in on many occasions suggests on the face of it that the authorities were responding unsympathetically. Yet it may have been as a last resort, for they knew the local popular resentment that would build up against such troops would not quickly evaporate. Again, as the fiasco at Carmarthen in June 1757 highlighted – when the mayor stood trial at the assizes for having ordered troops to fire on rioting colliers, killing five of them, but not before reading the Riot Act and several times asking them to disperse – the very uncertainty of the magistrates' proper course of procedure in forcefully encountering the mob discouraged them from acting resolutely. The want of reliability on the part of local constables and local military, which David Jones demonstrated was sometimes a factor during the years 1793–1801, was yet another constraint upon magistrates looking to call in troops.[29] In the south-west of England in 1800–1, at the beginning of the riots the authorities took a pacific stance. Whereas at Rhuddlan in spring 1740 three magistrates were for promptly calling in the military, the sheriff and their justices preferred to meet the mob on Monday, 26 May, to try to pacify them. Some gentlemen, perhaps many, throughout the century clung to the old paternalist model and were conscious that the malpractices of corn factors, badgers, farmers and the like were harming the poor.[30] Efforts were made on their part to prevent corn from being exported; thus at the behest of the local justices corn was not cleared from the mouth of the River Conwy in March 1757. Glyn Parry has shown that such magistrates were warmly praised by the people, one contemporary ballad acclaiming that Humphrey Meredith from Pengwern would have 'a proper lodging in the kingdom of Heaven' for his vigilance in stopping corn exports. Contrariwise, those who neglected to do so were subjected to verbal attack, even physically assaulted, as were six justices at Llannerch-y-medd in Anglesey during the provisions crisis in 1757.[31] On occasions, too, magistrates were intent upon punishing forestallers. The Anglesey justices were certainly siding with the people in the crisis of 1757, William Bulkeley recording in his diary on 8 February 1758:

The new Justices viz. – Sir Nicholas Baily, Jones of Henllys, Brisco the Collector of Beaumaris, Lloyd of Hirdrefaig and Wangle of Llwydiarth are greatly suspected to encourage and set them on, that ever since last Hillary Quarter, they have adjourned the Quarter to the Shire Hall, Beaumaris, every week ever since, where all the farmers that have sold any corn and those that bought it have been several times summoned to attend at the peril of their lives from a mob of 200 to 300, who fill the Hall and insult and abuse all those attending there upon their Summons who are kept there to answer the same questions asked over and over again by those threatening inquisition who from the Bench bully them, while the rude mob behind insult and abuse them, when between threats, noise and insults they at last are tired and confounded that they confess on themselves and are accordingly convicted and unmercifully fined.

By contrast, during the recent corn riot in Anglesey in January 1757 the authorities had acted leniently towards the rioters, for of the sixty-five or so prisoners arrested from an estimated mob of 150, all but the 'General' were set free the following day.[32] Such unwillingness to bring them before the courts chimes with 'the reluctance to prosecute, or at least to arraign suspects on capital charges' on the part of the magistrates of south-west England in 1800–1. Overall, however, no general conclusion can be reached about the nature of the sentences imposed on the rioters in Welsh courts. Whereas sentences ranging from a 6*d.* fine and a day's imprisonment to 1*s.* fine and a week in gaol were meted out by the Caernarfonshire Great Sessions on the men and women who stole barley at the parish of Llanbeblig on 7 February 1758, seven rioters, two of them man and wife, were sentenced to transportation for seven years for their part in the riots in May 1740 at Rhuddlan and the surrounding countryside. At the same time, it is impossible to ascertain the sentences passed on their numerous fellow rioters arraigned before the courts of both Denbighshire and Flintshire in 1740 (some 130 names appear in the Flintshire gaol files alone). Whatever the reason for the stiff sentences meted out to the Rhuddlan seven, the harsh punishment of three or four years' imprisonment together with sureties for seven years' good behaviour imposed by the magistrates on some six men for their part in the Denbigh corn riot in 1795 arose from their assaulting a magistrate and unlawfully imprisoning him. Similarly, in the wake of the serious corn riot at Merthyr in

September 1800, two were hanged, in this case doubtless to warn
against any future large-scale damage to property.[33]

Even if a number of magistrates were sympathetic, order had to
be restored. Troops were thus used on a number of occasions, some
coming from outside the area as, for example, troops from
Cheshire during the Denbighshire and Flintshire riots of 1740, and
the Old Pensioners from Chester Castle during the Caernarfonshire
troubles in February 1758.[34] A riot or the *threat* of one also saw the
raising of subscriptions to buy large quantities of corn to be
distributed at cheap rates to the poor become a familiar response of
the propertied classes, especially in the 1790s and 1800–1. Similar if
less frequent action was taken earlier in Welsh counties. Such
conduct on the part of the Haverfordwest Corporation in 1757 was
looked upon as a necessary means to avoid 'dreadful consequences'
and, significantly, the county remained quiet in that tumultuous
year.[35] Again, subscriptions were raised in Denbighshire and
Flintshire in early 1783 when grain prices were exceedingly high in
consequence of the bad harvest of 1782.[36] The threat of disorder,
too, on one occasion at least brought greedy farmers to their
senses, those about Pembroke in early December 1795 having
'become alarmed and promised a constant supply'.[37] There is some
evidence, too, that in the wake of the riots coalowners mended their
ways towards their workforce. Thus within weeks of the riot at
Pembroke on 23 May 1740 the duke of Newcastle was informed
that 'such care is now taken by ye owners of ye collerys to supply ye
men with corn and to keep 'em in order yt no disturbance can
happen for ye future'. Again, following the disturbances in the
county in 1795, Pembrokeshire coalowners supplied their
workforces at reduced prices.[38]

As for England and Wales in general, it is difficult to discover
precise gender involvement in the food riots under discussion.
Edward Thompson argues that the 'sexually-indeterminate'
vocabulary like 'rioters', 'the mob', and 'the poor' frustrates
specific gender identification.[39] Nevertheless there is some evidence
of the presence of women and children at a number of the riots in
Wales as elsewhere in Great Britain. A crowd of 400 men, women
and children made for Rhuddlan on 21 May 1740, where they
prevented a wagon-load of wheat from being exported, while on 6
June 1740 a crowd comprising mainly women unloaded wheat
from a vessel about to sail from Flintshire.[40] According to one

account, the fracas at Llanfydd on 30 May 1740 ended with 'Denbigh men, women and children persuaded to return to Denbigh'. When two days earlier twelve men visited the house of John Edwards of Henllan, five or six boys, the youngest about thirteen, accompanied them.[41] Giving evidence in court on 29 March 1758 concerning a food riot, John Hughes of Llanwenllwyfo, Anglesey, stated that in December 1757 he saw 'a great multitude of people, some women amongst them, coming to Redwharf in Anglesey armed with clubs and staves'.[42] There is difficulty in relying on gender differentiation emerging from an analysis of legal indictments for it is possible that, apart from cases where women played a leading role, there was rather more willingness on the part of the authorities to prosecute men than women.[43] The indictments brought before the Great Sessions for the Welsh circuits suggest that this was so. Of the 130 people indicted for rioting at Rhuddlan in May 1740, just six were women (one of whom, with her husband, was transported); in the Denbigh riots of May 1740 some sixty males, but no female, were indicted (yet we hear elsewhere of women present at Llanfydd on 30 May); some eighty males and eight females were indicted for riot in the Anglesey disturbances in early 1758; and there was just one female indicted, as against some fifty-five males, for theft of food before the Caernarfonshire Great Sessions in 1758–9. A somewhat larger contingent of females was to be found among the corn rioters tried before the Welsh courts between 1793 and 1801 for, as David Jones reveals, of the total 103 people indicted and convicted at the Great Sessions some fourteen were female.[44]

In most Welsh, as in English, food riots, women were certainly not more prominent than men. As far as Wales was concerned, in all probability men were to the fore in the majority of cases, but at the same time women constituted a significant presence in a number of them, no doubt, as Bohstedt suggests, 'partly because they were essential partners as bread-winners in the household economies of pre-industrial society and partly because bread riots were still effective politics in stable small-to-medium-sized traditional towns'. Moreover, at Haverfordwest on 18 August 1795, at Hay on 23 August 1795 and in the marches from Llangyfelach to Swansea in February 1793 and from Llangattock to Beaufort in March 1800, women were prominent participants even if the leaders of the last two marches were men. Women demonstrated on their own at Swansea on Monday, 20 April 1801, against high corn prices, John Bird on a visit to the town recording:

> About 4 o'Clock in the Afternoon a number of poor Women with two Common Girls of the Town at their head assembled and paraded the Streets, and being joined by a number of poor Children whom the Women encouraged to Holloa and Scream, the whole body proceeded to a Corn Warehouse, in which was a large quantity of Barley belonging to Messrs. Grove and Co., and forced open the Door, but did not attempt taking any of it away.

As in other instances we have met, it seems they were simply intent on making a point against the unfairness of rigging the market. Upon the calling out of the Cardigan militia quartered there, the women were sent home, and, tellingly, the two prostitute ringleaders, who were taken into custody and delivered to the Swansea Independent Volunteers, were permitted to escape.[45]

For all the threats made to fire Pembroke and Rhuddlan in 1740 and to cause physical harm to the gentlemen of Rhuddlan, these, as for similar outbursts across Britain, were so much rhetoric.[46] It seems that certain gentlemen aroused particular resentment through overzealous activity in arresting leading culprits. At both Rhuddlan and Pembroke in 1740, and at Conwy in February 1758, those arrested were forcibly released and David Ffoulkes Esq. in Rhuddlan and Mr Justice Holland in Conwy came in for hostile treatment.[47] Even so, there was no general undercurrent of anti-gentry ideology present in the riots before the 1790s, even if at times the mobs were the tools of political faction. The riots were grounded in the hunger of the people and their resentment of unfair profiteering at their expense. At Rhuddlan the people's wretchedness had reached such depths that they would rather be 'Hanged than Starvd' and local JP William Price distilled the essence in observing: 'We must attribute the Comotion to ye necessity of the People.'[48] A perceptible change in the chemistry of food riots was to occur in the 1790s for, as we have earlier observed, with the heightening of radical consciousness food riots in Wales as elsewhere in Britain were sometimes driven, in part at least, by Jacobinical sentiments.[49]

2. Smuggling

Public disorder and resistance occurred, too, when the authorities attempted to confiscate contraband cargo landed by smugglers in the isolated bays and creeks stretching along the entire Welsh coastline. For smuggling was seen as a legitimate activity, sanctioned by custom, by English and Welsh communities alike and, as Carl Winslow has persuasively argued, should be viewed as one among many 'of the traditions of resistance, carried on by the poor, to the laws and institutions of their rulers'.[50] That the eighteenth century witnessed a veritable explosion in smuggling can be explained by the high duties levied even on basic goods like tea, coal and salt, a state of affairs that clearly hurt the poor. While poverty was doubtless the main motivation, there was also the feeling that the harsh duties were unfair and, perhaps so far as Welsh people were concerned, that they were imposed by an alien, 'Saxon' government.[51] The comfortable sense that only the government was the loser when goods were smuggled further disinclined the community to perceive smuggling as a crime.[52] There was, too, doubtless point to the claims of both the Neath and the Swansea collectors that smuggling was on the increase from the 1730s to satisfy the thirst for spirits of the Welsh collier. Likewise, the collector at Cardiff complained of 'the many little tobacco shops in this country' and contended that they got all their supplies from smugglers.[53]

The country people providing a ready market for the smugglers embraced a wide spectrum of the local neighbourhood, the hard core comprising cottagers, craftsmen, farmers, and doubtless women and children. Farmers' horses and carts were got ready on the beaches to convey goods into the countryside.[54] Clergy and gentry, too, in perhaps a large number of instances were indulgent. Certainly the Revd J. Collins of Oxwich, Gower, displayed a distinct want of moral judgement in recording in his diary for 13 March 1794: 'Smugglers chased into the bay by the "Speedwell" Cutter, and then taken . . . Sixteen men landed and saved some casks . . . several of the parishioners got very drunk on gin.' Collins reveals not just his own tolerance but the undoubted popularity of the smuggler among his neighbours when recording on 15 March 1794 the burial of 'poor Thomas Matthew', a smuggler who had died from drinking too much smuggled gin, at which 200 people had turned out to pay their last respects.[55] Certain Anglesey gentry, too, and doubtless those of other counties were ready to purchase cheap smuggled goods.[56]

If smuggling was widely condoned by the lower orders and often brought some ease to its members, it had its darker side. For all the severity of the 1736 Act bringing in the death penalty for attacking a customs officer and the offer of lucrative rewards to informers, the authorities stood little chance of curbing smuggling in the face of the violent smuggling gangs, stout physical resistance from the local inhabitants excitedly filling the beaches and, as recorded in popular legend, the tricks got up to in order to outsmart the authorities. Indeed customs officers, small in numbers, and sometimes local gentlemen, ran the risk of severe injury if overzealous. Thus when a West Indiaman making for Bristol offloaded a large supply of rum, sugar and molasses onto the beach at Rhosili during broad daylight sometime in 1759, the customs officers could not reach the shore because there was 'a mobb of nigh on four hundred' who had gathered to carry away, in local parlance, the *stuff*. Barry Island in the late 1730s, reported the Customs Board official, was 'a most hazardous district over-run by ruffians'.[57]

It was the same westwards and northwards. Thus a riot occurred at New Quay on 5 August 1704 when salt smugglers were waylaid at 3 a.m. by eight Aberdovey customs officers, the 150 or so men waiting on shore to convey the bags inland attacking the officers with stones and sticks. Firing in self-defence, the officers hurt several of the crowd, one seriously. Remarkably, at daybreak the 'rabble' left the shore but quickly returned with several constables who arrested two and carried them before a local justice. The latter bound one of them to appear at the assizes, the mob charging him with badly injuring one of their number.[58] Two customs officers were violently assaulted, one mortally, at night-time on 19 May 1741 when attempting to prevent several local people from carrying away salt off an English vessel anchored in Dinas creek, north Pembrokeshire.[59] The north Wales coast was notorious for smuggling activity: one observer described Bangor in 1757 as 'a great thoroughfare for smugglers', smuggling went on in Pwllheli harbour in the full light of day, while, in Anglesey, Amlwch and Moelfre were veritable nests of smuggling activity. As a letter written in 1783 reveals, the customs officers were helpless to do much about it.[60]

The propensity to violence is further reflected in the heavily armed vessels used by the smugglers and in the fierce characters who headed the gangs, like the notorious John Connor ('Jack the Bachelor'), leader of the 'Rush gang', Thomas Field, another Irish smuggler, John Creemans who commanded an Irish wherry, Stephen and Thomas Richards, in charge of an Irish wherry and its crew of 'desperate ruffians', and Thomas Knight, the bane of the Cardiff customs officers. The extensive smuggling along the bays of Gower was dominated by William Arthur whose lawlessness and defiance were such that when a combined customs and excise raid was made on his farmhouse in Pwll-ddu in 1788 the revenue officers were confronted by fifty persons 'armed with pokers, iron-bars, large knives, loaded whips and other offensive weapons'.[61] Large-scale smuggling in Sussex in the 1740s had seen the deployment of troops, but when a request was made for help from the army to deal with the lawless situation in south Wales at the end of the 1780s the reply was terse: 'the situation of forces at present will not admit any detachment being sent into South Wales.'[62]

3. Wrecking

In wrecking, as in smuggling, the conflict of custom with law was clearly in evidence and rendered the enforcement of the criminal law an almost impossible task.[63] Indeed, here as in so many areas of eighteenth-century society, communities were 'ungovernable'.[64] Coastal neighbourhoods looked upon wrecking as their natural right, believing that it was no great moral offence, indeed that a vessel cast upon rocks in a storm was the work of Providence. Thus a Customs officer testified in 1745 that when present at the wreck of a vessel on the coast of Anglesey he had met with the tart claim from certain wreckers that they had as much right to be there as he had.[65] Similarly, the Revd John Evans was to comment in 1803 on the practice of wrecking along the coast of Glamorgan:

> These people, in other respects, are for the most part harmless and inoffensive . . . but when a wreck occurs, which they call a God send, looking upon it as a special favour sent to them in the course of providence, their nature seems changed, and they seize with rapacity, and defend with ferocity, what they conceive to be peculiarly their own.

Given that the last days of winter were a time of crisis for the poor, a period when desperation rendered them careless about obeying the law, it is not surprising that February was the main month of wrecks, at least as far as the Glamorgan coast was concerned.[66]

The main participants crowding about and clambering over wrecked ships – and opportunities for such plundering grew over the course of the century with the steep rise in merchant shipping – would have been drawn from the lower orders of society. Thus the thirty-six people indicted in 1745 for a riot at the scene of a wrecked vessel in Anglesey comprised twenty yeomen, six labourers, eight artisans, one mariner and one housewife.[67] Five yeomen from Castlemartin parish were indicted at the Pembrokeshire spring assizes, 1769, for stealing from a ship wrecked in Freshwater West bay. Later, in 1783, three farm servants of Abergele parish (Denbs.) were indicted at the assizes for stealing on 13 March 1782 from the wreck of the *Lady Maria Anna* of Ostend, lying on Gwrych beach, a ten-gallon cask of geneva, a feather bed, 3 tin cannisters, some clothing, a pair of shoes and chocolate.[68] The poorer sort of people also stood to gain by stripping the vessel of sails, cordage and rigging, either by using it in their own homes or selling it.[69] Upon the *Loveday and Betty* running aground in a storm near the mouth of the River Crigyll in south-west Anglesey on 31 December 1739 the Liverpool master went for help, only to discover on his return that in his absence the rigging and sails had been removed. The culprits were eight local people, including a tailor, one of their number calling out on board: 'If you do not make a hundred pounds of it tonight you will never make it.'[70] Fate dealt kindly with the wreckers, for we learn from William Bulkeley's diary that they escaped justice because the sessions judge was drunk.[71]

If most were from the lower orders, on occasion richer people were wreckers, underlining the fact that local community traditions and ways of thinking could be as important determinants as social status.[72] Thus at the Shrewsbury assizes for 1774 bills of indictment were brought against three 'opulent' inhabitants of Anglesey – one, indeed, the owner of a 'considerable' estate – for taking part, along with others, in the plundering of the *Charming Jenny* at Crigyll on 11 September 1773. The Hereford assizes of the following year convicted and sentenced to death a prosperous farmer living near Cardiff for plundering a wreck on the local coast.[73]

John Rule contends that the aforementioned wreck of the *Charming Jenny* 'provides us with one of the most disturbing accounts of inhumanity towards survivors'. If we recall the Crigyll robbers of the *Loveday and Betty* over thirty years earlier, it becomes clear that the area had a tradition of wreck plundering.[74] The barbarity surrounding the wreck of the *Charming Jenny* emerges in the account carried in the *Annual Register*. It appeared in the course of the depositions [at the Shrewsbury trial] that

> On the 11th of September last, in very bad weather, in consequence of false lights being discovered, the Captain bore for shore, when his vessel . . . went to pieces, and all the crew, except the captain and his wife, perished, whom the waves had brought on shore upon part of the wreck. Nearly exhausted they lay for some time, till the savages of the adjacent places rushed down upon the devoted victims. The lady was just able to lift a handkerchief up to her head, when her husband was torn from her side. They cut his buckles from his shoes, and deprived him of every covering. Happy to escape with life, he hastened to the beach in search of his wife, when horrible to tell! her half-naked and plundered corpse presented itself to his view.[75]

Captain Chilcot's exhausted wife drowned in a rock pool, and it was his anguish and rage which stirred the Anglesey magistrates to conduct inquiries. A search led to the discovery of looted goods in certain local cottages. Two men were put in gaol, and in response to the captain's continuing impatience at the local magistrates' want of urgency the case was moved to Shrewsbury. The two accused, John Parry, a person of fortune, and William Williams were condemned to death, Parry going to the gallows in April 1774 while Williams had his death sentence respited.[76]

Accounts of other wrecks testify to the violence of the crowds. When the *Pye* making for Bristol with tobacco, sugar and cotton, went aground on the rocks off Nash Point (Glam.) in 1737, almost immediately 'three to four hundred people from all parts of the Country towards the Hills' gathered on the beach to plunder the vessel and stoutly resisted the efforts of the customs officers to secure the cargo. A strong contingent of wreckers were known to have lived in Bridgend, 'most of them shoemakers', but (a telling circumstance) efforts at capturing the ringleaders were frustrated because:

an officer dares not enter the town to take them, for they have a bell for
a signal, which they have agreed to ring if any of them shall be
apprehended, and that the whole town may rise to rescue the prisoners
and punish the officers for their insolence in coming among them.[77]

A graphic description of a wreck off Break-Sea Point on the
Glamorgan coast at the turn of the nineteenth century was penned
by the Revd John Evans in 1803, an account which once again
highlights the barbarity of the wreckers and the seeming
helplessness of the magistrates to enforce the law. Not that the late-
century Glamorgan squires were inactive; from the 1770s there was
a new determination on the part of certain of their number to catch
and punish the wreckers, diarist William Thomas noting on 9
February 1775 how in consequence 'folks run to woods and away
like fools'. At the ensuing sessions in Hereford in August four were
acquitted but the hapless lately married Lewis William was
condemned to be hanged. Later, on 5 September 1782 another was
hanged for his part in plundering a Venetian vessel off the
Glamorgan coast the previous November.[78]

4. Poaching

The increasing tendency from the beginning of the eighteenth
century for offences against the game laws to be tried by one or two
justices 'out of sessions' – by mid-eighteenth century it had become
common practice – means that surviving eighteenth-century legal
records of poaching offences are thin on the ground. Yet, given the
widespread opposition of both middling men and poor farmers and
labourers to the game laws, conferring on the gentry and
aristocracy a monopoly on game, as selfish and unfair, poaching
was done with a free conscience. Both poachers and the wider
community held the view that the taking of animals was legitimate,
a customary right of the poor on a par with smuggling, wrecking or
taking wood from a common.[79]

  If records are not plentiful, enough survive to point to the
prevalence of poaching on the open hills, and to the Welsh gentry's
concern to uphold their privileges under the game laws. Evidence
survives for informers about poachers being entitled to a 'penalty'.
Poachers were seen as a low form of life by the gentry, and there

can be no doubt of the harm done to relations between them and the lower orders by the game laws. Thomas Lewis Esq. of Harpton Court (Rads.) thus referred in 1773 to 'those notoriously wicked vagabonds' who were destroying his rabbit warren upon the Forest of Radnor so that 'night and day' he was obliged to keep people to look after it: 'Sheen found two men about 3 in the morning who ran away hearing their coming and in a hurry left a net of 60 yards long behind them with a rabbit in it.' Lewis was prepared to prosecute those who interfered in this way, three men appearing before the Radnorshire Great Sessions in 1775 to answer a charge of having the previous December broken into his warren and killed rabbits.[80]

Their manorial courts allowed the gentry to take away the means of poaching by confiscating dogs, nets and other 'engines' belonging to the unqualified. The duke of Beaufort's leet courts for the manors of Crickhowell and Tretower, both in Brecknock, at mid-century received presentments of juries concerning fishing with nets, shooting game and keeping of guns by unqualified persons. Likewise, at the Chirkland manorial court for October 1734 six men were fined 20*s.* a piece for keeping and using greyhounds for the destruction of game, while at the Easter leet court of 1739 a carpenter was fined £5 for carrying a gun.[81]

Summary trial of poachers before one or perhaps two justices who, on the oath of a 'credible' witness, could imprison a culprit if he could not pay the fine imposed, was, in contrast to Quarter Sessions, 'fast, simple and relatively cheap'.[82] If complaints were made to Quarter Sessions that unqualified persons were destroying game, the court could issue warrants to high constables in the county to apprehend offenders and bring them before a local JP, as, for example, happened in the case of the Denbighshire Hilary Quarter Sessions of 1729 in response to complaints that 'several persons' in the county were unlawfully destroying game.[83] The magistrates acting individually 'out of sessions' used much discretion as to the best mode of proceeding against guilty offenders, in the process of which it appears that the inclinations of the prosecutor weighed heavily. Thus on 12 August 1782 magistrate J. Lloyd wrote to Ellis Yonge Esq. of Acton (Denbs.): 'I have convicted Thomas Williams of chasing and taking a rabbit in your warren, and have made out his commitment, unless he makes you ample amends for the trespass and you should be disposed to dispense with his imprisonment.'[84] Similar accommodation is evident in the punishment of poachers for destroying game on Talacre warren belonging to Sir Edward Mostyn between 1752 and 1759. Hugh Williams of Gwesbyr (Flints.) was committed to Flint gaol on 6 February 1752 for three months by Justice Lloyd of Holywell for destroying rabbits on the said warren while John Jones, also of Gwesbyr, labourer, was gaoled by the same magistrate four days later for selling two dozen rabbit skins – the rabbits taken from the same warren – to Thomas Parry of Northup. The killing of the rabbits had been done jointly by Hugh Williams, John Jones and Thomas Parry on Monday night, 20 January 1752, using a net. Parry the following morning sold a couple of rabbits for 6*d.* to William Humpherys at Mostyn. But while in prison Jones executed a bond jointly with Richard Giles providing security for his good behaviour, upon which guarantee Sir Edward was willing to let him go free.[85]

As Munsche demonstrates, security being given for future good behaviour was often enough to prevent a landowner whose property rights had been infringed from going to law. In December 1753 John Jones and William Jones, inhabitants of Gwesbyr, labourers (perhaps the same John Jones imprisoned in February 1752), were caught destroying game on Sir Edward Mostyn's warren at Talacre. Their confession of 26 December 1753 and the response to it tell us much about eighteenth-century mentalities:

> Whereas we John Jones and William Jones both of Gwesbyr, labourers, do hereby acknowledge and confess ourselves to have been guilty of committing trespass upon the warren of Sir Edward Mostyn of Talacre, bart., by chaising, killing and distroying Rabbets upon the 12th and 13th Inst. to the quantity of from 3 to 5 Couples each The property of the said Sir Ed. Mostyn. Now know all persons to whom this shall come that we the sd. John Jones and William Jones being heartly sorry for such offence do promise to pay upon demand unto Matts. Bertwisle for the use of the sd. Sir Ed. Mostyn each of us one pound and one shilling for satisfaction of the said offence and further promise to give such other satisfaction and security for our future behaviour as the sd. Sir Ed. Mostyn shall at any time hereafter require.

Upon the two paying £1. 1*s.*, Sir Edward ordered the recipient to return them each 10*s.* 6*d.*, which was duly done on 1 February 1754.[86]

If most were from the lower orders, not all poachers were drawn from their ranks.[87] Some were gentlemen and clergymen who coursed and shot game on manorial property where they had no rights. The earl of Powis received detailed information at the close of 1770 about gentlemen, including attorneys and clergymen, illegally shooting and coursing on his lands in north-east Wales. Later, in February 1782 George Read was writing from Llanerfyl to a fellow Powis Castle employee asking him to 'tell his Lordship that Parson Worthington has been continually Coursing in this neighbourhood since his Lordship left the Hills in a very ungenteel poaching manner and has by all accounts killed a hundred and fifty hares'.[88] Strains between members of the landed élite were obviously opened up, and for the gamekeeper the situation was obviously a tricky one. Thus Mr Price, gamekeeper of the Chirk Castle estate, desired to know from his employer in summer 1735 'how to use Gentlemen if some shall happen to come' to take game on the hills and who were unqualified.[89] Such conflict within the ranks of the gentry and aristocracy over killing game was just one more manifestation of the souring of relations between lords of manors and neighbouring freeholders which stemmed from the encroachment – as manorial lords saw it – of their manorial rights.

5. Clashes over manorial 'rights'

Perhaps indeed the most frequent dispute in eighteenth-century Wales, and hardly surprising given the vast areas of open moorland, occurred over manorial rights, particularly rights of common. Both private and crown manors witnessed clashes between the lords of those manors and the general body of the rural community, the latter including freehold or customary tenants of those manors as well as the numerous propertyless poor, over what each party perceived to be their 'rights'. As the century progressed there was a perceptible and growing insistence on the part of manorial lords on their legal rights of property in the face of what they deemed to be an increasing erosion of their manorial franchises by local freeholders and the propertyless alike. Not only were they concerned over encroachment and enclosure of commons but also the making of bricks upon the commons, the digging and burning of lime and the cutting of turfs without the lord's permission. Manorial lords saw part of the trouble of such encroachment on manorial franchises as stemming either from past neglect on the part of agents in enforcing rights like the collection of commortha rents – perhaps in part owing to the 'obstinacy and perverseness of the inhabitants' – or the wish on their own part to be popular, the resulting leniency giving rise to rights being perfunctorily enforced, if at all.[90] The attempt – increasingly made from the mid-eighteenth century – to arrest the decay of manorial franchises and to lay claim to concealed and lost rights was met with hostility by the rural populace who, perceiving their 'rights' to be grounded in customary usage and traditional practice, accused the manorial lords of harassment and oppression and offered resistance in the form of petitions, resort to legal action, or riot.[91]

One compelling reason for manorial lords to pay greater attention to their manorial franchises over the course of the century was the growth of industrial enterprise, mineral rights accordingly taking on a whole new significance. Bitter and protracted disputes consequently arose between lords of manors and freeholders over the right to work these mineral deposits. Fiercely contested during the 1740s and 1750s was the 4th duke of Beaufort's reassertion of his mineral and other rights in the lordship of Gower, local gentlemen-tenants of the seigniory like Thomas Price of Penlle'r-gaer, Robert Popkin of Forest and Richard Dawkins of Kilvrough denying the duke's right to coal, and claiming for themselves rights to the waste and to work the coal mines therein. Grievances were aired by the gentlemen-tenants as a body, at least thirty of them, at a meeting at the Guildhall, Swansea, on 8 December 1747, when Thomas Price opened the proceedings by directly attacking the duke's rights.[92] Later, in August 1749 some twenty-two tenants of the manor of Oystermouth petitioned the duke that they were customary free-holders rather than copyholders – so claiming the right to work mines under their lands – and the same claim was to be made in June 1755 by tenants of the manor of Pennard, who filed a bill to establish this mode of tenure.[93] While tenants of Pennard and Trewyddfa claimed that their reduced status as copyholders had been an innovation of recent years, the duke's formidable agent, Gabriel Powell, disputed this, earlier contending in 1742 that 'it seems to be a settled rule amongst the tenants to rob the Lord as much as they can'.[94]

Disputes of a much more violent nature occurred over the mining of lead ore in the Crown lordships in Cardiganshire, occasioned by Lewis Morris, deputy steward of the Crown lands there, attempting at mid-century to reassert the Crown's right to ore lying under the open wastes against the often blatantly illegal claims and encroachments of private owners like the squires of Nanteos, Gogerddan and Crosswood, who viewed such open lands as part of their freeholds. So, aided and abetted by rioting justices at the head of their dependent, subservient but loyal countrymen, violence surged unchecked and lawlessness ran amok.[95]

Mineral disputes apart, resistance to the lords' attempts to recover lost rights after a spell of slackness or to assert their right to make the most of their manorial property was a familiar occurrence. The Morgans of Tredegar House encountered resistance in the 1780s from Brecknock freeholders over Charles Morgan's attempt to recover his perceived right of collecting commortha rents in the manor of Brecon, through the neglect of agents not collected since 1752. Unwilling to reach any accommodation with Morgan, the freeholders entered a combination of allegedly 150 or more to try the right at law.[96] Waxing 'warm' on both sides in 1784, the whole matter, we have seen, was complicated by considerations of the approaching parliamentary election.[97] Morgan, as Crown lessee, also fell foul of the freeholders of Devynock Hundred in the late 1770s and 1780s over his insistence on the right of depasturing strange cattle from different counties like Glamorgan on the Great Forest of Brecon in order to make up the Crown rent, the freeholders as borderers on the forest claiming an exclusive right to the pasturage thereon. Their protest took the form of impounding the strange or 'foreign' cattle and refusing to release them on 'fair' terms, which in turn led to lawsuits. While for their part, as we have shown, the Devynock freeholders reproached Morgan for not giving them as his tenants and constituents preferable treatment to strangers, he defended his actions thus:

> I hope you and they [i.e. his 'friends' within his political interest] think better of me than to suppose I would give the preference to strangers or that anybody should be indulged before my tenants and constituents but at the same time I also hope you cannot object to my maintaining my right as tenant of the crown and whereby no injury will be sustained by the tenants.[98]

In similar vein, John Morgan of Tredegar House in November 1791 was anxious to maintain his right to cut timber on Coedmoeth

Common in the parish of Bedwellty (Mons.) in the face of the parishioners claiming such a right as belonging to themselves and their ancestors 'time out of mind'. Morgan's response to their twenty-one-strong petition was typical of the resistance put up by lords of the manor to claims to rights of common by neighbouring inhabitants, his agent replying:

> he will accede as far as he can to your request therein [not to cut timber into cordwood on the common]; and that as you do not claim the said wood, or the cutting of them, as a matter of Right, but of Favour only; He will oblige you so far as to order the cutting of them as favourable as possible to your Interest; I mean so as to leave a sufficient quantity for the purpose you mentioned remaining – for the value of them is not his whole object in cutting them, but the maintenance of his undoubted Right therein and thereto as Lord of the Soil.[99]

Much community conflict arose, too, over manorial lords resorting to eviction or rent increases in an effort to put a stop to the growing numbers of trespasses by cottagers on the open wastes. Again, two opposing views of 'legal' *vis-à-vis* 'customary' rights were in collision. The right to dig turf led to many disputes. From time to time the Lloyds of Bronwydd (Cards.) as lords of the manor were in dispute with people encroaching on their commons to dig turf. Summer 1718 thus saw trespassers on the Cemais Commons within the lordship of Cemais (Pembs.) being summoned to appear before the lord's court to clear themselves or to acknowledge their trespass; significantly, those making such acknowledgement were to be 'kindly used', but those refusing to appear would be prosecuted with rigour both by the lord and by other gentlemen having right of common. Later, in 1777, four Cardiganshire men renounced before the autumn Great Sessions of the county their right to Cilcennin moor 'and all . . . right of turbury and of digging turves in said common or moor'. Doubtless information about encroachments onto the wastes was made known to the lords by informers, sometimes paid ones. William Maurice, for example, received a one-guinea gratuity in May 1730 from the Chirk Castle family 'for informing against the burners of the Mountain'.[100]

Lords of the manor, private and Crown alike, were also concerned to prosecute those who made encroachments of small parcels of land on the commons, the rising population from mid-century witnessing a growth in the practice. In the late 1760s, for example, the lessee of the Crown lordship of Cantremelenith in Radnorshire, in order that the king should 'reap the benefit of his own lands', sought to make the great number of those who had erected cottages and made small enclaves on the commons turn tenants upon pain of having ejectments served on them. Such ejectments were indeed found to be necessary, John Lewis of Harpton, the Crown agent, commenting in 1768 on 'the natural dispositions of people being averse to turn tenants and acknowledge any Lord'. Freeholders as well as small cottagers were involved, and the former petitioned in 1773 against the claims of the Crown's lessee, 'who now terribly harasses your petitioners having sued several of us as trespassers for privileges which we have heretofore peaceably enjoyed'. By 1779 the efforts to assert the Crown's rights had proved ineffectual, for despite having served several ejectments and brought three successful trials at Hereford 'the commoners have immediately prevented his [John Lewis, the agent] possessing the recovered land by throwing down their inclosure and claiming their common.' It will be recalled that, as was the case with the Morgans of Tredegar, this dispute over manorial rights was seen by the Lewis family as having possible damaging political repercussions.[101]

Encroachments onto wastes by cottagers were disliked by freeholders and their tenant farmers, and so landowners along with manorial lords were anxious to put a stop to such 'depredations'. Significantly, those same freeholders of the manors of Gower Supraboscus and Pennard who were challenging the duke of Beaufort's mineral and other rights in the seigniory of Gower, drew up a remonstrance in 1747 intended to be sent to the duke complaining of the 'numberless encroachments of the commons . . . by erecting multitudes of cottages and making divers enclosures thereon within a few years past'.[102]

Various responses to this colonization of the wastes by the poor were instituted. Thus freeholders, often in response to the complaints of their tenant farmers, banded together to throw down the cottages and small enclosures of the squatters, the latter in Cardiganshire and seemingly elsewhere believing, it was stated in 1797, 'that cottages erected on the waste with each a portion of land annexed to them cannot be pulled down'.[103] Given this notion it is not surprising that concerted efforts by landowners at throwing down enclosures were by no means invariably effective. In March 1759 William Owen of Porkington (Shropshire) was informed:

> There are great complaints made by your tenants of Dolbenmaen and Penmorva [Caerns.] against several cottages and enclosures erected lately on the common called Garn Dolbenmaen. I've waited on purpose upon Mr Wynne of Wern and Mr Lloyd of Gessel, who has a Right there, Mr Wynne said he had been to throw down some of them. But it proved to no purpose for they were soon repaired, and for that reason he thinks it better to have them indicted and he will join in it.[104]

Recourse to law against squatters, even if successful, did not guarantee a peaceful outcome, however, as the marquess of Bute's clerk, John Bird, found to his cost when proceeding after a legal hearing to take down twelve illegal cots and enclosures on Cardiff Heath in June 1799. Fierce resistance was encountered from the squatters, none more so than that offered by their wives, Bird's diary recording that 'the Women for some time acted the part of Amazonians, having armed themselves with Pitchforks, etc. etc.'[105]

Enclosure of common lands on the part of the burgesses in certain Welsh boroughs met with riotous opposition from the poor,[106] who justifiably felt cheated of their right of common. Carmarthen borough, especially, witnessed a number of disturbances, demolition of enclosures occurring in 1726, 1786 and late March 1789 when a mob broke down all the enclosures of the commons about the town.[107] Disputes occurred in other boroughs. Five labourers and one gentleman were indicted at the Glamorgan spring assizes 1768 for having on eleven separate occasions between 6 and 25 April 1767 entered a piece of ground in Swansea called Goat Street, otherwise 'the waste', in possession of the burgesses for the previous ten years, and destroyed the ground and removed the burgesses from their possession.[108] On occasion, substantial landowners would challenge the enclosing burgesses. Thus spring 1783 saw landowners possessed of estates about Caernarfon borough enter an agreement to be at joint expense in taking steps to preserve their right of common called Rhospadrual, enclosed by the corporation.[109]

Enclosure by Act of Parliament did not witness the same degree of friction and resort to rioting as occurred over encroachments onto the wastes by squatters. Rioting in Flintshire on 22–3 April 1793 over the Hope Enclosure Act of 1791 was exceptional not only for its violence but because the poor were allegedly incited by their leaders to 'murmur against all order and to be dissatisfied with their situation'. (If Thomas Lovett, influential estate agent in north Wales, is to be believed, it was exceptional, too, in that it was 'composed chiefly of Women and Children'.)[110] However, if actual violent resistance to parliamentary enclosure was rare, there may well have been much ill-feeling engendered.[111] Certainly this was the case with regard to the enclosure of Narberth and Templeton commons in 1787. Isaac Callen of Monkton parish, yeoman, swore an affidavit in early summer 1787 condemning the harshness of the main landowner-beneficiary of the Act, Mr Knox of Slebech: 'Oh! my heart does still ach for the oppression that people have suffer'd by the tyranny of the Irish wolf' (Knox was born in 1732 in Co. Monaghan) who had not 'the least right for such tyrannical barbarous proceedings . . . And the hard hearted wretch obliged 'em to put away all their sheep from these mountains.' Consequently, he averred, about eighty people had fallen ill, so that they could not labour to support themselves. Another strident critic was Thomas Davies of Narberth, gent., who had a case brought against him at the 1789 autumn assizes for Pembrokeshire for insinuating that the three local enclosure commissioners had acted 'illegally and unjustly' in the execution of their offices.[112]

6. *Militia Riots*

Militia riots occurred in late eighteenth-century English and Welsh communities following the Acts of 1757, 1762, 1769 and 1796.[113] Undoubtedly rural communities experienced financial loss and hardship arising from the militia laws. Thus in May 1778 it was claimed that the absence of Brecknock men serving in the militia meant that poor rates in their native county were mounting.[114] In the wake of the Act of 1769 which attempted to tighten up on defaulters,[115] a riot broke out in Chirk, Denbighshire, on 3 March 1770 on the occasion of a subdivision meeting for Chirk Hundred at which the constables were to prepare lists of all men fit to serve in the militia. Upon the constable of Llanrhaeadr-ym-Mochnant being called into the Hand public house -- where the magistrates

had convened the meeting – to present his list, the noisy 400–500-
strong mob gathered outside, armed with knotted ash clubs,
pitchforks and rakes, broke the window of the room occupied by
the magistrates and declared they would take away their lives if
they persisted in the execution of the warrants to ballot for militia
men. When the justices went outside to reason with the people their
efforts proved in vain. It fell to John Evans of Llanrhaeadr, a
blacksmith, to bargain with John Edwards of Glynn, Denbighshire, one of the magistrates, that the people should be given a
discharge from militia service for the remainder of the three years.
The matter did not rest there, however, for shortly afterwards
Thomas Roberts of the parish of Llanrhaeadr, 'after stating all the
hardships he and his neighbours had endured by the militia laws',
informed Edwards that a discharge for three years was not enough
and demanded they must have a discharge for ever. Upon Edwards
responding that under the law he could not permit this and exhort-
ing them to go home, they soon dispersed, but only after warning
that next time the authorities should meet for the purpose they
would come down with ten times the number and kill all of them.
During the course of the disturbance the militia lists from the
several parishes were forcibly taken from the constables and torn
into pieces or burned.[116]

Mobilization of the militia led to riots in Merioneth in 1779,
when in early summer about 300 to 400 people so abused the
magistrates and deputy lieutenants that they were unwilling to raise
the militia without having some regular troops or militia at their
disposal to keep the mob quiet.[117] The impassioned face-to-face
confrontation between people and magistrates that took place
during these latter riots at Chirk and in Merioneth, as on countless
other occasions, underlines the fragile equilibrium that obtained at
this time between deference and defiance.

As David Jones indicated, the 1790s saw a heightening of
hostility against balloting of men for the militia, for now the war
situation saw a merging of all the grievances against high taxation,
rising food prices, the Navy Act of 5 March 1795 and the Act of 11
November 1796 for augmenting the militia. On 1 April 1795 there
was a serious riot at Denbigh against the Navy Act and balloting
for the militia, when significantly the ringleaders were alleged to
be 'seditious men' seeking to stir up 'Discontent amongst the
Ignorant'. Later, in November and December 1796 anti-militia

disturbances broke out in Carmarthenshire, Merioneth and Flintshire. In these militia riots, as in the case of food riots, we often see,
as Bohstedt demonstrates, 'local political bargaining' being played
out. Riots, then, 'were quintessentially local politics'. Through
them the crowd sought instant relief from immediate pressures and
threats, and sought to exploit their close 'vertical' relationship with
local magistrates to rouse them into taking remedial action to
defend the community.[118]

7. Hostility to Strangers

Resistance in Welsh neighbourhoods was often directed at
'strangers' who were perceived as constituting a threat to order,
harmony and tradition in the community. One interesting manifestation of this was the fight between Welshmen and Englishmen
in Henllan parish near Denbigh on Sunday evening, 1 September
1754, the affray taking place during the journey home from Cappel
Wakes where people from the town of Denbigh and the parish of
Henllan had spent the day drinking. Some ritualistic posturing and
menacing behaviour preceded the 'promiscuous hott fight', in the
form of both sides holding sticks and staves above their heads,
shouting and bawling, and crying out 'Dinbech' (some using the
Anglicized 'Denbigh') and 'Henllan' respectively. In the subsequent
trial a Denbigh sawyer alleged that when he attempted to quieten
both sides, the Welsh people answered: 'We are not for [i.e. against]
the Denbigh people but for [against]the Englishmen.' A further
Denbigh witness, likewise attempting to cool tempers, addressed
the country people (allegedly in pursuit of the Denbigh contingent)
as follows: 'For God's sake be quiet, let the Strangers alone, for the
Factory people pay sixty pounds a week wages and the people
[meaning the Factory people] spend it all in the Country.' It is clear
that the resentment of the Welsh-speaking country people of
Henllan parish was aimed at the English strangers, the 'Factory'
people, of the neighbouring town.

The attempts at containing the situation failed. In the ensuing
mêlée John Ffoulke, a Henllan blacksmith, who had at the outset
declared 'he would have the Englishmen beaten before they went
from thence', was knocked down with a stick and subsequently
died from the wound. Perhaps of significance is the fact that in the

evidence taken from both sides not a single witness claimed to have seen who struck the mortal blow, the nearest form of identification using the following words: 'he was knocked down by a tall person who had a stick or stake in his hand and who then was either in his shirt or waistcoat without sleeves'.[119]

A. H. Dodd likewise reminds us how the north-east Wales colliers in the eighteenth century 'were ever resentful of the intrusion of strangers'. On 3 October 1776 riots broke out for half an hour on Harwood mountain when colliers objected to the employment of Englishmen in the collieries in the Wrexham district.[120] An unusual manifestation of this suspicion of and resistance to strangers was instanced in Dolgellau at the close of the eighteenth century when pandemonium broke out over the arrival there of a gentleman with a black servant. Such was the level of antagonism displayed towards the servant wherever he went by the townspeople on this their first experience of a coloured person in their midst that the two were forced to leave the place sooner than intended.[121]

8. Unruly Factions

The nature of the electoral system meant that eighteenth-century politics in Britain were shot through with violence in the form of the threat of eviction as a means of persuasion, physical intimidation of voters, and rioting.[122] Riots occurred at Llanidloes on 26 December 1721 in the build-up to the 1722 election for the Montgomery boroughs seat and at the Carmarthenshire election of the same year.[123] The most spectacular disorder arising from political faction, however, was to occur in Carmarthen borough at mid-century, the fierce struggle between Whigs and Tories there from 1746 culminating in the Tory-gentry-sponsored riots and mob violence of 1755, which reduced the town to fire, smoke and tumult.[124] Violence also frequently characterized borough politics, gentry factions paying scant attention to public order. Vanity and a prickly sense of parochialism meant that at least on one occasion local officials fell out in public over the area of their respective authority. Fair days were times of heavy drinking and often fighting, and in the evening of the Cardigan fair of 25 March 1729 a riot broke out in the street, several persons beating one another with cudgels. John Morgan Esq., a JP for Cardiganshire, required the Peace, and with the help of two other county magistrates attempted to seize the cudgel of the ringleader, Charles Thomas John, a yeoman of the town. The latter, resisting, was with the help of others conveyed to the gaol. But standing at the door was the deputy mayor, William Jones, mercer, who declared that nobody should put any man in gaol in his corporation, proceeded to rescue the prisoner and, upon the latter mounting a bench and brandishing a staff at the justices who had arrested him, took to 'embracing and caressing' him. Challenged a little later by Morgan to explain his conduct, Jones replied: 'No Justice shall intermeddle in my Corporation. I'll wipe his Commission in my Backside.' The riot went on for nearly another hour, and for half an hour none of the constables of the town intervened.[125]

9. Defiance of the Authorities

Public disorder was also manifested when neighbours came to the defence of one of their number who was being taken into custody by a local official. In Welsh communities as elsewhere society, we have noted, was in a very real sense 'ungovernable'. Certainly Prendergast on the outskirts of Haverfordwest then, as later, was something of a 'no-go' area for the authorities. The attempted arrest in late 1771 of one William White of Prendergast, butcher, to answer to a suit of debt brought at the Court of Exchequer by the prosecutor John Mathias, a farmer, with the help of special bailiffs, ended in failure. Following his arrest in a public house, the woman who kept it quickly raised a mob who surrounded the house and threatened to murder Mathias and the bailiffs 'and that their bones should be carried home in bags' if they attempted to arrest White. In the uproar the latter shouted that neither they 'nor all the devils in hell' should get him from thence and that 'Prendergast was not easily managed'. Frustrated on that occasion, a second attempt on Friday, 20 December 1771 at 4 a.m. to 5 a.m., backed by six special bailiffs and several other persons armed with guns, was likewise to no avail, the mob proving too strong for them.[126] Earlier, in March 1731, Edward Parry, a high constable of Bromfield Hundred in Denbighshire, having apprehended Phoebe Leadbeter, spinster, on suspicion of felony, was forcefully robbed of his prisoner and

knocked down by William Barber, whom he had just before
charged to assist him, Parry 'having a great mob of women about
him' at the time Barber attacked him. Women here were clearly
coming to the stout defence of their own gender. Nor did the Vale
of Glamorgan populace take kindly to the attempted committal in
May 1765 of Moll Goch, 'the common whore' about Llandaff, to
Cowbridge Bridewell; once she had stolen the commitment out of
Edward the Carrier's pocket, 'the mob rose in her part, and
Mobbed him out of Town'.[127]

Forestalling merchants and greedy farmers, government or local
officials attempting to interfere with smuggling and wrecking,
manorial lords reasserting their lapsed rights, freeholders and
tenant farmers insisting on guarding their rights to common land
against the encroachments of cottagers, all help to explain the
remarkable degree of public disorder at this time, an incipient
lawlessness often provoked and participated in by the ruling class.
A number of the riots constituted collective popular political
bargaining. In the light of such easy resort to physical violence and
to verbal threats, insults and downright saucy conduct on the part
of the lower orders, it is difficult not to conclude that deference
could not be taken for granted; it had to be earned and was quickly
withdrawn. Lawlessness was often fortified by drink, and at times
driven by passionate attachment to one political faction or
another, such friendship and reciprocal bonds embracing not just
gentlemen and lesser freeholders but tenant farmers and dependants in the entire neighbourhood. There was scant hope indeed of
any illegal acts being redressed by impartial justice when sheriffs,
who ran elections and decided on the composition of juries, were
the creatures of a clique. Much of the lawlessness sprang either
from painful hunger or from the wish on the part of freeholders
and peasantry alike to enjoy old usages, or from the urge among
overweening, vain gentry families to make trials of strength with
one another. Down to the 1790s there was no ideological
underpinning to speak of. Neighbourhood harmony, too, was
constantly disrupted by interpersonal violence and chronic levels of
theft, activities that will be examined in the next chapter.

Violent and Light-Fingered Neighbourhoods

In the absence of a police force, the responsibility for discovering the perpetrators of crime in a community and for prosecuting them through the courts fell to the victims themselves, their families and immediate circle of friends and neighbours. Such was the need felt for watching out for the comings and goings of others that we are justified in thinking in terms of a 'peeping tom', meddling society. Any behaviour on the part of individuals that seemed suspicious to others in a neighbourhood would immediately lead to searching questions being asked of the suspects along the lines of where they had come from, where and from whom they had come by a particular article in their possession and so on. It was this rich seam of neighbourhood information which was tapped by victims and their immediate circle when setting out to discover the identity of a thief, for instance. (In addition, basic detective work would be undertaken as looking for the track of a shoe.) Much face-to-face inquiry would be done among neighbours, local markets and fairs would be visited in the hope that someone had spotted something, and the loss might be cried in neighbouring churches and at open market, or the theft advertised in one or other of the English border newspapers which were widely read in Welsh communities. Once suspects were identified, the injured party would acquire a warrant to take them into custody with the help of a constable, and bring them before a magistrate. Not infrequently, the very process of capturing suspects met with violent resistance, sometimes with the help of neighbours.

It has been firmly established that for the British Isles as a whole those offences which were brought before the courts represented a mere fraction of the total number committed, for many went 'undetected or unreported by the victim'.[1] Apart from both the cost incurred and the practice of out-of-court settlements in deterring prosecutions, to some extent the problem was compounded by the neglect of duty on the part of parish constables to arraign offenders before the courts, a dereliction of duty in Cardiganshire

Table 7: Offences known to the Court of Great Sessions for eight Welsh counties

OFFENCES	1730	1735	1740	1745	1750	1755	1760	1765	1770	1775	1780	1785	1790	1795	1800
1. Violent offences															
Murder	1	7	3	7	3	6	4	5	3	10	7	1	1	1	6
Manslaughter	0	0	1	0	0	0	0	0	3	0	2	3	5	0	0
Infanticide	2	1	2	1	1	3	0	3	0	1	0	1	1	5	1
Assault and riot and assault	31	54	38	37	37	46	31	20	22	30	25	25	16	14	9
Assault against authority	1	2	0	0	1	0	0	0	2	2	0	4	2	3	2
Sexual assault	0	0	0	0	2	2	1	2	1	2	4	0	1	1	2
2. Property offences															
Larceny	32	33	35	48	38	65	27	35	47	41	19	53	50	25	86
Breaking, entry and theft	6	2	0	1	5	3	2	0	5	0	0	2	2	2	3
Burglary	1	4	5	2	7	2	0	3	2	3	1	5	10	3	3
Obtaining by false pretences	0	0	1	2	0	1	0	1	1	0	0	2	2	0	1
3. Food, militia and election riots	0	1	12	0	0	0	0	0	2	0	0	0	3	14	1
4. Other offences															
Forcible entry and assault	1	4	0	0	0	0	0	1	2	0	0	0	0	0	0
Breaking and entry	4	0	1	0	2	0	0	1	0	1	0	0	0	0	0
Unlawful entry	2	2	5	6	4	3	2	0	4	1	1	3	1	0	4
Damage to property	3	3	4	2	4	3	2	0	5	3	1	0	1	2	0
Arson	0	0	0	0	0	0	0	2	0	0	0	0	0	0	0
Uttering	0	1	0	2	0	0	0	3	0	2	0	0	0	1	0
Forgery and extortion	0	0	0	3	1	2	0	0	0	0	0	4	2	1	3
Sowing discord	1	2	1	0	0	3	0	1	0	0	0	0	0	0	0
Nuisance	0	0	4	0	0	3	3	0	1	0	0	1	0	0	1
Engrossing	1	0	0	0	0	0	0	0	0	0	0	0	0	0	0
Contempt of court and perjury	0	2	4	4	2	1	0	2	1	3	2	3	0	1	5
Bestiality	0	0	0	0	0	0	0	0	0	0	0	0	2	0	0
Livestock maiming	2	1	1	2	2	0	1	0	0	0	4	0	1	0	0
Rescue	0	0	3	2	2	1	1	1	4	0	4	2	3	0	0
Abuse of office	2	0	0	2	2	0	0	4	2	2	0	1	3	2	1
5. Sundry	1	6	9	4	2	3	1	3	5	1	1	6	5	2	2
		128	109	113	113	147	75	87	110	102	67	116	108	77	131

communities approved of by the general public: 'instead of condemning and punishing the constables for neglect of duty, their conduct was applauded, and the condonation of crime was well and highly appreciated by the masses.'[2] Bearing in mind this severe limitation on the usefulness of statistics of reported offences committed, I have classified in table 7 the offences (a small number of which were not indicted) known to the Great Sessions of eight Welsh counties for selected years between 1730 and 1800.[3] As these are the assize courts held twice yearly and concerned with serious crimes, the number of charges brought represent just a portion of all offences arraigned before eighteenth-century Welsh courts as a whole. Yet they are useful in depicting the relative incidence of the various crimes committed, and in suggesting the pattern of crime.

For much of this chapter, two prominent types of offences will be discussed that seriously disrupted social harmony, namely, violent offences and theft. So far as violent crimes were concerned, table 7 reveals that most comprised assault, and riot and assault, although murder, manslaughter, infanticide, assault against authority and sexual assault all took place to a small extent. Similarly most property offences (the taking of property) fell within the category of larceny, the others of breaking, entry and theft, burglary and obtaining by false pretences occurring far less frequently. That together violent and property crimes dominated the offences committed can be seen by calculating the ratios of each to the total number of offences known to the courts (see table 8).

Between them, generally comprising four-fifths of all the offences known to the Great Sessions to have been committed, on balance theft-of-property offences comprised the majority. While this dominance of theft among the various felonies in Welsh counties accords to some extent with the pattern elsewhere in Britain – where larceny, burglary, housebreaking, highway robbery, robbery and pickpocketing 'normally accounted for between two-thirds and three-quarters of prosecuted felony' in the various English assize circuit courts between 1550 and 1750[4] – there was a far higher level of assault offences known to the Great Sessions courts in Wales. It appears, nevertheless, that violent crimes in Wales were falling gradually towards the close of the eighteenth century, and, according to David Jones, the proportion of offences against the person 'remained low for a short while [down to the late 1820s] in the nineteenth century'.[5]

*Table 8: Ratios of violent and theft-of-property offences to total offences
known to the Great Sessions in eight Welsh counties, 1730–1800*

	Violent offences			Theft-of-property offences	
Year	No.	% of total offences	Year	No.	% of total offences
1730	35	38	1730	39	42
1735	64	51	1735	39	31
1740	44	34	1740	41	32
1745	45	37	1745	53	43
1750	44	39	1750	50	44
1755	57	39	1755	71	48
1760	36	48	1760	29	39
1765	30	34	1765	39	45
1770	30	27	1770	55	50
1775	45	44	1775	44	43
1780	38	57	1780	20	30
1785	34	29	1785	62	53
1790	26	24	1790	64	59
1795	24	31	1795	30	39
1800	20	15	1800	93	71

So far as these two categories of violent and theft-of-property
crimes brought as either presentments or indictments before the
various Quarter Sessions courts were concerned, they related exclusively to the two categories of assault/riot and assault and larceny,
the more serious and violent offences like murder, infanticide,
breaking, entry and theft and burglary going to the Great Sessions.
The scale of violence emerges even more emphatically from the
combined presentments and indictments before the Quarter
Sessions: at certain of the Denbighshire courts selected at five-yearly
intervals between the mid-1730s and 1800, the total of seventy-two
property offences was far outstripped by the 108 assault ones.[6] It is
important to note that, unlike the Great Sessions, at Quarter
Sessions the overwhelming number of offences were not to do with
violence or theft but rather with minor offences like failure to
upkeep roads and bridges and the illegal sale of alcohol.

1. Violent Crimes

The resort to violence was wholly in character with the bruising confrontational tone of eighteenth-century neighbourhoods, much of the criminal activity dealt with at the lower and higher courts pertaining to assault on persons and attacks on property like breaking of fences, arson and maiming of livestock. A reading of the eighteenth-century gaol files of the Great Sessions leaves the strong impression that this was a rough, brutal and unsqueamish society, in which men and women alike turned naturally to assaulting those who in any way offended them. For many, life was held cheaply. When on 20 May 1741 Eynon Harry, a customs officer, was violently beaten in Dinas creek (Pembs.) in attempting to apprehend the illegal carrying away of salt from an Irish vessel, he begged his life of his assailant Daniel William, 'notwithstanding which the said Daniel William gave him some strokes afterwards and so left him'. The hapless Harry later died on 24 June.[7]

Alcohol played an important part in sparking off a large number of the many brutal fights that took place between men, fighting as individuals or in groups. A significant number of fatal brawls took place in alehouses, both among the regular drinkers[8] and at organized public festivities held on their premises like a night of merrymaking and dancing, a wedding rejoicing or a goose-eating.[9] Fair nights also saw many fights in the streets, which sometimes, as in the case of alehouse quarrels, led to fatalities. For instance, Abergele (Denbs.) fair night on 20 August 1793 witnessed fighting on the street in the late evening, in which Shadrack Jones, a farm servant, was kicked to death.[10]

Gaol-file depositions reveal the cause of many fights, in which men, stripped to the shirt and sometimes naked, anxious to 'bang' or to 'try' with an adversary, occasionally beat one another to death, often with sticks. (An injury from a fight, even if not fatal, could physically disable a man to the point of preventing him from continuing in the practice of his trade.)[11] A fight sometimes erupted in an alehouse or at a fair in response to a man bragging of his fighting valour and flaunting himself as the champion.[12] Again, such provocations as impugning the honesty of another, settling an old grudge, advising a drinking companion not to abuse his wife, disputes touching payment for ale or over the ownership of a stave, and bad blood between rival suitors for the affections of a maidservant, would each serve to start a fight leading to a fatality.[13]

Men fought one another to death on other occasions too. Upon meeting with a group of men about 7 p.m. on his homeward journey from a wake at Llanidan (Denbs.) on 22 June 1729, Thomas Edwards of Ruthin, blacksmith, was asked jestingly whether he was returning early because of want of money or because he wanted his supper. The thin-skinned blacksmith's taking offence to such teasing led to words and then a fight with John Griffith, blacksmith of Llanfwrog, who beat Edwards over the head with a stick and killed him. Again, a quarrel on Easter Monday 1772 at Denbigh over payment for the loan of tools led to John Samuel (in drink) and Simon Salusbury stripping and fighting in a street, Samuel sustaining mortal injuries. As a final example of trivial irritations sparking brutal combat leading to death, Monday, 15 May 1780 saw John Jones and David David, both stripped in their shirts, quarrel on the Abergavenny–Brecon turnpike road over Jones's allegedly having broken some earthenware of David's sister, whereupon David, asking Jones if he would fight him, in the same breath struck Jones with his fist, causing his death on 25 May.[14]

Those indicted for murder following the death of an adversary in a fight or brawl were normally sentenced for manslaughter. Killings adjudged to be murder were far fewer. Desire for gain was the motivation for a number of murders. It was thus greed to lay his hands on his old uncle's money that drove Edward Morgan of St Mellon's parish (Mons.), labourer, to murder Rees Edward David of Llanfabon (Glam.), his wife and daughter in their beds on the night of 3 January 1757. Similarly, after drinking with a man in an alehouse during the morning of 16 March 1770 and noticing his purse, Henry Thomas of Ystradgynlais (Brec.), labourer, robbed and murdered him some way along the road to Pontardawe.[15]

Family quarrels and feuds between neighbours in some instances spilled over to murder. Barbarous, indeed, were the assaults committed by Thomas Athoe, recently mayor of Tenby and a prosperous tenant farmer of Manorbier (Pembs.), and his son, Thomas, upon their close kinsmen, brothers George and Thomas Marchant, likewise farmers in Manorbier, on their journeying home from selling cattle at Tenby fair on the night of 23 November 1722. So brutal were the assaults that George was killed, for which homicide both the Athoes were executed the following year in Surrey. At the root of Athoe senior's malice lay an earlier quarrel between one of the Marchants (his nephew) and the young Thomas Athoe, who sustained a beating. Advised to bring an action against Marchant, the 58-year-old Thomas Athoe senior replied, 'No, he would pay him his own coin.' In their defence the Athoes submitted a number of (perhaps spurious) injuries they had received from the Marchants: that they had detained an estate from them, that they had bought certain livestock out of their hands at the previous October Wiston fair, that they had opposed their elections to borough office in Tenby and, perhaps the root of the squabble between the cousins, George Marchant had married the sweetheart of young Thomas Athoe.[16] Bad blood between farming neighbours in the parish of Llanafan Fawr (Brec.) in the early 1780s led to the premeditated murder of Thomas Price on the hillside of Esgair-Nevill in that parish on the Monday morning of 31 October 1784. 'Worrying of his cattle upon the hill' had led the said Thomas Price to bring a legal action against his neighbours, the Lewis family of Argod, farmers and shepherds. So vengeful was Lewis Lewis senior in the wake of this that he incited his sons, Lewis and Thomas, to murder Price, the said Lewis the younger and a neighbour, Evan Davies, actually carrying this out, with Thomas acting as an accomplice. Honourably refusing to the end to implicate his vendetta-driven, selfish father, Lewis the younger was later hanged. Although the Lewis family were a rough lot of sheep-stealers, of whom their neighbours supposedly lived 'in perpetual fear', Thomas Price himself, according to his grandson, was 'a perfect villain on the hill' and 'it was no uncommon thing', he admitted, 'for Lewis Lewis the elder to find seven or eight of his sheep dead on the hill and placed head to tail in a row – killed by Price and his dogs.'[17]

Emotional entanglements, as in all eras, gave rise to a number of murders. Men visiting houses to court sweethearts on occasion met a violent death. One such victim was William Maurice of Llansilin (Denbs.), who, on visiting his lover, Catherine Thomas of Llan-rhaeadr on Sunday night, 29 July 1753, 'found he was not to be received that night, the said daughter having other lovers then with her', an examinant was informed. A quarrel thereupon erupting between him and David Maurice, a servant to Catherine's mother, led to the said David striking him from behind with a pole while on horseback, the blow knocking him off his mount and causing him to expire on 10 August. A similar fate befell Thomas Owens on the occasion of his visiting the house of Robert Prichard at Morton in the parish of Rhiwabon on Sunday night about Old Christmas, 1766, to court Elizabeth, the daughter. The latter's brother-in-law repeatedly struck him with his fist and asked him 'what business such a one as him had to come to see for her'. Owens had the consolation of the guiltless Elizabeth's remorse, but died on 20 June 1767.[18]

Men also occasionally murdered young females with whom they were emotionally involved. By first striking her over the head with a stick and then strangling her, Josiah Hugh of Pen-marc parish (Glam.), farm labourer, murdered Mary Rees sometime between 5 p.m. and 7 p.m. on 11 June 1755 when she was milking the sheep of her master, John Holland. Mary had once claimed that the said Hugh was constantly following her and that he had told her that if he could not have her he would end her or himself. Margaret Docker, spinster, housemaid at Wynnstay was told by her spurned suitor John Harris in mid-August 1778: 'If you won't have me I'll take care you shall have nobody else', and it was her belief that the attack he then made on her with an iron nail would have killed her had he not been interrupted by her mistress approaching. A young woman's pregnancy in certain instances led to her murder. In late September 1788, for example, Margaret Thomas, spinster, a servant of Evan Evans, farmer of Garreg Fawr in Ystradfellte parish (Brec.), was murdered by a fellow male servant, William Williams, whose child she was carrying, Williams being fearful of her intention of swearing the child before a magistrate. A similar harsh end lay in store for Margaret Matthews upon being made pregnant by Edward Pugh the younger, of Evenjob, who was indicted for strangling her on 28 August 1756 but found not guilty.[19]

Far more numerous, of course, as table 7 clearly reveals, were the assaults that did not result in the death of the victim. Assault, whether with fists, feet, clubs, sticks or guns, and sometimes along with it abuse with foul language, was carried out sometimes by a single person or at other times by many 'riotously assembled'. Men had no qualms about assaulting women. Particularly nasty in this respect was the attack by John Davies, glover, on the pregnant Sarah Jones, wife of a Carmarthen tailor, in Carmarthen market on Saturday, 27 May 1776, the said Davies, cursing and swearing, throwing down her standing on which she was displaying bread and cakes for sale and striking her in the belly, by which beating she claimed, one of the twins later delivered of her was born dead.[20] Sometimes the extent of the injury from assaults was appalling: one man's thumb was bitten off, another lost the sight of his left eye, while another had his nose totally destroyed.[21] The hatred inspiring some assaults, physical and verbal, and the fear of intended future harm being done them, led some to pray for sureties of the peace against the menacing assailant.

Assault had many diverse causes. Eviction from a farm sometimes led to an attack on the party attempting to expel the occupant under notice. When Joseph Richards of Merthyr parish (Carms.), gent., entered his farm of Cwm on 29 September 1787 in order to gain possession and to hand it to a new lessee, he was attacked by Thomas Mathias with a hatchet and kicked on the ground by both Mathias and his wife, who declared they would never deliver up the farm.[22] We have earlier observed that driving of cattle to a common pound could lead to assault.[23] Again, assault sometimes preceded theft. Two labourers from Aberafan parish (Glam.) assaulted James Curson and William Todd in Baglan parish on 28 October 1755, first accosting them (in Welsh), 'Stand God damn you, I want your money', and then 'violently assaulting them with intent to rob them'. Charles Ellis, farm servant, was returning home from an alehouse in Gresford (Denbs.) with a drinking companion in the early hours of the morning of 2 December 1776 only to be attacked by him with stick and knife and then robbed of a silver watch.[24]

Disputes between neighbours occurred for all manner of reasons, some predictably boiling over into assault. The quarrel between Elizabeth Brown of Ruabon, widow, and Peter Magloughlen of Rhiwabon, tanner, and his wife, over putting bread in an oven common to them both which occurred in summer 1741 promptly led to Elizabeth's collier family the next day breaking into the Magloughlen's house and assaulting them, Sarah Pierce, Elizabeth's sister, 'with her knees upon her [Mrs Magloughlen's] belly and beating her as hard as she could'.[25]

Frequent assaults, too, were made upon officers of the law like constables, bailiffs and customs officers and those charged with accompanying them in the performance of their duties, signifying that if the local neighbourhood objected to certain actions and recourses on the part of the authorities as in their perception unjust, then the community stoutly resisted.[26] Assaults took place on those attempting to take people into custody, family, friends and neighbours forcibly releasing the captive.[27] In this category, one such person sometimes released from his captors by others in the community was the father of an illegitimate child. When John Hughes, a Wrexham tailor, was arrested by an overseer of the poor on 9 January 1766 as the sworn father of a bastard child to be born of Jane Jones of the parish of Caerwys (Flints.) in order to indemnify the said parish where the baby would become chargeable, his custodian was assaulted by John Hughes, the elder, tailor, and three others including a widow, thereby securing his freedom.[28] A constable and overseer ventured on a similar mission in mid-July 1751 in search of John Wynne of Ystrad, parish of Llanrhaeadr (Denbs.), and, having him in their custody, called at an alehouse on their way to bringing him before a magistrate. There they were assaulted, significantly on account of being 'strangers'. The local community attempted to rally round their own, and one of its members, a miller, upon being told of the official status of the custodians, retorted that 'he did not care what they were'.[29] Officials were also sometimes attacked when attempting to evict from farms or to distrain on goods either for arrears of rent or for debt. John Ralph of Wrexham, for instance, in accompanying on 1 June 1754 the constable of Stansty (Denbs.) to assist him in taking into custody William Parry and his wife of Stansty, tenants of a farm owned by Peter Edwards, for their earlier resistance to their landlord's distraining on them for rent arrears, was struck by Parry with a spade and wounded with a halberd. Similarly, officials attempting to serve notice of eviction or of impending actions to be brought against individuals in the courts were targets for attack. For example, after David Thomas of Cardigan, yeoman, employed by one of the attorneys of the Pembrokeshire Great Sessions in early 1743 to deliver a notice of actions to be brought in the forthcoming spring Great Sessions against Lewis Thomas, farmer, of Llanfyrnach parish (Pembs.), had left the notices on a rail in the barn in the presence of two farm servants and was setting off homewards, he was attacked with clubs by a pursuing group comprising Lewis Thomas's wife and son, the two aforementioned farm servants and two other women, the three women standing at a distance shouting, 'Kill him or make him come back to eat the paper.'[30]

We have seen that magistrates were assaulted during eruptions of public disorder. But even in less highly charged moments they were quite often verbally insulted or even physically assaulted in the execution of their office. Over the course of the eighteenth century a number of individuals were ordered to appear before the Denbighshire Quarter Sessions to answer for such abusive behaviour, as, for example, was Edward Bennion of Ruabon, wood collier, for insulting John Yale Esq. in the performance of his duties on 12 June 1769. Seemingly Yale was an unpopular justice, for in late summer of that year he received three incendiary letters threatening to take his life if he did not leave 'justice business'. Similarly, William John Probert was ordered to appear before the Breconshire Great Sessions of spring 1751 to answer for having behaved himself before justice Owen Evans Esq. on 19 May 1750 'in a very impudent, insulting . . . manner highly abusing and reflecting on the authority of the said Owen Evans during the execution of his office'. Emphasizing the non-class nature of such anti-magistrate abuse and defiance, gentlemen themselves sometimes objected to the behaviour of certain justices. Upon Sir Humphrey Howorth's committing Jeremiah Watkins, gent., of Newchurch parish (Rads.) in 1741, the latter had said in his presence that 'that was not the first time he had been wrongfully committed by some of the family'. Howorth had likewise so upset Thomas Johnson of Llangoed Castle (Brec.), clerk, that the latter challenged him on Sunday 1 June 1740 immediately after Divine Service in the churchyard of the parish of Aberllynfi to meet him in Dderrow Wood the following Tuesday at 5 a.m. to fight with pistols. Again, Denbighshire Trinity Quarter Sessions for 1728 ordered that Robert Lloyd, gent., of Maesaimod, 'having given approbrious language in this court', be put in gaol.[31]

Although the great majority of assaults in early modern Wales, as in England, were committed by men, reference to table 9 reveals that women were also not infrequently indicted for this offence. Of the total of 834 people presented before our selected counties' assizes in the sample years between 1730 and 1800 for assault or riot and assault, some 745 (89 per cent) were men and eighty-nine (11 per cent) women. Sometimes the women were found to have acted in the company of men, in certain instances their husbands;

Table 9: Number of people by gender known to eight Welsh assize courts, 1730–1800, as having committed crimes of violence

	1730		1735		1740		1745		1750		1755		1760		1765		1770		1775		1780		1785		1790		1795		1800	
	m	f	m	f	m	f	m	f	m	f	m	f	m	f	m	f	m	f	m	f	m	f	m	f	m	f	m	f	m	f
Murder	0	1	7	2	3	0	9	0	4	1	5	1	4	0	5	3	3	0	11	0	6	1	0	1	0	1	1	0	6	1
Manslaughter	0	0	0	0	1	0	0	0	0	0	0	0	0	0	0	0	3	0	0	0	3	0	3	0	4	0	0	0	0	0
Infanticide	0	2	0	1	0	2	0	1	0	1	1	2	0	0	0	6	0	1	0	1	0	0	0	1	0	1	0	5	0	1
Assault and riot and assault	70	6	100	13	56	4	73	5	49	4	82	14	51	3	41	11	36	11	45	4	37	5	52	7	19	0	18	1	16	1
Assault v. authority	1	0	19	0	0	0	0	0	0	0	0	0	0	0	0	0	11	0	2	0	0	0	9	1	5	1	50	2	6	1
Sexual assault	0	0	0	0	0	0	0	0	3	0	2	0	1	0	2	0	1	0	2	0	5	0	0	0	1	0	1	0	2	0

at others they acted without them, either individually or with other women. Thus in the sample, of the eighty-nine women presented for assault, thirty-five acted on their own or with others of their own sex, while fifty-four were in mixed groups. Assaults were made by them on both men and other women. A particularly violent case of this last description was the assault made on Mary Price on 6 March 1748 in the parish of Wrexham Abbot (Denbs.) by Anne Williams, a labourer's wife, Mary expiring on 15 March from the beating she got with a stick.[32] Although the indictment was found a true bill, the jury returned a verdict of not guilty, an inclination to leniency on this as on many other occasions we shall observe later.

Furthermore, as the aforementioned attack on David Thomas of Cardigan reveals, women sometimes incited men to violence. To cite a further instance, upon the refusal of John Ellis of Wrexham, yeoman, on 16 March 1754 – having been entrusted by Peter Edwards to watch over the distrained goods of his aforementioned tenant, William Parry, stored in the barn – to leave the building at Parry's request, William Parry's wife said to her husband, 'God damn him fall upon him and force him out', which he then proceeded to do. Nor is it unlikely that the women crowding round the earlier-mentioned Edward Parry, Bromfield's high constable, in March 1731 upon his taking up Phoebe Leadbeter, suspected of felony, were not instrumental in urging on William Barber to attack the friendless constable, releasing the prisoner in the process.[33]

Although, as in English regions, women in Wales (see table 9) were involved in far fewer homicides than men (thirty-seven against seventy-six),[34] a form of homicide peculiar to women was in-fanticide, one of the saddest manifestations of female insecurity and vulnerability in the early modern period. That newborn babies were more frequently got rid of than the small number of court cases would suggest is hinted at in the grisly entry of the Denbighshire Trinity Quarter Sessions, 1795: 'Account of costs of a search of all pools in a place in the parish of Ruthin for bodies of children supposed to have been thrown there'. Young unmarried women sometimes became pregnant before marriage as a consequence of the system of trial marriages discussed earlier, and any faltering in resolve to form a permanent union on the part of the father pushed young women to extremes because of their awareness of the dire consequences that would follow. Again, as in

English regions, many young women were servants, and as such enjoyed a relatively large degree of freedom to form sexual relationships.[35] An unmarried pregnant woman knew that once discovered she would be turned out of her present service or lodging place and, hounded by parish officials anxious to establish a place of her settlement, stood a chance of being sent out of the parish. Moreover, they may in some cases have been afraid of the shame they would bring on themselves and their families. In January 1788 Magdalen Bowen of Llywel (Brec.) threw her child into a pool near the River Senny 'being afraid of her father and mother'.[36] Small wonder that concealment of the pregnancy and ultimate doing away with the infant were often attempted.

Rumour and gossip about a girl's condition were open and rife in the neighbourhood, the more so upon her adamantly denying her pregnancy. Yet to disown a suspected pregnancy was of no avail, for it seems that the suspicion of it would lead to her dismissal from service or being turned out of a lodging house.[37] When Jane Edwards went to lodge in early 1742 with John Rowland and his wife at Trebrys in the parish of Llanrhaeadr-ym-Mochnant (Denbs.), having been recently dismissed from service in a neighbouring farmhouse in the same parish on the grounds, I suspect, of her pregnancy, the said John, hearing of the neighbourhood's suspecting her to be with child, warned her that she should not continue in his house but that he would take her to the parish officers unless she would own up to her pregnancy and name the father (who turned out to be a fellow servant in her last employment). She denied it, saying she would trouble him no further and, a little later, upon giving birth to the infant under a hedge, she proceeded to throw the male child into a bog. Returning to the Rowlands' home she found the door closed against her, the meat she had requested was handed to her through a window, and she was refused admittance till some neighbouring women came to charge her with having been delivered of a child.[38]

Although in Jane's, as in all other like cases, the consequences of having a bastard child were so daunting as to make concealment and doing away with the infant a risk worth taking, there was little chance of escaping the watchful eye of a suspicious neighbourhood. Jane's attempts at concealment were of no avail. We can only sympathize with Jane Evan of Tŷ yn y Felin in the parish of Cerrigydrudion (Denbs.) who on Monday, 14 March 1768 was to be pursued by an angry neighbourhood. They had noticed that on the previous Thursday, 10 March, she left home about 9 a.m. and did not return till the evening of the following day, and suspected she had been delivered of a child. On the morning of 14 May she had gone to the home of Jane Roberts for a drag load of turf,

> and on observing a great number of people coming towards her she drove the horse through a little river with the drag and endeavoured to make her escape but she was soon overtaken by this informant's [Jane Roberts'] servant and the [church] warden and brought to Ty yn y Felin

where certain women, upon examining her, concluded that she had recently given birth.[39]

The neighbourhood was ever watchful of young unmarried women because they, along with widows, constituted a threat to the social harmony and stability of a community. The model female was the one who married and produced children within wedlock.[40] If under this watchful, intrusive regime an unmarried female was suspected of being pregnant, the neighbourhood became agitated lest marriage should fail to take place and the abandoned pregnant woman should produce a bastard offspring that became a burden on the parish rates. Servants, enjoying much freedom for sexual relationships as we have seen, and having unmarried status, were particularly scrutinized on this score. Their attempts at concealment only served to heighten the resentment of the locality, for this, in turn, frustrated detection of the father and thus the neighbourhood's ability to secure itself against an extra unwelcome charge on the rates. When suspicion ripened that the suspected-pregnant female had given birth privately (to the extent that some had their babies out of doors and, in one instance in Clyro (Rads.) in a cow house) and murdered the infant, a search for the body was got under way, for the neighbourhood was anxious to prosecute for murder, Jackson argues, partly at least in order 'to deter women from producing bastards and from burdening the parish in the future'. It is this which can explain why at considerable time and expense to themselves the neighbourhood prosecuted even when they knew the chance of conviction was low.[41] As in English areas so, too, in Welsh ones, juries very rarely returned a verdict of guilty, their reluctance no doubt stemming from humanitarian motives.[42]

Reference to table 7 reveals that a very small number of assaults were sexual ones, mainly attempted or actual rape of women and, in some instances, young girls. With regard to the latter, in one horrible instance a 'Mr Jones' was found guilty at the Brecknock Great Sessions in autumn 1791 of raping a six-year-old girl, Catherine Wilkins. That the neighbourhood was outraged is reflected in the fact that the same David Jones the younger of Llanwrthwl parish (Brec.), gent., accused three farmers of his parish on 9 August 1791 with having recently threatened 'to quarter and draw [him] to pieces and to drag him into the river'.[43]

Women were raped in different settings, but certain assaults and ravishings had similar backgrounds. Farm servants were vulnerable when going into fields either to milk cows or to fetch them home for milking. Twenty-year-old Mary *verch* Thomas, spinster, servant to Jane Williams in the town of Ruthin, was on 10 November 1728 going to milk her mistresses' cows kept in the outskirts of the town when Thomas Dennis and John Francis, local men, each several times raped her in a field. In similar vein, Elizabeth Jones, spinster, servant of John Hughes of Park Eyton (Denbs.), was raped in summer 1770 by a neighbouring farmer, John Jones, on the way to fetching cows home. Jones was fortunate in his friends, for through the influence of her mistress and the local magistrate, the Revd J. Yale, she was persuaded to make matters up and to refrain from prosecuting him.[44] The custom of 'sending' people to show them the way was, again, the occasion for rape. Hannah Sargeant of Gwersyllt (Denbs.), a young girl, was raped on 15 February 1781 when (at her master's bidding) showing Stephen Taylor the road from her house to the turnpike. Significantly, once again, she did not immediately tell her father and mother for 'she was afraid . . . lest they should beat her'.[45] Similarly, in the event of sending him out of the town of Builth on 24 December 1774, Anne Williams of that town, a candle and lantern in her hand, only narrowly escaped being raped in a pigsty by William Price of Merthyr parish, tailor, through a passer-by coming to her rescue.[46] Although the instances I have cited involved spinsters, some of the victims were married.[47]

So far as family discipline was commonly enforced by physical means, with men beating their wives and children for misbehaving, a certain level of domestic violence was communally accepted as the natural order of things.[48] When deemed appropriate, the community had its own informal means of dealing with family quarrels and violence in its shaming rituals and by the balm applied through the intervention of neighbours.[49] Even so, there was domestic violence in a few instances of sufficient seriousness to warrant resort to the courts. Husbands were prosecuted for violence to their wives, even for murder in a number of isolated cases, as when Thomas Edwards of Llangollen (Denbs.), barber, was indicted for stabbing to death his schoolteacher wife, Maria, in front of her pupils, children under the age of eight, on 4 March 1739. Allegedly the couple had quarrelled frequently in the past, Edwards violently beating and abusing her. According to the pupils, he was angry that the pork he was eating was not sufficiently roasted and flung it into the ashes before going on to attack his wife with a knife.[50] In one case at least, domestic violence led to suicide. Margaret Crynfryn's detestation of her husband, Lewis, of Crickhowell (Brec.), came to a head in a row on the night of 12 June 1755 both outdoors and then in the house in the hearing of their frightened children. After accusing him of being a thief and a coward, that he wouldn't 'stand before a man but beat or abuse a woman', she shortly afterwards took her own life.[51]

Domestic disputes sometimes led to battered wives seeking sureties of the peace against their violent husbands. Two at least who did so were abandoned wives. Kathrine Roberts of Denbighshire at different times in the fifteen years before 1743, and Emilia Obrien of Tenby in 1787 and 1788 had to put up with deserting husbands returning to the family home and proceeding to beat and abuse them. Suspicion of infidelity lay at the root of Joseph Studley's (of Pentre'r-felin, Denbs.) violence to his wife, which led to her seeking sureties of the peace; only three months after their marriage in January 1727 he had begun to call her a whore and a bitch and to commence beating her.[52]

No doubt drink caused many such domestic quarrels. Bickering in the household of John David, miller of Llangwyllog parish (Angl.), late on the fateful Saturday night of 11 January 1735 followed a day's drinking by the miller at a local alehouse. Fetched home by his wife, he was heard to say that he must go to work in his mill to escape his wife's 'peevish language' and, irritated with the help she received from the maidservant, Margaret Thomas, and voicing his annoyance that 'two lazy Judies of you do very little', he insisted on the said Margaret accompanying him and his male servant to the mill, once there pushing the hapless maidservant for letting the candles fall from a window, whereby she fell to a lingering death.[53]

In this patriarchal society, the stern rule of the father over the children could erupt into undue violence. Thirteen-year-old John Lloyd's attempt to breach a barrel of small beer on 11 December 1770 led to his father, Robert, farmer, of Morton (Denbs.), berating him for his misbehaviour and striking him on the head so hard with a rake that a surgeon was needed to attend the wound.[54]

Some in the community, males and females alike, were quarrelsome and sowers of discord between neighbours. Presentment by grand juries at the Great Sessions of 'common barrators' was the neighbourhood's way of dealing with its worst wranglers. Such offenders in Radnorshire at mid-century were Hannah Jones of Presteigne, widow, prosecuted by John Thomas with the backing of eight witnesses as 'a common scold and disturber of the peace', and Winifred Lewis of Rhayader, spinster, presented for being an 'idle, turbulent, quarrelsome and a disorderly person and used and accustomed to upraid and disturb the peace of her neighbours'. Similarly, Richard Thomas of Llanddewi Brefi parish (Cards.), yeoman, and Morgan Richard of Llanbadarn Odwyn parish in the same county were both presented at the Cardiganshire Great Sessions in spring 1764 for being common barrators.[55]

Malicious damage against another person's property out of revenge for an actual or an imagined hurt was yet another manifestation of the easy resort to violence in the rural world. Arson, committed as much by women as men, if rare, was one such offence.[56] We have earlier shown (in chapter 6) that people harbouring a deep resentment against someone else entering a tenancy they themselves desired sometimes put outbuildings and corn belonging to the farm concerned to the torch. Other occasions of strife led to fires. A row with Thomas Roberts of Ffrithddu in Caerhun parish (Caerns.), farmer, on 25 January 1797 was sufficient to induce Mary Williams of that parish to set fire to a stack of hay of his that night, while the nasty, vengeful John James was presented in 1783 for setting alight John Bevan's house in Brecknock allegedly because he had assisted Ann Pugh against him in obtaining administration of her son's effects.[57] Once again, a romantic entanglement could drive a hurt party to take revenge through arson. Elizabeth Owen, servant girl of Humphrey

Williams of Whaern-ddu in Llantrisaint parish (Angl.), whose unborn child she was carrying, upon discovering her master's courting Ellin Owen of Pensherri in Llanfaelog parish, set off from Whaern-ddu on Sunday, 20 October 1799, and at dusk set fire to the corn ricks of her rival at Pensherri.[58]

Revenge, too was occasionally visited by the heinous crime of maiming of livestock. James Elias of Gelli-gaer parish (Glam.), labourer, with an accomplice, maimed a heifer belonging to Jenkin Thomas of the same parish on the night of 17 October 1738 because he had been the occasion of his spending money at law. Again, the aforementioned unsavoury arsonist John James also stooped to cattle maiming, destroying James Morgan's cattle in a beast house at Cwmpenllech (Brec.) in summer 1782 out of pique that Morgan had not fallen for a deception he attempted to play on him over a missing sheep.[59]

Damage was done to property in other forms such as breaking down hedges and fences of closes, destroying man-made water courses supplying water corn mills, breaking into property and cutting down trees, forcefully entering land and putting cattle to consume the corn and grass, and destroying boundaries between farms. If, as yet, but a darkening cloud on the horizon, turnpike gates, too, were destroyed in a few instances in Radnorshire, Breconshire and Flintshire from the 1760s. (Meanwhile in Denbighshire, two instances occurred in 1766 of a vicar and gentleman respectively forcibly taking a team through a turnpike gate at Llangollen without payment.)[60]

2. Theft

Besides physical assault and violence to property out of revenge, theft of property, as revealed in table 10, was frequent in both the deep countryside and in market towns and villages. Fairs and markets in the latter were, indeed, obvious places for light fingers to get to work, often through stealing from standings or booths. Thieves hung about alehouses, too, where goods were often pilfered from drinkers and lodgers alike, the task rendered the easier by virtue of the fact that lodgers frequently slept in the same chamber, indeed commonly sharing the same bed. Besides, the stables or storehouses of inns were places where vendors deposited

Table 10: Property offences known to Great Sessions in eight Welsh counties

	1730		1735		1740		1745		1750		1755		1760		1765		1770		1775		1780		1785		1790		1795		1800	
	m	f	m	f	m	f	m	f	m	f	m	f	m	f	m	f	m	f	m	f	m	f	m	f	m	f	m	f	m	f
Theft	30	11	30	12	42	1	51	12	35	6	60	15	22	8	29	10	73	7	44	7	18	3	63	9	44	13	19	7	70	26
Breaking, entry and theft	5	2	2	0	5	0	5	1	36	0	3	1	3	0	0	0	4	1	0	0	0	0	2	0	2	0	1	1	3	2
Burglary	1	1	5	0	3	1	0	2	7	2	1	1	0	0	2	1	2	0	3	1	1	0	7	0	7	3	2	1	3	4
Obtaining by false pretences	0	0	0	0	1	0	2	0	0	0	1	0	0	0	0	0	0	0	0	0	0	0	2	0	3	0	0	0	0	1
Total	36	14	37	12	51	2	58	15	78	8	65	17	25	8	31	11	79	8	47	8	19	3	74	9	56	16	22	9	76	33

their goods during the times of fairs. Some of those robbed at markets and fairs and in alehouses or upon leaving the latter were the victims of pickpockets. Another common place for thieving was the loft or outhouse of a farm comprising the sleeping quarters of the male farm servants, whose possessions presented somewhat easy targets for fellow servants and outsiders. They certainly did so for John Davies of Rhiwabon, labourer, who in summer 1728 was said to be one that 'used to go to chambers where young men used to lye out of the house and take from thence some clothes'.[61] Not only did servants pinch from one another; well placed to notice what was to be had on the premises, they sometimes stole money and goods from their employers, their occasional abrupt departure from the farm drawing natural suspicion upon themselves. By the same token, they were able to tip off family and friends as to what was on the premises worth stealing, as did Alice Thomas, servant at Merrixton farm, Amroth parish (Pembs.), whose information led to the theft of corn and geese on the night of 27–8 January 1790.[62] On a few occasions, too, knowledgeable past servants returned to steal from the premises of their erstwhile employers, in one such instance the servant having been recently discharged.[63] More than once, servants naively gave themselves away by purchasing new fineries clearly beyond their normal means or by wearing clothes they had stolen. Again, the fact that at busy seasons like harvest all the farm household would be at work in the fields meant that the empty farmhouse posed an irresistible temptation to the thief. Similarly, robberies were carried out during the known absence of families at Divine Worship on Sundays or, in the case of Rebecca John Harry of Llandeilo Fawr parish (Carms.), while she was out for the day on 20 February 1781 at Llandeilo fair.[64] Craftsmen were inclined to filch one another's raw materials, sometimes a one-time apprentice having set up on his own returning to steal from his former master. New developments, too, in industrial workings and by way of the big expansion of shops in towns offered widening temptations and opportunities for theft.

Theft in the community, as shown in table 11, covered a wide range of items including cattle, sheep, horses, corn, turnips, butter, cheese, meat, wool, timber, coal, farm implements, cloth, clothes, household utensils, fineries like jewellery and silk handkerchiefs, money and much besides. Although the motivation for stealing is difficult to ascertain, the reasons are sometimes volunteered in the depositions

Rough and Rebellious Communities

Table 11: Categories of theft known to the Great Sessions in eight Welsh counties

		1730	1735	1740	1745	1750	1755	1760	1765	1770	1775	1780	1785	1790	1795	1800
Livestock	sheep	10	4	5	17	18	11	8	3	21	19	7	6	6	11	20
	horses	2	2	3	1	2	6	2	4	4	4	0	11	8	1	4
	cattle	1	0	1	6	0	0	0	0	0	0	2	6	2	1	3
Food		1	6	1	1	3	3	3	1	3	2	0	5	4	1	10
Household goods		7	5	5	4	2	7	0	3	3	2	3	4	11	2	9
Clothing		2	4	4	3	6	6	1	3	4	1	0	2	7	5	13
Crops		1	1	1	0	0	1	1	2	1	1	0	2	4	1	9
Implements		0	0	0	1	2	0	0	0	1	1	1	0	1	0	0
Personal effects		6	5	14	9	8	8	9	10	10	10	1	10	7	3	6
Metal		0	0	1	1	0	6	1	1	0	0	0	0	1	0	4
Timber		0	0	0	0	0	0	0	3	1	0	2	0	0	0	1

and confessions sworn before magistrates. On occasions, theft was committed out of a sense of grudge. Upon being asked in mid-1748 by a companion why he had just taken from a part of the Black Mountain in Hay parish (Brec.) two white sheep belonging to William Gwyn Vaughan Esq., Thomas Prosser of Shephouse (Brec.) replied that they 'were the sheep of a person that made me spend a great deal of money'. William Roberts ran away from his service with David Foulkes Esq. of Gwerneigron in St Asaph parish (Flints.) on 16 November 1735 taking with him his livery clothes and a hat, because he was 'so severe to him that he could not serve his said master'. Found drunk at his farm work on 22 January 1766, Thomas Parry, hired by the week, was ordered by his employer Samuel Woodhouse, farmer, of St John's parish (Glam.) to go to his room and sleep, but instead he went there and took away a number of goods.[65]

A craving for drink, too, could drive a man to steal money. Foulk Williams filched money from a farm servant, William Roberts of Bodlyman in the parish of Betws-yn-Rhos (Denbs.) on 24 January 1733 in order to buy ale in Glascoed. Again, after drinking for some time with Evan Jones in late September 1765 in an alehouse in Radnorshire, Evan Evans suggested they should go home, having spent enough money on drink, but Jones replied: 'No boy, I have 6d. more to spend before we go, I shall not want 6d. soon. I know where to have one after this is gone.' By this he meant the £16 in the bedchamber of his master and mistress at Vedow house in Glasgwm parish (Rads.), a sum he later stole on 15 October. Similarly, in spring 1783 David Prytherch, labourer, was drinking at a public house in the parish of Llanhamlach in Brecknock, 'and being short of money' he recollected that there was a large brass pan in a kiln at Blaenant in Llanfigan parish in the same county, 'which he resolved to steal which he did at night-time'. A poor man with wife and family, John Basset of Denbigh, weaver, stole from the poor box in Denbigh church in the early hours of Easter Monday 1728, in all likelihood in order to get money to drink. The previous Good Friday or Easter Eve he had attempted unsuccessfully to pawn his wife's bodice for 3s. at a Denbigh inn, declaring he wanted the money to buy bread for his children. On Easter Monday morning, however, he was drinking at a public house in Henllan village, while later in the evening he was to be found with a friend in a Denbigh public house, refusing to return with his wife who had come to fetch him home.[66]

People sometimes stole, too, to enable them to move away from their home area. Elizabeth Roberts of Llangoed parish (Angl.), spinster, claimed that she stole a sum of money from a leather cutter's house on 25 September 1784 because, pregnant by Henry Humphreys and being threatened by the parishioners of Llangistyn, where she lived, with being turned out of the parish, she decided she needed money to be able to leave Anglesey with her partner and go to some place where they would not be molested. Similarly Edward Brees of Llangedwyn (Denbs.), yeoman, who had stolen money on 20 December 1750 from a local shop, said that he had done so because he had been teased by his father for not going abroad to seek for work, and that he wanted money to carry him away. Again, fifteen-year-old Thomas Williams of Llanaber (Mer.) stole a horse off the mountain on 20 August 1764 with the intention of selling it to raise the money to carry him to Liverpool.[67]

Sheer necessity born of poverty was a powerful impetus behind a significant amount of theft in these years. Upon being charged with unlawfully entering the house of John Lloyd Esq. of Vachdeilog on Saturday night, 17 December 1737, Gaynor Thomas of Llanfrothen parish (Mer.) stated that being over-hungry, she entered the premises 'only for a bit of meal' which she set out on the dresser to eat but was then discovered. It was his family's wanting meat which drove William Pritchard of Glasbury parish (Brec.), labourer, to steal two pigs from the sty at Gwernevett in 1738. In evidence given on 22 December 1740 concerning sheep-stealing in

Denbighshire, Samuel Walker alleged that John Parry had told him that he and his namesake father, a cobbler, 'had gone out and catched four sheep at a time and they would bring the best two home, and if they had not done so they might have starved for there was no work to be had'. It was his want of meal, of which he stole five quarts, that drove Hugh Owen of Llanddeusant (Angl.), tinker, to break into a house in Llanrhuddlad parish on 8 October 1744. Charged with taking pieces of iron from the shop at the mill at Esclusham (Denbs.) in 1758, Evan Williams confessed that he was 'in great need and distress'. Upon being taken up by a constable for theft of beef from the house of Anne Parry, widow, of Llanfydd parish (Denbs.) on the night of 22–3 January 1764, Thomas Griffith, labourer, confessed upon his knees that he had stolen the beef, 'and that his poverty had occasioned it'.[68] Edward John was convicted of sheep-stealing at Merioneth spring assizes for 1793 and his execution was fixed for 13 May, but a last-minute petition of 12 May comprising ninety-eight signatures of the leading citizens of the county miraculously procured a conditional pardon. Significantly, the petition urged: 'That the said Prisoner was tried and convicted at the last Great Sessions held at Bala . . . of stealing one Sheep . . . That it appear to us, that the said convict having a Wife and Children was pressed by extreme want and Poverty to commit the said offence.'[69]

Nor can there be much doubt that the theft of small coals from coalworks by men and women alike and theft of timber were a necessary form of self-help on the part of the poor. Difficult conditions for the lower orders in the last years of the 1730s thus accounted for Griffith Parry's observation from Clenenney (Caerns.) to William Owen at Porkington (Salop) on 11 December 1738: 'the writer is hard pressed to prevent "Glyn Wood" from being all stolen for fuel this winter.' Again, theft of turnips among the poor was so rife in south Pembrokeshire and in Anglesey at the close of the century that farmers simply would not grow them.[70]

Dislike of strangers, of foreigners, has already been encountered. Such was the antipathy shown to Scottish packmen and travelling Jews among the natives of the Vale of Glamorgan that they were often robbed and occasionally murdered. March 1765 and April 1784 saw travelling Jews robbed in the Vale. At least they escaped with their lives, no such clemency being shown to four Scotsmen in the Vale who, on separate occasions, were murdered in the first six decades of the eighteenth century. Similar fates befell two Scottish pedlars in Montgomeryshire in 1735, both murdered by an ale seller of Llanfair Caereinion parish who afterwards stole their possessions.[71]

The problem of theft in Welsh neighbourhoods in the later decades of the century was giving rise to sufficient concern among the propertied elements to warrant their joining in groups to bear jointly the cost of prosecuting felons, the expense attending prosecutions of suspected offenders having in the past frequently prevented such suspects from being brought to justice. As early as 1772 the Llanrhystud parish vestry (Cards.) passed a resolution 'that we the inhabitants of this parish do hereby jointly agree together to prosecute on all fellony that whomsoever will be found within this parish'. In entering such an agreement in January 1788, the Llangeler parish vestry (Carms.) resolved that a reward of two guineas 'will be paid to the person who shall give information against anyone that shall steal anything from either of the subscribers or their servants to be paid on conviction of the offender'. Concern that too many were escaping justice for want of pursuit and prosecution was also reflected in the elaborate articles agreed on for apprehending and prosecuting horse-stealers, housebreakers and the like among six parishes in Flintshire in 1779; 'for the more speedy pursuit and apprehending' of offenders the treasurer was to engage one person from each parish to be in readiness to go in pursuit, receiving half a guinea a year for his trouble.[72]

A certain amount of theft was the work of outsiders, particularly so in the later decades of the eighteenth century. Frightening to the maidservant who stumbled upon them was the robbery about 8 p.m. on Friday, 29 December 1775 by three Surrey labourers, their faces blackened and armed with pistols and a cutlass, of the house of Arthur Bennett Esq. in Denbighshire. Allegedly, one of the robbers, Henry Rowland, had told his accomplices that he knew the house of Bennett, 200 miles from London, where '£400 or £500 might be got'. Answering a charge before the Montgomeryshire spring Great Sessions, 1785, for stealing two horses in the county, John Atley of Bristol said he worked with a certain John Morris in the Three Crowns in Cheese Lane, in the city, 'whose ideas it was to steal horses from the Welsh mountains'. In certain instances, it was to some extent concern over outside gangs committing certain burglaries that led in part to the launching of such joint efforts on the part of ratepayers of parishes or groups of parishes or associations for the prosecution of felons. 'The fear that a numerous and desperate gang of villains are concerned therein [Cardiganshire and adjacent counties], who under various and specious disguises and appearances have lately introduced themselves into this County to the Great Terror of his Majesty's well disposed subjects' was thus an important consideration leading to the agreement to prosecute thieves entered into by the parishes of Llanwnnen and Lampeter in Cardiganshire in 1788. Suspicion of strangers and an inclination to cast blame on them for social ills was, of course, a characteristic of all the myriad autonomous inward-looking neighbourhoods of early modern Europe. To such an extent was this so in Carmarthenshire by the 1770s that suspicion had reached the point of suspecting all Englishmen! And it was infectious. John Price of Talgarth (Brec.) was thus writing to his neighbour, a certain Revd Jones, in summer 1773:

> We have shocking accounts in the weekly papers of a desperate gang of thieves in Devonshire and I have great reason to suspect their having crossed the Channel, for yesterday at Hay fair there were several strangers, part of some notorious gang (known to Sankey of Llyswen). I think that we who are on the confines of England should follow the example of the Carmarthenshire gentry and ask every Englishman that comes among us his business.[73]

That the countryside and small towns were much traversed by strangers, whether beggars, people in search of work, migrant Irish workers crossing Wales to and from the English harvest, or distant vendors of goods in Welsh markets, is a feature that needs underlining, and some of these committed theft.[74] But the overwhelming number of felonies were perpetrated by local people of both sexes, albeit the substantial majority were men. Of the 927 offences against property known to the Great Sessions of the eight selected Welsh counties at five-yearly intervals between 1730 and 1800, some 81 per cent were committed by males and just 19 per cent by females. Furthermore, whereas women as well as men stole food, clothes, shoes, household utensils, wool, cloth, jewellery and other fineries, and money, they did not generally steal livestock. Occasionally men and women jointly committed a theft, sometimes as husband and wife. Of the men who stole, the largest category were labourers, but significant numbers, too were yeomen (though here caution is needed as men signing themselves as such were sometimes merely farm servants), farmers and craftsmen.

Of particular seriousness within the prevailing pastoral economy of Wales was theft of livestock. Table 11 reveals that theft of livestock comprised 242 offences (166 of them sheep, 54 horses and 22 cattle), some 41 per cent of the total of 584 theft offences in the sample of years chosen. This kind of offence was rendered the more tempting by virtue of the open moorlands and commons that abounded. For all the watchfulness of the community, the determined tracking down of suspects by those robbed and the deterrent of a harsh criminal code, theft of livestock was endemic. Farmers stole sheep, horses and cattle from their neighbours, butchers spirited away animals, particularly sheep, and labourers and craftsmen stole horses, cattle and sheep, sometimes to survive. Certain thefts of livestock were on a breathtaking scale. Richard Phillips was thus found guilty at the Montgomeryshire autumn Great Sessions for 1795 of stealing from three separate parties on 5 and 12 June of that year as many as forty-one sheep and ten lambs, for which he was given sentence of death, although, as we shall see was commonly the practice, judgement was respited. So far as horse-theft was concerned – a felony considered second only to burglary as a serious property offence because horses were a vital means of transport and were also easy to steal – none was more flagrant in his flouting of the law than Harry Richard Robert otherwise Henry Roberts of Llangollen parish (Denbs.), who appeared before the Denbighshire Great Sessions at Easter 1762 to face charges of having in the preceding years stolen horses from no fewer than eighteen people. One person who had his horse taken from his premises by Harry Robert on 12 October 1761 was Richard Palfrey of Llanbadarn Fawr parish (Rads.), yeoman, 'and that after he and two sons of his had travelled about 400 miles in pursuit of the said gelding', he found him on Wednesday, 21 October at Robert's farm at Hafodgyn Fawr.[75]

Certain individuals like Harry Robert and in some cases, whole families, had bad reputations among their neighbours as thieves, and they, like strangers, quickly fell under suspicion once a theft had come to light. Dorothy Williams of Arllwyd in the parish of Llafannan (Denbs.), in giving evidence on 9 March 1728 against

John Lewis of Arllwyd for theft of barley from her father's barn, stated that she had a poor opinion of Lewis and did 'in some measure suspect him in particular not only because he was a near neighbour but that he was obnoxious to the whole neighbourhood for various criminal practices and particularly suspected for having formerly robbed this same barn', when Arllwyd was held under a previous tenant.[76] Thomas John Jenkin, yeoman, of the parish of Llanwrtyd (Brec.), 'a person of ill-fame', was in early 1750 suspected by his neighbours in the parish of Llanddewi Abergwesyn of having stolen several sheep in the district. Two men took him into custody at break of day and a magistrate, after hearing testimony, committed him for felony to Brecon gaol, but he escaped his captors on the journey to the prison.[77] On the night of 17 June 1756 Griffith Ellis of Glaswed in the parish of Llanddeiniolen (Caerns.) was informed of someone driving his lambs, whereupon he got out of bed and went with his servant towards the house of Maurice Evan, 'being a person of ill fame and much suspected'. Waiting in the adjoining house, they saw him return with a bag containing four quarters of lamb which turned out to be that of Griffith Ellis.[78] Thomas Pritchard of Llandrillo-yn-Rhos parish (Denbs.) bought some beef at Llangernyw fair on 29 November 1781 only to have it stolen off the butcher's standing while fetching his horse. In response to inquiries, Ellen Humphreys informed him that she had seen two persons in the fair that day 'commonly called John Honest (alias John Jones) and his daughter who live in a cottage on Moelfra mountain in the parish of St George . . . who had very bad characters', and, taking her advice to follow them home, he found that they had indeed stolen the sack of beef. John Honest persisted in his evil ways, stealing geese from Morris Pritchard, farmer of the parish of St George, on 17 February 1788; on that occasion the constable expressed his willingness to search for the geese 'as he knew the family to have a very bad character', in the process finding not only geese but eight quarters of mutton, but his efforts to secure John Honest were frustrated by the family pelting him and his assistants with stones.[79]

3. Punishment

It is certainly the case that the punishments laid down by statute were harsh in this century of the Bloody Code. Whipping for petty

larceny, burning the hand for manslaughter and felony, transportation to the colonies for seven years and more for burglary and
grand larceny, and hanging for capital offences like murder, the
theft of animals, burglary and breaking and entering and theft,
were all aimed at retribution and deterring others. Landowners
sitting on juries were sensitive to any threat to property. W. Jones
in reporting to the absentee J. G. Philipps of Cwmgwili (Carms.) on
the spring Great Sessions for 1789 at Carmarthen, observed:

> It is reported that the judges mean to leave two or three for execution. It
> was an observation made in Court that if he did not it would lower the
> price of lands, for no person would choose to purchase among us. PS. I
> find that one convict only is left for execution, to be executed on
> Saturday fortnight.[80]

Deterrence and example-setting informed the sentiments of a
Carmarthen writer when commenting on the four prisoners
sentenced to death for burglary and theft at the Carmarthen spring
assizes for 1787: 'The ignorance and brutality of our lower class,
unhappily seem to point out the necessity of such sacrifices. How
much better would it be, could a plan be adopted for obviating this
terrible necessity, by some degree of cultivation in the early part of
life.'[81]

Although it is impossible to determine accurately the verdicts
and sentences for indictments returned true bills at the Great
Sessions,[82] sufficient evidence exists to indicate that a significant
number of executions did take place and that many more convicts
were transported. Some sense of the severity of punishment is
conveyed in a few chosen examples from the court records. After
John Thomas alias John Jeffrey was convicted of assault and theft
of a silver watch and money at the Denbigh spring Great Sessions,
1777, he was hanged and then placed in chains upon a gibbet on
Rosset Green in Gresford parish to deter others, his widow and
another woman later (illegally) cutting down the gibbet.[83] Or take
again the harsh treatment meted out to Robert Owen of
Llandysilio (Angl.) in spring 1739 for stealing corn out of a local
mill in Llanddona, the diarist William Bulkley recording that 'the
mill thief was burnt in earnest, the Iron burning half way through
his hand'.[84] In this latter instance, as in others, we can discern
particularly harsh treatment slapped on those considered to be

deserving of it. John Price explicitly alluded to this tendency when writing to Richard Myddelton of Chirk Castle in October 1764 about the recent Quarter Sessions for Denbighshire: 'A Felon was tried and convicted, and was most severely scourg'd the next day publicly, being a person of a bad character.'[85] Although very few women were hanged in eighteenth-century Wales, a depressing number were transported as, for example, were Margaret Jones, aged twenty, and Ann Jones, aged fifteen, convicted at the Denbighshire Hilary Quarter Sessions, 1793, for together stealing at night five slippings of linen yarn.[86]

Yet it has been established by historians of crime, Beattie and Hay for instance, that punishments were often less severe than they might have been, that the courts on grounds of humanity or, perhaps, demonstrating the ruling élite's astute manipulation of the law to forge obedience, gratitude and deference, frequently saw fit to reduce the full severity of the sentence.[87] Thus with regard to larceny, goods stolen in Welsh and English communities were often undervalued to less than a shilling in order to reduce the offence from one of simple grand larceny to the lesser one of petty larceny.[88] In practice this meant that many who would have been transported were instead whipped. Many were the instances, too, in Welsh as in English counties, of judges granting a condemned convict a reprieve and allowing him to appeal for the king's mercy, usually given, and the death sentence thereupon commuted to transportation. Indeed, if the other Welsh circuits mirrored the practice of the Brecon one in the late eighteenth century, then reprieving of prisoners for capital offences was a very common occurrence – as many as nine in ten. For whatever reason this high ratio was significantly more marked than in English circuits.[89]

Reprieves were given throughout the century largely for sheep-stealers, horse-thieves and perpetrators of serious felonies like burglary, highway robbery and grand larceny, though not for murderers, with the singular exception of mothers guilty of infanticide.[90] So much so were convicts in these areas of theft afforded leniency that the chief justice of Chester (whose circuit took in Montgomeryshire, Denbighshire and Flintshire) urged in 1785 the necessity for hanging in face of the prevalence of horse-theft in Montgomeryshire.[91] Four years later Judge Hardinge, uneasy at the lack of capital punishment in his Brecon circuit for sheep-stealing over the previous twenty or thirty years, ordered two executions to serve as a future deterrent. (In 1813 he was to recall that such firmness on his part, opposing 'very powerful intercession for them', meant that in the quarter of a century following not a man was executed for this offence and very few were convicted. For him 'prevention by the warning of terror' had worked.)[92]

During the trials themselves character witnesses were busy seeking to sway the courts' verdicts, a practice condemned in the *Cambrian Register* for 1795:

> Those persons who are in the habit of attending courts of justice, must observe, that there are few criminals who are brought to the bar, that are not able to prevail upon some friend or neighbour, out of false compassion (for it is cruelty to the public) to speak to their characters.[93]

David Jones has persuasively shown that such character references could and did sway verdicts. Demonstrably the 'sex, age, status, record and behaviour of prisoners' weighed in a number of respects: 'very few' women were hanged in eighteenth-century Wales; if older men were 'respectable and religious family men' they made a favourable impression; and, contrariwise, hardened offenders and miscreant members of gangs met with an unsympathetic hearing.[94] Mr Davies of Pennyland's tenant in Carmarthenshire, found guilty of sheep-stealing at the county's spring Great Sessions for 1785 and ordered to be hanged shortly afterwards, was, significantly, also tried a year previously.[95]

If despite all efforts to dispose the courts to leniency, the death sentence was passed, then outsiders, drawn from sheriffs, magistrates, the gentry, clergymen, freeholders, the grand jury, attorneys, employers, friends and neighbours of the condemned, petitioned the judges and secretaries of state for a pardon.[96] A notable exception was the case of John Hugh, a notorious and feared sheep-stealer found guilty and condemned to death at the Cardiff Assizes in spring 1795, for 'though diligent inquiries were made with the hopes of discovering some favourable instances, which might induce a recommendation to mercy, not one man could be found who wished him to live'.[97] Despite the frustration felt by judges at each importunate clamour,[98] many appeals for pardon, as we have noted, were successful. However, a group in a peculiarly favourable position to steal, servants, were seemingly excluded from this feast of clemency, the *Cambrian Register* for

1796 remarking: 'Judges have very seldom recommended mercy to be extended to servants, convicted of robbing their masters.' For example, when John Collins, a labourer of Lampeter parish (Cards.), was hanged for theft of his employer the passionate, quick-tempered Sir Herbert Lloyd of Peterwell's possessions in 1765, it was observed: 'Crimes of this sort are too frequent in families where servants are kept and call for exemplary punishment.'[99]

~ 11 ~

Epilogue
'The Old Order Changeth'

As the eighteenth century moved into its later decades the fabric of the old society was showing increasing signs of strain and, by the 1790s, crisis. The rising population, with no such easy escape outwards as was later furnished by the railway, saw increasing pauperization at the base of society and much attendant social rupture. Not only did the pressure of escalating poor rates sow discord between neighbouring parishes. *Within* parishes the social tension developing in the decades from the 1760s was reflected in the quarrels among the poor themselves for a share of the relief. Overseers, too, sometimes defied the justices' instructions to pay relief to certain claimants, and better-off parishioners complained at having to pay higher rates, in a couple of parishes at least, and doubtless in others refusing to pay. It was the banding together of parish rate-payers from the 1760s to bear jointly the expense of going to law to protect themselves against unwanted pauper intruders, and also to prosecute all felons within their parishes, that as much as anything else mirrors the huge strains threatening the traditional stability of rural society. Perhaps, too, in this context, as Melvin Humphreys has invited us to contemplate, the growing number of parishes late in the century without resident gentry families meant that an alternative, less paternalist sway by small freeholders and large tenant farmers over what has been termed these 'parish states' effected a bleak exacerbation of pressing local problems.[1] Certainly the waning of customary hospitality and the dispensing of charity and the fall in the provision of employment in the wake of gentry non-residence would have placed extra pressure on the poor.

Increasing 'boiling for a tenancy'[2] among rural dwellers accompanying population growth was another manifestation of worsening relationships as farmers overreached themselves in the process of outbidding one another. Indeed the very poisoning of the countryside which David Williams saw as a consequence of 'reckless bidding' in the years before Rebecca[3] was as early as the

1760s in its prodromal stage. Simmering resentment could erupt into quarrels, and more extreme, arson.

Notwithstanding that there was a close interface between gentry and people, at once familiar and symbiotic, and that for all their neglect to attend Quarter Sessions those JPs who were resident were 'available to all' in frequently putting to right outside a lawcourt the innumerable petty squabbles between neighbours,[4] there were regular attacks by all groups in society upon magistrates and lords of manors alike who were perceived to be falling down on their duties as paternalists and obstructing the enjoyment of customary rights. Indeed mounting conflict over two opposing perceptions of 'rights' was to occur from mid-century as, too, over balloting for the militia. Rising farm rents from the 1760s likewise saw composers of ballads criticize greedy, selfish landlords, and there is no mistaking the upset of the north Walian tenantry at this new departure even if, as we have argued, both groups were to an extent naive.

There is no mistaking the growing resentment in Welsh society of the gentry in the 1790s, a disaffection masterfully analysed by David Jones.[5] It is equally clear that the mounting criticism of the magistrates – to such a pitch that even the radical mouthpiece *Seren Tan Gwmwl* condemned the violence that had been displayed in certain areas of Wales – sprang from the extraordinary conditions of that decade, above all *drudaniaeth* (costliness) and hunger.[6] As in the past the thin line between deference and defiance was easily crossed when the people deemed their magistrates to be behaving against the popular interest or unfairly towards them as individuals. Riot in these years constituted the ultimate appeal to authority to behave justly in the best traditions of the paternalist social model. But in the 1790s the confrontations, witnessed above all in corn, militia and enclosure riots, were sometimes underpinned by Jacobinical anti-gentry, anti-government sentiment. Even so this turbulent, unstable decade witnessed no widespread breach of oligarchic control of politics, and no deep-seated challenge was mounted to traditional authority. Paternalism and deference were still powerful social adhesives down to the close of the century. For all the theft by servants from their masters, deference on the part of the lower orders in Wales was sustained the more by the persistence in this largely pastoral region of living-in servants, their decline in areas of the south and east of England from the 1770s going some way towards undermining paternalist work relations.[7]

A few qualifications need to be made about the growing conflict in Welsh rural society from mid-century. In the first place, it is unhelpful to think in terms of defiance and resistance in the community as exclusively a venting of anger of the lower orders against their rulers. For one thing, the great magnates were feared by the lesser gentlemen just as much as by the common people, a regime of arrogance and oppression occasionally giving rise to criticism long before the political movement for 'Independence' from the 1780s.[8] Moreover, much of the resentment in the rural community was turned against lords of manors bent upon reasserting (in their view) lost rights against a marauding community, the protest embracing lesser gentlemen, small freeholders, tenant farmers and cottagers alike. Defiance and resistance, too, were often directed against selfish large farmers and middlemen, and against government employees like customs officers, press gangs and land-tax commissioners.[9]

Secondly, although as part of their paternalist credo the Welsh gentry, like their English counterparts, were keen to enforce deference, expecting tenants not to be 'impudent' or 'impertinent', and to vote and worship in the way they were told, they were not bullying tyrants.[10] It is significant that those few wholly tyrannical justices who disgraced their office and incurred the odium of the populace also aroused the disgust of their fellow magistrates, as did unsavoury characters like Charles Richardes of Penglais (Cards.) in the 1730s, William Myddelton, a Denbighshire justice, before his dismissal in 1742, the four Cardiganshire magistrates George Jones of Rhoscellan, Herbert Lloyd of Peterwell and John Johnes senior and junior of Abermaid in the middle decades, Sir John Meredith of Brecknock in the 1760s and Edward Pryse Lloyd of Glansevin (Carms.) in the 1770s and early 1780s.[11]

Thirdly, for the late eighteenth century as a whole we must be careful not to exaggerate the extent of the crisis. There was nothing remotely resembling the rural unrest in Ireland with its organized campaigns of intimidation and violence waged by the spate of secret societies beginning with the Whiteboys in the early 1760s and continuing down to the politicized, revolutionary Defenders of the 1790s. Such societies, bound together by oaths of secrecy, enjoying the tacit support of their communities and rooted in the lower-class Catholic resentment of an Anglo-Irish Protestant landed élite, manifested a total contempt for authority in their effort to redress peasant grievances like high rents, tithes and the erosion of customary rights. If growing opposition to tithe payment was evident in eighteenth-century Wales the absence as yet of any widespread religious divide saw no such anti-tithe protest as was demonstrated in the Irish Whiteboy and Rightboy movements. Again there was no general uprising against high rents in Wales as was manifested in the Irish Steelboy and Rightboy movements. It is indicative of a real crumbling of deference that gentry homes in Ireland were raided for arms by the Defenders in the 1790s, and that in the anti-militia riots of 1793 a staggering 230 were killed in a matter of just two months or so. This reflected a level of lower-class disaffection from the ruling élite unmatched in 1790s Wales, and is to be explained by the politicization of lower-class Irish Catholics which constituted a mass revolutionary movement.[12]

Deference in the Welsh countryside across the eighteenth century had been sustained by the ancient Welsh stock of most gentry families and by the absence of any real religious cleavage. While their Welsh ancestry was to furnish part of the explanation for the less bitter relations between rural dwellers and landlords in Wales than obtained in Ireland over the whole of the nineteenth century, the widening religious divide from the early 1800s between Nonconformist common people and Anglican gentry prized apart the homogeneity of the old order in Wales at a time when paternalism, too, was for various reasons collapsing in the English countryside.[13] Besides the growth of Nonconformist Liberalism in Wales which was to be achieved only through a sustained campaign of educating the people (*y werin*) in politics undertaken by Nonconformist leaders in the mid-nineteenth century, there was a further decline in traditional deference through Nonconformity rendering its adherents in a sense conceited; believing themselves to be less sinful than the pleasure-loving gentry, they came to look down upon them as spiritually inferior people.[14]

Another weakening of the hold of the gentry came in the aftermath of their unwillingness to reduce the high wartime rents with the onset of depression after 1814. Writing in 1831 on 'the present state of society in Wales', one commentator observed:

The present rent of land was raised to its present average at a time when the tenant could afford to pay it, by the superior value of the produce of his farm; but now the value of that produce is diminished, every principle of justice demands that the rent should be adjusted to this fall of value.

According to the same writer the gentry's growing hauteur, 'their habits of sterness and reserve' and their disdain for Welsh peasant culture further increased their unpopularity.[15] The Revd William Jones, curate of Llanbeulan, Anglesey, addressing the 'Character of the Welsh as a Nation' in 1841, cited approvingly a contemporary comment that the gentry were failing to pay sufficient attention to the conduct and morals of the people, which had 'occasioned an habitual want of deference on the part of the poor to the authority of the laws of the nation'. Only by gentry deciding 'to live at home' could the situation be righted, a viewpoint endorsed by the Revd Lister Venables, vicar of Clyro in Radnorshire, in 1847.[16] It is perhaps here that the long-term damage to Welsh society inflicted by absenteeism that had been spawned in the eighteenth century was to be most keenly felt.

There is no mistaking the collapse of gentry standing in south-west Wales by the early 1840s in the face of their haughtiness and their unwillingness to lower rents in the unprecedented price collapse of 1842–3. With Rebecca's appearance we can speak of a collapse of deference; only now did there occur in the Welsh countryside the enforcement of communal laws or codes outside the state law – a process demonstrated by David Williams and David Jones in turn – the forcible imposition of which had occurred in Ireland during the Whiteboy protest in the 1760s.[17] Yet deference was to some extent at least won back by the efforts of landowners in the wake of Rebecca to renew paternalism in their building of new churches and Anglican national schools, taking greater care of the poor in years of hardship, and dealing equitably with all types of people as magistrates.[18] This would have been assisted by the coming of railways, which made it easier for landowners to remain for longer periods on their Welsh estates.[19] Notwithstanding the mounting game grievance in the Welsh countryside from the second quarter of the nineteenth century in response to the growing preservation of birds, game and fish,[20] the gathering economic prosperity from the mid-1850s, together with the quickening rural exodus, undoubtedly promoted improved relations between tenants and landlords, relations that were to come under severe strain once more only with the prolonged if

intermittent depression from the late 1870s, the spur of the Irish
and Crofter movements and landowners' siding with the clergy
over the bitter tithe issue. By the early 1890s support for land
reform was widespread, leaving Charles Fitzwilliams of Cilgwyn
(Cards.) to ruminate: 'The old ways are things of the past,
landlords and tenants are not now the same to each other.'[21] Even
so, down to the 1890s some traditional Welsh gentry were still well
liked and respected on a *personal* level as generous landlords, even
after they had been unsparingly rejected as inappropriate leaders of
the new Wales. The radical *Carnarvon and Denbigh Herald* exactly
depicted the Welsh *mentalité* in acknowledging, in the wake of the
defeat of Ellis Nanney at a parliamentary by-election in 1891:

> there is no more popular landed-proprietor in Caernarfonshire than the
> squire of Gwynfryn . . . a man may be and often is something else and
> much more than the political creed he professes. Regarded from a
> Liberal point of view, Mr Ellis Nanney has always been a really right
> sort of man, but, unhappily on the wrong side of politics.[22]

Just as deference towards the Welsh gentry, strained certainly in
the 1790s, was long in the unmaking, so, too, was the traditional
paternal relationship between farmers and their labourers. The
persistence of the indoor servant system and of married labourers
boarding at the farms down to the end of the nineteenth century
and beyond certainly made for a paternalist regime. While a
growing gulf was none the less discernible by the mid-nineteenth
century and widened in the later decades, it is by no means clear
that labourers were 'a class apart' by the 1880s.[23] For all the
tetchiness on both sides, a patron–client relationship arguably
prevailed down to the First World War, which effected a revolution
in relations between masters and men.

Notes

Introduction

[1] I owe this observation to Dr Prys Morgan.
[2] J. V. Beckett, 'The peasant in England: a case of terminological confusion?', *Ag. Hist. Rev.*, 32 (1984).
[3] Trefor M. Owen, 'Historical aspects of peat-cutting in Merioneth', *Jnl. Mer. Hist. and Rec. Soc.*, 7 (1973–6).
[4] Melvin Humphreys, *The Crisis of Community: Montgomeryshire Society 1680–1815* (Cardiff, 1996); Glyn Parry, 'Stability and change in mid-eighteenth century Caernarvonshire' (unpub. MA thesis, Univ. of Wales, 1978); R. F. Suggett, 'Some aspects of village life in eighteenth-century Glamorgan' (unpub. B.Litt. thesis, Univ. of Oxford, 1976).

Chapter 1 Prologue: Setting the Scene: The Land and the People

[1] L. Symons, *Agricultural Geography* (London, 1968), 21–57.
[2] A. W. Ashby and I. L. Evans, *The Agriculture of Wales* (Cardiff, 1944), 208.
[3] Symons, *Agricultural Geography*, 21; G. W. Robinson, 'Natural factors in Welsh agriculture', *The Welsh Outlook* (September 1931).
[4] M. E. Hughes and A. J. James, *Wales, A Physical, Economic and Social Geography* (London 1961), part i, 80–4.
[5] NLW MS 1760A.
[6] David Jenkins, *The Agricultural Community in South-West Wales at the turn of the Twentieth Century* (Cardiff, 1971), 40–1.
[7] B. E. Howells, 'Social and agrarian change in early modern Cardiganshire', *Ceredigion*, vii (1972–5), 267.
[8] W. Davies, *A General View of the Agriculture and Domestic Economy of South Wales* (London, 1814), i, 161, 309–10; W. J. Lewis, 'The condition of labour in early nineteenth-century Cardiganshire', *Ceredigion*, iv, 4 (1963), 321; Parry, 'Stability and change', 196–7; B. H. Malkin, *The Scenery, Antiquities and Biography of South Wales* (2nd edn, London, 1807), ii, 417–18.
[9] Frank Emery, 'Wales', in J. Thirsk (ed.), *AHE&W, V,* i (Cambridge, 1984), 409–28.

¹⁰ Ibid., 413; M. I. Williams, 'Agriculture and society in Glamorgan 1660–1760' (unpub. Ph.D. thesis, Univ. of Leicester, 1967), 71–4.

¹¹ Parry, 'Stability and change', 208–10.

¹² G. Kay, *General View of the Agriculture of Merionethshire* (London, 1794), 7.

¹³ For early clover cultivation see Frank Emery, 'The mechanics of innovation: clover cultivation in Wales before 1750', *Journal of Historical Geography*, 2, i (1976), 35–48. See also D. W. Howell, 'Landlords and estate management in Wales', in J. Thirsk (ed.), *AHE&W, V*, ii (Cambridge, 1985), 273–6.

¹⁴ R. J. Colyer, 'Livestock', in G. E. Mingay (ed.), *AHE&W, VI* (Cambridge,1989), 324–6.

¹⁵ Ibid., 340–2.

¹⁶ R. Warner, *Second Walk through Wales* (London, 1799), 196; see also praise of the Vale of Clwyd from Henry Wigstead, *A Tour to North and South Wales in the Year 1797* (London, 1798), 19; J. Fox, *General View of the Agriculture of the County of Glamorgan* (London, 1796), 15.

¹⁷ The Revd John Evans, *Letters Written during a Tour through South Wales in the Year 1803* (London, 1804), 231.

¹⁸ Joseph Cradock, *Letters from Snowdon* (Dublin, 1770), 109.

¹⁹ D. Thomas, *Agriculture in Wales during the Napoleonic Wars* (Cardiff, 1963), 181.

²⁰ J. A. Chartres, 'The marketing of agricultural produce', in J. Thirsk (ed.), *AHE&W, V*, ii, 453.

²¹ Parry, 'Stability and change', 177.

²² Ibid., 178, citing G. Kay, *General View of the Agriculture of Caernarvonshire* (London, 1794), 19; Colyer, 'Livestock', 341, n.200. However, William Williams, land surveyor, writing on Anglesey in 1807, doubted if local farmers, even if offered ready cash, could be weaned from their attachment to the native drovers: 'as their old customers would offer a higher price, a promise of a few shillings in the beast would tempt them to hazard all for a few weeks' credit. But to their sorrow, this bait has too often ruined them' (NLW MS 822C).

²³ The Revd John Evans thus remarked of south Wales in 1803: 'Many of the errors visible in the agriculture of this country, certainly arise from the ignorance, prejudice, indolence and poverty of the tenants; but there are others, which attach to the proprietors of estates' (*Letters . . . South Wales*, 427).

²⁴ W. Hutton, *Tours in North Wales, 1787 to October 1797* (Birmingham, 1803), 86.

²⁵ Frank Emery, *The World's Landscapes: Wales* (London, 1969), 64–6.

²⁶ See *Reports* on the various counties to the Board of Agriculture in 1794.

²⁷ Frank Emery, 'The farming regions of Wales', in J. Thirsk (ed.),

AHE&W, IV (Cambridge, 1967), 153; Thomas, *Agriculture . . . Napoleonic Wars*, 31; J. M. Powell, 'The economic geography of Montgomeryshire in the nineteenth century' (unpub. MA thesis, Univ. of Liverpool, 1962), 26–8.

28 Howell, 'Landlords and estate management in Wales', 278–9; A. H. Dodd, *The Industrial Revolution in North Wales* (Cardiff, 1933), 55.

29 NLW, Harpton Court MS C40.

30 NLW, SA/QA/7, bishop's visitation, diocese of St Asaph, 1791.

31 E. Davies, 'Hafod and lluest: the summering of cattle and upland settlement in Wales', *Folk Life*, 23 (1984–5), 84–8.

32 A. H. Dodd, 'The enclosure movement in north Wales', *BBCS*, iii (1926–7), 210.

33 Colin Thomas, 'Colonization, enclosure and the rural landscape', *NLW Jnl.*, 19 (1975–6), 142.

34 Ibid.; Emery, *The World's Landscapes: Wales*, 91.

35 Ibid.; Thomas, 'Colonization', 141–3.

36 Thomas, *Agriculture . . . Napoleonic Wars*, 140–1; J. W. Edwards, 'Enclosure and agricultural improvement in the Vale of Clwyd, 1750–1875' (unpub. MA thesis, Univ. of London, 1963), 167–241.

37 D. W. Howell, *Land and People in Nineteenth-Century Wales* (London, 1979), 39–40.

38 PP, v, 1833, *SC on Agriculture, Evidence*, Q5821; PP, xv, 1882, *RC on Agriculture, Report*, 7.

39 Humphreys, *Crisis of Community*, 96.

40 D. W. Howell, *Patriachs and Parasites* (Cardiff, 1986), 8–11; Parry, 'Stability and change', 3–4. The Glamorgan figures provided by Dr. Martin were: great landlords £3,000–£5,000 and wealthy gentry £1,000–£3,000, (J. O. Martin, 'The landed estate in Glamorgan, *circa* 1660–1760' (unpub. Ph.D. thesis, Univ. of Cambridge, 1978)). For Glamorgan see also Philip Jenkins, *The Making of a Ruling Class: The Glamorgan Gentry, 1640–1790* (Cambridge, 1983), 48; for English estates see G. E. Mingay, *English Landed Society in the Eighteenth Century* (London, 1963), 21; J. V. Beckett, *The Aristocracy in England 1660–1914* (Oxford, 1986), 4–9.

41 At the same time, some of the small estates in Denbighshire in 1706, too, were owned by large proprietors from outside the county. For Merioneth, see Keith Williams-Jones, *A Calendar of the Merioneth Quarter Sessions Rolls* (Merioneth County Council, 1965), lxiii–lxix.

42 For the process of consolidation of the large estates in Britain generally see H. J. Habakkuk, 'The rise and fall of English landed families 1660–1800: i', *Trans. RHS*, 5th ser., 29 (1979); idem, 'The rise and fall of English landed families 1660–1800: i', *Trans. RHS*, 5th ser., 30 (1980); Mingay, *English Landed Society*, ch. iii; J. V. Beckett, 'The pattern of

landownership in England and Wales, 1660–1880', *Econ. Hist. Rev.*, xxxvii (1984); C. Clay, 'Marriage, inheritance and the rise of large estates in England, 1660–1815', *Econ. Hist. Rev.*, xxi (1968); for Wales see Williams-Jones, *Calendar*, lxiii–lxiv, where we have the first perceptive reference in Welsh estate studies to the 'remarkable failure of the male line in many [Merioneth] families'; P. R. Roberts, 'The decline of the Welsh squires in the eighteenth century', *NLW Jnl.*, 13 (1963–4), 163–4; Philip Jenkins, 'The demographic decline of the landed gentry in the eighteenth century: a south Wales study', *WHR*, ii (1982–3), 31–49; Howell, 'Landlords', 259–60; idem, *Patriarchs*, ch.i; Martin, 'The landed estate in Glamorgan', 224; Leslie Baker-Jones, *Princelings, Privilege and Power: The Tivyside Gentry in their Community* (Llandysul, 1999), 51–2; Humphreys, *Crisis of Community*, 100ff; Parry, 'Stability and change', 17ff. Parry (p.18) notes there were more male heirs in Caernarfonshire after 1770 and accordingly the importance of marriage in estate compilation declined.

[43] Landed income groups have been derived for the counties from the various *Reports* to the Board of Agriculture in 1794. Walter Davies, writing on south Wales, observed: 'From £200 a year downwards, most of the proprietors occupy their own lands' (*Agriculture . . . South Wales*, i, 120).

[44] Humphreys, *Crisis of Community*, 98–9.

[45] Edmund Hyde Hall, *A Description of Caernarfonshire (1809–1811)* (Caernarvon, 1952), cited in Parry, 'Stability and change', 27; for a complementary comment in 1806 on 'withering' mansions in Caernarfonshire, see NLW MS 821; for Merioneth, see Williams-Jones, *Calendar*, lxiii–lxiv; for other contemporary observations on deserted houses, see Howell, *Patriarchs*, ch. 1; Humphreys, *Crisis of Community*, 97.

[46] Ibid., 98ff; Parry, 'Stability and change', 26; Jenkins, 'Demographic decline', 39.

[47] Cited in Parry, 'Stability and change', 26.

[48] Roberts, 'Decline of the Welsh squires', 169.

[49] Pembs. RO, land-tax returns for 1786. The figure of 18 per cent would have been marginally lower had tenements assessed at under 1s. been counted, but these were mere houses with a few fields attached.

[50] Colin Thomas, 'Rural settlements in the modern period', in D. Huw Owen (ed.), *Settlement and Society in Wales* (Cardiff, 1989), 254–5.

[51] Peter Smith, 'Rural buildings in Wales', in J. Thirsk (ed.), *AHE&W, V*, ii, 692; Iolo's comment is cited in Suggett, 'Some aspects of village life in eighteenth-century Glamorgan', 17.

[52] W. T. R. Pryce, The social and economic structure of north-east Wales, 1750–1890' (unpub. Ph.D. thesis, Lanchester Polytechnic, Coventry,

1971), 88; Martin Davies, 'Hanes Cymdeithawl Meirionydd, 1750–1859' (unpub. MA thesis, Univ. of Wales, 1988), reference kindly provided by Brinley W. Jones; M. I. Williams, 'Agriculture and society in Glamorgan', 39–40.

53 In R. Floud and D. N. McCloskey (eds.), *The Economic History of Britain since 1700* (2nd edn, London, 1994), vol.1, 61.

54 B. W. Jones, 'The population of eighteenth-century west Glamorgan – the evidence of the parish registers', in S. Williams (ed.), *Glamorgan Historian*, 12 (1981); D. Jenkins, 'The demography of late-Stuart Montgomeryshire, *c.*1660–1720', *Mont. Colls.*, 78 (1990); Humphreys, *Crisis of Community*, 68–76.

55 E. A. Wrigley and R. S. Schofield, *The Population History of England, 1541–1871* (1981 and 1989); M. Flinn (ed.), *Scottish Population History from the Seventeenth Century to the 1930s* (Cambridge, 1977); K. H. Connell, *The Population of Ireland, 1750–1845* (Oxford, 1950).

56 Parry, 'Stability and change', i.

57 Davies, 'Hanes Cymdeithawl Meirionydd'.

58 Jenkins, 'The demography of late-Stuart Montgomeryshire', 97.

59 Humphreys, *Crisis of Community*, 71.

60 Jones, 'The population of eighteenth-century west Glamorgan', 189–90.

61 Ibid., 189; Parry, 'Stability and change', iv.

62 Jenkins, 'The demography of late-Stuart Montgomeryshire', 87–9, 91; idem, 'Harvest failure and crisis mortality: the example of Montgomeryshire, 1699–1700', *Papers in Modern Welsh History*, 1 (1982), 17–24.

63 J. G. Penrhyn Jones, 'A history of medicine in Wales in the eighteenth century' (unpub. MA thesis, Univ. of Liverpool, 1957), 30–3.

64 J. E. Griffith, 'The diary of William Bulkeley, of Brynddu, Anglesey', *Anglesey Antiq. Soc. Trans.* (1931).

65 NLW MS 12, 373B; UCNW, Bangor, Penrhos MS 415.

66 NLW, Brogyntyn MS 1427; Penrhyn Jones, 'A history of medicine', 30.

67 Ibid., 33.

68 Parry, 'Stability and change', iv–v; Penrhyn Jones, 'A history of medicine', 37–8.

69 Ibid., 34–5; William Thomas's diary for 2 September 1762 referred to 'the present fever' raging so severe in Llantrisant that often two burials occurred the same day (R. T. W. Denning (ed.), *The Diary of William Thomas, 1762–1795* (Cardiff South Wales Record Society, 1995), 47).

70 NLW MS 22131C.

71 Innes, *Old Llanelly* (Cardiff, 1902), 165; NLW, Tredegar Park MS 116/219; Penrhyn Jones, 'A history of medicine', 34–5. For location of crisis years, I have drawn on Brinley Jones and Melvin Humphreys besides my own inspection of a sample of Carmarthenshire and

Cardiganshire parish registers. Glamorgan crisis years are vividly described in Denning (ed.), *The Diary of William Thomas*.

72 See Humphreys, *Crisis of Community*, 73; Jones, 'The population of eighteenth-century west Glamorgan', 195.

73 NLW MS 22131C.

74 Jona Schellekens, 'The role of marital fertility in Irish population history, 1750–1840', *Econ. Hist. Rev.*, 46 (1993), 369–78. I owe thanks to my colleague Mr N. C. W. Woodward for this reference and other helpful comments in this section on population.

75 For the anxiety of tradesmen, mariners and yeomen in Glamorgan to assert their social standing between 1660 and 1760, see Williams, 'Agriculture and society in Glamorgan', 45–6.

76 NLW, SA/QA/6, diocese of St Asaph, bishop's visitation, 1791; NLW, SA/QA/14, diocese of Bangor, bishop's visitation, 1801; for an excellent discussion on status see Suggett, 'Some aspects of village life in eighteenth-century Glamorgan', 123–6.

77 Howell, *Patriarchs*, 13–14; Williams, 'Agriculture and Society in Glamorgan', 49; P. Laslett, *The Worlds We Have Lost – Further Explored* (London, 1983), 62.

78 NLW, Cwrtmawr MS 182B.

79 NLW, SA/QA/6; SA/QA/10, diocese of St Asaph, bishop's visitations, 1791 and 1795.

80 Williams, 'Agriculture and society in Glamorgan', 46.

81 NLW, SA/QA/6; diocese of St Asaph, bishop's visitation, 1791.

82 The data are compiled from a number of sources, mostly bishops' visitations: NLW, SA/QA/6, 7, 9 and 10; SD/QA/61 and 120; LL/QA/2; B/QA/2; NLW, SD Misc. B39; Walter Davies, 'A statistical account of the parish of Llanymyneich in Montgomeryshire', *Cambrian Register*, i (1795).

83 NLW MS 1677B. This source is thoroughly worked in Humphreys, *Crisis of Community*, ch. iii. While working it independently, I am indebted to Dr Humphreys for directing me to the source. See also Walter Davies, *A General View of the Agriculture and Domestic Economy of North Wales* (London, 1810), 450–2.

84 Ibid.

85 NLW MS 1677B.

86 Laslett, *The Worlds We Have Lost*, 91–101.

87 Davies, 'A statistical account of the parish of Llanymyneich in Montgomeryshire', 266; Anne Whiteman, *The Compton Census of 1676* (Oxford, 1986), lxii, citing Schofield's contention; B. E. Howells, 'The historical demography of Wales', *Local Historian*, 10 (1972–3), 293.

88 P. Corfield, *The Impact of English Towns, 1700–1800* (Oxford, 1982), 7.

89 H. Carter, 'The growth and development of Welsh towns', in Donald

Moore (ed.), *Wales in the Eighteenth Century* (Swansea, 1976), 50–1; Neil Evans, 'The urbanisation of society', in T. Herbert and G. E. Jones (eds.), *Popular Protest, Wales 1815–1880* (Cardiff, 1988), 7.
90 Corfield, *English Towns*, 7; H. Carter, 'Urban and industrial settlement in the modern period, 1750–1914', in Owen (ed.), *Settlement and Society*, 269.
91 Hutton, *Tours in North Wales*, 27, 74.
92 NLW, William Dillwyn's diaries, 1743–1824, 1775 diary; Malkin, *The Scenery . . . South Wales*, ii, 142, 149; Evans, *Letters . . . South Wales*, 243, 359.
93 Peter Clark (ed.), *Country Towns in Pre-industrial England* (Leicester, 1981), 29–30.
94 Chartres, 'The marketing of agricultural produce', 413–14; Clark, *Country Towns*, 30.
95 Evans, *Letters . . . South Wales*, 359; Clark, *Country Towns*, 23–4. For the standing of professional men in English society, see Paul Langford, *A Polite and Commercial People: England 1727–1783* (Oxford, 1992), 72–3.
96 If Carmarthen is typical, however, by no means all the traders were incorporated in the lists, as is clear from a comparison with the Carmarthenshire land tax returns for 1798 (Carms. RO, IR23/114).
97 Mark Matthews, 'In Pursuit of Profit: local enterprise in south-west Wales in the eighteenth century' (unpub. Ph.D. thesis, Univ. of Wales, 1998), 39.
98 Caernarfon RO, XDI/745.

Chapter 2 Tenant Farmers and Small Freeholders

1 Evans, *Letters . . . South Wales*, 324. For land and status see Suggett, 'Some aspects of village life in eighteenth-century Glamorgan', 123–8.
2 Richard Williams ('Poet of Vanity'), 'A new song illustrating the way of the world at the present time and the difference which existed in days of yore' (Caernarfon, 1850). I owe thanks to Professor Merfyn Jones of University of Wales, Bangor, for providing the translation from the Welsh 'Cân Newydd . . .'
3 H. T. Evans, *The Gorse Glen* (Liverpool, 1948), 31.
4 This is the thrust of the information contained in the various Welsh county *Reports* of the Board of Agriculture in 1794. For a discussion of farm sizes in the early eighteenth century see Emery, 'Wales', in *AHE&W, V*, i, 403–4, and Howell, 'Landlords', 276.
5 PP, 1896, xxxiv, *Report of the RC on Land in Wales and Monmouthshire*, 328, 345–6; and, a valuable work, R. O. Roberts (ed.), *Farming in Caernarvonshire around 1800* (Caernarfon, 1973), 171.

⁶ NLW, Bronwydd MS 6804.

⁷ Davies, *Agriculture*... *South Wales*, ii, 162; C. Hassall, *General View of the Agriculture of the County of Carmarthen* (London, 1794), 11; T. Dineley, *Official Progress of the First Duke of Beaufort through Wales in 1684* (1888 edn), 276; C. Hassall, *General View of the Agriculture of the County of Pembroke* (London, 1794), 10; Carms. RO, Cawdor Vaughan MS: rental of the Pembs. estate belonging to Lord Cawdor in 1810: in Stackpole parish, Rowston farm, 400 acres; in Bosherston parish, Crickmail farm, 306 acres, Trevallen farm, 343 acres; in Castlemartin parish, Moor farm, 343 acres, Bullibar, 342 acres, Linney, 481 acres, Flimston, 467 acres; and in Wiston parish, West Dairy farm, 490 acres; G. Kay, *General View of the Agriculture of Montgomeryshire* (London, 1794), 15; Edwards, 'Enclosure and agricultural improvements in the Vale of Clwyd', 25.

⁸ Davies, *Agriculture*... *South Wales*, ii, 162; Williams, 'Agriculture and society in Glamorgan', 95–6.

⁹ Howell, *Land and People*, 69–70.

¹⁰ Dodd, *The Industrial Revolution in North Wales*, 59–60; O. Beynon, 'The lead mining industry in Cardiganshire from 1700 to 1830' (unpub. MA thesis, Univ. of Wales, 1937), appendix, 19.

¹¹ NLW, Wynnstay survey and valuation, 1763; for a further example of specified numbers of livestock granted individual commoners, see NLW, Margam and Penrice MS 1466: 'A note of those that are allowed to common on Margam Mountain, 1704'; altogether fourteen parties were named, a few including either 'the commoner or tenant'.

¹² *Parliamentary Debates*, 4th ser., i, 22 Feb. 1892, 947.

¹³ C. Vaughan, 'Lluestai Blaenrheidol', *Ceredigion*, v (1966), 246–63; Davies, 'Hafod and lluest', 76–96; T. Lloyd and D. Turnor, *General View of the Agriculture of the County of Cardigan* (London, 1794), 21–2.

¹⁴ NLW, Chirk Castle MS E2851: letter of J. Rees, 8 Nov. 1747 to R. Myddelton; Chirk Castle MS E4872: letter of 14 Nov. 1742 of J. Rees.

¹⁵ NLW, Powis Castle correspondence, letter of 20 Dec. 1762; Carms. RO, Cawdor/Vaughan MS 102/8029: letters of 19 April 1715 of R. Vaughan to Morgan and of 21 Sept. 1721 of J. Roberts to Morgan.

¹⁶ NLW, Wynnstay R10: Sir John Wynn Rentals, 3, 1706–13.

¹⁷ Martin, 'The landed estate in Glamorgan', 99.

¹⁸ Cited in Howell, *Land and People*, 71.

¹⁹ Carms. RO, Cawdor/Vaughan MS 8029: letter of 9 April 1713.

²⁰ NLW, Dolfriog MS 249.

²¹ Edwards, 'Enclosure and Agricultural Improvements in the Vale of Clwyd', 78–122.

²² Carms. RO, Cawdor/Vaughan MS 41/5770.

²³ For the 'inconvenience' of these intermixed holdings, see, for example, NLW, Crosswood MSS group i/1019.

24 Carms. RO, Cawdor/Vaughan MS 102/8029: letter of R. Vaughan, 7 Oct. 1718; Pembs. County Library, Survey of Harcourt Powell's estate, 1778.
25 Roberts, *Farming in Caernarvonshire*, 27, 30.
26 Davies, *Agriculture... North Wales*, 101, cited by R. Colyer, *The Welsh Cattle Drovers* (Cardiff, 1976), 2; Hereford RO, F/A iii/107.
27 Glamorgan RO, D/DP/877/6.
28 A. H. John, *The Industrial Development of South Wales* (Cardiff, 1950), 17.
29 Colyer, *The Welsh Cattle Drovers*, 11–13.
30 Humphreys, *Crisis of Community*, 45.
31 Williams, 'Agriculture and Society in Glamorgan', 152; G. N. Evans, 'The artisan and small farmer in mid-eighteenth century Anglesey', *Trans. Angl. Antiq. Soc.* (1933), 88; Davies, *Agriculture... South Wales*, ii, 294.
32 Idem, *Agriculture... North Wales*, 357; also partly cited in Humphreys, *Crisis of Community*, 45.
33 Martin, 'The landed estate in Glamorgan', 63, 71; T. M. Humphreys, 'Rural society in eighteenth-century Montgomeryshire'(Univ. of Wales Ph.D. thesis, 1982), 119–22; Evans, 'The artisan and small farmer', 89.
34 G. Kay, *General View of the Agriculture of Denbighshire*, 17; Davies, *Agriculture . . . South Wales*, ii, 170; Hassall, *Pembroke*, 33; idem, *Carmarthen*, 49; Lloyd and Turnor, *Cardigan*, 17; Fox, *Glamorgan*, 57.
35 G. Kay, 'Hints for the improvement of north Wales', appended to *Denbighshire*, 17–18; idem, *Caernarvonshire*, 9; Cradock, *Letters from Snowdon*, 112–13; NLW MS 1676B: Walter Davies's tour through north Wales, 1797.
36 For example, NLW, Wigfair 6: Thos. Williams to Ed. Lloyd, prob. 1685; NLW, Ruthin MS 1531.
37 Carms. RO, Cawdor/Vaughan MS 102/8029; NLW, Chirk Castle MS E286.
38 'Better' remedies against a bad tenant were thus introduced on the Golden Grove estate (Carms.) shortly before 1715 and were quickly copied on the Derwydd estate; thus in certain leases of Richard Vaughan of Derwydd a sum of 15s. a year was reserved for default of grinding corn at his mills (Carms. RO, Cawdor/Vaughan MS 102/8029).
39 NLW, Crosswood MSi/1021.
40 PP, 1896, xxxiv, 471–2.
41 Evans, 'The artisan and small farmer', 90; PP, 1896, xxxiv, 473.
42 NLW, Bronwydd MS i/619.
43 Evans, 'The artisan and small farmer', 89–91.
44 NLW, Powis Castle correspondence, MS 3566.
45 Williams, 'Agriculture and society in Glamorgan', 59.

46 A. H. John, 'Glamorgan, 1700–1750', in A. H. John and Glanmor Williams (eds.), *Glamorgan County History*, v, *Industrial Glamorgan* (Cardiff, 1980), 35.
47 I owe this reference to Dr Mark Matthews.
48 Wigstead, *A Tour to North and South Wales*, 32, 44; Eric Morgan, 'The economic, social and political life of the Hundred of Dewisland . . . *c.* 1790–1914' (unpub. M.Phil. thesis, Univ. of Wales, 1992), 33–4.
49 Kay, *Denbighshire*, 38–9; BL, Add. MS 35127, fos. 180–2, letter 14 September 1792. I owe thanks to Professor G. E. Mingay for this reference.
50 Howell, *Patriarchs*, 216–17; Fox, *Glamorgan*, 57–8; Davies, *Agriculture . . . South Wales*, i, 173–4.
51 Evans, *Letters . . . South Wales*, 427.
52 Colyer, *The Welsh Cattle Drovers*, 3; Hassall, *Carmarthen*, 31; idem, *Pembroke*, 37; NLW, Wynnstay deposit, 1952, i; Hassall, *Carmarthen*, 31–2.
53 Cradock, *Letters from Snowdon*, 111–12; Parry, 'Stability and change', 185–6.
54 Cited in ibid., 27; see also Humphreys, *Crisis of Community*, 128–9; Kay, *Flintshire*, 7–8.
55 Roberts, 'The decline of the Welsh squires', 164.
56 Many of these 'errors' are listed in Evans, *Letters . . . South Wales*, 427–8. Philip Yorke (1743–1804) of Erddig (Denbs.) was exceptional, however, in introducing improving husbandry clauses into his leases from 1767 onwards (Eric Griffiths, *Philip Yorke, (1743–1804) Squire of Erthig* (Wrexham, 1995), 53ff).
57 For this revisionism see F. V. Emery, 'The mechanics of innovation', 35–48; Martin, 'The landed estate in Glamorgan', 102; Humphreys, *Crisis of Community*, 148–52.
58 R. J. Colyer, 'Early agricultural societies in south Wales', *WHR*, 12 (1984–5), 567–8.
59 Dodd, *The Industrial Revolution in North Wales*, 61ff; Thomas, 'Colonization, enclosure and the rural landscape', 142.
60 PP, 1893–4, xxxvi, 58.
61 NLW, Harpton Court MS c/14.
62 NLW, Margam and Penrice MS L 1128; see also Margam and Penrice MS 1989; Carms. RO, Cawdor/Vaughan MS 102/8029: letter of 11 July 1717, Vaughan to Morgan.
63 NLW, Powis Castle MS 1030.
64 Carms. RO, Cawdor/Vaughan MS 102/8029: letters of R. Vaughan, 30 April, 23 Aug. 1715.
65 NLW, Ashburnham, MS 236.
66 NLW, Powis Castle correspondence, MS 1021.

67 Ibid., MS 1907.
68 For example, the comment of the steward of St Donats (Glam.) cited in A. H. John, *The Industrial Development of South Wales*, 17; see also Gwent RO, Medlycott D760/135; letter 29 May 1723 of E. Riggs to a Monmouthshire gentleman.
69 Carms. RO, Cawdor/Vaughan MS 8029, fo. 52.
70 For 1678–83, NLW, Wigfair 6; NLW, Wynnstay rental 1670–94; NLW, Kemeys-Tynte MSS 27 and 46; NLW, Herbert correspondence, no. 457; NLW, Chirk Castle MS E. 3670. For 1690–1, NLW, Rhual MS 63; NLW, Wynnstay rental 1670–94; NLW, Chirk Castle MS F5876. For 1694–9, NLW, Powis Castle correspondence, MS 22075; NLW, Brogyntyn MS 934; NLW, Clenennau MS 937; NLW, Wynnstay rental 1694–1705; NLW, Margam and Penrice MSS L312, L341; NLW, Owen and Colby MS 1959.
71 For 1700–3, NLW, Chirk Castle MSS E454, E6274; NLW, Powis Castle correspondence, MS 803. For 1708–9, NLW, Ashburnham MSS 228–9, 243–4; NLW, Picton Castle MS 1574; Flints. RO, Erddig MS D/E/539. For 1722–3, Gwent RO Medlycott D760.135; NLW, Margam and Penrice MS L1071. For 1726, University of Wales, Swansea, Mackworth MSS 248, 250. For 1728, NLW, Chirk Castle MS E1327. For 1731–8, NLW, Chirk Castle MS E1098; NLW, Bodewryd MSS 475, 487–90; UCNW, Bangor, Penrhos, i, MS 376; University of Wales, Swansea, Mackworth MSS 423, 458, 485; NLW, Brogyntyn MSS 607, 1432–3, 1439–40; Flints. RO, Erddig D/E/457; Carms. RO, Dynevor 155/i: letters of Thomas Williams, 1735–6. For 1740–2, NLW, Milborne MS 2259; NLW, Margam and Penrice MSS L1203, L1234, L1237; NLW, Bodewryd MS 704; NLW, Chirk Castle MSS F14063, F4529; NLW, Badminton MS 11233; NLW, Owen and Colby MSS 895, 909; NLW, Brogyntyn MS1443. For 1747–8, NLW, Brogyntyn MS 1563; NLW Chirk Castle MS F14063; UCNW, Bangor, Kinmel MS 1675. For 1750–1, NLW, Powis Castle correspondence, MSS 1958–9; Flints. RO, D/M/4289 and D/E/550. For 1755–6, Carms. RO, Cawdor/Vaughan: letters of Lewis Lewis to J. Vaughan, 26 Feb., 6 March, 24 May 1756; NLW, Chirk Castle MS E327.
72 NLW, Bodewryd MS 490.
73 NLW, Chirk Castle MS E3670; see also Flints. RO, D/KK762; NLW, Kemeys-Tynte MSS 30,46.
74 UCNW, Bangor, Kinmel MS 1675.
75 Gwent RO, D.760.135; University of Wales, Swansea, Mackworth MS 378.
76 UCNW, Bangor, Henblas MS A18; NLW, Bodewryd MS 704; Emery, 'Wales', in *AHE&W, V*, i, 405–6.
77 NLW, Brogyntyn MS 1443.

78 Carms. RO, Cawdor/Vaughan MSS, box 41/5720; see also NLW, Owen and Colby MS 2218 for a similar predicament in south-west Wales in May 1800.
79 Carms. RO, Dynevor MS 155/i.
80 NLW, Chirk Castle MS F14063.
81 NLW, Ashburnham MS 244.
82 NLW, Chirk Castle MS E5031. See also NLW, Bodewryd MS 488 for David Roberts's (Plas Eyton) sympathetic attitude in 1736 in the face of calls for tenants' payments from Dr Wynne at Bodewryd.
83 E.g. in terms of arrears, NLW, Margam and Penrice MS L659, letter of 16 Nov. 1709, William Phillips to Sir Thomas Mansell.
84 NLW, Powis Castle correspondence, MS 463; NLW, Chirk Castle MSS, F9351, F3949, F2803, F2804, F10724; L. Owen, 'The Letters of an Anglesey Parson, 1712–32', *Trans. Cymm.* (1961), part i, 93; NLW, Margam and Penrice MS 2544.
85 NLW, Wynnstay R9: rental, 1694–1705.
86 NLW, Wynnstay R8: rental, 1670–93; Chirk Castle MS F14063.
87 Gwent RO, Medlycott MS D760.135.
88 UCNW, Bangor, Kinmel MS 1675: letter of 5 Jan. 1747.
89 NLW, Bodewryd MS 475.
90 NLW, Brogyntyn MS 1443; see also Brogyntyn MS 1440.
91 NLW, Margam and Penrice MS L1203.
92 NLW, Ashburnham MS 225.
93 NLW, Wynnstay R9: rental, 1694–1705.
94 Ibid.; W. M. Myddelton (ed.), *Chirk Castle Accounts, 1666–1753* (Manchester, 1931), 230, n.1286.
95 NLW, Wynnstay R8: rental, 1670–93; Howell, *Land and People*, 54.
96 NLW, Wynnstay R8: rental, 1670–93.
97 NLW, Powis Castle MS 962; Carms. RO, Cawdor/Vaughan MS 77/7034.
98 NLW, Tredegar Park MSS 119/179 and 121/143; Denning (ed.), *The Diary of William Thomas*, 8 May 1763.
99 For arrears of rent in Carmarthenshire in the early 1780s see NLW, Owen and Colby MSS 425, 427 and NLW, D. T. M. Jones MS 8045.
100 NLW, Wynnstay MS 124, fo. 101; MS 125, fos. 65, 132–3, 147–8; MS 128, fos. 177–8; MS 126, fo. 83.
101 Humphreys, *Crisis of Community*, 131–2; Howell, *Patriarchs*, 84–7.
102 David Williams, *The Rebecca Riots* (Cardiff, 1955), 130; University of Wales, Swansea, Collins MSS Box 7: 'A terrier of the . . . houses, glebe-lands, tythes . . . belonging to the rectory of Rosilly, co. Glamorgan . . . 4th Day of October, 1720'; J. A. Stratton, 'The 1720 terriers of Cregrina and Llanfihangel Nantmelan', *Trans. Rads. Soc.*, xlviii (1978), 75–8; Williams, 'Agriculture and society in Glamorgan', 61.

[103] F. Green, 'Harries of Cryglas and Trevacoon', *WWHR*, viii, (1919–20), 128; NLW, Lucas MSS 2864–5.

[104] NLW, Powis Castle MS 1958; A. L. Cust, *Chronicles of Erthig on the Dyke* (2 vols., London, 1914), i, letter 7 Feb. 1750; Flints. RO, MSS D/E556, D/M4289.

[105] F. Jones, 'The Vaughans of Golden Grove: the duchess of Bolton', *Trans. Cymm.* (1963), part ii, appendix A, 248; NLW, Chirk Castle MS E1590; NLW, Wynnstay MS 125, fo. 65.

[106] NLW, Margam and Penrice MS 6080.

[107] Howell, *Land and People*, 69; UCNW, Bangor, Bodorgan MS 1580; NLW, Margam and Penrice MS 7228; NLW MS 6556E; NLW, Noyadd Trefawr MS 737; NLW MS 4703F; NLW, Slebech MS 7466.

[108] J. Geraint Jenkins, *The Welsh Woollen Industry* (Cardiff, 1969), 125, 171, 178–9, 216–18; NLW, Wynnstay MS 129, fo. 457, letter 16 May 1783 of F. Chambre; Humphreys, *Crisis of Community*, 47–8.

[109] UCNW, Bangor, Kinmel MS 1675; Sir Frederic Eden, *The State of the Poor* (London, 1797), iii, 887; Pryce, 'Social and economic structure of north east Wales', 12, citing T. Pennant, *The History of the Parishes of Whitford and Holywell* (London, 1796); T. Pennant, *Tours in Wales*, new edn, i, 22.

[110] Colyer, *The Welsh Cattle Drovers*, 14; Williams, 'Agriculture and society in Glamorgan', 286–90.

[111] Aled Eames, *Ships and Seamen of Anglesey 1558–191* (Anglesey Antiquarian Society, 1973), 115.

[112] Muriel Bowen Evans, 'The land and its people, 1815–1974', in D. W. Howell (ed.), *Pembrokeshire County History*, iv (Haverfordwest, 1993), 35. I am grateful to Dr Prys Morgan for underlining these privileges enjoyed by the freeholder. See also R. J. Moore-Colyer, 'Farmers and fields in nineteenth-century Wales: the case of Llanrhystud, Cardiganshire', *NLW Jnl.*, 26 (1989–90), 33.

[113] Williams, 'Agriculture and society in Glamorgan', 220.

[114] NLW, SA/QA/6: bishop's visitation, 1791.

[115] Parry, 'Stability and change', 64–9.

[116] Williams, 'Agriculture and society in Glamorgan', 165–6.

[117] Bowen Evans, 'The land and its people', 18–19.

[118] Humphreys, *Crisis of Community*, 46–7; Bowen Evans, 'The land and its people', 35–6.

[119] NLW MS 22131C: letter from Cardiganshire of Lewis Evans, dated Feb. 1791.

[120] D. Lleufer Thomas, *Welsh Land Commission: A Digest of its Report* (London, 1896), 137–8.

[121] Lloyd and Turnor, *Cardigan*, 20.

Chapter 3   Craftsmen and Artisans

1   J. Geraint Jenkins, *Life and Tradition in Rural Wales* (pbk edn, Stroud, 1991), 24–5, 30–2; idem, 'Rural industry in Cardiganshire', *Ceredigion*, 6 (1968–71), 91; L. S. Andrews, 'Vaynor lands in the eighteenth century', *Mont. Colls.*, 46 (1940), 134–5.

2   Angus McInnes, 'A forgotten people: the craftsmen of pre-industrial England', in Colin Richmond and Isobel Harvey (eds.), *Recognitions: Essays Presented to Edmund Fryde* (Aberystwyth, 1996), 439–52.

3   *The Universal British Directory of Trade, Commerce and Manufactures, compiled for the years between 1793 and 1798* (Castle Rising, 1993).

4   NLW MS 1677B.

5   Sir Leonard Twiston Davies and Averyl Edwards, *Welsh Life in the Eighteenth Century* (London, 1939), 113–14.

6   Cited in Howell, *Land and People*, 153.

7   Evans, 'The artisan and the small farmer', 87; NLW, Owen of Orielton MSS., parcels 10 and 7.

8   NLW, Chirk Castle MS E2893.

9   PP, 1893–4, xxxvi, *RC on Labour, the Agricultural Labourer, Wales*, 165, para. 35.

10   Jenkins, *Life and Tradition*, 19; Jenkins, *The Agricultural Community in South-West Wales at the Turn of the Twentieth Century*, 43.

11   BL, Add. MSS 35127, letter from Hagley to Arthur Young, 14 September 1792.

12   UCNW, Bangor, Mostyn MS 6507; NLW, Wynnstay rental, 1736–9.

13   Cited by A. Davies, 'Wages, prices, and social improvements in Cardiganshire, 1750–1850', *Ceredigion*, 10 (1984–7), 31.

14   I owe thanks to my research student Dr Mark Matthews for providing me with this information.

15   G. Nesta Evans, *Social Life in Mid-Eighteenth Century Anglesey* (Cardiff, 1936), 156.

16   Humphreys, *Crisis of Community*, 48–9.

17   Emery, 'Wales', *AHE&W, V*, i, 407–8.

18   Williams, 'Agriculture and society in Glamorgan', 109.

19   Parry, 'Stability and change' 151–2.

20   Ibid., 158–60

21   NLW, GS4.44.2.

22   Parry, 'Stability and change', 151–2.

23   Williams, 'Agriculture and society in Glamorgan', 117–19.

24   Ibid., 118; F. Green, 'The fortunes of Leweston', *WWHR*, xii (1926).

25   Richard Colyer, 'Of lime and men: aspects of the coastal trade in lime in south-west Wales in the eighteenth and nineteenth centuries', *WHR*, 14 (1988–9), 55; F. Green, 'Dewisland coasters in 1751', *WWHR*, viii

(1919–20), 159–60; Hassall, *Pembroke*, 18; P. B. S. Davies, *Dewisland Limekilns* (Haverfordwest, 1989).
26 R. Pococke, *Travels*, ii, Camden Soc. (1889), 184.
27 This can be seen in Davies, *Dewisland Limekilns*, 26.
28 See, for example, GS.4.812.6.
29 Ruthin RO, QSD/SR/19, SR/39, SR/116, SR/194; for the death through starvation in 1773 of a twelve-year-old apprentice to a Bridgend shoemaker, see Denning (ed.), *The Diary of William Thomas*, 16.
30 GS.4.517.5, 4.48.4 and 4.49.5.
31 D. J. V. Jones, *Before Rebecca* (London, 1973), 31–3.
32 Ibid., 64–5.
33 H. M. Davies, ''Very different springs of uneasiness': emigration from Wales to the United States of America during the 1790s', *WHR*, 15 (1990–1), 373–81.

Chapter 4 The Labouring Poor

1 R. W. Malcolmson, *Life and Labour in England 1700–1780* (London, 1981), 35.
2 Walter Davies was informed by T. F. Lewis concerning Radnorshire: 'Labourers, in most places, have their diet at the farm houses' (*Agriculture . . . of South Wales*, ii, 289).
3 Ibid., 383–4.
4 John Rule, *The Labouring Classes in Early Industrial England 1750–1850* (London, 1986), 109.
5 NLW MS 1766E; John, 'Glamorgan, 1700–1750', 35.
6 Howell, *Land and People*, 101.
7 PP, 1919, viii, 905.
8 John, 'Glamorgan, 1700–1750' 38; Malcolmson, *Life and Labour*, 37–8; Alan Armstrong, *Farmworkers: A Social and Economic History 1770–1880* (London, 1988), 30.
9 Fox, *Glamorgan*, 46; Lloyd and Turnor, *Cardigan*, 14; J. Clark, *General View of the Agriculture of Brecknock* (London, 1794), 24; J. Clark, *General View of the Agriculture of Radnorshire* (London, 1794), 22; Hassall, *Pembroke*, 26; Kay, *Montgomeryshire*, 18; idem, *General View of the Agriculture of Anglesey*, 23; idem, *Caernarvonshire*, 20.
10 UCNW, Bangor, Mostyn MS 6423: Bodidris account books; Griffith, 'The diary of William Bulkeley of Brynddu', appendix A., 88–90; Carms. RO, Cawdor Box 71, Abermarles Accounts, Michaelmas 1731–2; F. R. Lewis, 'Lewis Morris and the parish of Llanbadarn Fawr, Cardiganshire, in 1755', *Arch. Camb.*, xciii (1938), 20, cited in Davies, 'Wages, prices, and social improvements in Cardiganshire, 1750–1850', 31; John, 'Glamorgan, 1700–1750', 38–9.

[11] F. Green, 'Pembrokeshire in bye-gone days', *WWHR*, ix (1920–3), 105–6, cited in John, *The Industrial Development of South Wales*, 16.

[12] Cited in Parry, 'Stability and change', 86.

[13] Flints. RO, D/E/558, D/E/888.

[14] Dodd, *The Industrial Revolution in North Wales*, 336.

[15] A. Young, *A Six Weeks Tour through the Southern Counties of England and Wales* (3rd edn, London, 1772), 156, 163.

[16] John, 'Glamorgan, 1700–1750', 39.

[17] D. J. Davies, *The Economic History of South Wales prior to 1800* (Cardiff, 1933), 146, citing A. Young, *Annals of Agriculture*, iii.

[18] Fox, *Glamorgan*, 46; Kay, *Denbighshire*, 15; Kay, *Anglesey*, 23; Kay, *Montgomeryshire*, 18; Clark, *Radnorshire*, 22; Kay, *Caernarvonshire*, 20; Kay, *Merioneth*, 16; Hassall, *Carmarthen*, 24; Lloyd and Turnor, *Cardigan*, 14, 31; Hassall, *Pembroke*, 25.

[19] Armstrong, *Farmworkers*, 48–52.

[20] Samuel Rush Meyrick, *History and Antiquities of the County of Cardigan* (London, 1808), cited by Davies, 'Wages, prices, and social improvements in Cardiganshire', 33.

[21] NLW MS 1762B.

[22] Davies, *Agriculture... South Wales*, ii, 284–5, 289; idem, *Agriculture... North Wales*, 353.

[23] Davies, *The Economic History of South Wales*, 145; John, 'Glamorgan, 1700–1750', 38–9.

[24] Davies, *The Economic History of South Wales*, 146; A. L. Bowley, 'The statistics of wages in the United Kingdom during the last hundred years', *Journal of the Royal Statistical Society*, 61 (1898), 702–22; Dodd, *The Industrial Revolution in North Wales*, 335.

[25] NLW, G. E. Owen MS 162, reference kindly provided by Dr Mark Matthews; J. Hucks, *A Pedestrian Tour through North Wales, 1795* (London, 1795), 14.

[26] Dodd, *The Industrial Revolution in North Wales*, 338.

[27] Ibid.

[28] Ibid.

[29] Young, *Annals of Agriculture*, iv, 23 (1785), 361–91; Dodd, *The Industrial Revolution in North Wales*, 339; Parry, 'Stability and change', 242.

[30] Armstrong, *Farmworkers*, 31; Malcolmson, *Life and Labour*, 145; Humphreys sees this as having been the case in Montgomeryshire, *Crisis of Community*, 83.

[31] Armstrong, *Farmworkers*, 33.

[32] NLW, Chirk Castle MS E5197; PP, 1896, xxxiv, *Royal Commission on Land in Wales and Monmouthshire*, 626.

[33] Davies, *Agriculture... North Wales*, 360–1.

[34] Eden, *The State of the Poor*, iii, 887–91; Dodd, *The Industrial Revolution in North Wales*, 348.

[35] Ibid.

[36] Ibid.

[37] Armstrong, *Farmworkers*, 57.

[38] Carms. RO, Cawdor MSS., Box 2/119.

[39] Lloyd and Turnor, *Cardigan*, 15; Fox, *Glamorgan*, 45.

[40] Eden, *The State of the Poor*, iii, 904.

[41] Davies, *Agriculture . . . South Wales*, ii, 284n.; for the ameliorating cushion of perquisites generally during the period of the French Wars and thereby helping maintain living standards, see Armstrong, *Farmworkers*, 54.

[42] W. J. Lewis, *Lead Mining in Wales* (Cardiff, 1967), 265–8; Lewis, 'Lewis Morris and the parish of Llanbadarn Fawr', 20; Lloyd and Turnor, *Cardigan*, 31; NLW, Powis Castle MS 1626.

[43] Ibid., MS 3954; Lewis, *Lead Mining*, 271–3; for the system in England, see Rule, *The Labouring Classes*, 64.

[44] Lewis, *Lead Mining*, 267, 274.

[45] Carms. RO, Cawdor MSS., Box 2/39: letter of 13 Nov. 1799; Lewis, *Lead Mining*, 275–6.

[46] John, 'Glamorgan, 1700–1750', 14–15.

[47] Ibid., 14, 35–7.

[48] John, *The Industrial Development of South Wales*, 18.

[49] Howell, *Patriarchs,* 100; NLW, Picton Castle MSS, journal of colliers' turns, 28 December 1776–22 February 1777 and estate rental, 1789. For Glamorgan, see John, 'Glamorgan, 1700–1750', 28–9.

[50] John, 'Glamorgan, 1700–1750', 35, 39; idem, *The Industrial Development of South Wales*, 17–18.

[51] Carms. RO, Cawdor/Vaughan MS 8029: letter of 17 Jan. 1758.

[52] NLW, Wynnstay MS 128, fos. 167, 250–1, 253.

[53] Pembs. RO, Haverfordwest Corporation Records, 1641, fo. 2.

[54] PRO, HO/67/22/280: crop returns, 1801; NLW, Tredegar Park MS. 292.

[55] P. H. Gosden, *Self-Help: Voluntary Associations in Nineteenth-Century Britain* (London, 1973), 4–9.

[56] For a good example see the 'rules and orders' of the 'True Briton' society in the parish of Llanfihangel Penbedw (Pembs.), Pembs. RO, PQ/RF/1.

[57] PP, 1803–4, xiii, 1714–15.

[58] Davies, *Agriculture . . . South Wales*, ii, 466–7; Eden, *The State of the Poor*, iii, 889.

[59] Ibid.

[60] Davies, *Agriculture . . . South Wales*, ii, 467.

[61] Eden, *The State of the Poor*, iii, 900; Pembs. RO, PQ/RF.

264

Notes

62 An argument put by A. Davies for Cardiganshire clubs, in 'Wages, prices, and social improvements in Cardiganshire, 1750–1850', 45. That the contribution of members of Llanfihangel Penbedw was merely 6*d*. compared with a charge of 10*d*. at clubs like Narberth, Newport and Fishguard in Pembrokeshire may reflect its less well-off *rural* membership.

63 R. U. Sayce, 'Popular enclosures and the one-night house', *Mont. Colls.*, 47 (1942), 109–20.

64 NLW, Harpton Court MS 1721.

65 A. E. Davies, 'Enclosures in Cardiganshire, 1750–1850', *Ceredigion*, viii (1976–9), 104–6; NLW, Crosswood MSS, group i, 1174.

66 NLW, Bronwydd MSS., i, 558; Howell, *Land and People*, 29.

67 Lloyd and Turnor, *Cardigan*, 28; W. Marshall, *The Rural Economy of the Southern Counties* (1798), i, cited in Malcolmson, *Life and Labour*, 36–7; Armstrong, *Farmworkers*, 51.

68 Olwen Hufton, 'The rise of the people: life and death among the very poor', in A. Cobban (ed.), *The Eighteenth Century: Europe in the Age of the Enlightenment* (London, 1969), 298; an excellent treatment is John Williams-Davies, 'Merched y gerddi: a seasonal migration of female labour from rural Wales', *Folk Life*, 15 (1977).

69 Ibid., 15, 18.

70 Jenkins, *The Welsh Woollen Industry*, 125, 171, 178–9, 216–18.

71 Ibid., 231–2, 236–7, 246–7, 314, 316, 328–30; for an excellent treatment see also M. Tibbott, 'Knitting stockings in Wales: a domestic craft', *Folk Life*, 16 (1978), 61–73.

72 Hutton, *Tours in North Wales*, 37; Tibbott, 'Knitting stockings in Wales', 62.

73 Jenkins, *The Welsh Woollen Industry*, 210–12.

74 Evans, *Letters . . . South Wales*, 348–50, 357–8.

75 Jenkins, *The Welsh Woollen Industry*, 330–1, 334; Clark, *Brecknock*, 45–6.

76 The Revd David Davies, *The Case of the Labourers in Husbandry Stated and Considered* (1795), 188–91, cited in Dodd, *The Industrial Revolution in North Wales*, 420–1; Eden, *The State of the Poor*, iii, 890.

77 E. J. T. Collins, 'Dietary change and cereal consumption in Britain in the nineteenth century', *Ag. Hist. Rev.*, 23 (1975), 105.

78 Hugh Owen (ed.), *Additional Letters of the Morrises of Anglesey* (*Y Cymmrodor*, xlix, 2 parts, 1947, 1949), ii, 581.

79 Pococke's *Travels through England*, ed. J. J. Cartwright, i, 1751, Camden Society (1888), 238; and ii, 1754, 1756, 1757, Camden Society (1889), 177.

80 NLW, Powis Castle MSS. 3646, 3673.

81 Davies, *Agriculture . . . South Wales*, ii, 292; Collins, 'Dietary change', 100–1.

82 UCNW, Bangor, Henblas A, 18, entry for 9 May 1735.

83 *Pococke's Travels*, ii, 1754, 1756 and 1757, 177; T. Pennant, *Tours in Wales* (3 vols., London, 1810), *Tour in North Wales*, 1773, 22.

84 BL, Add. MSS 35127: Dr J. Simmonds to Arthur Young.

85 Lloyd and Turnor, *Cardigan*, 28; Eden, *The State of the Poor*, iii, 898.

86 Davies, *Agriculture... South Wales*, ii, 292.

87 PP, 1865, xxvi. I owe thanks to Dr Eric Morgan for this reference.

88 *Pococke's Travels*, i, 238 and ii, 177; for the reference to butter, see Flints. RO, D/M 4289: letter of Sir Thomas Mostyn from Gloddaeth, 7 Dec. 1756 wherein: 'butter which our country people chiefly live on is very dear.'

89 Eden, *The State of the Poor*, iii, 898, 904.

90 Evans, *Letters... South Wales*, 436.

91 B. H. Malkin, *The Scenery... South Wales* (2nd edn, London, 1807), ii, 238. Similarly, in Cornwall, by the close of the eighteenth century fish and potatoes had become the staple foods of the labouring population (Rule, *The Labouring Classes*, 53).

92 Evans, *Letters . . . South Wales*, 436; Davies, *Agriculture . . . South Wales*, ii, 294; Eden, *The State of the Poor*, iii, 890.

93 C. S. Read, 'On the farming of south Wales', *Journal of the Royal Agricultural Society of England*, x (1849), 148.

94 Lord George Lyttleton, *An Account of a Journey into Wales* (London, 1756), 239–40; Pennant, *Tours in Wales*, 2, 386; H. M. Vaughan, 'A synopsis of two tours made in Wales in 1775 and 1811', *Y Cymmrodor*, xxxviii (1927), 49, 57; Evans, *Letters . . . South Wales*, 185–6, 348–9; H. P. Wyndham, *A Gentleman's Tour through Monmouthshire and Wales, 1774* (London, 1775), 44, referring to the whitewashed cottages of Glamorgan; Davies, *Agriculture . . . North Wales*, 82; NLW MS 1766E: Walter Davies's notebook on south-west Wales.

95 Read, 'On the farming of south Wales', 149; for a detailed examination of cottage structures in one Welsh county in the eighteenth and nineteenth centuries, see Eurwyn William, ' "Home-made homes": dwellings of the rural poor in Cardiganshire', *Ceredigion*, xii, 3 (1995), 23–40.

96 Smith, 'Rural building in Wales', 696–98; ample evidence concerning the poor quality of farm buildings emerges from the many estate surveys of the late eighteenth century.

97 For the poor accommodation of farm servants in the late nineteenth century see PP, 1893–4, xxxvi, *Royal Commission on Labour, The Agricultural Labour, Wales*; NLW, Behrens MS 368A; Smith, 'Rural building in Wales', 698.

98 Lloyd and Turnor, *Cardigan*, 15.

99 Pennant, *Tours in Wales*, ii, 226–7.

[100] A. Armstrong, 'Food, shelter and self-help', in G. E. Mingay (ed.), *AHE&W, VI,* 1750–1850 (Cambridge, 1989), 749.

[101] Davies, *Agriculture . . . South Wales,* ii, 353–4.

[102] E.g. Lloyd and Turnor, *Cardigan,* 15: 'As the value of land has rapidly increased, fields are cultivated, which in former times supplied the poor with furze, thorns, etc. for fuel.'

[103] Armstrong, 'Food, shelter and self-help', 748.

[104] NLW, Tredegar Park MS 64/29.

[105] NLW, Badminton, ii, MSS. 1930, 1932.

[106] NLW, Picton Castle MS 1678 and Cilcennin PV book, 1734–90.

Chapter 5 The Dependent Poor

[1] Flints. RO, D/E/1296; Denning (ed.), *The Diary of William Thomas,* 180.

[2] T. P. Ellis, 'The Dolgelley parish registers', *Y Cymmrodor,* xl (1929), 184, appendix i; Eden, *The State of the Poor,* iii, 904.

[3] Carms. RO, Cwmgwili MSS., i/172.

[4] NLW., Leeswood MS 1663.

[5] E. Parkinson (ed.), *The Glamorgan Hearth Tax Assessment of 1670* (Cardiff, South Wales Record Society, 1994), xxxvii–xxxix.

[6] PRO, E/179/220/165; Humphreys, *Crisis of Community,* 56–7; Francis Green (ed.), 'Pembrokeshire hearths in 1670', *WWHR* (1920–3, 1924, 1926), based on PRO, E/179/224/532; Gerald Morgan, 'Bottom of the heap: identifying the poor in west Wales records 1600–1680', *Llafur* (1996), 27; Parkinson, *The Glamorgan Hearth Tax Assessment,* xxix.

[7] A. H. Dodd, 'The old poor law in north Wales', *Arch. Camb.,* lxxxi (1926), 112–13; PP, *Reports of Commons,* 1715–1801, ix, 719ff.

[8] For enclosure in lowland Cardiganshire creating employment, see Lloyd and Turnor, *Cardigan,* 29–30.

[9] PP, 1803–4, xiii, *Abstract of the Answers and Returns Relative to the Expense and Maintenance of the Poor.*

[10] The table is adapted from HC 1839, xliv, 8–9.

[11] J. P. Huzel, 'The labourer and the poor law, 1750–1850', in G. E. Mingay (ed.), *AHE&W, VI,* 1750–1850 (Cambridge, 1989), 761–6.

[12] See, for example, NLW, Cenarth PVB, 1743–1818; NLW, Llangedwyn PVB, 1755–1801; Ruthin RO, Erbistock PVB.

[13] The Aber-nant and Cenarth parish vestries clearly reveal this late-1770s surge in expenditure (NLW, Aber-nant PVB, 1732–1802; NLW, Cenarth PVB, 1743–1818).

[14] Ruthin RO, Henllan PVB, 1744–74.

[15] NLW, Aber-nant PVB, 1732–1802; the figures for Meifod are carried in *Cambrian Quarterly Magazine*, 1829, 92ff.

[16] NLW, Lampeter PVB, 1777–1803.

[17] Carms. RO, Newchurch PVB, 1736–1810.

[18] Humphreys, *Crisis of Community*, 88.

[19] On 1 February 1793 an overseer of the parish of Llanbister and two others unlawfully promised John Moss of the parish of Llanfihangel Nant Melan (Rads.) £10 if he would marry Mary Griffiths of Llanbister parish, a poor person and unable to support herself; the marriage duly took place on 12 February whereby the responsibility for the future maintenance of Mary fell on her husband's parish (GS4.531.3; for similar cases see GS.4.60.4 and GS.4.63.2).

[20] Thus the Lampeter vestry on 10 June 1794 ordered the churchwardens and overseers of the poor to compel Mary Jenkins of Wern and Mary James of Berthlwyd to swear to their respective parishes and to have them removed for fear they should become chargeable to the parish, 'as they were inform'd that they are in a state of pregnancy' (NLW, Lampeter VB, 1777–1803).

[21] NLW, Cenarth VB, 1743–1815; Ruthin RO, Henllan PVB, 1744–74. Similar resolutions to maintain only those that were settled and belonged to the parish were made by fourteen parishioners of Llanfihangel Bachellaeth parish (Caerns.) on 7 September 1766 (NLW, Broom Hall MS 1275), and by the vestry of Llandysiliogogo parish (Cards.) on 7 July 1767 (NLW, Llandysiliogogo PVB, 1766–79).

[22] NLW, Lampeter PVB, 1777–1803; NLW, Llanfihangel Ystrad PVB, 1791–1805.

[23] Ruthin RO, QSD/SR/111, Michaelmas 1736.

[24] See, for Carmarthenshire, T. I. Jeffreys Jones, 'The parish vestries and the problem of poverty, 1783–1833', *BBCS*, 14 (1950–2), 222–4, who employs the term 'chronic paupers'.

[25] Ibid.

[26] Ruthin RO, Henllan PVB.

[27] Ruthin RO, Erbistock PVB.

[28] Caernarfon RO, XPE 55/26.

[29] A. Davies, 'Some aspects of the operation of the old poor law in Cardiganshire, 1750–1834', *Ceredigion*, vi (1968), 17.

[30] NLW, Lampeter PVB, 1777–1803; NLW, Llanfair-ar-y-bryn PVB, 1791–1800.

[31] NLW, Aber-nant PVB, 1732–1802.

[32] NLW, Llanfair-ar-y-bryn PVB, 1791–1800; NLW, Llanrhystud PVB, 1737–1802, no. i.

[33] E. N. Bennet, *Problems of Village Life* (London, 1914), 144–6; Alun Davies writes of Cardiganshire between 1750 and 1834: 'Many persons

often informed the vestries that they were too poor to maintain their relatives' (Davies, 'Some aspects of the operation of the old poor law', 27).

[34] NLW, Lampeter PVB, 1777–1803; Davies, 'Some aspects of the operation of the old poor law', 22–3.

[35] Ibid.

[36] NLW, Llanfair-ar-y-bryn PVB, 1791–1800.

[37] The parish vestry books I have consulted, like those of Llannor (Caerns.), Gwyddelwern (Mer.), Aber-nant, Llanfair-ar-y-bryn, are replete with such cases of child care; Denning (ed.), *The Diary of William Thomas*, Editor's Introduction, 16.

[38] Davies, 'Some aspects of the operation of the old poor law', 26.

[39] Jeffreys Jones, 'The parish vestries and the problem of poverty', 231.

[40] Davies, 'Some aspects of the operation of the old poor law', 26.

[41] Jeffreys Jones, 'The parish vestries and the problem of poverty', 225; Davies, 'Some aspects of the operation of the old poor law', 20. An excellent treatment for Montgomeryshire is provided in Humphreys, *Crisis of Community*, 87–95, who speaks of the parish authorities from the 1780s being 'overwhelmed by the desperation of hungry labouring families'.

[42] Dodd, 'The old poor law in north Wales', 117–18; Humphreys, *Crisis of Community*, 86–7; Hucks, *A Pedestrian Tour through North Wales, 1795*, 26.

[43] Davies, 'Some aspects of the old poor law', 20–2, Jeffreys Jones, 'The parish vestries and the problem of poverty', 225–8; Ellis, 'The Dolgelley parish registers', 149–51.

[44] Ruthin RO, Henllan PVB, 1744–74; NLW, Lampeter PVB, 1777–1803; Jeffreys Jones, 'The parish vestries and the problem of poverty', 226; NLW, Llanfair-ar-y-bryn PVB, 1791–1800.

[45] Jeffreys Jones, 'The parish vestries and the problem of poverty', 227.

[46] Ibid.; Dodd, 'The old poor law in north Wales', 114; for commendation of such vestry initiatives in Montgomeryshire as propping up the cottage economy there, see Humphreys, *Crisis of Community*, 91.

[47] Davies, 'Some aspects of the operation of the old poor law', 24–5, 29.

[48] NLW, Llandysiliogogo PVB, 1766–79; NLW, Llanrhystud PVB, 1737–1802, no. i; NLW, Aber-nant PVB, 1732–1802.

[49] J. P. Huzel, 'The labourer and the poor law', in G. E. Mingay (ed.), *AHESW, VI*, 1750–1850, 757.

[50] Ibid., 772.

[51] PP, *Report of Commons*, 1715–1801, ix, 519; a valuable essay on the unreformed workhouse in Britain is James S. Taylor, 'The unreformed workhouse 1776–1834', in E. W. Martin (ed.), *Comparative Development in Social Welfare* (London, 1972), 57–84.

52 PP, 1803–04, xiii, 712.
53 Taylor, 'The unreformed workhouse', 61.
54 Dodd, *The Industrial Development of North Wales*, 387–90.
55 Davies, 'Some aspects of the operation of the old poor law', 16.
56 Dodd, 'The old poor law in north Wales', 122.
57 Davies, 'Some aspects of the operation of the old poor law', 16; NLW, Llawhaden parochial records (reference kindly provided by my research student, Dr Eric Morgan); Jeffreys Jones, 'The parish vestries and the problem of poverty', 233.
58 Dr Eric Morgan kindly drew my attention to the Llawhaden evidence; Eden, *The State of the Poor*, iii, 901; NLW, Llanfair-ar-y-bryn PVB, 1791–1800.
59 Pembs. RO, PQ/7/1800. I am again indebted to Dr Eric Morgan for access to his photocopy of this report.
60 Taylor, 'The unreformed workhouse', 64, 74; NLW, Llanfair-ar-y-bryn PVB, 1791–1800. However, Llandyfaelog vestry (Carms.) on 20 October 1795 made residence in the almshouse compulsory if paupers were to receive parish charity: only poor widows·and their children were to be excepted from this ruling. But the order was rescinded on 24 August 1802. Similar strictness as to paupers having to enter the workhouse or poorhouse was taken by the Llangyndeyrn vestry on 15 September 1797 and 12 October 1797, with the exception of idiots and the bedridden (Jeffreys Jones, 'The parish vestries and the problem of poverty', 233–4).
61 Olwen H. Hufton, *The Poor of Eighteenth-Century France, 1750–1789* (Oxford, 1974), ch.iv.
62 Cited in G. Nesta Evans, *Social Life in Mid-Eighteenth-Century Anglesey* (Cardiff, 1936), 196.
63 Wigstead, *A Tour to North and South Wales*, 17.
64 NLW, Wynnstay rentals, 1695 and 1699, in Rental 1694–1705.
65 Evans, *Social Life in Mid-Eighteenth-Century Anglesey*, 197; GS4.47.6.
66 Dodd, 'The old poor law in north Wales', 113, citing the *North Wales Gazette*.
67 Cited in Davies, *The Economic History of South Wales*, 144.
68 Evans, *Letters . . . South Wales*, 222.
69 Davies, 'Some aspects of the operation of the old poor law', 15; PP, *Reports of Commons*, 1715–1801, ix, 293.
70 D. W. Howell, *Patriarchs and Parasites: The Gentry of South-West Wales in the Eighteenth Century* (Cardiff, 1986), 150.
71 Pembs. RO, Pembrokeshire treasurers' vouchers, 1782–9.
72 GS.4.817.4; GS.4.55.3; for similar fates in Glamorgan see Denning (ed.), *The Diary of William Thomas*, 16, 160–1.
73 Trefor M. Owen, *The Customs and Traditions of Wales* (Cardiff, 1991), 55.

74 Carms. RO, Cawdor Vaughan MSS. 22/647, 103/8061 and 63/6575; F. Jones, 'The Vaughans of Golden Grove', *Trans. Cymm.* (1966), 162; NLW, Tredegar Park MSS. 117/206, 50/114 and 43/31; NLW, Chirk Castle MS E.6271; NLW, Wynnstay MSS, rental and accounts, 1736–9, 1743–4, and MS 122, fo. 421.

75 PP, 1803–4, xiii, 1714–15; NLW, Llangedwyn PVB, 1755–1801; NLW, Aber-nant PVB, 1732–1802; Ruthin RO, Erbistock PVB; Caernarfon RO, XPE 55/26.

76 NLW, Glynllivon MSS. 380 and 533.

77 NLW MS 821: survey of Caernarfonshire.

78 Malkin, *The Scenery . . . South Wales*, ii, 23–4.

79 Humphreys, 'Rural society in eighteenth-century Montgomeryshire', 250–1.

80 In reaching this conclusion I obviously disagree with K. D. M. Snell's contention that as far as settled inhabitants of parishes in England were concerned, 'before about 1780 relief policy was usually generous, flexible and humane' (*Annals of the Labouring Poor* (Cambridge, 1985), 106–7).

81 NLW, Cenarth PVB, 1743–1818; Ruthin RO, Henllan PVB, 1744–74; NLW, Aber-nant PVB, 1732–1802.

82 GS4.64.5.

83 NLW, Noyadd Trefawr MS 1678.

84 T. I. Jeffreys Jones, 'Parochial administration in Carmarthenshire', *Trans. Cymm.* (1952), 73; NLW, Llangedwyn PVB, 1755–1801; NLW, Llanfair-ar-y-bryn PVB, 1791–1800; NLW MS 1676B: journal of tour through part of north Wales, 1797.

85 NLW, Chirk Castle MS E4082.

86 GS4.373.6.

Chapter 6 *Relations in Working the Land*

1 Geraint H. Jenkins, *The Foundations of Modern Wales, 1642–1780* (Oxford, 1987), 225.

2 Ibid., 223, 225–6.

3 NLW, Chirk Castle MS E2893.

4 F. Jones, 'The Vaughans of Golden Grove', *Trans. Cymm.* (1964), ii, 202.

5 NLW, Chirk Castle MS E2089.

6 Carms. RO, Cawdor/Vaughan, box 40, collection i, letter of 1 Nov. 1756 from Lewis Lewis to Vaughan.

7 UCNW, Bangor, Mostyn MS 7539.

8 UW, Swansea, Mackworth MS 513.

9 Glam. RO, D/DP/877/2, 877/9.

10 NLW, Chirk Castle MS E5570.
11 NLW, Wynnstay MS 123, memorandum, August 1777.
12 Ibid., MS 122, fos. 501–2.
13 NLW, Chirk Castle MS E2747.
14 UCNW, Bangor, Mostyn MSS. 7725 and 7726.
15 NLW, Tredegar Park MS 291: letter of 14 July 1799 of Henry Brown to Morgan.
16 NLW, Chirk Castle MS E871; NLW, Badminton, ii, MS 11241.
17 Introduction to *Casgliad o Bregethau*, translation kindly provided by Martin Davies, Aberystwyth.
18 Jenkins, *Foundations*, 268–9.
19 Ibid., 275.
20 E. D. Evans, *A History of Wales, 1660–1815* (Cardiff, 1976), 224.
21 NLW, Wynnstay MS 126, fo. 283, memo of F. Chambre.
22 Ibid., MS 125, fo. 547; MS 129, fo. 483; NLW, Burdon Deeds and Documents, MS 23.
23 NLW, Wynnstay MS 132, fos. 73–4.
24 Ibid., MS 123, fos. 169–70; MS 129, fos. 217–18.
25 Davies, ' "Very different springs of uneasiness": emigration from Wales to the United States', 377–82; PP, 1896, xxxiv, 51; R. Colyer, *A Land of Pure Delight* (Llandysul, 1992), 155.
26 Carms. RO, Cawdor/Vaughan MSS. 8029 and 8057; Jones, 'The Vaughans of Golden Grove', *Trans. Cymm.* (1964), ii, 203; BL, Hardwicke papers, cclii, Add. MSS. 35,600, fos. 29–32, source kindly indicated by Paul Langford.
27 NLW, Tredegar Park MS 121/144.
28 NLW, Wynnstay MS 122, fo. 509; GS4.193.2.
29 NLW MS 11774 (Behrens MS 15): letter of 12 March 1825 of L. P. Jones to D. Davies; PP, 1896, xxxiv, 470–1.
30 Hilary M. Thomas (ed.), *The Diaries of John Bird, 1790–1803* (Cardiff, South Wales Record Society and Glamorgan Archive Service, 1987), 89.
31 Carms. RO, Cwmgwili MSS. i/185; Humphreys, *Crisis of Community*, 145–6.
32 NLW, Chirk Castle MS E777. See also NLW, Eaton Evans and Williams (Haverfordwest) MSS. 959–60, relating to an 'impudent' tenant, William Williams.
33 UCNW, Bangor, Mostyn MS 7643.
34 Both passages cited in Jenkins, *Foundations*, 268, 271.
35 Howell, 'Landlords', 267–8.
36 GS4.900.2 and 903.1.
37 Carms. RO, Dynevor MS 155/i: letters of 19 Nov. and 7 Dec. 1735; NLW, Brogyntyn MS 1433.
38 For Ireland, see Thomas Bartlett, 'An end to moral economy: the Irish

militia disturbances in 1793', in C. H. E. Philpin (ed.), *Nationalism and Popular Protest* (Cambridge, 1987), 216. I am grateful to Mrs Claire Boucher, my research student, for this reference.

39 NLW, Bronwydd MS 6804.
40 NLW, Wynnstay MS 123, fo. 81: letter of 9 May 1777; NLW, Tredegar Park MS 116/218 and 224.
41 Cited in J. G. W. Scheltinga, 'The Gwydir estate 1814–1914' (unpub. Ph.D. thesis, Univ. of Wales, 1992), 166.
42 NLW, Margam and Penrice MS L1034; NLW, Chirk Castle MS E822; see also NLW, Badminton ii, MS 11241: petition of William Watkins.
43 NLW, Wynnstay MS 124, fo. 397.
44 NLW, SD/CCCM (G), 254–9; NLW, Leeswood schedule, 25–7; NLW, Badminton MSS. 9848 and Badminton, ii, MS 11234.
45 David Williams, *The Rebecca Riots* (Cardiff, 1955), 131; NLW, Lucas schedule, 72.
46 Flints. RO, Lloyd Kenyon papers, MS206; NLW, Mayberry MSS. 4252, 4354–6; NLW, Cilybebyll MSS.1402–13.
47 NLW, Brogyntyn MS 910.
48 Parry, 'Stability and change', 76.
49 NLW, Wynnstay MS 124, fo. 445, MS 123, fo. 457.
50 NLW, Tredegar Park MS 291; NLW, Margam and Penrice MS 2544.
51 Davies and Edwards, *Welsh Life in the Eighteenth Century*, 6.
52 NLW, Wynnstay MS 129, fo. 565: letter of Francis Chambre, 28 April 1786.
53 Suggett, 'Some aspects of village life in eighteenth-century Glamorgan', 100.
54 NLW, Brogyntyn MS 1427.
55 For example, Carms. RO, Cawdor/Vaughan MS 102/8029: letter of R. Vaughan, 7 Oct. 1718 to Morgan; UCNW, Bangor, Bodrhyddan MS 2153.
56 NLW, Brogyntyn MS 1444.
57 Ibid., MS 1461.
58 GS.4.895.4; UCNW, Bangor, Mostyn MS 7632.
59 GS.4.377.4.
60 GS.4.273.4; GS.4.52.2.
61 Suggett, 'Some aspects of village life in eighteenth-century Glamorgan', 106–8.
62 Cited ibid., 106–7; see also Denning (ed.), *The Diary of William Thomas*, 17 June 1763, 30 May 1764.
63 GS.4.272.4.
64 GS.4.255.3.
65 *The Merioneth Miscellany, 1955*, 'A report of Penllyn and Edeirnion', *Cylchgrawn Cymdeithas Hanes a Chofnodion Sir Feirionydd*, 1–3 (1952–5), 16.

[66] I owe thanks once again to Martin Davies, Aberystwyth, for this reference.

[67] GS.4.250.5.

[68] GS.4.47.4; GS.4.384.4; GS.4.380.7; GS.4.387.10.

[69] R. J. Moore-Colyer, 'Horses and equine improvement in the economy of modern Wales', *Ag. Hist. Rev.*, 39, 2 (1991), 126.

[70] GS.4.301.4.

[71] Denning (ed.), *The Diary of William Thomas*, 29 July, 1785.

[72] Thomas (ed.), *The Diaries of John Bird*, 168.

Chapter 7 *Popular Culture, Religion and Alternative Belief*

[1] Matthews, 'In pursuit of profit: local enterprise in south-west Wales in the eighteenth century' (unpub. Ph.D. thesis, Univ. of Wales, 1998), 113; Suggett, 'Some aspects of village life in eighteenth-century Glamorgan', 8; Jenkins, *Foundations*, 277; Denning (ed.), *The Diary of William Thomas*, 48.

[2] Jenkins, *Foundations*, 397–9; idem, Richard Suggett and Eryn M. White, 'The Welsh language in early modern Wales', in Geraint H. Jenkins (ed.), *The Welsh Language Before the Industrial Revolution* (Cardiff, 1997), ch. ii.

[3] For the best account of educational progress in eighteenth-century Wales see Gareth E. Jones, *Modern Wales* (2nd edn, Cambridge, 1994), ch. 6; Jenkins, *Foundations*, 370–81.

[4] R. S. Schofield, 'Dimensions of illiteracy in England 1750–1850', *Explorations in Economic History*, 10, iv (1972), 437–54.

[5] These figures were generously made available to me by Mr Brinley W. Jones.

[6] Jenkins, *Foundations*, 379–80, 409.

[7] Bob Bushaway, ' "Tacit, unsuspected, but still implicit faith": alternative belief in nineteenth-century rural England', in Tim Harris (ed.), *Popular Recreations in England, 1500–1850* (London, 1995), 192; Prys Morgan, *The Eighteenth Century Renaissance* (Llandybïe, 1981), 45–6.

[8] Robert Malcolmson, *Popular Recreations in English Society* (Cambridge, 1973), 15.

[9] NLW, Cardiganshire QSOB, July 1773, where the 'great increase' in unlicensed alehouses for Cardiganshire was noted; see also NLW, C. in W. MSS SD/QA/121: incumbent of Begelly parish (Pembs.) reporting in 1799 on the great deal of 'drunkenness and revelling' at unlicensed alehouses in his district.

[10] For example, Robert Hughes of Brymbo (Denbs.) was attacked with tongs by Edward Jones of Hope (Flints.) yeoman on 1 January 1742 in

the evening at a public house at Hope, from which blow he was to die on 16 January (GS4.47.8); again, Hugh Davies, a turner of Denbigh, on 23 July 1742 was involved in a fight with Edward Jones at an alehouse in Ruthin, the latter receiving a nasty gash to his temple (GS4.49.3). The diary of William Thomas refers to certain individuals dying through overdrinking.

11 GS4.382.6, Breconshire gaol file, autumn 1760, attesting to Peter Powell's wife going to Bwlch alehouse 'for her husband' and sitting down with them by the kitchen fire; GS.4.52.7, Denbs. gaol file, Autumn 1759, testifying to Edward Morris and his wife being in the Sign of the Hand in Chirk sometime in Feb. 1759; GS4.50.6, Denbs. gaol file, March 1752, testifying to Ellis Jones and Jane Williams being at the alehouse in Llanrhaeadr in Kinmerch in mid-July 1751.

12 Pennant, *Tours in Wales*, 2, 210, referring to Merioneth; Peter Burke, *Popular Culture in Early Modern Europe*, Aldershot, revised reprint, 1994, 50 and chs. 4 and 5; Isser Woloch, *Eighteenth-Century Europe: Tradition and Progress, 1715–89* (London, 1982), 216, 221; William Thomas's diary for 6 November 1763, in recording the burial of Zephania Jones, tyler, noted that he was 'a great diverter of vain folks in winter nights in telling them old stories'.

13 Malcolmson, *Popular Recreations*, 15.

14 Pennant, *Tours in Wales*, 2, 243.

15 Malcolmson, *Popular Recreations*, ch. ii; idem, 'Leisure', in G. E. Mingay (ed.), *The Victorian Countryside* (London, 1984), ii, 603–4; Bob Bushaway, *By Rite: Custom, Ceremony and Community in England, 1700–1880* (London, 1982), 44, 107; J. M. Golby and A. W. Purdue, *The Civilisation of the Crowd: Popular Culture in England, 1750–1900* (London, 1984), ch. i.

16 Owen, *Customs and Traditions*, 67; Malcolmson, *Popular Recreations*, 52.

17 *Lleuad yr Oes* (Williams, Abertawy, 1827), cited by Hugh Owen, 'Introduction' to Griffith, 'The diary of William Bulkeley', 26; see also Bulkeley's entry for 15 March 1741 referring to football matches between adjacent parishes in Anglesey in the years around 1740.

18 Davies and Edwards, *Welsh Life in the Eighteenth Century*, 46; G. J. Williams, 'Glamorgan customs in the eighteenth century', *Gwerin*, i (1955), 100, 102–3; Owen, *Customs and Traditions*, 92–4; Malcolmson, *Popular Recreations*, 16–19, 52–3.

19 Richard Suggett, 'Festivals and social structure in early modern Wales', *Past and Present*, 150 (Feb. 1996), 79–112; Denning (ed.), *The Diary of William Thomas*, 206.

20 Evans, *Letters . . . South Wales*, 437–8; Malcolmson, *Popular Recreations*, 49.

21 See, for gambling, Bulkeley's diary, 4 June 1734 relating to a cock-fight at Llandyfrydog (Angl.). There are a number of references to theft of cocks in the eighteenth-century sessions rolls of the Denbs. Quarter Sessions housed at Ruthin RO; see also Merioneth Quarter Sessions, Easter 1784: case of Robert Owen, labourer, stealing a fighting cock from an esquire.

22 The Revd Pegge, 'A memoir on cock-fighting', *Archaeologia*, iii, cited in Davies and Edwards, *Welsh Life in the Eighteenth Century*, 44–5. For English cock-fights, see Malcolmson, *Popular Recreations*, 50.

23 Autobiography of Matthew Owen of Llanrhwydrus (Angl.), in *Cymru*, xxxiv, cited in Davies and Edwards, *Welsh Life in the Eighteenth Century*, 47–8; Owen, *Customs and Traditions*, 80, 94.

24 Malcolmson, *Popular Recreatons*, 20–5; C. D. Morgan, *Wanderings in Gower* (Swansea, 1886), 27–8 for a description of Penrice 'Harvest fair'.

25 Bushaway, *By Rite*, 148–60; T. M. Owen, *Welsh Folk Customs* (new edn, 1987), 27, 46–7, 69.

26 Bushaway, *By Rite*, 126.

27 Suggett, 'Festivals and social structure', 108–9.

28 Golby and Purdue, *The Civilisation of the Crowd*, 18, 51ff.

29 Davies and Edwards, *Welsh Life in the Eighteenth Century*, 62; Owen, *Customs and Traditions*, 99; G. Nesta Evans, *Religion and Politics in Mid-Eighteenth Century Anglesey* (Cardiff, 1953), 63–4.

30 For Elizabeth Baker's diaries, see Ben Bowen Thomas, *The Old Order* (Cardiff, 1945), 17; Suggett, 'Festivals and social structure', 85.

31 Owen, *Customs and Traditions*, 100; Edmund Hyde Hall, *A Description of Caernarvonshire (1809–11)* (Caernarfon, 1952), 317, 319; Thomas Edwards (Twm o'r Nant), *Bannau y Byd* (c.1800).

32 Golby and Purdue, *The Civilisation of the Crowd*, 43. Yet it is often difficult to discern the precise reason for decline, as, for example, of revels in the Vale of Glamorgan noted for the year 1764 by William Thomas (Denning (ed.), *The Diary of William Thomas*, 117).

33 GS4.824.1, 825.1.

34 Suggett, 'Festivals and social structure', 89.

35 Ibid., 110.

36 Golby and Purdue *The Civilisation of the Crowd*, 25–6; Cradock, *Letters from Snowdon*, 42–3.

37 Thomas, *The Old Order*, 38–9, 50.

38 S. P. Menefee, *Wives for Sale* (Oxford, 1981), 32; E. P. Thompson, *Customs in Common* (Penguin, 1993), 409. This paragraph owes much to conversation with my research student, Mrs Wilma Thomas.

39 Owen, *Welsh Folk Customs*, 234; Catrin Stevens, 'The funeral wake in Wales', *Folk Life*, 14 (1976), 27–45.

40 The authoritative works are J. R. Gillis, *For Better, for Worse: British*

Marriages, 1600 to the Present (Oxford 1985); Stephen Parker, *Informal Marriage, Cohabitation and the Law, 1750–1989* (London, 1990); R. B. Outhwaite, *Clandestine Marriage in England, 1500–1850* (London, 1995); Lawrence Stone, *Uncertain Union and Broken Lives: Marriage and Divorce in England, 1660–1857* (Oxford, 1995).

[41] J. R. Gillis, 'Conjugal settlements: resort to clandestine and common law marriage in England and Wales, 1650–1850', in J. Bossy (ed.), *Disputes and Settlements: Law and Human Relations in the West* (Cambridge, 1983), 261–86, cited in Outhwaite, *Clandestine Marriage*, 139.

[42] Roger L. Brown, 'Clandestine marriages in Wales', *Trans. Cymm.* (1982), 74–5; 'A report of Penllyn and Edeirnion', *Cylchgrawn Cymdeithas Hanes a Chofnodion Sir Feirionydd*, 1–3 (1952–5), 8.

[43] See, for example, NLW, SD/CCC m (G), 316 a–f, consistory court, archdeaconry of Carmarthen, the case of Morgan Beynon and Elizabeth Lewis.

[44] The Revd J. Evans, *A Tour through Part of North Wales in the Year 1798, and at Other Times*, 359–60; idem, *Letters . . . South Wales*, 354.

[45] Parker, *Informal Marriage*, 25; Gillis, *For Better, for Worse*, 97.

[46] Stone, *Uncertain Unions and Broken Lives*, 12–13.

[47] Parker, *Informal Marriage*, 26; Gillis, *For Better, for Worse*, 30–1, 109, 114, 120–1.

[48] Hyde Hall, *A Description of Caernarvonshire*, 323.

[49] Parker, *Informal Marriage*, 19–20.

[50] E. W. Jones, 'Medical glimpses of early 19th century Cardiganshire', *NLW Jnl.*, xiv (1965–6), 260–75, cited in Gillis, *For Better, for Worse*, 31.

[51] Gillis, *For Better, for Worse*, 198–9; Outhwaite, *Clandestine Marriage*, 139.

[52] Gwennith Gwynn, 'Besom wedding in the Ceiriog Valley', *Folk Lore*, xxxix (1928), 150–1, 160–4; Gillis, *For Better, for Worse*, 198; Parker, *Informal Marriage*, 18; Menefee, *Wives for Sale*, ch. ii, 'Jumping the broom – and back'.

[53] Parker, *Informal Marriage*, 19.

[54] Gwynn, 'Besom wedding in the Ceiriog Valley', 158.

[55] The consistory court of the archdeaconry of Carmarthen thus dealt with restitution of conjugal rights in the case brought by Morgan Beynon of Mothvey against Elizabeth, his wife, in 1746 and, again, in the case brought around 1750 by John Rees of Llangennech against his wife, Mary (NLW, SD/CCCM (G), 316 (a–f) and 355 (a–k)).

[56] Gillis, *For Better, for Worse*, 73–81.

[57] Denning (ed.), *The Diary of William Thomas*, 14, 133: John y Nel was John O'Neil, a legendary Irish pirate, who used to play a crucial part in

the Llantwit Major Annwyl Day Celebrations; see also Owen, *Customs and Traditions*, 64–6.

58 Williams, 'Glamorgan customs', 106–8.

59 The quotation is from Edward Pugh, *Cambria Depicta* (1816), 438–9, cited in Owen, *Customs and Traditions*, 66; Gillis, *For Better, for Worse*, 79–80.

60 The provision of Welsh services is shown in the bishops' queries and answers, as for example, bishop's visitation, archdeaconry of Carmarthen, queries and answers, clergy, 1755 (NLW, SD/QA/61). For a masterful analysis of the visitation returns across Wales see Eryn M. White, 'The established Church, Dissent and the Welsh language *c.*1660–1811', in Jenkins (ed.), *The Welsh Language before the Industrial Revolution*, 234–87.

61 Carms. RO, Dynevor MS 154/3, letter 27 September 1776.

62 Jenkins, *Foundations*, 180; Lewis Lewis, curate of a Carmarthenshire parish behaved scandalously at Easter 1750, through intoxication, and in the months following, which led to the churchwardens hauling him before the consistory court (NLW, SD/CCCM (G), 348–54).

63 For a different view concerning the standing of the clergy in the minds of parishioners, see Parry, 'Stability and change', 305 and 311 where he argues that immorality and misbehaviour meant 'many undoubtedly failed to command the respect of their parishioners'.

64 Davies and Edwards, *Welsh Life in the Eighteenth Century*, 48.

65 Jenkins, *Foundations*, 181; Parry, 'Stability and change', 316.

66 Ibid.

67 Ibid., 316–17.

68 NLW, SD/QA/61: archdeaconry of Carmarthen, bishop's visitations, 1755. The numbers of communicants and total number of families in each parish are in many cases no more than estimates. Numbers of families stated were translated into total numbers of inhabitants by using a multiplier of 4.1/3.

69 GS4.250.4; GS4.1005.13.

70 Jenkins, *Foundations*, 356; Parry, 'Stability and change', 337–44.

71 G. H. Jenkins, *Literature, Religion and Society in Wales* (Cardiff, 1978), 237.

72 I owe this observation to my colleague at Swansea, Dr Prys Morgan.

73 The Morris quotation is cited in Parry, 'Stability and change', 310; Thomas, *The Old Order*, 45.

74 Jenkins, *Foundations*, 342.

75 Parry, 'Stability and change', 342–3; Jenkins, *Foundations*, 356.

76 Kay, *Caernarvonshire*, 20–1.

77 Evans, *Letters . . . South Wales*, 354.

78 Jenkins, *Foundations*, 357; Parry; 'Stability and change', 344. Valuable

insights into women's place and role in Methodism have been provided by Dr Eryn White.

79 G. H. Jenkins, 'The new enthusiasm', in G. E. Jones and T. Herbert (eds.), *The Remaking of Wales in the Eighteenth Century* (Cardiff, 1988), 45.

80 Ibid., 45–7; idem, *Foundations*, 355–6.

81 Ibid., 195–6, 382–4.

82 Davies and Edwards, *Welsh Life in the Eighteenth Century*, 125–6; Jenkins, *Foundations*, 185.

83 Ibid., 358; for examples of persecution, see William Williams, *Welsh Calvinistic Methodism* (2nd edn, London, 1884), chs. v and vi.

84 Jenkins, *Foundations*, pp. 358–9.

85 Ruthin RO, DD WY/6962; Williams, *Welsh Calvinistic Methodism*, 85.

86 Ibid., 86–7.

87 Bushaway, 'Alternative belief in nineteenth-century rural England', 195; Charles Phythian-Adams, 'Rural culture', in G. E. Mingay (ed.), *The Victorian Countryside* (London, 1981), ii, 616ff. For the authoritative analysis of folk beliefs in Wales see Geraint H. Jenkins, 'Popular beliefs in Wales from the Restoration to Methodism', *BBCS*, xxvii (1977–8), 440–62.

88 Phythian-Adams, 'Rural culture', 621; Bushaway, 'Alternative belief', 208–9; Edmund Jones, *Account of the Parish of Aberstruth in the County of Monmouth* (Trevecka, 1779), 68–77.

89 Ibid., 77; Wigstead, *A Tour to North and South Wales*, 20; Evans, *Letters . . . South Wales*, 439–40.

90 Owen, *Welsh Folk Customs*, 111.

91 Ibid., 98, 111, 130.

92 Phythian-Adams, 'Rural culture', 620–3; Bushaway, 'Alternative belief', 210.

93 Phythian-Adams, 'Rural culture', 622; J. Ceredig Davies, *Welsh Folk Lore* (Aberystwyth, 1911), 207; Jones, *Account of the Parish of Aberstruth*, 72–3; Peter Roberts, *The Cambrian Popular Antiquities of Wales* (London, 1815), 169–72; Meyrick, *The History and Antiquities of the County of Cardigan*, 55–6.

94 Phythian-Adams, 'Rural culture', 622; Jones, *Account of the Parish of Aberstruth*, 77; Owen, *Welsh Folk Customs*, 47–8.

95 Hyde Hall, *A Description of Caernarvonshire*, 321; Jenkins, *Foundations*, 279.

96 Ceredig Davies, *Welsh Folk Lore*, 230; Jenkins, 'Popular beliefs', 447–8.

97 Ibid., 450–2; Ceredig Davies, *Welsh Folk Lore*, 230–46; GS4.529.9; Denning (ed.), *The Diary of William Thomas*, 203; Roberts, *Cambrian Popular Antiquities*, 268–9; GS4.47.3; William Edward of the Vale of Glamorgan (d.1768) could also discover a thief's identity (Denning (ed.), *The Diary of William Thomas*, 203).

[98] Jenkins, *Foundations*, 368.

[99] Bushaway, 'Alternative belief', 200, 213–15.

Chapter 8 The People and Politics

[1] The standard works here are the many articles by P. D. G. Thomas, starting with his 'Eighteenth century politics', in A. J. Roderick (ed.), *Wales through the Ages* (Llandybïe, 1960), ii; Philip Jenkins, 'Political quiescence and political ferment', in Herbert and Jones (eds.), *The Remaking of Wales in the Eighteenth Century*; and Jenkins, *Foundations*, ch. 8.

[2] Jenkins, 'Political quiescence and political ferment', 16–17; idem, 'Jacobites and freemasons in eighteenth century Wales', *WHR*, 9, no. 4 (1979), 402–5; Jenkins, *Foundations*, 312–13; Gwyn A. Williams, 'Beginnings of radicalism', in Herbert and Jones (eds.), *The Remaking of Wales in the Eighteenth Century*, 121.

[3] Jenkins, 'Political quiescence and political ferment', 17; Jenkins, *Foundations*, 312–13, 319–20.

[4] Carms. RO, Cwmgwili MSS i/226, 292; Plas Llanstephan MS 333.

[5] Evans, *A History of Wales, 1660–1815*, 212–15.

[6] Jenkins, 'Political quiescence and political ferment', 17.

[7] Ibid., 17, 29–30; Jenkins, *Foundations*, 314; Howell, *Patriarchs*, 120–1.

[8] For an excellent discussion, see Jenkins, *Foundations*, 322–3.

[9] D. V. J. Jones, *Before Rebecca* (London, 1973), 27, 52–5; Williams, 'Beginnings of radicalism', 111–47; idem, *The Search for Beulah Land*, 22–3.

[10] Idem, 'Beginnings of radicalism', 137–8; Jones, *Before Rebecca*, 53.

[11] GS4.256.4; Williams, 'Beginnings of radicalism', 138–9.

[12] Ibid., 134–6; Jones, *Before Rebecca*, 52.

[13] Ibid., 27, 60.

[14] Williams, *The Search for Beulah Land*, 22–3.

[15] Evans, *Letters . . . South Wales*, 329.

[16] Frank O'Gorman, *Voters, Patrons and Parties: The Unreformed Electoral System of Hanoverian England 1734–1832* (Oxford, 1989), 58–62; Sir Lewis Namier and J. Brooke (eds.), *The House of Commons, 1754–90* (3 vols., London, 1964), i, 36.

[17] NLW, Nanteos collection, unscheduled; Myddelton (ed.), *Chirk Castle Accounts*, 443–4.

[18] O'Gorman, *Voters, Patrons and Parties*, 53–5; E. Porritt, *The Unreformed House of Commons* (Cambridge, 1909), i, 118; Carms. RO, Cwmgwili MS 109.

[19] O'Gorman, *Voters, Parons and Parties*, 9; also H. Perkins, *The Origins of Modern English Society, 1780–1880* (London, 1969), 38–51.

20 Carms. RO, Cwmgwili i/MS 281; Roland Thorne, 'The political scene, 1660–1815', in B. E. Howells (ed.), *Pembrokeshire County History*, iii (Haverfordwest, 1987), 346.
21 NLW, Chirk Castle MS E5355; NLW, Tredegar Park MS 66/27.
22 NLW, Wynnstay rental 1745–7.
23 Humphreys, *Crisis of Community*, 208.
24 NLW, Margam/Penrice MS L1199.
25 Ibid., MS L590.
26 Ibid., MS L1014, also cited in full in Jenkins, 'Political quiescence and political ferment', 22–3.
27 NLW, Chirk Castle MS E4356.
28 NLW, Chirk Castle MS E2890.
29 Jenkins, *Foundations*, 304–5.
30 NLW, Chirk Castle MS E4904; Jenkins, *Foundations*, 305; Carms. RO, Cawdor/Vaughan MS 102/8029.
31 O'Gorman, *Voters, Patrons and Parties*, 237.
32 NLW, Badminton ii, MS 14827; Carms. RO, Cwmgwili i, MS 304.
33 A. W. Jones, 'Agriculture and the rural community of Glamorgan, circa 1830–1896' (unpub. Ph.D. thesis, Univ. of Wales, 1980), 441.
34 NLW, Chirk Castle MSS 3724, E663, E865.
35 Humphreys, 'Rural society in eighteenth-century Montgomeryshire', 581; idem, *Crisis of Community*, 207.
36 Ibid., 210.
37 Flints. RO, D/E/1158; Humphreys, *Crisis of Community*, 212–13; Thorne, 'The political scene, 1660–1815', 342; Jenkins, *Foundations*, 305.
38 NLW, Wynnstay MS 124, fos. 95–6 and MS 122, fo. 214.
39 O'Gorman, *Voters, Patrons and Parties*, 248ff.
40 NLW, Gogerddan MSS: unscheduled letters; see also Carms. RO, Abergwili i, MS 228.
41 Howell, *Patriarchs*, 128–9; F. Jones, 'The Vaughans of Golden Grove', iv, *Trans. Cymm.* (1966), 183.
42 NLW, Brogyntyn MS 1548; Tredegar Park MS 121/145.
43 NLW, Chirk Castle, MS E320.
44 R. D. Rees, 'Electioneering ideals current in south Wales, 1790–1832', *WHR*, 2, 3 (1965), 242.
45 NLW, Harpton Court MS C138.
46 NLW, Wynnstay MS 125, fo. 325. Chambre accordingly subscribed £50 on behalf of his master.
47 NLW, Tredegar Park MS 292.
48 Carms. RO, Cwmgwili i, MS 168; O'Gorman, *Voters, Patrons and Parties*, 90–105; David Eastwood, 'Contesting the politics of deference: the rural electorate, 1820–60', in Jon Lawrence and Miles Taylor (eds.), *Party, State and Society: Electoral Behaviour in Britain since 1820*

(Aldershot, 1997), 31–3; Matthew Cragoe, 'The Golden Grove interest in Carmarthen politics' (unpub. MA thesis, Univ. of Wales, 1986).
49 NLW, Badminton ii, MSS 2120, 2123.
50 NLW, Tredegar Park MSS 124/529, 66/166.
51 Ibid., MS 124/526.
52 NLW, Harpton Court MSS 1845, c/89.
53 *Trans. Carms. Antiq. Soc.*, i (1905–6), 96; NLW, Badminton MS 1326. From the mid-1780s Robert Morris of Clasemont, campaigning on behalf of Swansea freeholders, argued for their rights of common, which were being eroded by the duke of Beaufort's illegal encroachments (R. Sweet, 'Swansea politics and reform, 1780–1820', *WHR*, 18, i (1996), 22).
54 O'Gorman, *Voters, Patrons and Parties*, 252–3; Carms. RO, Dynevor MS 155/2, reference kindly provided by Dr Mark Matthews; Denning (ed.), *The Diary of William Thomas*, 96.
55 P. D. G. Thomas, 'A Welsh political storm: the Treasury warrant of 1778 concerning Crown lands in Wales', *WHR*, 18, iii (1997), 433.
56 Ibid., 434–9.
57 NLW, Noyadd Trefawr MS 1808.
58 Thomas, 'A Welsh political storm', 439–43.
59 NLW, Pentypark MS 58.
60 Thomas, 'A Welsh political storm', 444–9.
61 John Bohstedt, *Riots and Community Politics in England and Wales 1790–1810* (Cambridge, Mass., 1983), 5.

Chapter 9 Riots and Popular Resistance

1 An earlier version of part of this chapter appeared in David W. Howell and Kenneth O. Morgan (eds.), *Crime, Protest and Police in Modern British Society: Essays in Memory of David Jones* (Cardiff, 1999).
2 Cradock, *Letters from Snowdon*, 49–50.
3 D. J. V. Jones, 'The corn riots in Wales, 1793–1801', *WHR*, 2 (1964–5), 323.
4 Emery, 'Wales', *AHE&W*, *V*, i, 405 citing the diarist Owen Thomas; Griffith, 'The diary of William Bulkeley', entry for 15 April 1757.
5 GS4.299.1.
6 Denning (ed.), *The Diary of William Thomas*, 172–3; see also GS4.810.7; Pembs. RO, Haverfordwest Corporation records, 2143, fo. 52.
7 Edward Thompson, 'The moral economy of the crowd', *Past and Present*, 50 (1971), 78.
8 Flints. RO, D/M 4289.
9 J. Stevenson, *Popular Disturbances in England, 1700–1870* (London, 1979), 95.
10 At Wrexham: Flints. RO, D/E/539; at Loughor and Swansea: John,

'Glamorgan, 1700–1750', 42; at St Asaph: UCNW, Bangor, Penrhos, i, 807; at Beaumaris (1728): UCNW, Bangor, Penrhos, i, 367; at Pembroke: PRO, SP 36/50, part 3, fos. 88–9; at Denbigh: GS4.47.3; at Rhuddlan, Rhyl, Prestatyn and St Asaph: PRO, SP. 36/50, part 3, fos. 92–7 and K. Lloyd Gruffydd, 'The Vale of Clwyd corn riots of 1740', *Flintshire Historical Society Publications*, 27 (1975–6), 38–9; at Caernarfon in 1752: W. H. Jones, *Old Karnarvon* (Caernarfon, 1882), 135–6; at Laugharne and Carmarthen: Howell, *Patriarchs*, 135, 161; at Holyhead, Redwharf, Llanbedr-goch and Beaumaris: Evans, *Social Life in Mid-Eighteenth Century Anglesey*, 185–6; GS4.252.3; Griffith, 'The diary of William Bulkeley', entry for 8 Feb. 1758; at Caernarfon in 1758: J. H. Davies, *The Morris Letters* (Aberystwyth, 1909), ii, 62, kindly provided in translation by Dr Prys Morgan; Caernarfon RO, M/1705: letter of Edward Bridge of Aberwheeler, Bodfari, 21 Feb. 1758; at Conwy: Caernarfon RO, M/1705; at Pwllheli: GS4.273.1; at Llanishen and Ely: Denning (ed.), *The Diary of William Thomas*, 132; at Flint and across the north Wales coalfield in 1778 and 1789: Dodd, *The Industrial Revolution in North Wales*, 400; at Aberystwyth in 1783: Lewis, *Lead Mining in Wales*, 277.

11 Stevenson, *Popular Disturbances in England*, 96.

12 Eden, *The State of the Poor*, iii, 904; Roger Wells, 'The revolt of the south-west, 1800–1', *Social History* (October, 1977), 740–1.

13 NLW, Chirk Castle MS E87; Dodd, *The Industrial Revolution in North Wales*, 400; also GS4.1012.3, Flintshire gaol file, April 1790, concerning riot in parish of Bangor-on-Dee, Flints., 24 July 1789; Lewis, *Lead Mining in Wales*, 277; Davies, *The Morris Letters*, letter of 13 Feb. 1758.

14 Lloyd Gruffydd, 'The Vale of Clwyd corn riots', 42.

15 GS4.816.3.

16 Griffith, 'The diary of William Bulkeley', entry for 8 Feb. 1758.

17 PRO, SP.36/50, part 3, fos. 92–7; GS4.47.3; GS4.252.3; Thompson, 'The moral economy', 114.

18 Griffith, 'The diary of William Bulkeley', entry for 8 Feb. 1758.

19 Wells, 'The revolt of the south-west', 726; GS4.299.1, NLW MS 1352B, fo. 321, Dudley Ackland to Mr [John] Campbell, 10 March 1796.

20 Thompson, 'The moral economy', 112; David Jones made the same claim for the riots in Wales in the 1790s and 1800–1 ('The corn riots in Wales', 339); Wells, 'The revolt of the south-west', 723.

21 Parry, 'Stability and change', 105.

22 J. Bohstedt, 'Gender, household and community politics: women in English riots 1790–1810', *Past and Present*, 120 (1988), 105.

23 PRO, SP 36/50, part 3, fos. 94, 96.

24 Davies, *The Morris Letters*, 62. The Welsh phrase used by William Morris in his letter of 13 Feb. 1758 was 'a chware mas y riwl'; GS4.64.4.

25 Bohstedt, 'Gender, household and community politics', 106.

26 Thompson, 'The moral economy', 113–14.

27 Lloyd Gruffydd, 'The Vale of Clwyd corn riots', 41; PRO, SP 36/50, part 3, fo. 94.

28 *Gentleman's Magazine*, 27 (1757), 591–2; A. J. Hayter, *The Army and the Crowd in Mid-Georgian England* (London, 1978), 17.

29 Thompson, 'The moral economy', 121–2; Jones, 'The corn riots in Wales', 339.

30 NLW, clerk of the peace correspondence, Pembroke County Records, 1795–7: in February 1796 the Pembrokeshire magistrates resolved: 'All persons going from farm to farm to purchase up the corn storehousing the same in order to export it for profit in these times of scarcity are enemies in the country and the real authors and instigators of the riotous disposition of the people.' Wells, 'The revolt of the south-west', 724 comments that 'magisterial indifference to the claims of the free market was one of the reasons for the survival of the "moral economy" '.

31 NLW MS 12501E (Wigfair 101): Parry, 'Stability and change', 101.

32 Evans, *Social Life in Mid-Eighteenth Century Anglesey*, 185–6.

33 Wells, 'The revolt of the south-west', 743; GS4.273.1; GS4.1002.5; Lloyd Gruffydd, 'The Vale of Clwyd corn riots', 40–2; GS4.47.3; GS4.64.4; my thanks to Glyn Parry for the reference to Merthyr. The hanging of the pig gelder for his part in the Caernarfon corn riot of April 1752 after a 'drumhead court martial' held on the spot was perhaps done out of pique by the authorities at the effrontery of the riot taking place during the sitting of the Sessions (I owe this information and idea to a conversation with Glyn Parry, and for details see Jones, *Old Karnarvon*, 134–5).

34 Parry, 'Stability and change', 106; Caernarfon RO, M/1705.

35 Pembs. RO, Haverfordwest Corporation records, 2143, fo. 52.

36 NLW, Wynnstay MS 125, fos. 299, 317–18, 325, MS 128, fos. 167 and 253.

37 NLW MS 1352B, fo. 310.

38 T. S. Ashton and J. Sykes, *The Coal Industry of the Eighteenth Century* (Manchester, 1929), 119; NLW MS 1412D (Henry Owen MSS).

39 E. P. Thompson, *Customs in Common* (Harmondsworth, 1993), 308ff.

40 Lloyd Gruffydd, 'The Vale of Clwyd corn riots', 37–9.

41 NLW, Chirk Castle MS E4894; GS4.47.3.

42 NLW, GS4.252.3.

43 Thompson, *Customs in Common*, 327.

44 Lloyd Gruffydd, 'The Vale of Clwyd corn riots', 40, 42; NLW, GS4.47.3; NLW, Chirk Castle MS E4894; GS4.252.3; GS4.273.1 and 273.3.

45 Bohstedt, 'Gender, household and community politics', 89; W.

Thwaites, 'Women in the market place: Oxfordshire c. 1690–1800', *Midland History*, ix (1984), 35–6; N. Rogers, *Crowds, Culture and Politics in Georgian Britain* (Oxford, 1998), 229; Jones, 'The corn riots in Wales', 344–5, 350; Thomas (ed.), *The Diaries of John Bird 1790–1803*, 131.

46 Thompson, *Customs in Common*, 246–8.
47 PRO, SP 36/50, part 3, fos. 88–9 for Pembroke; PRO, SP 36/50, part 3, fos. 92–3 for Rhuddlan; NLW MS 12501E for Conwy.
48 Lloyd Gruffydd, 'The Vale of Clwyd corn riots', 42.
49 Jones, 'The corn riots in Wales', 336–7, 343; Thompson, *Customs in Common*, 248.
50 Carl Winslow, 'Sussex smugglers', in D. Hay, P. Linebaugh and E. P. Thompson (eds.), *Albion's Fatal Tree* (London, 1975), 121.
51 Graham Smith, *Smuggling in the Bristol Channel 1700–1850* (Newbury, 1989), 141.
52 *Crime and Punishment: A Welsh Perspective: Crime and the Sea, A Maritime Dimension* (Gwynedd Archives and Museums Service, 1987), 29.
53 Smith, *Smuggling in the Bristol Channel*, 141.
54 *Crime and Punishment: A Welsh Perspective*, 28; there is an oral tradition that women in Rhosili, Gower, took part in the smuggling and joined in the attacks on customs officers: see David Rees (ed.), *A Gower Anthology* (Swansea, 1977), 121.
55 'Incidents at Oxwich', *Gower*, 22 (1971).
56 *Crime and Punishment: A Welsh Perspective*, 29; Griffith, 'The diary of William Bulkeley', entry for 21 Sept. 1742.
57 Smith, *Smuggling in the Bristol Channel*, 137, 141.
58 A. Stanley Davies, 'Cardiganshire salt smugglers – an xviii century riot', *Arch. Camb.*, xci (1936), 312.
59 GS4.813.3.
60 *Crime and Punishment: A Welsh Perspective*, 28.
61 Smith, *Smuggling in the Bristol Channel*, 142–4.
62 Winslow, 'Sussex smugglers', 142–4; Smith, *Smuggling in the Bristol Channel*, 143–4.
63 John Rule, 'Wrecking and coastal plunder', in Hay et al. (eds.), *Albion's Fatal Tree*, 185–6.
64 For the notion of an 'ungovernable' people, see J. Brewer and J. Styles (eds.), *An Ungovernable People: The English and their Law in the Seventeenth and Eighteenth Centuries* (London, 1980).
65 Rule, 'Wrecking and coastal plunder', 177.
66 Evans, *Letters... South Wales*, 113; Philip Jenkins, 'Times and seasons: the cycles of the year in early modern Glamorgan', *Morgannwg*, xxx (1986), 26–7.

67 Rule, 'Wrecking and coastal plunder', 182.

68 GS4.818.3; GS4.60.3.

69 Rule, 'Wrecking and coastal plunder', 170, 173, 186.

70 GS4.251.1.

71 *Crime and Punishment: A Welsh Perspective*, 39.

72 Rule, 'Wrecking and coastal plunder', 182.

73 Ibid., citing *Annual Register*, xvii (1774), 113–14 and *Annual Register*, xviii (1775), 154; *Crime and Punishment: A Welsh Perspective*, 37–44.

74 Ibid., 39.

75 *Annual Register*, xvii (1774), 113–14.

76 *Crime and Punishment: A Welsh Perspective*, 38; *Annual Register*, xviii (1775), 113, which mistakenly refers to the *Charming Nancy*.

77 Smith, *Smuggling in the Bristol Channel*, 139; John, 'Glamorgan, 1700–1750', 34.

78 Evans, *Letters . . . South Wales* 111–12; Denning (ed.), *The Diary of William Thomas*, 268, 270, 315; Jenkins, *The Making of a Ruling Class*, 98, was the first to recognize this gentry vigilance.

79 Douglas Hay, 'Poaching and the game laws on Cannock Chase', in Hay et al. (eds.), *Albion's Fatal Tree*, 192, 208; P. B. Munsche, *Gentlemen and Poachers* (Cambridge, 1981), 77–8, 87, 107.

80 For entitlement to a 'penalty' see NLW, Brogyntyn MS 1104; NLW, Harpton Court MS C/82: letter of 5 Dec. 1773; GS4.527.2.

81 NLW, Badminton manorial records, Crickhowell and Tretower manors, MSS 224, 231, 240, 148; NLW, Chirk Castle MS D104.

82 Munsche, *Gentlemen and Poachers*, 87.

83 Ruthin RO, Denbs. Quarter Sessions OB, Hilary, 1728/9.

84 UNCW, Bangor, Bodrhyddan MS 2158.

85 Flints. RO, D/MT/568, 569.

86 Munsche, *Gentlemen and Poachers*, 92; Flints. RO, D/MT/571.

87 The same observation is made by Hay for Cannock Chase, in Hay et al. (eds.), *Albion's Fatal Tree*, 213.

88 NLW, Powis Castle MSS 2956, 2785.

89 Ibid., MS E5283.

90 NLW, Tredegar Park MS 66/166: 6 December 1784, concerning Charles Morgan's right to collect commortha rents in the manor of Brecon; Carms. RO, Vaughan MS 8029: letter of John Vaughan of Golden Grove, 28 December 1756, which talks of the lord's right having been 'shamefully neglected' in Golden Grove manors; NLW, Wynnstay Deposit, 1952, i, concerning collection of fines and amerciaments in the manor of Cyfeiliog, 1763.

91 Ibid.; NLW, Wynnstay MS 127, fo. 57, F. Chambre to Sir Watkin W. Wynn, 10 April 1788; the whole complex problem of 'custom, law and

common right' is the title of Edward Thompson's awe-inspiring chapter 3 in his *Customs in Common*. For a petition from a body of freeholders complaining of harassment on a Crown manor in Radnorshire from the 1760s see NLW, Harpton Court MS 1791.

[92] NLW, Badminton ii, MS 1930: Gabriel Powell's answer, 15 Feb. 1748.

[93] Ibid., MSS 1455, 1457, 1458, 2061.

[94] Ibid., MSS 2363–8, 1457, 2334. The disputes have been analysed in detail in Joanna Martin, 'Private enterprise *versus* manorial rights: mineral property disputes', *WHR*, 9 (1978–9), 155–75.

[95] Beynon, 'The lead mining industry in Cardiganshire', 84–106 and appendix, 18ff; Meyrick, *History and Antiquities of the County of Cardigan*, appendix, nos. 18, 19; Lewis, *Lead Mining in Wales*, ch. 5.

[96] NLW, Tredegar Park MSS 70/226, 70/227, 66/166.

[97] Ibid., MSS 70/266, 66/166.

[98] Ibid., MS 119/624, 116/230, 114/526, 124/527.

[99] Ibid., MS 64/29.

[100] NLW, Bronwydd i, MS 569; GS4.900.6; see also for a legal dispute in 1779 between Madam Lloyd and V. Thomas and his 'gang' over the right of cutting turf in Nevern parish, Bronwydd, i, MS 568; Myddelton (ed.), *Chirk Castle Accounts*, 484.

[101] NLW, Harpton Court MSS 1721, 1784, 1802, 1785, 1843, 1791, 1853, 1739, 1844, 1845, c/89.

[102] NLW, Badminton ii, MS 1932.

[103] NLW, Crosswood i, MS 1174.

[104] NLW, Brogyntyn MS 1274.

[105] Thomas (ed.), *The Diaries of John Bird 1790–1803*, 113–14.

[106] See Thompson, *Customs in Common*, 121ff for urban protests over common rights.

[107] Carms. RO, Cwmgwili i, MS 283; for a 1786 'notice' drawn up by the Carmarthen rioters of that year see Carms. RO, Plas Llanstephan MS 337.

[108] GS4.621.3.

[109] NLW, Wynnstay MS 128, fo. 173.

[110] Jones, *Before Rebecca*, 45–6; NLW, Leeswood MS 1758; NLW, Chirk Castle E542.

[111] Roger Wells, 'Social protest, class, conflict and consciousness in the English countryside, 1700–1880', in Mick Reed and Roger Wells (eds.), *Class, Conflict and Protest in the English Countryside, 1700–1880* (London, 1990), 155–6; J. M. Neeson, *Commoners: Common Right, Enclosure and Social Change in England, 1700–1820* (Cambridge, 1993), 280–1.

[112] Pembs. RO, Lewis of Henllan MS 1/83; GS4.842.2.

[113] J. R. Western, *The English Militia in the Eighteenth Century* (London, 1965), chs. 6, 7, 8 and 9.

[114] NLW, Tredegar Park MS 52/230. For the financial burden in Anglesey,

see Jones, *Before Rebecca*, 51; for the refusal of the overseers of
Newchurch parish, Carmarthenshire, to relieve the family of an absent
militiaman, see Carms. RO, Cwmgwili ii, MS 379.

[115] Western, *The English Militia*, 197–9, 298.

[116] GS4.57.3; PRO, SP 44/142, fos. 262–6.

[117] PRO, WO 1/1005, fos. 927–8.

[118] Jones, *Before Rebecca*, 52–3; W. Lloyd Davies, 'The riot at Denbigh in
1795: Home Office correspondence', *BBCS*, iv (1928–9); Bohstedt,
Riots and Community Politics in England and Wales, 1790–1810, ch. 1.

[119] GS4.51.4.

[120] Dodd, *The Industrial Revolution in North Wales*, 399; Ruthin RO,
QSD/SR/267.

[121] Wigstead, *A Tour to North and South Wales*, 48.

[122] Ian Gilmour, *Riot, Risings and Revolution* (Pimlico, 1993), ch. 10.

[123] T. M. Humphreys, 'The Llanidloes riot of 1721', *Mont. Colls.*, 75
(1987), 107–15; P. D. G. Thomas, 'County elections in eighteenth-
century Carmarthenshire', *Carmarthenshire Antiquary*, iv (1962), 35–7.

[124] Howell, *Patriarchs*, 134–5.

[125] GS4.889.4.

[126] GS4.819.5.

[127] NLW, GS4.45.2; Denning (ed.), *The Diary of William Thomas*, 139; for
the difficult position of 'plebeian constables . . . obliged to enforce an
essentially patrician concept of order', see David Eastwood, *Governing
Rural England: Tradition and Transformation in Local Government
1780–1840* (Oxford, 1994), 226–30.

Chapter 10 *Violent and Light-Fingered Neighbourhoods*

[1] J. M. Beattie, *Crime and the Courts in England 1660–1800* (Oxford,
1986), 199; see also, for the problems presented by the 'dark figure' and
other difficulties in measuring crime, J. A. Sharpe, *Crime in Early
Modern England, 1550–1750* (London, 1984), ch. 3.

[2] Howell Evans (Chief Constable), *Cardiganshire Constabulary: A
Retrospect of the Nineteenth Century relating especially to Crime and its
Prevention* (Aberystwyth, 1901), 3–5.

[3] The counties were selected on the basis of the survival of records for the
years concerned and are Brecknock, Cardiganshire, Denbighshire,
Flintshire, Glamorgan, Montgomeryshire, Pembrokeshire and Radnorshire. The five-year interval in the case of Brecknock was not possible
for 1760 (instead 1761), of Cardiganshire for 1770 (instead 1771) and of
Pembrokeshire for 1745 (instead 1744), 1755 (instead 1754), 1760
(instead 1761) and 1765 (instead 1767). The statistics were derived from

offences known to the courts and catalogued by Mr Glyn Parry at the National Library of Wales.

⁴ Sharpe, *Crime in Early Modern England*, 53–6. Beattie indicates that in England assault cases were heard in the Quarter Sessions (*Crime and the Courts in England*, 5).

⁵ David Jones, *Crime in Nineteenth-Century Wales* (Cardiff, 1992), 66.

⁶ Ruthin RO, Denbs. QS rolls. At the Denbighshire Great Sessions, even, violent offences outnumbered theft ones by 77 to 69 over the five-yearly intervals between 1735 and 1800 but even here, it is apparent, the difference in level of violence shown in the offences was not so great as in the Quarter Sessions. In the Great Sessions of the eight counties at five-yearly intervals between 1735 and 1800 theft exceeded violent offences by 692 to 536.

⁷ GS4.813.3.

⁸ Many examples are to be found in the Great Sessions gaol files including: GS4.47/8, fight between Robert Hughes (killed by a tongs) and Edward Jones on 1 Jan. 1742; GS4.375.2, fight between William Davies (killed) and Edward Prosser; GS4.377.2, fight on 8 Oct. 1740 between Thomas David (killed) and William Owen, Thomas William Hopkin intervening and stabbing Thomas David in the neck; GS4.385.7, fight on 25 Sept. 1774 in which Thomas Parry was killed; GS4.519.1, fight on 23 April 1739 in which William Price was mortally wounded.

⁹ GS4.57.6, a quarrel between Griffith Jones and Thomas Edwards following a night of merrymaking and dancing, wherein Edwards lost his life; GS4.251.2, a fight on Sunday 27 June 1742, following a wedding party, between Richard Matthew and George Warmingham who was fatally wounded; GS4.56.1, March 1768, a fight at a goose-eating between two miners, John Jones and Robert Lloyd, Jones sustaining fatal wounds.

¹⁰ GS4.64.1.

¹¹ GS4.49.3, Hugh Davies, fighting with Edward Jones in a Ruthin ale-house on 23 July 1742 allegedly rendered Jones incapable of continuing as a tanner.

¹² For example, GS4.375.3, a fight between the 'bragger' William Davies and Edward Prosser, Davies receiving mortal injuries; GS4.382.6, a fight between Philip Jeremy, the boaster, and Peter Powell, smith, who was killed.

¹³ GS4.61.1, a fight between William Jones and Edward Hughes; GS 4.54.1, a fight at Abergele fair; GS4.377.2, a fight on 8 Oct. 1740 in which Thomas David was killed; GS4.382.6 and 385.7, fights over payment of ale; GS4.519.1, a fight leading to William Price's death; GS4.50.8, fight over a girl between Owen Ellis and Andrew Williams.

¹⁴ GS4.44.5; GS4.57.5; GS4.386.7.

15 GS4.617.4; GS4.621.7.

16 NLW, Castell Gorfod MS 32.

17 NLW Facs. 600: A typescript copy of a transcript by John Price, Dolfelin, Llanafan Fawr, of 'a circumstantial account of the evidence produced on the trial of Lewis Lewis, the younger . . . before the Court of Great Sessions in Brecon, 26 August 1789'. See also NLW MS 9954C.

18 GS4.51.2 and GS4.55.4.

19 GS4.617.1; GS4.59.2; GS4.388.5; GS4.523.4.

20 GS4.742.4.

21 GS4.57.4; GS4.49.4; GS4.47.8.

22 GS4.748.1.

23 For example, GS4.819.6.

24 GS4.617.2; GS4.58.7; see also GS4.45.4: assault by Richard Williams on John Owen and the theft of breeches, and GS4.58.7, assault on John Williams, tailor, and theft of 3*s*. off his person; GS4.748.1, attack upon and robbery of two elderly women, 24 January 1789, in area about Crwbin (Carms.) by two soldiers.

25 GS4.47.5.

26 For the like situation in English counties, see Brewer and Styles (eds.), *An Ungovernable People: The English and their Law in the Seventeenth and Eighteenth centuries*.

27 For example, GS4.738.4, concerning the rescue of John Jenkins at Llandeilo by his two sons in late August 1766.

28 GS4.55.1; for other Denbighshire examples, see GS4.50.7, forcible release of John Wynne of Ystrad in mid-July 1751; GS4.55.2, forcible release of John Clark, Ruabon parish, husbandman, on 6 July 1766 out of custody of John Lloyd, a special constable, by David Jones, collier; GS4.61.2, forcible release of Thomas Peters, flaxdresser, on 5 April 1785, by two labourers.

29 GS4.50.7.

30 GS4.51.5; GS4.813.6.

31 Ruthin RO, QSD/SR/238; SR/70; SR/102; SR/143; SR/229; SR/256; Flints. RO, D/E/888; GS4.380.1; GS4.519.5; GS4.377.1; Ruthin RO, QSD/OB/1714–34.

32 For the reference to early-modern England see Sharpe, *Crime in Early Modern England*, 109; GS4.49.5. Other Denbighshire examples of a woman attacking another female are: GS4.44.3, attack by Elizabeth Wilkinson on Elianora Matthews, 4 July 1728; GS4.45.2, attack by Dorothea Matthew on Anna Roberts, 20 March 1732; Wales 4.50.2, attack by Margaret Salusbury on Margaret Gittins, 17 March 1750; GS4.52.5, attack by Dorothy Pennant on Anna Jones, 20 July 1758; Ruthin RO, QSD/SR/99, attack by Elizabeth Humphreys on Dorothy Jones.

[33] GS4.51.5; GS4.45.2.

[34] For England, see Beattie, *Crime and the Courts in England*, 106; F. McLynn, *Crime and Punishment in Eighteenth-Century England* (London, 1989), 117ff, is informative on murders by women in English counties.

[35] M. Jackson, *New-Born Child Murder* (Manchester, 1996), 49; the Denbighshire QS citation is from Ruthin RO, QSD/SR/342.

[36] GS4.388.4; see also, Jackson, *New-Born Child Murder*, 48.

[37] Ibid., 49.

[38] GS4.47.6.

[39] GS4.56.1.

[40] Jackson, *New-Born Child Murder*, 47.

[41] Ibid., 46.

[42] This conclusion is based on an inspection of eighteenth-century Welsh gaol files for all Welsh counties.

[43] GS4.388.10; as far as other young girls were concerned: GS4.48.5; GS4.53.1 and GS4.302.2.

[44] GS4.44.4 and GS4.57.2.

[45] GS4.59.7.

[46] GS4.378.4.

[47] Examples of rape of married women are to be found in: GS4.47.6; GS4.51.1; GS4.385.2; GS4.528.7.

[48] Beattie, *Crime and the Courts in England*, 74.

[49] For an example of the making up of a quarrel by the mediation of neighbours, see GS4.50.8, quarrel between Roger Lewis and John David.

[50] GS4.47.2 and GS4.47.3. For other examples of men killing their wives see GS4.748.3; GS4.620.6; GS4.45.3.

[51] GS4.381.3.

[52] GS4.48.2; GS4.823.6; GS4.44.3. For other seeking of sureties from battered wives see GS4.738.3; GS4.51.6.

[53] GS4.250.5.

[54] GS4.57.3.

[55] GS4.522.5, 522.7; GS4.897.7; see also GS4.898.4; GS4.47.5, concerning John Johnson and Peter Williams; GS4.50.5, concerning Robert Sockett and Thomas Griffiths.

[56] For example, GS4.743.4, conviction of Daniel Morgan Rees at Carms. spring sessions, 1780, of burning an outhouse; GS4.49.1, presentment of Hugh Ellis for firing a barn; GS4.45.3, presentment of Catherine *uch* Richard for firing farm buildings and barley, oats and hay; for a follow-up to the last case see Ruthin RO, QSD/SR/101; GS4.377.4, presentment of Ann Watkins for firing a barn and two wainhouses; GS4.387.3, presentment of John James for firing a house; GS4.276.1, presentment

of John Evans for firing a house; GS4.274.3, presentment of Jonnet Jones for firing ricks; GS4.278.1, presentment of Mary Williams for burning a stack; GS4.256.4, presentment of Elizabeth Owen for firing corn ricks and a cart house.

57 GS4.278.1; GS4.387.3.
58 GS4.256.4.
59 GS4.376.5; GS4.387.3. For horse stabbing see GS4.817.1 and 818.6.
60 GS4.528.4; GS4.384.3; GS4.1005.13 and GS4.1008.3; Ruthin RO, QSD/SR/230.
61 GS4.44.3.
62 GS4.824.3; see also GS4.47.4, the confession of Richard Holbrook who on 29 January 1740 let William Forrester into his master's farmhouse to steal money.
63 GS4.59.3, John Rowland stole from John Edwards of Stansty, farmer (Denbs.), on 30 Jan. 1779, lately dismissed from his employer's service; see also GS4.617.2, theft by David Yorath, a former servant of Richard Jones, yeoman, of St Nicholas parish, on 25 Jan. 1756; GS4.57.3, theft by Edward Peter from his former fellow servants at the farm of Thomas Jones of Llanarmon in late Jan. 1771; GS4.609.6, a confession of William Jenkin, parish of Wenvoe (Glam.), labourer, that on 17 Nov. 1729 he stole from the house of Mary James of Radir parish, spinster, where he had formerly lived as a servant.
64 GS4.744.1.
65 GS4.380.1; GS4.298.4; GS4.620.5.
66 Ruthin RO, QSD/SR/101; GS4.525.1; GS4.387.4; GS4.44.3.
67 GS4.255.1; GS4.50.4; GS4.54.2.
68 GS4.298.5; GS4.375.4; GS4.47.4; GS4.251.2; Ruthin RO, QSD/SR/199; GS4.54.1.
69 E. Vaughan Jones, 'Sheep stealing at Llangelynin in 1792', *Jnl. Mer. Hist. and Rec. Soc.*, 7 (1973–6), 394; GS4.64.5.
70 NLW, Brogyntyn MS 1440; for the theft of small coals from a colliery on the Chirk Castle estate in early 1746, see NLW, Chirk Castle MS E4883; PRO, HO 67/22/26: crop returns, 1801; Kay, *Agriculture of Anglesey*, 15.
71 Denning (ed.), *The Diary of William Thomas*, entry for 24 December 1763; GS4.178.4.
72 NLW, Llangibby MS A832: Llangevelach and Languick Association, 1784; NLW, Llanrhystud Vestry Book, i, 1737–1802; NLW, Llangeler parish register, 1777–1804; *Articles, Agreed on, for Apprehending and Prosecuting of Horse-Stealers, House-Breakers, etc. in the County of Flint* (Wrexham, 1779); see also *Shrewsbury Chronicle*, 17 March 1787, concerning the launch of the Kerry Association (Mont.) for prosecuting felons; NLW, Baker Gabb MS 953, concerning the Abergavenny

Association for the prosecution of felons; NLW, Lampeter Vestry Book, meeting 22 Oct. 1787.

73 Evans, *Rules, Orders and Guide to Cónstables and a Short History of the Cardiganshire Police Force*; NLW, D. T. M. Jones MS 1212.

74 Examples can be cited from the gaol files of the Great Sessions; for example GS4.745.1, theft by a stranger of the goods of Thomas Walter, farm servant, of the parish of Llandybïe.

75 *The ˙Cambrian Register for the Year 1795* (London, 1796), 456–7; GS4.53.3; Beattie, *Crime and the Courts in England*, 167–70; McLynn, *Crime and Punishment*, 93.

76 GS4.44.2.

77 GS4.380.6.

78 GS4.273.1.

79 GS4.60.1 and GS4.62.1. John Honest in 1788 was called John Edwards, not Jones, but was doubtless the same as the John Honest indicted in 1782.

80 Carms. RO, Cwmgwili i, MS 231a.

81 *Shrewsbury Chronicle*, 21 April 1787. For similar sentiments, see Lewis Evans's letter to his brother in London, written from Cwmgwili, 3 May 1791 (NLW MS 22131C).

82 Even as far as the helpful Brecknock Circuit Black Books are concerned, there are shortcomings. A. A. Powell in 'Crime in Brecknockshire 1733–1830 as revealed by the records of the Great Sessions' (unpub. MA thesis, Univ. of Wales, 1990), 79–80, shows that in a sample of indictments filed between 1733 and 1830, of the 354 indictments returned true bill only in 210 cases is the verdict known; further, that of the 104 guilty verdicts, sentences are known for just seventy-nine.

83 GS4.58.8.

84 Griffiths, 'The diary of William Bulkeley', *Angl. Trans.* (1933), entry for 28 April 1739.

85 NLW, Chirk Castle MS E6162.

86 GS4.63.5. William Thomas's diary records the execution on 7 October 1791 at Cardiff of 31-year-old Catherine Griffith for breaking the house of Mrs Price of Park in Llanilltern, St Fagans.

87 J. M. Beattie, 'Crime and courts in Surrey 1736–1753', in J. S. Cockburn (ed.), *Crime in England 1550–1800* (London, 1977), 170, 181; D. Hay, 'Property, authority and the criminal law', in Hay et al. (eds.), *Albion's Fatal Tree*, 40–9; Sharpe, *Crime in Early Modern England*, 63–70; McLynn, *Crime and Punishment*, xivff.

88 See the lists of offences known to the eighteenth-century Great Sessions for all Welsh counties extracted from the gaol files and compiled by Glyn Parry at the MSS Dept., NLW.

89 D. V. J. Jones, 'Life and death in eighteenth-century Wales: a note',

WHR, 10, 4 (1981), 537–8: on the Brecon circuit between 1753 and 1819 a mere 9 per cent of convicted prisoners were executed, and in Montgomeryshire and Carmarthenshire between 1800 and 1818/19 just 7 per cent and 11 per cent respectively of those capitally convicted were hanged.

90 The reprieves and pardons are scattered among the many gaol files of the Great Sessions. David Jones reached the same conclusion in his 'Life and death' article, 542. Reprieves for murderers were few indeed: GS4. 901.5, royal pardon for John Jenkins (Cards.), cobbler and militia man; GS4.735.1, royal pardon for John Lewis of Carmarthen, tailor, for murdering his wife.

91 Jones, 'Life and death in eighteenth-century Wales', 542.

92 Ibid.; E. Vaughan Jones, 'Sheep stealing at Llangelynin', 384.

93 *The Cambrian Register for the Year 1795* (London, 1796), 450.

94 Jones, 'Life and death in eighteenth-century Wales', 543–4.

95 Carms. RO, Cwmgwili i, MS 196, letter of 28 March 1785.

96 Jones, 'Life and death in eighteenth-century Wales', 545.

97 *The Cambrian Register for the Year 1795*, 450.

98 Jones, 'Life and death in eighteenth-century Wales', 545.

99 *The Cambrian Register for the Year 1796* (London, 1799), ii, 570–1; Jones, 'Life and death in eighteenth-century Wales', 541; for the indictment against Collins, see GS4.898.2.

Chapter 11 Epilogue: 'The Old Order Changeth'

1 Humphreys, *Crisis of Community*, 256–7; for the notion of the 'parish state' see David Eastwood, *Government and Community in the English Provinces, 1700–1870* (London, 1997), ch. 2.

2 Hughes Jones (of Maesglasau), *Garddy Caniadau* (1776) cited in Humphreys, *Crisis of Community*, 254–5.

3 Williams, *The Rebecca Riots*, 105–6.

4 Suggett, 'Some aspects of village life in eighteenth-century Glamorgan', 95ff; for eighteenth-century Anglesey justices carrying on the tradition of the old 'mediators' or even older daldeu see Evans, *Religion and Politics in Mid-Eighteenth Century Anglesey*, 206 and appendix C.

5 Jones, *Before Rebecca*, chs. 1 and 2; see also Humphreys, *Crisis of Community*, 'Conclusions'; Williams, *The Search for Beulah Land*, 22–3.

6 E. D. Evans, *A History of Wales 1660–1815* (Cardiff, 1976), 219, 224–5.

7 Douglas Hay and Nicholas Rogers (eds.), *Eighteenth-Century English Society* (Oxford, 1997), 196; Wilfrid Prest, *Albion Ascendant: English History 1660–1815* (Oxford, 1998), 165.

8 See, for example, UCNW, Bangor, Plas Coch MS 1324: criticism of Viscount Bulkeley in 1709 by Anglesey gentry.

[9] For the British-wide dimension to this see Frank O'Gorman, *The Long Eighteenth Century: British Political and Social History 1688–1832* (London, 1997), 328.

[10] G. E. Mingay, *Land and Society in England 1750–1980* (London, 1994), 31–5.

[11] For Charles Richardes, see BL, Hardwicke papers, cclii, Add. MSS 35, 600, fos. 29–32 (my thanks to Paul Langford for directing me to this source); for Sir John Meredith, see NLW, Tredegar Park MSS 116/127, 130, 132; for Edward Pryse Lloyd, see NLW, Eaton Evans and Williams MSS 4404–94.

[12] My observations for Ireland are primarily based on Jim Smyth, *The Men of No Property: Irish Radicals and Popular Politics in the Late Eighteenth Century* (London, 1992), chs. 1 and 2 and pp. 101 and 104; see also Samuel Clark and James Donelly, Jr. (eds.), *Irish Peasants: Violence and Political Unrest 1780–1914* (Manchester, 1983), 15.

[13] Hay and Rogers (eds.), *Eighteenth-Century English Society*, 208, where it is claimed that by 1820 a new social order had come about wherein paternalism was marginal; Eastwood, *Governing Rural England*, 261–5, where it is argued that the remodelling of the English poor law in the 1830s saw the landed élite much shorn of its traditional ascendancy in local administration by the institution there of a 'new kind of paternalism', that of central government; Alun Howkins, *Reshaping Rural England. A Social History 1850–1925* (London, 1991), 74, which refers to 'the destruction of the old paternalist order' between the 1800s and 1840s; Mingay, *Land and Society in England*, 35; John Archer, *By a Flash and a Scare: Incendiarism, Animal Maiming, and Poaching in East Anglia 1815–1870* (Oxford, 1990), 30–1. But for a claim that paternalism was not a strong motivation among most nineteenth-century English landowners towards maintaining the rural social order – indeed that most were indifferent to the well-being of their communities – see F. M. L. Thompson, 'Landowners and the rural community', in Mingay (ed.), *The Victorian Countryside*, ch. 33.

[14] Glanmor Williams, *Religion, Language and Nationality in Wales* (Cardiff, 1979), 165; I have also benefited from conversation on this point with Dr Prys Morgan. For the mid-nineteenth-century politicization of the *Gwerin* see I. G. Jones, *Explorations and Explanations* (Llandysul, 1981), 294–6 and Ryland Wallace, *Organise! Organise! Organise!* (Cardiff, 1991).

[15] Anon., 'The present state of society in Wales', *Cambrian Quarterly Magazine*, 3 (1831), 126, 128–9.

[16] The Revd William Jones, *A Prize Essay . . . on the Character of the Welsh as a Nation* (London, 1841), 153; PP, xxvii, 1847, *Reports of the Commissioners of Inquiry into the State of Education in Wales, Brecknock, Cardigan and Radnor*, no. 63.

[17] Claire Boucher, 'Working the land: land and politics in Ireland, England and Wales in the 1880s' (unpub. MA thesis, Univ. of Wales, 1998), 137–44; R. B. McDowell, 'Colonial nationalism, 1760–82', in T. W. Moody and W. E. Vaughan (eds.), *A New History of Ireland*, iv (Oxford, 1986), 201–2.

[18] David Jones, *Rebecca's Children* (Oxford, 1989), 360–1; Matthew Cragoe, *An Anglican Aristocracy* (Oxford, 1996), 89. Dr Cragoe makes a strong case for continuing gentry paternalism in Carmarthenshire down to the 1880s.

[19] John Gibson, *Agriculture in Wales* (London, 1879), 19.

[20] Jones, *Crime in Nineteenth-Century Wales*, 128–32; Gerald Morgan, *A Welsh House and its Family: The Vaughans of Trawsgoed* (Llandysul, 1997), 231–5; Baker-Jones, *'Princelings, Privilege and Power'* . . . *The Tivyside Gentry in their Community*, 292–7.

[21] Cited in J. H. Davies, 'The social structure and economy of south-west Wales in the late nineteenth century' (unpub. MA thesis, Univ. of Wales, 1967), 87.

[22] *Carnarvon and Denbigh Herald*, 3 April 1891: editorial. My understanding of late nineteenth-century Welsh rural society owes much to K. O. Morgan, *Rebirth of a Nation: Wales 1880–1980* (Oxford and Cardiff, 1981) and Jenkins, *The Agricultural Community of South-West Wales at the Turn of the Twentieth Century.*

[23] The notion is forwarded in David Pretty, *The Rural Revolt that Failed: Farm Workers' Trades Unions in Wales, 1889–1950* (Cardiff, 1989).

Bibliography

1. MANUSCRIPT COLLECTIONS

Caernarfon Area Record Office, Caernarfon
XM/1705, letter of Edward Bridge of Aberwheeler (Bodfari), 1758
XD1/745, Caernarfon borough census, 1794

Parochial collections:
Gwyddelwern
Llannor

Carmarthenshire County Record Office, Carmarthen
IR23/114, Carmarthenshire Land Tax, 1798

Deposited collections:
Abergwili
Cawdor/Vaughan
Cwmgwili
Dynevor
Plas Llanstephan

Parochial collections:
Newchurch

Denbighshire County Record Office, Ruthin
Order books and sessions rolls of Denbighshire Quarter Sessions

Parochial collections:
Erbistock
Henllan

Flintshire County Record Office, Hawarden
D/E/539, letters from John Williams to Joshua Edisbury, 1707–15
D/E/556, letters from John Caesar to Simon Yorke, 1750
D/E/558, letter from Thomas Birch to Philip Yorke of Erddig, 1768
D/E/888, letter of 28 May 1769 from Mrs Dorothy Yorke to her son Philip
D/E/1158, copy of letter of 31 December 1720 from John Meller at Erddig to Sir Philip Yorke of Hardwicke
D/E/1296, John Meller's notices to Wrexham overseers, March 1729
D/M/4289, letters from Sir Thomas Mostyn to Edmund Herbert of Gray's Inn, 1739–56
D/KK/762, letter of 22 February 1678 from Thomas Williams to Edward Lloyd of Gray's Inn
D/MT/568, memorandum of men poaching rabbits at Talacre warren, 1752
D/MT/571, confession, 26 December 1753, of two labourers of Gwesbyr for poaching

Glamorgan County Record Office, Cardiff
D/DP/877, Margam estate correspondence

Gwent County Record Office, Cwmbran
Deposited collection:
Medlycott

National Library of Wales
Deposited collections:

Ashburnham	Kemeys-Tynte
Badminton	Leeswood
Baker Gabb	Llangibby
Behrens	Lucas
Bodewryd	Margam and Penrice
Brogyntyn	Mayberry
Bronwydd	Milborne
Burdon	Nanteos
Chirk Castle	Noyadd Trefawr
Cilybebyll	Owen and Colby
Clenennau	Pentypark
Crosswood	Picton Castle
Cwrtmawr	Powis Castle
Dolfriog	Rhual
Eaton Evans and Williams	Ruthin Lordship
Glynllivon	Slebech
Gogerddan	Tredegar Park
Harpton Court	Wigfair
Herbert Correspondence	Wynnstay
D. T. M. Jones	

NLW MSS:
821C, William Williams's survey of Caernarvonshire, 1806
822C, William Williams's survey of Anglesey, 1807
1352B, Stackpole Letters
1412D, letter of John Campbell of Stackpole to Major Ackland, 1796
1676B, Walter Davies's journal of a tour through north Wales
1677B, Walter Davies's journal of a tour through north Wales
1762B, diaries of tours in north and south Wales by Walter Davies
1766E, Walter Davies's notebook on south-west Wales
4703F, a survey of the Caerhun estate in north Wales, 1774
6556E, a survey of the estates of Sir Thomas Stradling, 1732
9954C, a photostat facsimile of the title page of *A Circumstantial Account of the Evidence Produced on the Trial of Lewis Lewis the Younger for the Murder of Thomas Price . . . of Llanafan Fawr, 1789*
11774E, documents, 1824–35, relating to the management of the estates of L. P. Jones in Carmarthenshire
12373B, transcript of Lampeter parish register
12501E, letter book of Robert Howard, customs collector at Conwy
22131C, letters from Cardiganshire of Lewis Evans

Diocesan Records (Bangor, Llandaff, St Asaph and St Davids):
Consistory Court papers
Visitation papers

Parochial collections:

Aber-nant	Llanfihangel Ystrad
Cenarth	Llangedwyn
Lampeter	Llangeler
Llandysiliogogo	Llanrhystud
Llanfair-ar-y-bryn	

Quarter Sessions records:
Cardiganshire Quarter Sessions order books

Great Sessions records:
Detailed examination was made of many of the following:
GS4.250.4 to 255.3, Anglesey gaol files, 1733–90
GS4.375.1 to 388.8, Breconshire gaol files, 1733–90
GS4.270.4 to 277.2, Caernarfonshire gaol files, 1733–90
GS4.890.2 to 904.6, Cardiganshire gaol files, 1733–90
GS4.734.6 to 748.4, Carmarthenshire gaol files, 1733–90
GS4.45.4 to 62.6,   Denbighshire gaol files, 1733–90
GS4.610.4 to 627.6, Glamorgan gaol files, 1733–90
GS4.298.3 to 303.5, Merioneth gaol files, 1733–90
GS4.811.2 to 824.4, Pembrokeshire gaol files, 1733–90
GS4.516.6 to 530.2, Radnorshire gaol files, 1733–90

Pembrokeshire County Library, Haverfordwest
Survey of Harcourt Powell's estate, 1778

Pembrokeshire County Record Office, Haverfordwest
PQ/RT, Pembrokeshire land-tax returns, 1786
PQ/RF, Pembrokeshire friendly societies
Haverfordwest Corporation records, 1641 and 2143

Deposited collections:
D/LEW, Lewis of Henllan

Public Record Office
SP36/50, part 3
SP44/142
WO1/1005

University of North Wales, Bangor
D/M 4289, letter of Sir Thomas Mostyn from Gloddaeth, 1756

Deposited collections:
Bodorgan
Bodrhyddan
Henblas
Kinmel
Mostyn
Penrhos
Plas Coch

University of Wales Swansea
Deposited collections:
Collins
Mackworth

2. OFFICIAL PUBLICATIONS

Report of Commons (PP, 1715–1801, ix).
Abstract of Answers and Returns . . . Relative to the Expense and Maintenance of the Poor, 1802–3 (PP, 1803–4, viii).
Select Committee on Agriculture (PP, 1833, v).
Reports of the Commissioners of Inquiry into the State of Education in Wales (PP, 1847, xxvii).
Royal Commission on Agriculture (PP, 1882, xv).
Parliamentary Debates, 4th ser., i, 22 February 1892.
Royal Commission on Labour, Wales (PP, 1893–4, xxxvi).
Report of the RC on Land in Wales and Monmouthshire (PP, 1896, xxxiv).

3. WORKS OF REFERENCE

Jones, Philip Henry, *A Bibliography of the History of Wales* (3rd edn, Cardiff, 1989).
Rees, Eiluned, *Libri Walliae: A Catalogue of Welsh Books and Books Printed in Wales 1546–1820*, 2 vols. (Aberystwyth, 1987).
The Universal British Directory of Trade, Commerce and Manufactures, compiled for the years between 1793 and 1798, prepared by Peter Barfoot and John Wilkes (Castle Rising, 1993).

4. BOOKS AND ARTICLES PUBLISHED BEFORE 1850

Anon., *Articles Agreed on, for Apprehending and Prosecuting of Horse-Stealers, House-Breakers, etc. in the county of Flint* (Wrexham, 1779).
Anon., 'Sessions', *Cambrian Register for the Year 1795* (London, 1796).
Anon., 'Sessions', *Cambrian Register for the Year 1796* (London, 1799).
Anon., 'The present state of society in Wales', *Cambrian Quarterly Magazine*, 3 (1831).
Annual Register, xvii (1774), xviii (1775).
Clark, J., *General View of the Agriculture of Brecknock* (London, 1794).
Idem, *General View of the Agriculture of Radnorshire* (London, 1794).
Cradock, Joseph, *Letters from Snowdon* (Dublin, 1770).
Davies, Walter, 'A statistical account of the parish of Llanymyneich in Montgomeryshire', *Cambrian Register*, i (1795).
Idem, *General View of the Agriculture and Domestic Economy of North Wales* (London, 1810).
Idem, *General View of the Agriculture and Domestic Economy of South Wales* (London, 1814).
Eden, Sir Frederic, *The State of the Poor*, 3 vols. (London, 1797).
Evans, The Revd John, *Letters Written During a Tour through South Wales in the Year 1803* (London, 1804).
Fox, J., *General View of the Agriculture of the County of Glamorgan* (London, 1796).
Gentleman's Magazine, 27 (1757).

Hassall, C., *General View of the Agriculture of the County of Carmarthen* (London, 1794).

Idem, *General View of the Agriculture of the County of Pembroke* (London, 1794).

Hucks, J., *A Pedestrian Tour through North Wales 1795* (London, 1795).

Hutton, W., *Tours in North Wales, 1787 to October 1797* (Birmingham, 1803).

Jones, Edmund, *Account of the Parish of Aberstruth in the County of Monmouth* (Trevecka, 1779).

Jones, The Revd William, *A Prize Essay . . . on the Character of the Welsh as a Nation* (London 1841).

Kay, G., *General View of the Agriculture of Caernarvonshire* (London, 1794).

Idem, *General View of the Agriculture of Denbighshire* (London, 1794).

Idem, *General View of the Agriculture of Flintshire* (London, 1794).

Idem, *General View of the Agriculture of Merionethshire* (London, 1794).

Idem, *General View of the Agriculture of Montgomeryshire* (London, 1794).

Lloyd, T. and Turnor, D., *General View of the Agriculture of the County of Cardigan* (London, 1794).

Lyttleton, Lord George, *An Account of a Journey into Wales* (London, 1756).

Malkin, B. H., *The Scenery, Antiquities and Biography of South Wales* (2nd edn, London, 1807).

Meyrick, Samuel R., *History and Antiquities of the County of Cardigan* (lst edn, London, 1808).

Pennant, T., *Tours in Wales* (3 vols., London, 1810).

Pococke, Richard, *Travels through England during 1750, 1751 and Later Years* (2 vols., Camden Society edn, 1888–9).

Roberts, Peter, *The Cambrian Popular Antiquities of Wales* (London, 1815).

Warner, R., *Second Walk through Wales* (London, 1799).

Wigstead, Henry, *A Tour to North and South Wales in the Year 1797* (London, 1798).

Wyndham, H. P., *Gentleman's Tour through Monmouthshire and Wales, 1774* (London, 1775).

Young, Arthur, *A Six Weeks Tour through the Southern Counties of England and Wales* (3rd edn, London, 1772).

Young, Arthur (ed.), *Annals of Agriculture*, iv, 23 (1785).

5. BOOKS PUBLISHED SINCE 1850

Anon., *Crime and Punishment – A Welsh Perspective: Crime and the Sea – A Maritime Dimension* (Gwynedd Archives and Museums Service, 1987).

Archer, John, *By a Flash and a Scare: Incendiarism, Animal Maiming, and Poaching in East Anglia 1815–1870* (Oxford, 1990).

Armstrong, Alan, *Farmworkers: A Social and Economic History 1770–1880* (London, 1988).

Baker-Jones, Leslie, *Princelings, Privilege and Power: The Tivyside Gentry in their Community* (Llandysul, 1999).

Beattie, J. M., *Crime and the Courts in England 1660–1800* (Oxford, 1986).

Beckett, J. V., *The Aristocracy in England 1660–1914* (Oxford, 1986).

Bohstedt, John, *Riots and Community Politics in England and Wales 1790–1810* (Cambridge, Mass., 1983).

Brewer, J. and Styles, J. (eds.), *An Ungovernable People: The English and their Law in the Seventeenth and Eighteenth Centuries* (London, 1980).

Burke, Peter, *Popular Culture in Early Modern Europe* (Aldershot, revised reprint, 1994).

Bushaway, Bob, *By Rite: Custom, Ceremony and Community in England, 1700–1880* (London, 1982).

Clark, P. (ed.), *Country Towns in Pre-industrial England* (Leicester, 1981).

Clark, S. and Donelly, Jr, James (eds.), *Irish Peasants: Violence and Political Unrest 1780–1914* (Manchester, 1983).

Corfield, P., *The Impact of English Towns, 1700–1800* (Oxford, 1982).

Cragoe, Matthew, *An Anglican Aristocracy* (Oxford, 1996).

Cust, A. L., *Chronicles of Erthig on the Dyke* (London, 1914).

Davies, D. J., *The Economic History of South Wales prior to 1800* (Cardiff, 1933).

Davies, J. Ceredig, *Welsh Folk Lore* (Aberystwyth, 1911).

Davies, Sir Leonard Twiston and Edwards, Averyl, *Welsh Life in the Eighteenth Century* (London, 1939).

Denning, R. T. W., *The Diary of William Thomas, 1762–1795* (Cardiff, South Wales Record Society, 1995).

Dodd, A. H., *The Industrial Revolution in North Wales* (Cardiff, 1933).

Eastwood, David, *Governing Rural England: Tradition and Transformation in Local Government 1780–1840* (Oxford, 1994).

Idem, *Government and Community in the English Provinces, 1700–1870* (London, 1997).

Emery, Frank, *The World's Landscapes: Wales* (London, 1969).

Evans, E. D., *A History of Wales, 1660–1815* (Cardiff, 1976).

Evans, G. Nesta, *Social Life in Mid-Eighteenth Century Anglesey* (Cardiff, 1936).

Idem, *Religion and Politics in Mid-Eighteenth Century Anglesey* (Cardiff, 1953).

Gillis, J. R., *For Better, for Worse: British Marriages, 1600 to the Present* (Oxford, 1985).

Gilmour, Ian, *Riot, Risings and Revolution* (Pimlico, 1993).

Golby, J. M. and Purdue, A. W., *The Civilisation of the Crowd: Popular Culture in England, 1750–1900* (London 1984).

Gosden, P. H., *Self-Help Voluntary Associations in Nineteenth-Century Britain* (London, 1973).

Griffiths, Eric, *Philip Yorke (1743–1804), Squire of Erthig* (Wrexham, 1995).

Hay, D. and Rogers, N., *Eighteenth-Century English Society* (Oxford, 1997).

Hayter, A. J., *The Army and the Crowd in Mid-Georgian England* (London, 1978).

Howell, D. W., *Land and People in Nineteenth-Century Wales* (London, 1979).

Idem, *Patriarchs and Parasites: The Gentry of South-West Wales in the Eighteenth Century* (Cardiff, 1986).

Howkins, Alun, *Reshaping Rural England: A Social History 1850–1925* (London, 1991).

Hufton, Olwen, *The Poor of Eighteenth-Century France, 1750–1789* (Oxford, 1974).

Humphreys, Melvin, *The Crisis of Community: Montgomeryshire Society 1680–1815* (Cardiff, 1996).

Hyde-Hall, Edmund, *A Description of Caernarvonshire (1809–1811)* (Caernarfon, 1952).

Jackson, M., *New-Born Child Murder* (Manchester, 1996).

Jenkins, David, *The Agricultural Community in South-West Wales at the Turn of the Twentieth Century* (Cardiff, 1971).

Jenkins, Geraint H., *Literature, Religion and Society in Wales* (Cardiff, 1978).

Idem, *The Foundations of Modern Wales, 1642–1780* (Oxford, 1987).

Jenkins, J. Geraint, *The Welsh Woollen Industry* (Cardiff, 1969).

Idem, *Life and Tradition in Rural Wales* (paperback edn, Stroud, 1991).

Jenkins, Philip, *The Making of a Ruling Class: The Glamorgan Gentry, 1640–1790* (Cambridge, 1983).

John, A. H., *The Industrial Development of South Wales* (Cardiff, 1950).

Jones, D. J. V., *Before Rebecca* (London, 1973).
Jones, Gareth E., *Modern Wales* (2nd edn; Cambridge, 1994).
Jones, I. G., *Explorations and Explanations* (Llandysul, 1981).
Jones, William Henry, *Old Karnarvon* (Caernarfon, 1882).
Laslett, P., *The Worlds We Have Lost – Further Explored* (London, 1983).
Lewis, W. J., *Lead Mining in Wales* (Cardiff, 1967).
Malcolmson, Robert, *Popular Recreations in English Society* (Cambridge, 1973).
Idem, *Life and Labour in England 1700–1780* (London, 1981).
McLynne, F., *Crime and Punishment in Eighteenth-Century England* (London, 1989).
Menefee, S. P., *Wives for Sale* (Oxford, 1981).
Mingay, G. E., *English Landed Society in the Eighteenth Century* (London, 1963).
Idem, *Land and Society in England 1750–1980* (London, 1994).
Moore-Colyer, R., *The Welsh Cattle Drovers* (Cardiff, 1976).
Idem, *A Land of Pure Delight* (Llandysul, 1992).
Morgan, C. D., *Wanderings in Gower* (Swansea, 1886).
Morgan, Gerald, *A Welsh House and its Family: The Vaughans of Trawsgoed* (Llandysul, 1997).
Morgan, K. O., *Rebirth of a Nation: Wales 1880–1980* (Oxford and Cardiff, 1981).
Morgan, Prys, *The Eighteenth Century Renaissance* (Llandybïe, 1981).
Munsche, P. B., *Gentlemen and Poachers* (Cambridge, 1981).
Myddelton, W. M. (ed.), *Chirk Castle Accounts, 1663–1753* (Manchester, 1931).
Neeson, J. M., *Commoners: Common Right, Enclosure and Social Change in England, 1700–1820* (Cambridge, 1993).
O'Gorman, Frank, *Voters, Patrons and Parties: The Unreformed Electoral System of Hanoverian England 1734–1832* (Oxford, 1989).
Idem, *The Long Eighteenth Century: British Political and Social History 1688–1832* (London, 1997).
Outhwaite, R. B., *Clandestine Marriage in England, 1500–1850* (London, 1995).
Owen, Hugh (ed.), *Additional Letters of the Morrises of Anglesey* (*Y Cymmrodor*, xlix, 2 parts, 1947, 1949).
Owen, T. M., *Welsh Folk Customs* (new edn, Llandysul, 1987).
Idem, *The Customs and Traditions of Wales* (Cardiff, 1991).
Parker, Stephen, *Informal Marriage, Cohabitation and the Law, 1750–1989* (London, 1990).
Prest, Wilfrid, *Albion Ascendant: English History 1660–1815* (Oxford, 1998).
Roberts, R. O., *Farming in Caernarvonshire around 1800* (Caernarfon, 1973).
Rogers, N., *Crowds, Culture and Politics in Georgian Britain* (Oxford, 1998).
Rule, John, *The Labouring Classes in Early Industrial England 1750–1850* (London, 1986).
Sharpe, J. A., *Crime in Early Modern England, 1550–1750* (London, 1984).
Smith, Graham, *Smuggling in the Bristol Channel 1700–1850* (Newbury, 1989).
Smyth, Jim, *The Men of No Property: Irish Radicals and Popular Politics in the Late Eighteenth Century* (London, 1992).
Snell, K. D. M., *Annals of the Labouring Poor* (Cambridge, 1985).
Stevenson, J., *Popular Disturbances in England, 1700–1870* (London, 1979).
Stone, Lawrence, *Uncertain Union and Broken Lives: Marriage and Divorce in England, 1660–1857* (Oxford, 1995).
Thomas, Ben Bowen, *The Old Order* (Cardiff, 1945).
Thomas, David, *Agriculture in Wales during the Napoleonic Wars* (Cardiff, 1963).
Thomas, Hilary M. (ed.), *The Diaries of John Bird 1790–1803* (Cardiff, South Wales Record Society, 1987).
Thompson, E. P., *Customs in Common* (Penguin, 1993).

Wallace, Ryland, *Organise! Organise! Organise!* (Cardiff, 1991).
Western, J. R., *The English Militia in the Eighteenth Century* (London, 1965).
Williams, David, *The Rebecca Riots* (Cardiff, 1955).
Williams, G. A., *The Search for Beulah Land* (London, 1980).
Williams, Glanmor, *Religion, Language and Nationality in Wales* (Cardiff, 1979).
Williams, William, *Welsh Calvinistic Methodism* (2nd edn, London, 1884).
Williams-Jones, Keith, *A Calendar of the Merioneth Quarter Sessions Rolls* (Merioneth County Council, 1965).

6. ARTICLES IN JOURNALS AND CHAPTERS

Anon., 'A report of Penllyn and Edeirnion, *Cylchgrawn Cymdeithas Hanes a Chofnodion Sir Feirionydd*, 1–3 (1952–5).
Anon., 'Incidents at Oxwich', *Gower*, 22 (1971).
Armstrong, A., 'Food, shelter and self-help', in Mingay, G. E. (ed.), *AHE&W, VI, 1750–1850* (Cambridge, 1989).
Beattie, J. M., 'Crime and courts in Surrey 1736–1753', in Cockburn, J. S. (ed.), *Crime in England 1550–1800* (London, 1977).
Beckett, J. V., 'The pattern of landownership in England and Wales, 1660–1880', *Econ. Hist. Rev.*, xxxvii (1984).
Idem, 'The peasant in England: a case of terminological confusion?', *Ag. Hist. Rev.*, 32 (1984).
Bohstedt, J., 'Gender, household and community politics: women in English riots 1790–1810', *Past and Present*, 120 (1988).
Brown, Roger L., 'Clandestine marriages in Wales', *Trans. Cymm.* (1982).
Bushaway, Bob, ' "Tacit, unsuspected, but still implicit faith": alternative belief in nineteenth-century rural England', in Harris, T. (ed.), *Popular Recreations in England, 1500–1850* (London, 1995).
Carter, H., 'The growth and development of Welsh towns', in Moore, Donald (ed.), *Wales in the Eighteenth Century* (Swansea, 1976).
Idem, 'Urban and industrial settlement in the modern period, 1750–1914', in Owen, D. Huw (ed.), *Settlement and Society in Wales* (Cardiff, 1989).
Chartres, J. A., 'The marketing of agricultural produce', in Thirsk, J. (ed.), *AHE&W, V*, ii (Cambridge, 1985).
Clay, Christopher, 'Marriage, inheritance and the rise of large estates in England, 1660–1815', *Econ. Hist. Rev.*, xxi (1968).
Collins, E. J. T., 'Dietary change and cereal consumption in Britain in the nineteenth century', *Ag. Hist. Rev.*, 23 (1975).
Davies, A. E., 'Some aspects of the operation of the old poor law in Cardiganshire, 1750–1834', *Ceredigion*, vi (1968).
Idem, 'Enclosures in Cardiganshire, 1750–1850', *Ceredigion*, viii (1976–9).
Idem, 'Wages, prices, and social improvements in Cardiganshire, 1750–1850', *Ceredigion*, x (1984–7).
Davies, A. Stanley, 'Cardiganshire salt smugglers: an XVIII century riot', *Arch. Camb.*, xci (1936).
Davies, E., 'Hafod and lluest: the summering of cattle and upland settlement in Wales', *Folk Life*, 23 (1984–5).
Davies, H. M., ' "Very different springs of uneasiness": emigration from Wales to the United States of America during the 1790s', *WHR*, 15 (1990–1).
Davies, W. Lloyd, 'The riot at Denbigh in 1795 – Home Office correspondence', *BBCS*, iv (1928–9).

Dodd, A. H., 'The old poor law in north Wales', *Arch. Camb.*, lxxxi (1926).

Idem, 'The enclosure movement in north Wales', *BBCS*, iii (1926–7).

Eastwood, David, 'Contesting the politics of deference: the rural electorate, 1820–60', in Lawrence, Jon and Taylor, Miles (eds.), *Party, State and Society: Electoral Behaviour in Britain Since 1820* (Aldershot, 1997).

Ellis, T. P., 'The Dolgelley parish registers', *Y Cymmrodor*, xl (1929).

Emery, Frank, 'The mechanics of innovation: clover cultivation in Wales before 1750', *Journal of Historical Geography*, 2, i (1976).

Idem, 'Wales', in Thirsk, J. (ed.), *AHE&W, V*, i (Cambridge, 1984).

Evans, G. Nesta, 'The artisan and small farmer in mid-eighteenth century Anglesey', *Trans. Angl. Antiq. Soc.* (1933).

Evans, Muriel Bowen, 'The land and its people', in Howell, D. W. (ed.), *Pembrokeshire County History*, iv (Haverfordwest, 1993).

Evans, Neil, 'The urbanisation of society', in Herbert, T. and Jones, G. E. (eds.), *Popular Protest: Wales 1815–1880* (Cardiff, 1988).

Griffith, J. E., 'The diary of William Bulkeley, of Bryndddu, Anglesey', *Trans. Angl. Antiq. Soc.* (1931).

Gruffydd, K. Lloyd, 'The Vale of Clwyd corn riots of 1740', *Flintshire Historical Society Publications*, 27 (1975–6).

Gwynn, Gwennith, 'Besom wedding in the Ceiriog Valley', *Folklore*, xxxix (1928).

Habakkuk, H. J., 'The rise and fall of English landed families, 1600–1800: i', *Trans. RHS*, 5th ser., 29 (1979).

Idem, 'The rise and fall of English landed families, 1600–1800: ii', *Trans. RHS.*, 5th ser., 30 (1980).

Hay, D., 'Poaching and the game laws on Cannock Chase', in Hay, D. et al (eds.), *Albion's Fatal Tree* (London, 1975).

Idem, 'Property, authority and the criminal law', in Hay, D. et al (eds.), *Albion's Fatal Tree* (London, 1975).

Howell, D. W., 'Landlords and estate management in Wales', in Thirsk, J. (ed.), *AHE&W, V*, ii (Cambridge, 1985).

Hufton, Olwen, 'The rise of the people: life and death among the very poor', in Cobban, A. (ed.), *The Eighteenth Century: Europe in the Age of the Enlightenment* (London, 1969).

Humphreys, Melvin, 'The Llanidloes riot of 1721', *Mont. Colls.*, 75 (1987).

Huzel, J. P., 'The labourer and the poor law, 1750–1850', in Mingay, G. E. (ed.), *AHE&W, VI, 1750–1850* (Cambridge, 1989).

Jenkins, D., 'Harvest failure and crisis mortality: the example of Montgomeryshire, 1699–1700', *Papers in Modern Welsh History*, 1 (1982).

Idem, 'The demography of late-Stuart Montgomeryshire, c. 1660–1720', *Mont. Colls.*, 88 (1990).

Jenkins, Geraint H., 'Popular beliefs in Wales from the Restoration to Methodism', *BBCS*, xxvii (1977–8).

Idem, 'The new enthusiasm', in Jones, G. E. and Herbert, T. (eds.), *The Remaking of Wales in the Eighteenth Century* (Cardiff, 1988).

Idem, Suggett, Richard and White, Eryn M., 'The Welsh language in early modern Wales', in Jenkins, Geraint H. (ed.), *The Welsh Language before the Industrial Revolution* (Cardiff, 1997).

Jenkins, Philip, 'The demographic decline of the landed gentry in the eighteenth century: a south Wales study', *WHR*, 2 (1982–3).

Idem, 'Times and seasons: the cycles of the year in early modern Glamorgan', *Morgannwg*, xxx (1986).

Idem, 'Political quiescence and political ferment', in Herbert, T. and Jones, G. E. (eds.), *The Remaking of Wales in the Eighteenth Century* (Cardiff, 1988).

John, A. H., 'Glamorgan, 1700–1750', in John, A. H. and Williams, Glanmor (eds.), *Glamorgan County History*, v, *Industrial Glamorgan* (Cardiff, 1980).

Jones, B. W., 'The population of eighteenth-century west Glamorgan: the evidence of the parish registers', in Williams, S. (ed.), *Glamorgan Historian*, 12 (1981).

Jones, D. J. V., 'The corn riots in Wales, 1793–1801', *WHR*, 2 (1964–5).

Idem, 'Life and death in eighteenth-century Wales: a note', *WHR*, 10, 4 (1981).

Jones, E. Vaughan, 'Sheep stealing at Llangelynin in 1792', *Jnl. Mer. Hist. and Rec. Soc.*, 7 (1973–6).

Jones, F., 'The Vaughans of Golden Grove: the Duchess of Bolton', *Trans. Cymm.* (1963).

Idem, 'The Vaughans of Golden Grove', *Trans. Cymm.* (1964).

Idem, 'The Vaughans of Golden Grove', *Trans. Cymm.* (1966).

Jones, T. I. Jeffreys, 'The parish vestries and the problem of poverty, 1783–1833', *BBCS*, 14 (1950–2).

Idem, 'Parochial administration in Carmarthenshire', *Trans. Cymm.* (1952).

Lewis, F. R., 'Lewis Morris and the parish of Llanbadarn Fawr, Cardiganshire, in 1755', *Arch. Camb.*, xciii (1938).

Malcolmson, Robert, 'Leisure', in Mingay, G. E. (ed.), *The Victorian Countryside* (London, 1984).

McDowell, R. B., 'Colonial nationalism, 1760–82', in Moody, T. W. and Vaughan, W. E. (eds.), *A New History of Ireland*, iv (Oxford, 1986).

McInnes, Angus, 'A forgotten people: the craftsmen of pre-industrial England', in Richmond, C. and Harvey, I. (eds.), *Recognitions: Essays Presented to Edmund Fryde* (Aberystwyth, 1996).

Moore-Colyer, R. J., 'Early agricultural societies in south Wales', *WHR*, 12 (1984–5).

Idem, 'Of lime and men: aspects of the coastal trade in lime in south-west Wales in the eighteenth and nineteenth centuries', *WHR*, 14 (1988–9).

Idem, 'Livestock', in Mingay, G. E. (ed.), *AHE&W, VI* (Cambridge, 1989).

Idem, 'Farmers and fields in nineteenth-century Wales: the case of Llanrhystud, Cardiganshire', *NLW Jnl.*, 26 (1989–90).

Owen, L., 'The letters of an Anglesey parson, 1712–32', *Trans. Cymm.* (1961).

Owen, Trefor M., 'Historical aspects of peat-cutting in Merioneth', *Jnl. Mer. Hist. and Rec. Soc.*, 7 (1973–6).

Phythian-Adams, Charles, 'Rural culture', in Mingay, G. E. (ed.), *The Victorian Countryside* (London, 1984).

Rees, R. D., 'Electioneering ideals current in south Wales, 1790–1832', *WHR*, 2 (1965).

Roberts, P. R., 'The decline of the Welsh squires in the eighteenth century', *NLW Jnl.*, 13 (1963–4).

Rule, J., 'Wrecking and coastal plunder', in Hay, D. et al. (eds.), *Albion's Fatal Tree* (London, 1975).

Sayce, R. U., 'Popular enclosures and the one-night house', *Mont. Colls.*, 47 (1942).

Smith, Peter, 'Rural buildings in Wales', in Thirsk, J. (ed.), *AHE&W, V*, ii (Cambridge, 1985).

Stevens, Catrin, 'The funeral wake in Wales', *Folk Life*, 14 (1976).

Suggett, Richard, 'Festivals and social structure in early modern Wales', *Past and Present*, 150 (1996).

Sweet, R., 'Swansea politics and reform, 1780–1820', *WHR*, 18, i (1996).

Taylor, James S., 'The unreformed workhouse 1776–1834', in Martin, E. W. (ed.), *Comparative Development in Social Welfare* (London, 1972).

Thomas, Colin, 'Colonization, enclosure and the rural landscape', *NLW Jnl.*, 19 (1975–6).

Idem, 'Rural settlements in the modern period', in Owen, D. Huw (ed.), *Settlement and Society in Wales* (Cardiff, 1989).

Thomas, P. D. G., 'Eighteenth century politics', in Roderick, A. J. (ed.), *Wales through the Ages*, ii (Llandybïe, 1960).

Idem, 'County elections in eighteenth-century Carmarthenshire', *The Carmarthenshire Antiquary*, iv (1962).

Idem, 'A Welsh political storm: the Treasury warrant of 1778 concerning Crown lands in Wales', *WHR*, 18, iii (1997).

Thompson, Edward, 'The moral economy of the crowd', *Past and Present*, 50 (1971).

Thompson, F. M. L., 'Landowners and the rural community', in Mingay, G. E. (ed.), *The Victorian Countryside* (London, 1981).

Thwaites, W., 'Women in the market place: Oxfordshire c. 1690–1800', *Midland History*, ix (1984).

Vaughan, C., 'Lluestai Blaenrheidol', *Ceredigion*, v (1966).

Wells, Roger, 'The revolt of the south-west, 1800–1', *Social History* (October, 1977).

Idem, 'Social protest, class, conflict and consciousness in the English countryside, 1700–1880', in Reed, Mick and Wells, Roger (eds.), *Class, Conflict and Protest in the English Countryside, 1700–1880* (London, 1990).

White, Eryn M., 'The established Church, Dissent and the Welsh language c. 1660–1811', in Jenkins, Geraint H. (ed.), *The Welsh Language before the Industrial Revolution* (Cardiff, 1997).

Williams, Eurwyn, ' "Home-made homes": dwellings of the rural poor in Cardiganshire', *Ceredigion*, xii, 3 (1995).

Williams, G. A., 'Beginnings of radicalism', in Herbert, T. and Jones, G. E. (eds.), *The Remaking of Wales in the Eighteenth Century* (Cardiff, 1988).

Williams, G. J., 'Glamorgan customs in the eighteenth century', *Gwerin*, i (1955).

Williams-Davies, John, 'Merchedd y gerddi: a seasonal migration of female labour from rural Wales', *Folk Life*, 15 (1977).

Winslow, Carl, 'Sussex smugglers', in Hay, D. et al. (eds.), *Albion's Fatal Tree* (London, 1975).

7. UNPUBLISHED THESES (University of Wales unless otherwise stated)

Beynon, O., 'The lead mining industry in Cardiganshire from 1700–1830'. MA, 1937.

Boucher, Claire, 'Working the land: land and politics in Ireland, England and Wales in the 1880s'. M.Phil., 1998.

Cragoe, Matthew F., 'The Golden Grove interest in the politics of Carmarthenshire, 1804–21'. MA, 1987.

Davies, Martin, 'Hanes Cymdeithawl Meirionydd, 1750–1790'. MA, 1988.

Edwards, J. W., 'Enclosure and agricultural improvement in the Vale of Clwyd, 1750–1875'. MA, London, 1963.

Humphreys, T. M., 'Rural society in eighteenth-century Montgomeryshire'. Ph.D., 1982.

Jones, A. W., 'Agriculture and the rural community of Glamorgan, circa 1830–1896'. Ph.D., 1980.

Jones, J. G., Penrhyn, 'A history of medicine in Wales in the eighteenth century'. MA, Liverpool, 1957.

Martin, J. O., 'The landed estate in Glamorgan, *circa* 1660–1760'. Ph.D., Cambridge, 1978.

Matthews, Mark, 'In pursuit of profit: local enterprise in south-west Wales in the eighteenth century'. Ph.D., 1998.

Morgan, Eric, 'The economic, social and political life of the Hundred of Dewisland . . . c. 1790–1914'. M.Phil., 1992.

Parry, Glyn, 'Stability and change in mid-eighteenth century Caernarvonshire'. MA, 1978.

Powell, A. A., 'Crime in Brecknockshire 1733–1830 as revealed by the records of the Great Sessions'. MA, 1990.

Powell, J. M., 'The economic geography of Montgomeryshire in the nineteenth century'. MA, Liverpool, 1962.

Pryce, W. T. R., 'The social and economic structure of north-east Wales, 1750–1890'. Ph.D., Lanchester Polytechnic, Coventry, 1971.

Scheltinga, J. G. W., 'The Gwydir estate 1814–1914'. Ph.D., 1992.

Suggett, R. F., 'Some aspects of village life in eighteenth-century Glamorgan'. B.Litt., Oxford, 1976.

Williams, M. I., 'Agriculture and society in Glamorgan 1660–1760'. Ph.D., Leicester, 1967.

Index

Note: The index is primarily a subject index. Minor place names and people have not been included. Bold page numbers refer to Tables.

English language 116, 137
English, the
  hostility towards 205, 206, 234
  landholdings in Wales 12
estates
  craftsmen on 59, 60
  labourers' wages 67, **68**, 69
  size of 10–11
  see also landowners
Evans, Revd John 5, 33, 43, 86, 161,
  191

fairies, belief in 154–5
fairs 47, 142
  fighting at 206, 213
famine 93–4, 178, 242
farm labourers and servants 20, 24, 90,
  246
  absence from food riots 180
  hierarchy of 67, **68**
  hiring systems 66
  indoor 66, 72, 246
  outdoor married 66, 72, 246
  relations with gentry 127–8
  relations with tenant farmers 132–4
  in social hierarchy 20, 22
  theft by 128, 133, 229, 239–40
  wages 67, **68**, 69
  see also labouring poor
farmers
  and Methodism 153–4
  relations between 60, 129–32
  in social hierarchy 20–1
  social relations with labourers 33–4
  supplementary incomes 29, 53–4
  wrecking by 192
  see also freeholders; tenant farmers
farming
  agricultural improvements 4–6, 43–5,
    118–19
  arable 2–3
  bad harvests 46–8, 51
  dairy 3
  depressions 49–51
  open arable fields 7
  pastoral 1–2, 3–4
  poor level of 38–9, 43–4
  see also crops; livestock
farming regions 3–4
farms
  enlargement 36, 37
  fragmented and intermixed 38, 51
  improvements 118–19

shared tenancies 38
  size of 34–5, 37–9
fertility rates 19–20
Ffoulkes, David, magistrate 183–4, 188
ffriddoedd (rough pastures) 8
fights and brawls 213–14
flannel manufacture 53
  see also woollen industry
Flint, food riots 180
Flintshire 9, 14, 18
  farm wages 70
  friendly societies 83
  poor relief **96**
  riots 64, 203, 204
Foley, Paul, landowner 38–9
food riots 161, 177, 178–88
  craftsmen in 64
  lead miners in 77–8
  political provocation in 183–4, 188
  protests against exports 179–80
  punishments 185–6
  thefts of cargoes 180–1
  use of troops 184, 186
  violence 182–3
  women participants 186–8
Franklen, John, Llanmihangel 44
freeholders 20, 54–7
  electoral support for landowners
    167–70, 171–2
  lack of agricultural improvements
    56–7
  landownership 11
  provision for heirs 56
  and right to vote 33, 54
  and rights of common 172–3
  in social hierarchy 21–2, 55–6
  see also farmers; tenant farmers
French Wars
  effect on poor relief 103
  farm wage rises 72–3, 76
  increase in arable farming 2–3
  price rises 76
  riots 64–5
friendly societies 82–3, **82**
fuel
  coal 91–2
  peat 90–1
  right to take 80–1, 91–2

gambling 139, 141
Game Laws 122, 194, 245
gaols 109
gavelkind (division of inheritance) 34, 38

labour supply 72, 75, 105
labourers *see* craftsmen and artisans;
    farm labourers and servants
labouring poor
    income levels 66–81
    indoor farm servants 66, 72
    material conditions 87–92
    props against indigence 81–7
    see also farm labourers and servants;
        poor relief
Lampeter 27, 103, 104, 163
land reform, support for 246
landowners
    assistance for tenant farmers 48–9
    charity 111–12, 169–70
    and consolidation of tenant farms
        36–7
    deforestation by 6
    electoral support for 162, 163–70
    encroachment by 7
    growing unpopularity of 161, 242–3
    and increased rents 51–2, 119–20
    involvement in farming 43–4, 48–9
    reassertion of manorial rights 7,
        197–203
    relations with tenant farmers 116–27,
        245–6
    renewal of paternalism 245
    and repair of buildings 42–3
    and right to take fuel 91–2
    see also gentry
landowners, absentee 12, 116, 241, 245
    and decline of tradition 112–13
    and poor farming methods 44
    protests against 159
landownership
    gentry estates 10–11, 12
    intermixture of farm holdings 38,
        129, 130
    large estates 10–11
    owner-occupation 12
landscape
    and land use 1–2, 3–4
    and population density 13–14
Laugharne 2, 5, 180
lead miners
    in food riots 77–8, 180
    Methodism among 152
    wages (truck system) 78–9
lead-mining 14, 41, 75, 78
leases of farms 40–1, 125, 162
    auctions for 116, 132, 241
    and covenants 42, 121–2

for lives 40, 42, 163–4
and repairs 42–3, 117–18
for years 40
see also rents
leather trades 28, 62
lime-burning 63
literacy 137–8
livestock 52
    dairy cattle 3
    impounding 131–2
    maiming of 227
    sheep 3–4
    store cattle 2, 4, 6, 47
    theft of 235, 236, 238–9
Llanbrynmair (Mont.) 22, 160
Llandyfaelog parish, poor relief 103,
    104
Llanfair-ar-y-bryn parish 101, 103,
    114–15
Llanfechain (Mont.), social structure
    22, **22–3**, **24**, 26, 59, 66
Llangollen, child beggars 108–9
Llanishen, food riots 180
Lloyd, Bishop, *Notitiae* (1681–7) 26
lluest (shepherd's hut) 8
local politics, improvements 173–4
lower orders, use of term xiii–xiv

magistrates 168, 169, 242
    and administration of poor relief 115
    assaults on 184, 185, 219
    and food riots 184–5
    summary trial of poachers 194,
        195–6
    tyrannical 243
malicious damage 226
manorial courts, and poachers 195
manorial rights
    mineral extraction 198–9
    reasserted 178, 197–203, 243
Margam estate 49, 117, 164–5
marriage
    among freeholders 55
    broomstick 146, 147–8
    clandestine (little wedding) 146
    and courtship 142, 146, 147
    and domestic violence 224–6
    rates 19–20
    trial 146–7, 221–2
Meifod (Mont.)
    poor relief **98**
    social structure **23**, 24, **24**, 26, 59, 66
merchants 29